Also by Lidia Matticchio Bastianich

La Cucina Di Lidia

Lidia's Italian Table

Lidia's Italian-American Kitchen

Lidia's Family Table

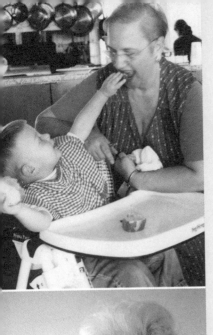

Lidia's Family Table

Lidia Matticchio Bastianich

with David Nussbaum

Photographs by Christopher Hirsheimer

 Alfred A. Knopf New York 2004

This Is a Borzoi Book Published by Alfred A. Knopf

Copyright © 2004 by Tutti a Tavola, LLC
All rights reserved under International and Pan-American Copyright Conventions. Published in the United States by Alfred A. Knopf, a division of Random House, Inc., New York, and simultaneously in Canada by Random House of Canada Limited, Toronto. Distributed by Random House, Inc., New York.
www.aaknopf.com

Knopf, Borzoi Books, and the colophon are registered trademarks of Random House, Inc.

The recipes for *Sugo* and Turkey Meatballs were previously published in *Gourmet* magazine.

Library of Congress Cataloging-in-Publication Data

Bastianich, Lidia.
  Lidia's family table/by Lidia Matticchio Bastianich; photography by Christopher Hirsheimer.—1st ed.
     p. cm.
  Includes index.
  ISBN 1-4000-4035-3
  1. Cookery, Italian.   I. Title.
TX723.B31897 2004
641.5945—dc22

                                                                          2004022411

Manufactured in the United States of America

First Edition

This book is in honor of my family,

all four generations that gather regularly at our table.

And as our fourth generation continues to sprout,

my two new angels are Ethan Bastianich and Julia Manuali.

May there always be in your life, my little angels,

a table full of love where family gathers,

and may you know that Noni's unconditional love

will be there with you eternally.

Contents

Acknowledgments

As you can see from the cover, I'm not the only cook in this book! Everyone in my family, of every age, has contributed to it in countless ways. And to each of them I want to express my love, gratitude, and happiness for the *family* effort that has brought this volume to completion. It is a true expression of our life as a family at our table.

The support and help I receive from businesses and individuals in the food and restaurant communities, the publishing world, and from my own staff have also been invaluable in the creation of this book. I heartily thank my friends at Colavita USA, Cuisinart, and Palm Bay Imports, and the producers of Grana Padano for their generous donation of products and equipment required in the hundreds of hours of recipe development—and for their longtime support of my projects.

The merchants that I and my book team turned to for the raw materials for our marathon cooking sessions are also worthy of recognition. We are fortunate that markets large and small across this country are responding to informed consumer demands for fresh, flavorful, nourishing food to feed our families. To my friends at Marino Fish Market in Astoria and Citarella in Manhattan, my thanks for exemplary seafood. We were delighted as well by the quality and variety of food we found at Fairway Markets, Gourmet Garage, and Whole Foods Market in New York City, and Stop and Shop supermarkets in both New York and Massachusetts, among others. Foster's Market in Greenfield, Massachusetts, provided many fine products for recipe and photo sessions, particularly their meats, cut to order with good cheer on short notice.

As an advocate of regional agriculture and a lover of really fresh food, I am glad that I can thank by name many small family farms who directly supplied us with their superb home-grown products. Many of these are in the Connecticut River valley of western Massachusetts (where David Nussbaum did much of our shopping) and I wish to salute the Hibbard Farm of Hadley, for their mouthwatering asparagus in the spring and tasty parsnips in the fall; also, the Butynski Farm of Greenfield, the Golonka Farm of Hatfield, and the Ciesluk Farm and Bars Farm in Deerfield, for sweet corn, tomatoes, and all manner of summer produce. I was delighted by the flavor of the naturally raised birds from the Diemand Turkey Farm in Wendell, Massachusetts. And our desserts were inspired by wild blueberries from The Benson Place in Heath and the apples, peaches, plums, pears, and quince (and ciders) from Clarkdale Fruit Farm in Deerfield. Appreciation to Margaret Schnall of Hatfield and her flock of hens for dozens of eggs in every size and color, as delicious as they are pretty. The Westminster (Vermont) Cheese Company supplied us with excellent fresh ricotta and rich butter from the milk of their grass-fed Jersey cows. And all of our days in Vermont, and several recipes here, were sweetened by the maple syrup produced by John Reynolds on his farm in Stannard, Vermont.

Many individuals labored to make this book a reality and as beautiful and big as it is. As always, I am indebted to my agent Jane Dystel for everything she has done for me; thanks also to her partner Miriam Goderich.

At Alfred A. Knopf, my publisher, I know that Judith Jones brings a superb team together to work on my manuscript. I want to thank assistant editor Ken Schneider for his unflagging and expert effort to keep everything together and his good cheer at all times, Carol Carson, who so understood the essence of this book in creating the cover, and Cassandra Pappas for the lively and expressive interior design. Kathleen Fridella for her careful work coordinating the copyediting and Tracy Cabanis for overseeing production, and Paul Bogaards and Sheila O'Shea, who always do such a great job promoting my books.

And to my dear friend Christopher Hirsheimer, whose photography I love, thank you for capturing the spirit of my family and the essence of my food. All with natural light.

In my own office and downstairs in Felidia—in the dining room and kitchen— I thank all who keep our flagship sailing successfully. I would not have been able to work on this book and other projects were it not for you: Executive chef Fortunato Nicotra, for Formula Uno performance in the kitchen and helping me on those special needs for the book; Genji Ridley and Mario Pincic, for their commitment in managing the dining room in my absence; and Shelly Burgess, for keeping me in line with my business and special appearance commitments.

In particular, I want to thank Miguelina Polanco for coordinating the many cooking and photo sessions for this book and for organizing the manuscript as well as handling all my other affairs while I was on book duty. Though the cooking for this book was done at home, we could count on emergency help and recipe supplies from my sous-chef Todd Curtis, and our cooks, whenever we asked.

A Special Thanks for a Very Special Team

I want in particular to recognize a group which made such an essential and unique contribution to this book that it acquired the name "Team Lidia". Almost all of the book's contents—both the recipes and my commentary—emerged from two dozen long, exciting days in the kitchen, from January to October 2003. On those days, I would meet my team in the kitchen early in the morning and we would cook for ten to fourteen hours.

With the support of Team Lidia, at each session I perfected the group of family dishes I wanted to see in the book and at the same time I explored and experimented with new ideas and ingredients. The team provided the many hands, eyes, and senses that allowed me to work on as many as fifteen different dishes in one day. The team also supplied and prepped the food and helped me keep an eye on a six-burner stovetop covered with simmering soup pots, often while two or three casseroles baked in the oven. The team constantly cleaned and kept order in my kitchen at home, and in Judith's kitchen when we worked at her home in Vermont and, for the first sessions, at her apartment in Manhattan.

Cooking help was only half the job, though: the team also documented the preparation of each dish and every change and modification I wanted in the finished dishes, recording each session with handwritten notes, audio tape recordings, and digital photographs. These were the resources that David and I later drew on to write the recipes and text. As you can imagine, it was hard work every day (though we enjoyed big lunches) but it provided me with an accurate record of what works and what doesn't, which has made this a better book. And the sessions themselves were for me an unprecedented opportunity to cook with freedom and focus—and receive immediate, informed feedback—that has taught me many new lessons.

So let me thank Team Lidia, for hundreds of hours of chopping, washing, notetaking, and encouragement. Team members included Judith Jones, my editor; David Nussbaum, my cowriter; Laura Supper (on most days my banquet manager at Felidia), sometimes holding the digital camera with one hand and arranging special dinners on the cell phone with the other. I depended greatly upon Lara Brumgnach, one of the pastry chefs at Felidia, to handle food prep chores as well as extensive note-taking. Kathleen Hackett was a valued team member until she went on the inactive list following the birth of her son, Finn. Hannah Lord helped us get started at our first sessions. In Vermont, Michelle Mackin joined the team for a couple of days and Chris Vandercook skillfully videotaped the sessions. Professor Eddie Brumgnach, Lara's father, handled the camera when Laura was on vacation and, despite the East Coast blackout in August 2003, he set a one-day record for most photos and best jokes. I want to thank Katie Mahoney, who assisted David in Massachusetts by transcribing the tapes and organizing the photographs.

Dear Judith, thank you for your unconditional support and encouragement. Thank you for rolling up your sleeves many a time and cooking along with me, and all along recognizing and bringing out my family's most intimate relationships, which culminate at our table.

David, you are a gem: tireless, witty, gregarious, and committed no end to this project. For this I thank you from the bottom of my heart.

And once again I want to thank my mother, Erminia Matticchio, and her partner, Giovanni Bencina, for their many hours of hard work on the team and their undisputed judgment about which dishes belonged on our family table.

LIDIA BASTIANICH
New York, May 2004

Introduction

I am fortunate indeed that cooking—something I've loved ever since I was a small child—has become my life's work. My days are filled with the challenges and delights of making wonderful food, whether I'm developing new menu items and teaching young cooks at my restaurants, testing and writing recipes for books, giving classes and demonstrations to home cooks, or getting dishes to come out just right on camera for my TV programs.

Yet I count it an even greater blessing that when I am home, in my free time, I get to cook again. But now it is for my family—and for fun: the cooking I truly love the most. While it's not every day that I am so lucky, at least several days a week, and always on Sunday, I get to play around in the kitchen and put a meal on the table for those I love dearly: my mother and her partner, Giovanni, both in their eighties, who have an apartment in my house; my two children, their spouses (my children-in-law), and my five grandchildren—who all live close enough that there's never a reason to miss a family meal. In an era when generations are separated by distance and the demands of hectic life more than ever before, when sitting down to supper seems a lost custom, I am amazed at how lucky I am. For hours on end, four generations of my family gather in the kitchen and dining room, cooking, eating, cleaning up, and always talking—while the kids run

MEET MY FAMILY

Let me introduce you now to the cast of characters who help in the kitchen and gather around the large pine table for family meals and festive occasions.

My mother, Erminia, eighty-plus, and her living partner, Giovanni, eighty-plus, who have their own apartment upstairs but are always on hand as sous-chefs and prep cooks.

My daughter, Tanya, and my delightful son-in-law, Corrado Manuali, and their two children, Julia, age one, and Lorenzo, five They live within five minutes' walking distance from us, so they appear regularly to see what's cooking.

Joseph Bastianich, my son; his loving wife Deanna Damiano; and their children: Olivia, seven; Miles, four; and Ethan, two. They live in Greenwich, Connecticut, about seventeen miles from us, and rarely a week passes by that they are not gathered around the table.

I have a brother, Franco Motika, who with his wife, Margaret, lives in Poughkeepsie, New York, with their three grown children—Paul, Estelle, and Eric—all of whom join us for many a meal.

To say nothing of family and friends from Istria and other parts of the world, friends of the children, and neighbors—there is always someone passing through.

At the table with my five grandchildren: left to right, Ethan, Miles, Olivia, Lorenzo, and Julia. (You'll meet the other members of my family as their pictures appear throughout the book.)

around laughing (or sometimes crying). These are the most precious moments of my life.

In this book, I want to share with you the cooking I do at home, in the midst of my busy work life, in a house where you never know how many people are going to come through, hungry. There are the fast, often improvised dishes that I make for my mother, Gianni, and myself if I get home early, or might make for their dinner before I leave for work. There are the family favorites, dishes that my brother and I grew up on and that the new generations now demand (and that my brother expects when he and his wife drive down from Fishkill, New York).

There are special-occasion and holiday dishes that for reasons of tradition and fabulous taste we must have at least once or twice a year. And there are a bunch of new dishes that came into being in the course of playing in my kitchen (and that of my editor Judith Jones), seeing what was in the cupboard and the refrigerator and following an impulse about how to put it all together. Some of these spontaneous inventions were so good that they may become family favorites in time; perhaps in your family too.

Explaining *how* I cook at home is another goal of this book. The recipes detail the techniques that I consider most important—the ones I rely on to make delicious dishes quickly. I describe why I use them so that you can better understand and adapt them to your own cooking. I tell you the specific pots, pans, and tools that I reach for again and again, sometimes for their effect on the food or because I cook in big quantities in order to have leftovers to send home with my children or to put in the freezer. Some of these will be suitable for your needs; others may not be. Also, the ingredients out of which I create dishes at home are flexible, depending on what is on hand in the fridge or freezer or what seasonal treat we may find at the supermarket. I want these recipes to serve as a guide so you will be flexible, too, and make your own substitutions, additions, or simplifications. No dish has to be done exactly the same way every time.

More than the specifics of any recipe or technique, however, I want this book to convey the joy and creativity I find in family cooking. Putting home-cooked food on the table—carefully purchased, consciously prepared, responding to the likes and dislikes of the people who look to us for nourishment—is a nurturing act. Through this effort we teach and share our emotions, wisdom, and love.

How we feel about our time in the kitchen, at the stove, is also part of the nurturing, I believe. When we approach the food before us as an organic connection to the world we live in, we share a deeper appreciation of the earth's magnificent gifts. Cooking is a rhythmic, changing, vital process and when we are in the kitchen we should sense the rhythm—and set the rhythm too. We should be engaged with the food in front of us and what is going on inside the pot, regardless of what the recipe says. Do the carrots need more moisture? or higher heat? Do they need more seasoning? What can you do to develop their best flavor and finest consistency?

In truth, I hope these recipes are just a starting point for you. Be innovative, be daring: add flavoring agents, change the textures—cook following your own tastes. Cook with your feelings and passion! Cook, too, with an eye on tomorrow: perhaps you'll make a bit more of something I've suggested, and the next day you'll extend it into an entirely new meal. Save, and savor, leftovers with zeal: a few big florets of broccoli, an asparagus or two, a handful of string beans, and a ½ pint of marinara sauce will become a great *primavera* sauce for pasta just when you thought you had nothing in the house to eat. I've put my cooking ideas and instincts, favorite tastes and pet passions everywhere in the book to show what moves me. But ultimately I want you to let yourself go in the kitchen: let the food lead you first and then follow your own senses and spirit of fun—this is the best way to add spice and sweetness to the food on your family table.

And now, *buon appetito* and *tutti a tavola a mangiare* (all to the table to eat).

Welcome to My Kitchen
Benvenuti nella mia Cucina

Welcome to my kitchen. I want to give you a look around this space—the heart of my home—and at the staple foods and equipment I cook with at home.

I have a comfortable kitchen, which after thirty years in the cramped galleys of restaurants is a dream. At last I have lots of work space atop the cabinets, which sit at either end of my double-oven commercial stove. Together they form an island which stretches across one side of the kitchen. My favorite work space is at the left of the island, with the stove burners immediately to my right, an easy reach to shake a skillet. Underneath my countertop prep area are cupboards with my essential seasonings. The refrigerator and freezer are a few steps to the left. The main sink is right behind me (with a view of my fig tree through the window); next to it, there's a hearth housing a wood-fired rotisserie and grill. From hooks and racks above the sink and hearth hang skillets, saucepans, and pot covers; sieves, spiders, tongs, ladles, and spatulas.

But the most delightful aspect of my kitchen is that the work counters and cook top are open to the eating area with the long pine table—my family table—at which we take most of our meals and do most of our living as well. When I am making supper, I can watch Tanya and Lorenzo doing art; keep an eye on Julia in her playpen and Ethan searching for cookies; see my mother picking fresh chives from the little garden bed outside the windows. Giovanni is peeling garlic for me and we're conversing in Italian. This is the way I cook!

The Foods I Cook with at Home

Most days when I cook lunch or supper at home I don't have time to shop, so I get my ideas by opening some of the dozens of doors in the kitchen—for the dry storage cupboards, the refrigerator, and the freezer—and seeing what's behind them.

Let's open some of these together, starting with the cooking staples I keep close by, in the cabinet right under my cutting boards and the cupboards on the other side of the stove island. I haven't included every item you might find on a given day since I do collect seasonings, condiments, and regional specialties on my trips, and incorporate them into dishes when I am improvising and having fun. And you don't need everything listed here to cook my recipes, though I have marked in bold the items that are, in my opinion, essentials to keep on hand at all times:

Basics for stovetop cooking, on and under the counter:

- **Extra-virgin olive oil: good grade for cooking; premium for seasoning**
- **Canola oil**
- **Vinegars—red wine vinegar; balsamic vinegar, medium grade (see page 39); distilled white vinegar;** cider vinegar
- **Sea salt, both granular (table grind) and coarse crystal (*sel de mer*); crystal kosher salt;** premium crystal sea salt (*fleur de sel*)
- **Whole black peppercorns,** whole white peppercorns
- *Peperoncino*—hot red pepper flakes, for that touch of spiciness we all like
- **Dried oregano (Greek); dried thyme**
- **All-purpose flour**

- **Dried bread crumbs**—dried bread crumbs can stay in an air-tight container in the cupboard; if seasoned with oil or cheese keep in refrigerator

The Vegetable Bin—a dark and cool place:

- **Garlic—lots!**
- **Shallots**
- **Common (yellow) onions, red onions,** sweet onions (such as Maui, Walla Walla, or Vidalia)
- **Russet (baking) potatoes, small red potatoes,** Yukon Gold potatoes

In the cupboards:

- **All-purpose flour, unbleached;** whole-wheat flour; semolina flour; buckwheat flour (oily specialty flours, like chestnut and chickpea, in the freezer).
- **Yellow polenta (imported);** buckwheat polenta (*taragna*); white polenta
- **Short-grain Italian rice for risotto (Arborio or Carnaroli); long-grain white rice;** brown rice, wild rice
- Dried pastas—long: spaghetti, linguini, perciatelli, capellini; tubular: ziti, rigati, rigatoni, cavatappi, radiatori, gomiti, campanelle; and for soups: tubetini, stellinie, orzo, ancini pepe. Plus dry whole-wheat linguini or ziti, and other different shapes to enjoy as you find them in the store.
- **Dried *cannellini* beans; dried *borlotti* or cranberry beans;** dried black-eye beans
- Dried lentils
- Split peas
- Farro-barley
- **Golden raisins, prunes, dried apricots,** dried cherries
- **Dried porcini** (my mother puts them in the freezer) (see page 140)
- **Pine nuts, walnuts,** pecans, hazelnuts (put them in the freezer, too, for long storage)

- **Sugar, granulated; honey;** *zucchero da canna* (page 389); maple syrup; brown sugar (dark and light)

In the cupboards in cans and jars (I check the fridge first for open jars!):
- **San Marzano plum tomatoes** (page 124)
- **Imported tomato paste (preferably in tubes)**
- **Sun-dried tomatoes, packed in olive oil**
- Imported tuna fish packed in olive oil (*tonno in olio*)
- **Imported anchovies, packed in olive oil (in the freezer, if opened)**
- **Tiny capers (*nonpareil*) in vinegar brine**
- *Peperoncini,* **whole small peppers in vinegar brine, preferably Tuscan**
- Hot cherry peppers in vinegar brine (for hot-lovers, like me)
- **Roasted sweet red peppers* (pimento) in brine**
- **Canned, cooked beans:** *cannellini;* garbanzo (*ceci*)
- **Apricot jam,** rose hip jam, plum jam, strawberry jam, peanut butter
- Baby gherkin pickles
- Dijon mustard
- Ketchup

In the refrigerator—everyday dairy and cheeses:
- **Milk:** whole, 2%, and skim
- **Butter, unsalted** (there's salted too)
- **All-the-time cheeses: Parmigiano-Reggiano, Pecorino, and Grana Padano** (cheese rinds are saved in the fridge as well)
- Some-of-the-time cheeses: fresh mozzarella, fresh ricotta, crumbly goat cheese; ricotta salata, aged pecorino

In the refrigerator—vegetables and herbs:
- **Carrots, celery, scallions, leeks, spinach, cabbage, mushrooms, lettuces,** chard, parsnips, turnips, celery root, squashes
- **Italian parsley, fresh basil, fresh rosemary, fresh bay leaves,** fresh thyme, fresh mint (fresh horseradish and other herbs when in season)

In the refrigerator—odds and ends:

- **Bacon** (preferably slab or thick-cut); **prosciutto ends** (see page 129)
- **All kinds of olives:** black and green; brine-cured, oil-cured, with pits and pitted

In the freezer—cooking staples in pints and quarts:

- **All-Purpose Turkey Broth, page 80** (and turkey wings for more broth!)
- **Simple Tomato Sauce, page 132**
- **Marinara sauce, page 130**
- Summer tomato sauce, page 256
- **Bolognese sauce, page 143**
- Frozen green peas
- Frozen berries

The Skillets, Pots, and Tools I Cook with at Home

Though there are dozens of skillets hanging near the stove and cupboards full of pots and saucepans, I use the same ones day after day. Probably, all of us cooks have our favorites—they feel familiar and comfortable in our hands; we know how much they hold and how fast they heat.

My everyday pots may be larger than the ones you use now, in part, as I mentioned before, because I always want to have food to send home with others. But large quantity cooking is also essential to my principle of building many dishes from elemental components, like sauces and soup bases, that I freeze for future meals. I hope you will become a convert to the efficiencies, conveniences, and creative possibilities that this style of cooking affords. In which case, you'll need the big saucepans and soup pots I use and specify in the recipes. A 12-quart stock pot, and 8- and 10-quart heavy saucepans or Dutch ovens, and cast-iron pan, make life much easier and more delicious.

It is also the case that my cooking techniques demand large surface or volume dimensions. This is true of almost every pasta dish I make, for which a 14-inch-diameter skillet is a must. I have two of them, and I use them for everything—meats, vegetables, sauces—so it's not unusual for both of those great old pans to be on the stove at the same time. I recommend this pan in dozens of recipes in this book, so I hope you will get at least one. I also depend on my heavy-duty roasting pans, 17 by 20 inches or even bigger for my main course roasts. The breadth is necessary, not for massive meat or poultry pieces, but to cook and caramelize a big quantity of vegetables and seasonings and to make a sauce in the roasting pan too.

I am *not* hooked on gadgets, though I have drawers full of them, often given to me as gifts. As you can glean from the recipes, which specify the cooking tools I use, there are a few things I must have nearby when I'm cooking. For pasta, I always use an Asian-made spider—the stir-fry tool with a wire basket on a long handle—to lift noodles from the cooking pot. I keep spiders in several sizes to use as tossers and stirrers. Metal tongs are also in my hands whenever I'm at the stove; several sizes are useful. Sieves and hand strainers, as well as larger draining baskets and colanders, are also essential implements, as are wooden spoons for mixing. There's nothing fancy about these things but they are the best extensions of my hands I have used—and hands and fingers are my favorite kitchen tools and the most important of all.

But my recipes, the recipes I share with you in this and other books, can be cooked in any size kitchen. Don't let this tour of my kitchen deter you. No matter how small your space, make it convenient and comfortable for you and your family. You can also reduce most of the recipes designed to serve six by cutting ingredients in half and using a somewhat smaller cooking vessel. Otherwise cook them as they are and you will have leftovers, which, when revisited creatively, can turn into delightful new dishes. I offer you some of those ideas throughout the book, but use your own imagination.

Lidia's Family Table

Welcoming Dishes—
Appetizers and Salads

Any of these dishes could be an antipasto, a salad, a side dish, or even the starring feature in the main course. They are put together with simple everyday ingredients that sparkle when treated with *amore* and just enough of the right condiments.

Take the roasted black olives, intense and crunchy with an orange twist: as well as being great snacks or the heart of an antipasto, they can be tossed into salads, folded into a sandwich, or added to enhance a pasta or risotto. What I truly get a challenge from is transforming seemingly plain vegetables into shining dishes. Any of these recipes will leave your guests' mouths puckering with flavors, and they'll be wanting more.

Top left: Cooked Carrot Salad with Pine Nuts and Golden Raisins; right, Mackerel Cured in Olive Oil; left, Roasted Acorn Squash Salad; right, Roasted Beet and Beet Greens Salad with Apple and Goat Cheese; third row, left, Roasted Black Olives and Pearl Onions, right, Pickled Peppers; fourth row, left, Roasted Eggplant and Tomato Salad, right (and above right), Mussels in Salsa Verde

Seafood Appetizers

One thinks of fish mostly as a main course. Not the Italians, not I. Marinated, pickled, whipped, or topped with a vinaigrette, fish makes a splendid welcome to the table, and a tasty addition to any antipasto or buffet spread.

Mackerel Cured in Olive Oil—*Sgombri sott'Olio*

Mackerel is a wonderful fish to buy when it is in season. It is inexpensive and intensely flavored, and when it is preserved in oil this way, you can keep it as long as a month; you'll have in your fridge a delicious treasure to draw on for a quick appetizer or lunch dish. The most common size is 11 to 12 inches, and the filleting and boning of these small fish can be quite a job. So, unless you are feeling ambitious, get your fishmonger to do the work.

SERVES 8

8 mackerel fillets (from 3 pounds whole mackerel)

Juice of 2 lemons, or more depending on size (about ½ cup)

1 teaspoon black peppercorns

1½ teaspoons salt

1½ to 2 cups extra-virgin olive oil

Lay the mackerel in a single layer in an 11- or 12-inch skillet, preferably stainless steel. The pan should be just big enough so that the fish fillets, nestled side by side, cover the bottom. Pour 2 cups or more water and the lemon juice over the fillets to cover them, and sprinkle half the peppercorns and 1 teaspoon of the salt over.

Set the pan over medium heat, and bring to a slow rolling boil. Turn down the heat, and simmer gently for 15 minutes.

Prop up a large wooden or plastic cutting board at a moderate angle, tipping toward the sink. When the fillets are done (to check: the point of a knife should slip through the center easily), remove them carefully from the pan with a slotted spatula and lay them on the board. Let them drain and cool completely.

Select a shallow glass or ceramic dish that will just hold the fillets in one layer, or you can use a smaller, slightly deeper dish that will accommodate two layers of fillets. Arrange the mackerel in whichever dish, sprinkle each layer lightly with salt and the remaining peppercorns, and pour in enough of the olive oil to cover the fillets.

If you are using the mackerel the same day, let it marinate for 2 to 3 hours at room temperature. Otherwise, cover securely with plastic wrap and store for up to a month in the refrigerator. Bring back to room temperature 2 hours before serving.

Marinated Mackerel and Red Onion Salad

6 fillets of Mackerel Cured in Olive Oil
  (preceding recipe)

2 tablespoons of the curing oil

1 medium Bermuda onion, thinly sliced
  and cut in ½-inch pieces
  (about 1 cup)

2 tablespoons red wine vinegar

2 tablespoons chopped fresh Italian
  parsley

Salt to taste

Break the mackerel up into bite-size pieces and toss with the oil, onion, vinegar, and parsley. Season with salt to taste. Divide among six salad plates and serve. You can also use it as a sandwich filling on a crispy roll; it is good on grilled bread, too, as in the next recipe (with or without mashed beans).

Bruschetta of Cured Mackerel and Beans

SERVES 4 OR MORE

4 fillets of Mackerel Cured in Olive Oil
  (page 3)

2 cups canned cannellini beans,
  drained and rinsed

18 thin slices red onion

2 tablespoons extra-virgin olive oil

Salt and freshly ground pepper to taste

4 large or 8 smaller slices country
  bread, grilled and brushed with
  olive oil

Lightly mash the mackerel and beans together, then toss with the red onions and oil, and season with salt and pepper. Spoon equal portions onto the slices of warm bruschetta (grilled bread).

Cured Mackerel and Tomato Salad

SERVES 4

Arrange two tomato slices in a line on each of four plates, and sprinkle lightly with sea salt.

Set one mackerel fillet on top of each row of tomato slices, sprinkle on a little more salt, and drizzle the curing oil and balsamic vinegar on top. Sprinkle chopped parsley over all.

8 slices ripe tomatoes

About ½ teaspoon sea salt

4 fillets Mackerel Cured in Olive Oil (page 3)

2 tablespoons mackerel-curing oil

4 teaspoons balsamic vinegar

1 tablespoon chopped fresh Italian parsley

THE TOUGH UGLY COD I LOVE THE BEST

Cod is preserved by different methods and in many forms. In Istria, the type we used were whole small cod, called stoccafisso, *which had been air-dried—not salt-cured—until hard as wood. When I was little, the long skinny bodies, with the heads cut off and the dry gills looking like gaping mouths, made me think of shriveled sea monsters. To soften them, first my father would beat the fish with a wooden mallet (and we'd all pitch in); then they were soaked for days and cooked for hours.*

Stoccafisso, in my opinion, makes the best baccalà mantecato (see next page). *Fortunately, I can buy it now at my favorite fish store in Astoria, Queens. It still needs lengthy soaking, cooking, and boning. But the electric mixer has eliminated almost all of the pounding!*

With either salt cod or stoccafisso, *I prefer an electric mixer for whipping the cooked fish into* baccalà mantecato, *rather than the food processor. The paddle of the mixer spreads and separates the softened fibers, emulsifying them with the potatoes, olive oil, and cream, whereas the food processor chops up the fibers. The mixer makes a spread with texture like the one I grew up with; the tactile sensation in the mouth makes it taste better.*

If you want to try stoccafisso *for a truly traditional* baccalà mantecato, *write to me for details at www.lidiasitaly.com.*

Baccalà Mantecato—A Savory Spread of Whipped Salt Cod

*T*his is one of our family's cherished holiday dishes, a creamy, garlicky appetizer spread, full of flavor, that we enjoy on everything—good crusty bread, grilled bread, crackers, crostini, bread sticks, carrot sticks, celery sticks, even spaghetti, gnocchi, risotto.

It is good as an hors d'oeuvre, an appetizer, or a main course, and great for parties. It brings lots of complex flavor to anything that it is spread on.

Baccalà mantecato *is important to our family, though, for more than its addictive savor. It is a link to Istria, my native region, where the imminent arrival of Christmas at our house (and everyone else's) was scented by the unmistakable vapors of dried codfish, cooking for hours and hours. These were not fish from our local waters, but a delicacy from Northern Europe, a fish that was brought in to be bartered and exchanged for olive oil and good Mediterranean wine, carefully selected and dearly bought. But despite the expense, or the time and labor in its preparation,* baccalà mantecato *always appeared on the table for the seafood feast on Christmas Eve, la Vigilia. And we devoured it at every holiday gathering, but always saving some for tomorrow. Making* baccalà mantecato *was the mark of a good cook in Istria, and many would stop in at a particular house not just for the holiday greetings but also for a taste of the* baccalà.

In our household, my father was the chief cook of baccalà mantecato—*it was his one culinary triumph—and that makes it all the more special to me. Though he has been gone for many years, his masterful touch with this dish remains with me and inspires me; every time I make it now, I remember him, with every bite. . . .*

MAKES ABOUT 4 CUPS

1 pound boneless *baccalà* (salt cod), soaked to remove salt (see box, page 9)

1 medium russet potato (about ½ pound)

2 plump garlic cloves, finely minced

1 cup extra-virgin olive oil

½ cup half-and-half or light cream

When the *baccalà* is sufficiently soaked, cut it into smaller pieces—6 inches or so—and put them in a saucepan or deep skillet with at least an inch of water to cover. Bring to a boil, set the cover ajar (rest it on a wooden spoon set on the rim of the pan), and cook at a steady bubbling boil for 20 minutes or more, until the cod is easy to flake but still has body and shape. Don't let it start to break apart. Lift it out of the cooking water, and let it drain and cool in a colander. Reserve a cup of the cooking water.

Meanwhile, rinse the potato but leave it whole and unpeeled. Put it in a small pot covered with cold water. Bring to the boil, and cook steadily until you can easily pierce the potato with a knife blade. Let it cool, and peel it.

Set up the electric mixer and flake all the fish into the bowl. Beat with the paddle at low speed to break the fish up more; drop in the minced garlic, and beat at medium speed while you pour in half the olive oil very gradually in a thin stream, then add the potato and incorporate it; continue beating at low speed as you gradually add the rest of the oil. Now raise the speed to high and whip the fish to lighten it. Reduce the speed to medium and incorporate the half-and-half gradually, then whip at high speed again. At this point the whipped cod should be smooth and fluffy, almost like mashed potatoes but with texture. If it is very dense, you can thin it with the cooking water (but be careful: too much water will make it too salty). Finally, season with pepper and beat it in to blend.

If you use a food processor instead of a mixer, follow the same order of additions, and process as needed to form a light, smooth spread.

Put the spread in containers and store sealed, in the refrigerator, for up to a week. You can also freeze *baccalà mantecato*; the texture will not be as creamy, but it will have good flavor and makes a delicious pasta sauce (recipe follows).

½ cup poaching water from cooking the *baccalà*

Freshly ground black pepper to taste

RECOMMENDED EQUIPMENT

A heavy-duty electric mixer with the paddle attachment or a food processor

How to Serve Baccalà Mantecato

I like *baccalà* best served with warm grilled country bread, but *baccalà* can be served on crackers, as a dip for crudités, on grilled polenta, or with anything crunchy that you might have in your fridge or cupboard. It is a wonderful condiment for dry or fresh pasta and delightful when whipped at the last minute into a simple basic risotto. *Baccalà* can be made into a patty, breaded, and fried, then served warm on top of a mixed salad.

Quick Pasta with Baccalà Mantecato

A great way to enjoy baccalà mantecato, before you eat it all as a spread or dip, is as a dressing for cooked pasta; 1 cup is enough to make a flavorful sauce for a pound of spaghetti, other long dry pasta, or fresh maltagliati pasta, which my father always liked. It is also good to dress potato gnocchi.

Transforming the baccalà mantecato into a pasta sauce is best done in a big skillet—14 inches in diameter—into which you can drop all the pasta, straight from the cooking pot, and dress it—see the first part of chapter 3 for the basics of skillet sauces and how pasta and sauce are finished together.

FOR 1 POUND OF PASTA OR GNOCCHI

⅓ cup extra-virgin olive oil

3 plump garlic cloves, sliced (about ¼ cup)

1 pinch to ½ teaspoon dried *peperoncino* (hot red pepper flakes)

1 cup or more *Baccalà Mantecato* (preceding recipe)

Hot water from the pasta-cooking pot

¼ teaspoon salt, or more to taste

Freshly ground black pepper

¼ cup chopped fresh Italian parsley

Start cooking your dry pasta in a big pot of salted water just before starting the sauce. If you are doing fresh pasta or gnocchi, don't put it in until after you start the sauce.

Pour the oil in the skillet, scatter the garlic in the oil, and put the pan over medium heat. Get the garlic sizzling, but don't let it get dark; stir it or shake the pan frequently. After a couple of minutes, sprinkle the pepper flakes in the oil, let them sizzle for a minute, then scrape in the *baccalà* spread and stir it well in the skillet.

Let the *baccalà* heat up for a few minutes; ladle 2 cups of boiling water from the pasta pot into the skillet and stir it, incorporating the *baccalà mantecato*, garlic, and oil into a thin sauce. Bring it to a boil, stirring, add the salt and pepper to taste, then adjust the heat to keep the sauce simmering actively until the pasta is almost *al dente*.

Add the drained pasta or gnocchi to the skillet, and toss to coat and finish cooking with the sauce (see page 92). Remove from the heat, toss with parsley, and serve.

TAKING THE SALT OUT OF SALT COD

Salt cod comes in fascinating variety. What you'll find in any market usually depends on the ethnic community in the neighborhood. There may be baccalà with bones or boneless; whole sides of fish or trimmed fillets; lightly or heavily salted fish; fish that's totally dry and hanging from the ceiling or moist fish in the refrigerator. But every kind must be soaked, for hours or even days, to purge it of salt. And then it must be cooked to soften it. Keep in mind: the thinner the piece of fish, usually the saltier it is. I prefer the thicker cuts.

For this small recipe—a fraction of what my father used to make—I suggest you buy moist Canadian salt-cod fillets, packed in 1-pound boxes and refrigerated. The boxes often give soaking instructions, but I recommend the following method for all types of boneless baccalà:

Put the fish in a large container, such as a plastic food-storage box or a big bowl that will fit in your sink but is big enough to keep the baccalà completely submerged. Run cold water into the container in the sink to cover the fish, fill it to the brim, and let it start spilling over (and running into the open drain). Close the tap so there's only the slightest steady drip of fresh water into the container, which will slowly but continuously wash out the salt. To minimize the dripping noise, drape a clean wet kitchen towel over the faucet, positioned to catch the drips, with one end in the water bath. The towel will silently conduct the fresh water down.

Soak under dripping water overnight—10 to 12 hours for most kinds of baccalà. It's OK to move the container if you need the sink, of course—if you do, dump the water and cover the fish with fresh. And if you can't keep the drip going, just dump and change the water completely at least every 4 hours.

Here's how I decide when baccalà is ready for cooking: I lift the flesh out of the water, press my finger against it at a thick part, then touch my finger to my tongue. If it's palatably salty, or very close, I can cook it, since more salt will come out during cooking. Don't soak baccalà longer than necessary, as you will start to lose the flavor of the fish.

Drain the baccalà well and cook it right away or within a day or so. Store it in the refrigerator, patted dry and well wrapped.

Tonno sott'Olio—Homemade Marinated Tuna in Olive Oil

*C*anned tuna is a staple in my kitchen—in one of the cupboards, there's always a tall stack of colorful cans of excellent Italian tonno in olio di oliva. Tuna packed in olive oil is the only kind to have, in my opinion, and I make it the basis for many meals, sometimes some pasta for lunch or dinner, or a salad for myself, my mother, and Gianni, or sandwiches for the kids.

But when I want the best marinated tuna, I make my own marinated tonno sott'olio: I poach thick tuna steaks gently for 15 minutes, let them cool and dry for a couple of hours, then pack the fish in jars in big chunks, submerged in extra-virgin olive oil. It is truly simple, as this recipe will show you.

If you love tuna, then I know you will make this recipe your own. Just a chunk of it on a plate, with nothing more than a drizzle of the marinating oil, makes a great antipasto. Or dress it up with onion or tomatoes, as I suggest for Marinated Mackerel (pages 4 and 5). Use it in the colorful salad I give you here with cherry tomatoes, red onion, and scallions, or see how tonno sott'olio takes your own favorite tuna salad to a new level. And don't miss the opportunity to make the outstanding pasta sauce with tomatoes on page 14.

With this recipe you'll have about 2 pounds of tuna, in jars or crocks of oil. Stored in the refrigerator, it will keep for a month or more, giving you plenty of time to try it in several different dishes. But I guarantee you'll want more: to make larger batches, just multiply the ingredients and follow the basic procedures.

MAKES 1½ TO 2½ POUNDS, ENOUGH FOR SEVERAL RECIPES

2 to 3 pounds tuna steaks, 1¼ to 1½ inches thick

1 to 1½ cups white vinegar

6 bay leaves

2½ teaspoons salt

2 to 3 cups best-quality extra-virgin olive oil, or more as needed

1 teaspoon whole black peppercorns

Set the pan on the stove and lay in the tuna steaks. Pour enough water over them just to cover them, then pour in the vinegar. Drop in the bay leaves and sprinkle on 2 teaspoons of the salt. Bring the liquid to a boil over medium-high heat, shifting the fish a bit to keep it from sticking to the pan bottom.

When it is boiling, partially cover the pan and adjust the heat to maintain a steady but gentle bubbling. Cook for 15 minutes or a little longer, until the steaks are cooked through. Test by inserting a toothpick: when the flesh is fully cooked, the toothpick will go all the way through, with only a little resistance.

Turn off the heat and lift out each steak with tongs and a wide spatula, supporting it so it doesn't break. Spill off excess water and lay the steaks on the wire rack. Sprinkle the remaining ½ teaspoon salt evenly over the tuna, and let the steaks cool and air-dry for about 2 hours, turning the pieces after an hour to facilitate drying. Meanwhile, remove the bay leaves from the poaching liquid, blot them on towels, and let them air-dry too; discard the poaching liquid.

When dry, slice the steaks in half or into several pieces that will fit into your jars. Put the pieces in a shallow bowl pour some of the olive oil over them, and turn them so they are well coated with oil. Layer the pieces into jars one at a time, pouring a bit more oil over to make sure there's a film of oil surrounding each piece.

As you pack in the fish, divide the bay leaves and peppercorns among the containers. When you've put as many pieces in each jar as you want—you don't have to fill them to the top—pour in more oil to cover the fish by at least ¼ inch.

Before refrigerating, tap repeatedly on the sides of the jars to shake loose air bubbles. You may also insert a table-knife blade down along the inside of the jar and slide it slowly all around the circumference, moving the contents very slightly to release trapped air. Now let the containers sit for 15 minutes or so, so the bubbles rise to the surface. Tap the jar gently on a hard surface so any remaining air bubbles will rise.

Cover the jars with plastic wrap and/or jar lids and set them in the refrigerator. Marinate 2 days before opening. As you take fish and oil from the jar, pour in more extra-virgin olive oil if necessary so that any remaining fish is completely covered with a layer of oil.

RECOMMENDED EQUIPMENT

A 10- or 11-inch sauté pan with 3-inch sides or other shallow pan (see box, page 13)

1 or 2 wire cooling racks large enough to hold the tuna steaks

Clean, dry wide-mouth glass jars or glazed crocks with a total capacity of 6 to 8 cups

Salad of Homemade Marinated Tuna, Small Tomatoes, and Red Onion

T his is a special salad worthy of your homemade tonno sott'olio. *You blanch the tomatoes and scallions, and briefly sauté the red onion to mellow pungency and soften textures. The salad needs a good hour of marinating to let the sweet and savory flavors mingle. Incidentally, leftovers make great juicy sandwiches.*

I recommend white balsamic vinegar here, to wilt the red onion and dress the salad. White balsamic is not a traditional product, but it comes from Modena, like any decent balsamic, and it has a clean taste and a light color that don't muddy dishes the way dark balsamic can. If you can't find it, use regular wine vinegar. You may also use top-quality canned tuna in this salad, but drain and discard the packing oil and substitute fresh extra-virgin olive oil in the dressing and sauté.

SERVES 6 AS A FIRST COURSE, 10 OR MORE AS PART OF AN ANTIPASTO SPREAD

8 ounces or so homemade *Tonno sott'Olio* (about ⅓ of a full batch: page 10) or imported Italian tuna packed in olive oil

4-ounce bunch of scallions (about a dozen)

1 pint cherry and/or pear tomatoes, preferably mixed colors and shapes

1 small red onion (3 or 4 ounces)

2 tablespoons *tonno*-marinating oil or fresh extra-virgin olive oil

¼ teaspoon salt

1 tablespoon white balsamic vinegar

3 tablespoons tiny capers in brine, drained, or less to taste

Prepping the Salad Ingredients

Drain the tuna: save the oil from homemade *tonno*; discard the oil from canned tuna. Trim the scallions and remove all loose or wilted layers (see photo, page 251), keeping all the tight and tender white and green; don't cut them.

Rinse the tomatoes and make a slit in the skin at the stem end of each. Bring 2 quarts of water to the boil in a saucepan; set up a bowl of icy water nearby. Drop in the tomatoes and blanch for about ½ minute; scoop them from the pot and drop into the ice water.

Now blanch the scallions in the boiling water for 2 to 3 minutes, just to soften them, then refresh in the ice water. Drain the chilled tomatoes; peel off and discard the skin. Lift out the chilled scallions, pat dry with paper towels, and slice crosswise into 1-inch lengths.

Peel the onion, trim the ends, and slice lengthwise in quarters; cut the wedges crosswise in half. If using a big onion, slice up a heaping cup of 1-inch wedge-shaped pieces. Put the onion pieces and the 2 tablespoons of olive oil in a medium skillet set over medium-high heat. Sprinkle on ¼ teaspoon salt, and cook, toss, and stir for 1 to 2 minutes, to get all the onion pieces sizzling and softening, then pour in the white balsamic vinegar. Toss the onion in the vinegar for a minute or so, then transfer to a mixing bowl.

Assembling, Dressing, and Marinating the Salad

When the onions have cooled a bit, break apart the drained tuna into 1-inch chunks and drop them in the bowl with the scallions and the capers. Toss together, then sprinkle the dressing ingredients over them and toss some more. Drop the peeled tomatoes into the bowl, and fold them into the salad so they're coated with dressing but don't break apart.

Let the salad marinate for an hour or so. Adjust the seasonings and dressings to taste, and serve on a big platter or individual plates.

FOR DRESSING

¼ teaspoon dried oregano

4 tablespoons *tonno*-marinating oil or fresh extra-virgin olive oil, or to taste

4 tablespoons white balsamic vinegar, or more to taste

¼ teaspoon salt, or to taste

Freshly ground black pepper to taste

TIPS FOR THE BEST HOMEMADE TONNO SOTT'OLIO

- Tonno sott'olio *needs time to marinate and develop flavor! Cook the tuna and put it in oil at least 2 days before you plan to serve it.*

- *Ask the fishmonger to cut all your tuna steaks 1¼ to 1½ inches thick, for uniform cooking. And the slices should be no more than 7 inches across at the widest point, so you can just cut them in half for pieces that will fit neatly into wide-mouth storage jars. Larger pieces also tend to break apart after cooking.*

- *I like the* ventresca, *the belly part of the tuna, the best, and it is cheaper. Being the belly, it is a bit fattier, but, then, that is what makes it good. So you might want to ask your fishmonger for it and try it.*

- *Poach the tuna in a wide shallow pan, such as a straight-sided sauté pan—but use the smallest one you have in which the steaks will fit in one layer. This will minimize the amount of cooking liquid needed, and so reduce the loss of flavor. For 2 to 3 pounds of tuna, a 10- or 11-inch pan should do.*

- *If the fish is wet when it goes into the marinating oil, it can ferment and spoil. Allow 2 hours for the fish to cool, drain, and dry after poaching.*

- *Air trapped in the marinating jar will also hasten spoilage. To avoid this, coat the fish with oil before packing and rid the jar of air bubbles, as instructed.*

Pasta with a Sauce of Tomato and Homemade *Tonno sott'Olio*

Though it cooks for only 15 minutes, this tomato sauce gets loads of flavor from both the tonno and the olio of your marinated tuna. But you don't want just to boil the tuna and tomatoes together: it is essential to add the fish, the oil, and all the other ingredients to the big skillet at the right time. The technique of skillet sauces, and how to finish pasta and sauce together, is explained in depth on pages 89 to 93.

For this chunky sauce, I recommend a short dried pasta with lots of nooks and crannies, like cavatelli or campanelle or conchiglie. These will catch some tuna for you with each bite, so you don't end up with all the tuna swimming in the bottom of your bowl.

FOR I POUND OF PASTA, SERVING 6

About I pound homemade *Tonno sott'Olio* (page 10), in marinating oil

About ¾ cup marinating oil

I medium onion, diced into ½-inch pieces (about I cup)

½ teaspoon salt, or more to taste

¼ to ½ cup tiny capers in brine, drained

¼ to I teaspoon dried *peperoncino* (hot red pepper flakes)

½ teaspoon dried oregano

I 28-ounce can (3 cups) San Marzano or other Italian plum tomatoes, with juices, crushed by hand into very small chunks

Hot water from the pasta-cooking pot

¼ cup chopped fresh Italian parsley

Lift a few chunks of tuna from the oil and hold them over a bowl (don't wipe or drain them—drips of oil are fine). With your fingers, break the chunks into flaky bits, ¾ inch wide or so, to get 4 cups total.

Meanwhile, bring a pot of salted water to a boil, and start cooking your pasta shortly after you've started the sauce (see box, page 98).

Pour ⅓ cup of the marinating oil into a 14-inch skillet, scatter in the onion, and set over medium-high heat. Sprinkle with ¼ teaspoon salt, and cook, stirring, for 1½ minutes or so, until the onion is sizzling. Clear one side of the skillet and drop in the capers, more or less according to taste, and stir to toast them in the hot spot for 1½ minutes, then stir and cook with the onion for another minute.

Drop in the flaked tuna and cook, still over medium-high heat, for 2 minutes, stirring occasionally. Sprinkle on another ¼ teaspoon salt and the oregano. Let the tuna caramelize lightly but not darken. (If the pan seems very dry, add another tablespoon or two of oil.) Drop *peperoncino*, to taste, into a hot spot, and toast for a minute, then stir in with the other ingredients.

Pour the crushed tomatoes and juices into the pan; slosh the tomato container with a cup or so of boiling pasta water and pour that in too. Now stir in 2 more tablespoons of tuna-marinating oil, and bring the sauce to an active bubbling boil.

Cook for 10 minutes or more, at the same time as the pasta. Lift the pasta from the pot while it is still slightly undercooked, and drop it into the skillet of simmering sauce. Toss and cook pasta and sauce together until the pasta is fully cooked and the sauce coats it well and is not soupy. Remove from the heat, and toss pasta with the parsley; drizzle over another tablespoon or two of tuna-marinating oil, and toss again.

Serve immediately in warm bowls.

COOKING WITH OLIO FROM TONNO SOTT'OLIO

To have fabulous tuna is not the only reason I make homemade tonno sott'olio. The fish marinates in my best extra-virgin olive oil; after a few days, the oil is loaded with flavor that I can incorporate in tuna dishes as well. With tuna taken from a can, however, this treasure is missing. Even with top imported brands, I have no idea how old the can is or what effects a deteriorated oil might have on a dish—so I always drain canned tuna and discard the packing oil.

Still, there's a challenge with my fresh, flavorful olio from the tuna jar, which applies to all oils in cooking: how do I retain all the taste of the marinating oil or the freshness and taste of uncooked olive oil? The pasta-sauce recipe illustrates how I do this, by adding the oil in stages.

Some of the oil goes directly into the skillet, to serve as a fat in which the other ingredients cook and caramelize. This oil contributes flavor to the dish, but the high temperatures effectively change many flavor elements.

Therefore, I add oil after, in this case, the tomatoes have provided a liquid base and lowered the temperature of the sauce. Most of the added oil's flavor remains and is not altered by higher temperatures.

Finally, after the pasta has been dressed in the skillet and comes off the heat, I toss in a couple of spoonfuls of even more oil. This last addition reinforces the flavor; it puts the "smile" on the pasta that you may have heard me talk about, by giving it a sheen as well as lending its own fresh note to the layered harmony of flavors.

Mussels in *Salsa Verde*

Here's a welcoming dish, *delicious and eye-catching*.

2 pounds mussels

3 or 4 bay leaves, preferably fresh

2 tablespoons sliced garlic

FOR SERVING

1 cup *Salsa Verde* (½ recipe on
 page 362)

1 cup or so *Salmoriglio* (page 366)

1 cup or so Smooth Sweet Red Pepper
 Sauce (page 364)

Lemon wedges

Sprigs of fresh parsley

Rinse and scrub the mussels well under running water. If the mussels have hairy beards attached, pick these off just before cooking.

Pour 2 cups of water into a 14-inch skillet or other wide shallow pot; drop in the bay leaves and garlic. Bring to the boil over high heat and cook, covered, for a couple of minutes, to release the flavors.

Lift the cover, dump in all the mussels, and cover again. Cook over high heat, shaking the pot frequently, for 4 to 5 minutes, or until all the mussels have opened. Remove from the heat. Scoop the mussels out of the pot with a spider, onto a platter or into a colander, to drain further and cool (save the cooking liquor for broth or other dishes). When cool, remove and discard the upper shells of the mussels, leaving the meats attached to the lower shells.

Before serving, top each mussel with a small spoonful of *salsa verde* or other sauce and arrange on serving platters—see the flowerlike presentation in the photo opposite page 1. Place lemon wedges on the platters if you like; a bunch of Italian parsley on the side of the dressed mussels is another nice decorative touch.

HEALTHY EATING

Use the best and the freshest ingredients, make your food healthful, prepare it with awareness, make it taste good, and diversify what you eat. That's the principle I keep in mind when I cook for my family, my guests, and myself.

We are all familiar with the food pyramid and how much we should eat of what and when. But eating should be pleasurable and approached with a positive state of mind and anticipation. There should be no guilt in eating; when we eat, we are nourishing our bodies, our minds, our souls. And we do it best in a context with others, be it family, friends, or strangers.

The two key words in healthy eating are diversity and moderation, and I think the Mediterranean-Italian way exemplifies this. In preparing an Italian meal, seasonal fresh products are paramount, and the preparation should be as simple as possible, using mostly olive oil as the fat of choice. These are two rather simplistic notions for such a huge topic, but they hold true.

What really makes the difference is how Italians eat their meals. An Italian meal is like a symphony. The first movement is antipasto—an array of vegetables, cured fish, meats, and cheeses, not an overload but just a tease to the senses. The second movement could either be some soup or pasta—tre forchettate, three forkfuls, as it is customary to say. The next movement is the main course, about a third part proteins always accompanied by contorni, mostly of vegetables. The closing is rarely an intricate dessert but, rather, a delightfully ripened fruit and/or a chunk of cheese.

Wine is always part of the table; it is food for Italians, and a glass is customary even with lunch. In a beautiful setting, sharing with family and friends, the meal is a joyous and rewarding experience.

The diversity of tastes and textures in such a meal satiates us mentally; we are content, and our brains signal our stomachs that we need no more food. If you bypass feeding the psyche, your stomach will require much more food to feel full.

Planning such a meal does not entail a tremendous amount of time. It is a state of mind, and a quest for living life well every day.

Shrimp and Scallops *Gratinate—Gamberi e Capesante Gratinate*

18 medium-large shrimp
(about 30 ounces)

18 sea scallops (about 18 ounces)

¼ cup extra-virgin olive oil

4 sprigs fresh thyme

8 garlic cloves, smashed

½ teaspoon salt

1 teaspoon dried *peperoncino*
(hot red pepper flakes)

Soft butter, for buttering baking dishes

⅓ cup lemon juice

⅓ cup dry white wine

1 recipe Garlic Butter (recipe follows)

1 recipe Seasoned Bread Crumbs
(recipe follows)

Lemon slices as garnish

RECOMMENDED EQUIPMENT

Nine 5-to-6-inch gratin dishes, or an
8-by-12-inch shallow baking dish

Shell the shrimp, leaving the tails on. Split lengthwise up to the last link of the tail, and scrape out any black veins. Feel each scallop, and if there is a small, hard muscle, trim it away.

Marinate the shrimp and scallops in the olive oil, thyme, garlic, salt, and pepper for 2 to 3 hours.

Preheat the oven to 450°.

Generously butter the nine gratin dishes (or the large baking dish, if you are using that), then sprinkle on ½ tablespoon each of lemon juice and white wine. Holding a shrimp by the tail, set it down in the dish so the split sides are splayed out to form a base and the tail is up-right. Arrange another shrimp next to it at one end of the dish, and two scallops at the other, for individual portions. (If you are using the large baking dish, put all the scallops at one end and all of the shrimps, tails up, at the other.)

Cut the garlic butter in nine equal parts. Then cut each part into cubes and distribute equal amounts over the seafood in the nine gratins. Sprinkle about 1½ tablespoons of the seasoned bread crumbs over each. (If using the large dish, scatter all the butter over, and then sprinkle all the bread crumbs on top.)

Bake in the preheated oven for 15 minutes, until the top is browned and crispy. If it is not sufficiently brown and crunchy, slip it under a hot broiler for a minute or so. Serve with a slice of lemon.

Garlic Butter

Heat the olive oil in a small pan and cook the garlic and shallots gently until soft but not brown. Pour in the white wine and lemon juice, bring to a boil, and cook until almost evaporated. Cool completely, then beat with the softened butter and parsley until blended. Refrigerate or freeze. Double or triple the amounts if you like, and keep a roll of this delicious butter frozen for future use.

1 ½ tablespoons extra-virgin olive oil

3 fat garlic cloves, finely chopped

2 shallots, finely chopped

¼ cup dry white wine

1 tablespoon lemon juice

4 ounces (1 stick) unsalted butter, at room temperature

1 tablespoon chopped fresh parsley

Seasoned Bread Crumbs

Mix all the ingredients together until the crumbs are evenly moistened with oil. If you want to make extra, increase the amounts and keep in a zip-lock bag in the freezer.

1 ½ cups bread crumbs (one- or two-day-old country bread preferred)

3 tablespoons extra-virgin olive oil

2 tablespoons chopped fresh Italian parsley

1 tablespoon chopped fresh thyme

Grated zest of a small lemon

⅛ teaspoon salt

Baked and Fried Appetizers

Baking and frying add a lot of texture to a dish. So, if you like crunchy, crispy ends, and caramelized and chewy bits and pieces, this is the section for you. Any of these recipes can be transformed from tantalizing hors d'oeuvres to a main course or accompaniment.

Egg-Battered Zucchini Roll-Ups

I have literally grown up on zucchini prepared in this simple way—sliced into thin strips, dipped in egg, and fried. It was one of my favorite vegetables when I was little, and quite often my mother made our lunch sandwiches with the strips too, for us to take to school. (It's still a great sandwich; see page 23.)

Crispy and sweet and soft at the same time, the strips are delicious warm or at room temperature, with just a sprinkle of salt—as I serve them to my grandkids—or dressed with capers and lemon juice, for adult tastes. Rolled up and secured with toothpicks, these are a great finger food for a party—a preferred morsel for martini drinkers, I've noticed. They're also a delicious side dish for grilled meats and fish. At summer suppers, I put a platter of roll-ups in the middle of the table, where everybody at any time can spear one with a fork.

SERVES 10 AS AN HORS D'OEUVRE, 6 AS A SIDE DISH

To Coat and Fry the Zucchini

Rinse and dry the zucchini and trim off the stem and blossom ends. With a sharp knife, slice the squash lengthwise into strips about ⅛ inch thick, flexible but not paper-thin. You should get five or six strips from each small zucchini.

Dump the flour into a wide bowl or shallow dish. In another wide bowl, beat the eggs well with ½ teaspoon of the salt and grinds of pepper. Set a wide colander on a plate, to drain the battered strips before frying.

Tumble five or six zucchini strips at a time in the flour, coating them well on both sides. Shake off loose flour and slide the strips in the beaten eggs. Turn and separate the strips with a fork, so they're covered with batter; pick them up one at a time and let excess egg drip back into the bowl; then lay them in the colander.

Dredge and batter all the zucchini strips this way, and let them drain. Add the egg drippings collected under the colander to the batter, if you need more.

Pour canola oil into the skillet to a depth of ⅓ inch, and set it over medium-high heat. Cover a baking sheet or large platter with several layers of paper toweling, and place it near the stove.

2 pounds (5 or 6) small zucchini

About 2 cups flour, for dredging

5 large eggs

¾ teaspoon or more salt

Freshly ground black pepper to taste

2 cups or more canola oil, for frying (amount depends on skillet size)

1 or 2 tablespoons well-drained tiny capers in brine

Freshly squeezed juice of ½ lemon or more

RECOMMENDED EQUIPMENT

A 12- or 14-inch skillet, for frying

Kitchen tongs

Toothpicks

When the oil is very hot (not smoking), test it by dropping in a half-strip of battered zucchini. It should sizzle actively and begin to crisp around the edges within ½ minute, but not smoke or darken. When the oil is right, quickly slip several strips into the skillet, using kitchen tongs or a long fork to avoid spatters of hot oil. Don't crowd the strips—no more than seven at a time in a 12-inch pan—so they crisp quickly and won't absorb oil.

Maintain the heat so the strips are sizzling actively. Cook on the first side for 1½ minutes or so, then flip them over. They should be nicely colored on the first side; if not, raise the heat slightly. Cook the second side for another 1½ minutes, until golden and crisp, then transfer the strips to the paper towels. Lay them flat in a single layer, and sprinkle them while hot with pinches of salt.

Fry all the strips in batches, and salt lightly right after (use ¼ teaspoon salt for all of them, or more to taste). It's best to let them cool uncovered, but if you need the space, lay paper towels over a sheet of strips to drain the next ones to come out of the skillet. Let the slices cool for a few minutes.

Forming the Roll-Ups

Place a fried strip pointing away from you on your worktable, with the wider end (from the blossom end of the zucchini) facing you. Place three or four capers on that end, then roll the strip tightly, enclosing the capers in the center. Stick a toothpick all the way through the roll-up, so it stays together. Roll up all the strips—or as many as you want.

Just before serving, stand the roll-ups on end and squeeze drops from a half-lemon (through a strainer to catch the seeds) all over the spiral tops. Arrange them on a serving platter. If you like capers as much as I do, scatter another teaspoon or so of drained capers all over.

What's wrong with zucchini in a sandwich? Since my mother made these all the time for my brother and me, I've always considered it a perfectly normal idea. So, when Joe and Tanya were little, I'd make them each a lovely sandwich of a crusty roll filled with egg-battered zucchini strips for lunch at school. Years later, they confessed to me that they were ashamed to take such a peculiar sandwich out of their lunchboxes—so they threw out the zucchini before other kids could see it! Now, of course, they love the combination of crisp bread and moist, flavorful zucchini, and regret all the empty rolls they had to swallow. I tell Olivia, Lorenzo, and Miles to eat whatever they like, and forget about what other kids think.

Here's how to make a great zucchini-strip sandwich. Fry up some strips, and get crusty European-style rolls or bread loaf, like ciabatta or baguette. Slice the bread open, crisp the insides a bit in the oven (or toaster oven), then pile zucchini strips in the middle—warm or room-temperature, lightly salted.

Plain, just like that, is still the way I make my zucchini sandwich. Countless embellishments would be good too: fresh pesto, spread like mayonnaise; a thick slice of fresh tomato; or shreds of fresh basil leaves, parsley, or arugula. A loaf-sized zucchini sandwich is a great picnic item: cut it crosswise in thin slices for an appetizer or snack or in thicker slices for a main course. Stick a toothpick in to hold the layers together.

Herb Frittata

These small *frittate* make a wonderful appetizer cut in wedges and served at room temperature. Or serve one per person as a nice lunch dish. We always thought they were best made in the springtime, when nettles, fennel fronds, young shoots of wild asparagus, or ramps could be gathered in the fields. But if you are more city-bound, you can infuse the eggs with fresh thyme leaves, parsley, and chives, which you can get year-round.

SERVES 2 AS AN APPETIZER, I AS A LUNCH DISH

2 large eggs

2 tablespoons milk

¼ teaspoon salt

2 tablespoons chopped fresh chives

1 ½ teaspoons chopped fresh thyme leaves

2 tablespoons chopped fresh parsley

1 teaspoon butter

2 teaspoons extra-virgin olive oil

RECOMMENDED EQUIPMENT

A small frying pan, about 5 inches on the bottom, 7 inches across the top

Whisk the eggs, milk, salt, and fresh herbs until just blended together.

Heat the butter and oil in the small frying pan until it just starts to sizzle, then pour in the eggs and turn the heat down very low. Cook gently for 3 to 4 minutes. The eggs will start to puff up and sizzle at the edges. Lift a corner of the frittata with a spatula, and check to see if the bottom has browned in splotches. When it has, flip the frittata over by giving the pan a firm, quick shake up and over toward you so that the egg mass dislodges and flips over in one piece. Or, if that unnerves you, turn the frittata over with a spatula. Cook the second side for 1½ to 2 minutes, again checking to see if the bottom has browned to your liking.

Serve right away, or let cool to room temperature and cut the frittata in wedges.

Good As . . .

A garnish for soup. If you have some leftovers—or you might want to make some just for this purpose—take the frittata and roll it like a jelly roll, then cut it in thin strips. Bring some flavorful meat or vegetable broth to a boil, add the frittata shreds and some grated cheese, and serve.

Mixing the eggs and parsley

Loosening the edges to turn the frittata over

Pouring the eggs into the hot, buttered pan

Cooked on both sides and ready

The frittata cut in wedges

Mushroom Custard

I love custards—when they are properly baked, that is, so each spoonful feels like velvet and truly melts on the tongue, releasing all its flavors. This is one of the most basic pleasures of eating, one that my family enjoys and that I want to share with you.

Here is a custard that has everything: lots of the flavor of fresh mushrooms, dried porcini, sage, garlic, and leeks, all concentrated and deepened in the skillet, and a creamy custard that holds all these flavors in suspension. When a spoonful of this melts on your tongue, you'll understand why I love custards. Serve it as a first course at a special dinner, or as the centerpiece of a holiday brunch. This recipe is for eight small custards and is easily multiplied to make more.

The recipe details the important steps in making any custard, so, if you haven't made one particularly successfully before, pay special attention.

For uniform baking, I recommend that you use identical molds to bake up a batch, if possible. If you don't have any, I encourage you to buy a set of inexpensive ½-cup ceramic molds—get eight or a dozen; either a small shallow soufflé shape or the taller traditional custard cup is fine. You'll use them forever, I hope.

MAKES 4 CUPS OF FILLING, ENOUGH FOR
8 SMALL BAKED CUSTARDS

FOR THE RAMEKINS

1 to 2 tablespoons soft butter

FOR THE MUSHROOM
FILLING

4 tablespoons soft butter

½ pound leek, trimmed and well
rinsed, finely chopped (1 ½ cups)

1 teaspoon salt

3 fresh sage leaves, finely chopped
(about 1 tablespoon)

1 plump garlic clove, peeled and
minced

Preheat the oven to 375° and set a rack in the center.

Butter the insides of the ramekins or custard cups generously. Set the ramekins in the empty baking dish.

Put the 4 tablespoons of butter in a medium skillet, and set over medium heat. When the butter is starting to foam, stir in the leek and ¼ teaspoon salt and cook for 3 minutes or so, until the leek is sizzling and softening. Stir in the chopped sage, and cook a couple minutes more; lower the heat if necessary so the leek doesn't brown. Push the leek aside to clear a space in the middle of the pan, and drop in the minced garlic. Stir the garlic in the hot spot for a minute, then stir in with the leek.

Now drop in all the mushrooms, sprinkle on another ¼ teaspoon salt, the porcini powder, and grinds of pepper. Raise the heat slightly, and cook for a minute or two, stirring frequently. Cover the pan, and cook for 3 minutes or so, shaking the pan occasionally, so the mushrooms release most of their liquid. Uncover the pan, and cook rapidly to evaporate the juices, stirring often, just until the mushrooms have started to caramelize and stick in the pan. Remove the pan from the heat, stir in the chopped parsley, and let the mushrooms cool a bit.

Beat the eggs and the remaining salt with a whisk in a large mixing bowl until smooth. Pour in the milk, whisking steadily to blend well. Scrape in the cooked mushroom mixture, and stir gently until every bit is dispersed. Pour or ladle the custard into the prepared cups, filling them evenly.

Pour very warm (not boiling) water into the baking pan, to come about halfway up the side of the cups, and carefully move it onto the oven rack. Or put the pan in the oven first and then pour in the warm water.

Bake for about 10 minutes, and check how the custard is cooking: shake the pan or a cup gently; if the custard is still loose, as is likely, the surface will slosh a bit. After 15 minutes, the custards should have started to set around the sides—this part will wobble, like Jell-O, though the center may still be sloshing. Check the custards every 2 to 3 minutes now. When the tops are all set (just wobbling), lay two fingers on them and press gently. At first, there may be liquid under the surface—cook slightly longer, until the custard feels set but soft, and moves beneath your fingers. Now they are done.

Remove the pan from the oven to a stable surface. Lift out the cups with dry towels (remove some of the hot water from the pan first, to make this job easier), and let them rest on a wire rack to cool briefly. Serve warm.

A Special Treat

This dish makes a great appetizer, but also makes an impressive brunch dish. To make it extraordinary, when truffles are in season grate a few shavings on top just before serving.

About 6 ounces firm small mushrooms (white buttons and cremini; or morels, porcini, or other fresh wild mushrooms), thinly sliced (2½ cups)

½ teaspoon porcini powder (page 140), from 1 tablespoon dried porcini pulverized in spice grinder or mini-chopper or by hand

Freshly ground black pepper

1 tablespoon chopped fresh Italian parsley

FOR THE CUSTARD

4 large eggs

2 cups milk

RECOMMENDED EQUIPMENT

8 small (4-ounce) soufflé ramekins or custard cups

A baking pan with 2½-to-3-inch sides, large enough to hold all the cups in a water bath

Cutting the onion in half

Cutting thin slices

Sweet Onion *Gratinate*

The inspiration for this recipe came on a recent visit to France. In a small bistro, I was served an elegant but amazingly simple gratin, just a thin layer of sautéed onions with grated Parmigiano-Reggiano on top, baked in a hot oven to form a crisp, fragile delicacy. When I got home, I decided to replicate it—but with a base of thin bread slices underneath the onions, to make it easier to assemble and serve. To my great delight, the bread became wonderfully crisp in the oven, adding more texture, and at the same time captured the delicious onion juices.

The key to wonderful flavor here is slowly cooking the onions in a big skillet—they should be meltingly soft without any browning, and moist without excess liquid. Sweet onions are the best—large Vidalia, Maui, Walla Walla, or any other of the fine varieties now available. A gratinate—the Italian term for a baking dish encrusted with cheese or other crisp topping—fills a big sheet pan. It will serve a large group as an appetizer or a lunch dish, or make a great hors d'oeuvre for a crowd, cut in small pieces. You can bake it ahead for convenience, and serve it at room temperature or briefly warmed in the oven.

MAKES 15 OR MORE APPETIZER SLICES, OR
SEVERAL DOZEN HORS D'OEUVRE PIECES

Cooking the Onions

Peel the onions and cut in half through the stem ends. Rinse the halves in cold water for a moment (see box on facing page for why!). Slice the halves crosswise into very thin half-moon shapes; you should have over 12 cups of onions.

Preheat the oven to 425°.

Put the oil and butter in the skillet, set over medium heat, and before the butter is all melted, dump in all the onions and turn them over to coat. Drop in the bay leaves, sprinkle with the salt, turn, and stir the onions a bit more, then cover the pan. Let the onions sweat and soften for about 10 minutes, stirring just once or twice, but otherwise keeping them covered.

Uncover the pan, and continue to cook the onions and to evaporate the juices gradually. Adjust the heat to keep the juices bubbling

FOR THE ONION TOPPING

3½ pounds large sweet onions, such as Vidalia or Walla Walla

¼ cup extra-virgin olive oil

4 tablespoons butter

4 bay leaves

½ teaspoon salt

FOR THE BASE AND THE GRATIN

8 tablespoons (1 stick) soft butter

9 or more thick slices (about ¾ pound) hearty white bread*

2 cups freshly grated Parmigiano-
   Reggiano or Grana Padano
   (about 12 ounces)

RECOMMENDED EQUIPMENT

A 12- or 14-inch skillet with a cover,
   for sautéing the onions
A 12-by-18-inch rimmed baking sheet

Sweet Onion Gratinate *(cont.)*

without risking burning the onions, and stir frequently. After 10 minutes or so, the onions should be very soft, wet, and glassy, but with hardly any liquid left in the pan. If there's a lot of liquid, raise the heat slightly and cook longer, stirring as the juices evaporate. But don't let the onions or the pan get completely dry. Remove it from the heat while the onions are still moist, and let them cool off just a bit.

Assembling and Baking the Gratin

Butter the baking sheet generously, using 3 to 4 tablespoons of the soft butter. Trim off the crusts of the bread slices, and lay the slices in one layer in the baking sheet, sides touching, to cover the bottom completely. Fill any empty spaces with pieces of bread cut to shape. Now press down gently over all the bread with your hand, to compress the layer slightly and close any gaps. Spread the remaining soft butter all over the bread with a rubber spatula or big spoon.

While the onions are still warm, spoon them onto the bread and spread in an even layer; scrape the flavorful cooking juices from the pan too. Sprinkle all the cheese evenly over the onions, covering the entire surface, but don't press the cheese down at all.

Bake for 10 minutes or so; rotate the pan for even cooking and bake another 10 to 15 minutes, until the cheese is a deep-brown-gold crust and the edges of the bread are also crisp and dark (but not burned).

Let the gratin cool for at least a few minutes (the pan will be very hot!). Serve it warm or at room temperature, cut in pieces of any size.

Note: A hearty home-baked or home-style white bread, in sandwich-loaf shape, is best here. A day-old or 2-day-old unsliced loaf from the bakery is perfect; cut ½-inch-thick slices yourself. Otherwise, a good-quality packaged white bread is satisfactory.

A LIGHT TOUCH WITH CHEESE MAKES A GOLDEN GRATIN

In order to produce a great gratin—the crust that makes the dish a gratin—you've got to let the grated or shredded cheese fall lightly and evenly on the surface. If you're using a lot of cheese, let it build up in a fluffy layer so the oven's heat penetrates the granules, baking them into a crisp and gorgeously colored crust. Resist the temptation to pat or press the cheese down, or it will turn into a gummy slab when it bakes.

Often cooks remove their lasagna or manicotti when they see the first streaks of gold, afraid that it will burn in another minute. When the cheese has been applied with a light touch, it will darken gradually for a long time without burning. Not only will longer baking produce a more spectacular-looking dish, but the deeper caramelization creates more flavor too. For me, a great gratin must be dark and deeply colored all over the top, like the Polenta Pasticciata in the photo on page 217.

Mushroom *Gratinate*

As with pizza or focaccia, the bread base of the gratinate can be covered with all manner of savories. A big batch of sliced mushrooms sautéed with lots of garlic and herbs makes a great topping. Use wild mushrooms if you have some or a mixture of wild and cultivated (see box on page 139 for suggestions). Use a whole-grain country bread as a base for a more gutsy flavor.

MAKES 12 OR MORE APPETIZER PIECES

3 tablespoons extra-virgin olive oil

4 tablespoons butter

6 plump garlic cloves, finely chopped

2½ pounds mushrooms, cleaned (for details, see page 139) and sliced

1 teaspoon chopped fresh thyme leaves

4 fresh sage leaves, chopped

1 teaspoon salt

½ cup freshly grated Parmigiano-Reggiano or Grana Padano

FOR THE BASE AND GRATIN

12 thick slices hearty wheat bread, lightly toasted

3 tablespoons soft butter

¼ cup chopped parsley

1 cup freshly grated Parmigiano-Reggiano or Grana Padano

RECOMMENDED EQUIPMENT

A 12- or 14-inch sauté pan

A large rimmed baking pan, 10 by 14 inches

Preheat the oven to 375°.

Heat the olive oil in the skillet over medium heat and sauté the garlic, stirring, until it just begins to color. Add the butter and, when it melts, toss in the mushrooms, sprinkle on the thyme, sage, and salt, and cook, stirring now and then, until the water evaporates and the mushrooms start to caramelize. Remove from the heat, then stir in the grated cheese.

Lay the bread slices in one layer in the baking pan to cover the bottom completely. Spread the soft butter all over the bread and spoon the mushrooms evenly on top, pressing them down into the bread. Sprinkle the parsley on and top with grated cheese.

Bake for 10 to 15 minutes until the cheese has browned and the edges of the bread are crisp. Let rest a few minutes, then cut into serving pieces.

Spooning mushrooms over the bread slices

Pressing the mushrooms into the bread

Sprinkling the freshly grated cheese all over

Salads

Today, beautiful salad greens, mesclun, baby lettuces, and hydroponic salads can be found year-round. When one orders a salad, it is always synonymous with a green salad. But there are many other vegetables that can also be made into luscious salads.

What I want to share with you in this section is my enthusiasm for marinating and making salads from raw, baked, and cooked vegetables: boiled Scallion and Asparagus Salad is fresh, sweet, and mellow; roasted beet with seasonal fruit diced in it and topped with crumbles of cheese is almost a meal in itself; carrots undergo a Cinderella transformation; and winter squash moves beyond pumpkin pie and jack-o'-lanterns to find a new flavorful and syrupy life here.

All of these delights and others in this section can make tempting appetizers, refreshing main-course salads, or side dishes to balance your meal—it's up to you.

Scallion and Asparagus Salad

This is a great spring salad with two long, lovely green vegetables that have a real affinity for each other (try the Asparagus, Green Pea, and Scallion Sauce for pasta in chapter 3). It is delicious as an antipasto or a first course, or as a side dish to grilled meat and fish.

You can serve this salad chilled, but I like it at room temperature.

If you haven't poached scallions before, be sure to note how nicely it brings out the flavors in a mellow way. And here's a thrifty cooking tip: scallion trimmings are some of the most useful scraps in the kitchen. A handful of leaves and the root ends can make an instant broth, as a substitute for stock—see my recipe for Simple Vegetable Broth, page 288.

SERVES 6

Cooking the Vegetables

With a vegetable peeler, shave off the skin from the bottom 3 inches or so of each stalk, so they cook evenly. (Save the stubs and peelings for soup base or asparagus-stub sauce, page 137.) Snap off the hard stubs at the bottom of the asparagus stalks—they'll break naturally at the right point.

Trim the root end of each scallion and the wilted ends of the green leaves. Peel off the loose layers at the white end too, so the scallions are all tight, trim, and about 6 inches long.

In a wide deep skillet, bring 1 quart of water (or enough to cover the vegetables) to a boil, and add the asparagus and scallions.

Adjust the heat to maintain a bubbling boil, and poach the asparagus and scallions, uncovered, for about 6 minutes or more, until they are tender but not falling apart, and cooked through but not mushy. To check doneness, pick up an asparagus spear in the middle with tongs; it should be a little droopy but not collapsing.

As soon as they are done, lift out the vegetables with tongs and lay them in a colander (any fat asparagus spears may take a little longer, so leave them in a few minutes more). Hold the colander

1 ½ pounds fresh asparagus

¾ pound scallions

3 ½ tablespoons extra-virgin olive oil

1 ½ tablespoons red wine vinegar

1 teaspoon salt, or more if needed

Freshly ground pepper to taste

3 hard-cooked eggs, peeled
   (see box next page)

Scallion and Asparagus Salad (cont.)

under cold running water to stop the cooking. Drain briefly, then spread on kitchen towels, pat dry, and sprinkle about ½ teaspoon salt over them.

Making the Salad

Slice the asparagus and the scallions into 1-inch lengths, and pile them loosely in a mixing bowl. Drizzle the oil and vinegar over them, then sprinkle on ½ teaspoon salt and several grinds of black pepper. Toss well, but don't break up the vegetables.

Quarter the eggs into wedges, and slice each wedge into two or three pieces; salt lightly and scatter the eggs in the bowl, and fold in with the vegetables. Taste and adjust the seasoning. Chill the salad briefly, then arrange it on a serving platter or on salad plates.

Peeling lemon with a vegetable peeler

Roasted Black Olives and Pearl Onions

T his might be considered a salad, but it is a wonderful stuzzichino (something to nibble on). Slow roasting intensifies the flavor of olives and gives them an unusual yet delightful crunch. Tossed with vinegar-poached pearl onions, they make a lively and beautiful salad-condiment (photo, opposite page 1). Serve this as an antipasto with cured meats and cheeses, or with grilled meats and fish. It is also a great garnish for sandwiches or with slices of grilled bread. All you need is a plate, a fork, and a glass of good red wine.

MAKES ABOUT 3 CUPS

Preheat the oven to 300°. Spread the olives on a large baking sheet, and bake for 20 minutes, or until they have shriveled a bit and are slightly crunchy but not crisped or burned. Let them cool in the pan (they'll dry more and become a bit crunchier).

Meanwhile, cut off the root end of each onion, but don't peel them. In a small saucepan, heat 2 cups water and the vinegar to a boil, drop in all the onions, and cook for 5 to 10 minutes, depending on their size, until they feel soft all the way through when you squeeze them but not mushy. Drain, and let them cool. Remove the skin (or pop the onion out of the skin by squeezing at the top). If the onions are ¾ inch thick or more, slice them open and flake them apart, separating the layers; tiny onions can be left whole.

Toss the olives, onions, and orange zest in a bowl; dress with the oil and juice to taste. Marinate briefly or overnight, refrigerated, if you want. Serve at room temperature in a shallow bowl with a serving spoon.

1 pound well-drained pitted brine-cured olives

½ pound tiny pearl onions (½ inch wide, or as small as possible)

½ cup red wine vinegar

2 tablespoons orange zest, in fine threads or julienne slivers (see box)

FOR DRESSING

1 to 2 tablespoons extra-virgin olive oil

1 to 2 tablespoons freshly squeezed orange juice

Roasted Acorn Squash Salad

Lightly caramelized slices of roasted squash make a tasty and pretty salad, dressed up with toasted almonds, crumbled cheese, and glistening swirls of Reduced Balsamic Vinegar (recipe follows), one of my favorite condiments. Serve this as an antipasto, a first course, or a side dish. With roast meat or poultry, it can be a main course salad too. How about a Thanksgiving leftover salad of roast squash and my roast turkey (page 332) with balsamic reduction and Quince Chutney (page 368)?

Any sweet-fleshed winter squash is suitable, but I find the scalloped edges of acorn squash slices look especially nice.

SERVES 4 TO 6

FOR BAKING THE SQUASH

3 pounds acorn squash
(1 large or 2 small ones)

2 tablespoons extra-virgin olive oil

½ teaspoon salt

FOR DRESSING

2 teaspoons extra-virgin olive oil

⅛ teaspoon salt, or more to taste

¼ cup slivered almonds, toasted in the oven or on a dry skillet (see procedure below)

1 tablespoon or so Reduced Balsamic Vinegar (recipe follows), thickened for drizzling

2 tablespoons or more crumbled cheese (optional), such as aged goat cheese, drained fresh ricotta, cottage cheese, or *ricotta salata*

Preheat the oven to 400°. (As soon as it's hot, you can toast the slivered almonds for garnishing the salad: spread them on a baking sheet and bake for 5 minutes, shaking them up once or twice, until lightly colored and fragrant. Or toast them while the squash is roasting, or after.)

To prepare acorn squash: With a sharp vegetable peeler or paring knife, strip off the peel from the protruding ridges of the squash. You don't need to peel more than this: leaving the rest of the peel will help the squash to retain its shape and looks nice too. (If you are roasting a smooth squash like butternut, remove all the peel.)

With a sharp heavy knife, cut the squash in half lengthwise, and scoop out all the seeds and fibers. Place each half cut side down; trim the ends, then cut semicircular slices of squash, all about 1 inch thick.

Put all the pieces in a pile on a large baking sheet, preferably non-stick or lined with parchment, or on a non-stick silicone baking mat. Drizzle the 2 tablespoons oil over the squash, sprinkle on the salt, and toss to coat with the seasonings, then spread the pieces out to lie flat, not touching.

Bake about 20 minutes, then flip the pieces over. Bake another 15 minutes or so, until the squash is just tender all the way through (poke with a fork to check) and nicely caramelized on the edges.

Assembling the Salad

Let the squash pieces cool on the pan until you're ready to serve. Arrange them—in a symmetrical design or in a casual pile—on a large serving platter or on individual salad plates, with two or three slices per portion.

Refresh them with drizzles of olive oil, sprinkles of salt. Scatter the almond slivers over, and then streaks or swirls of warm balsamic reduction. Finally, crumble bits of cheese all over.

Reduced Balsamic Vinegar for Drizzling
Sauce and Glaze

You may have heard me describe the extraordinary qualities of an authentic aceto balsamico tradizionale—*how it takes 20 years of careful concentration to develop its intense flavors; how a few drops make a dish taste magical; and how the price of a tiny bottle has caused many unsuspecting tourists to faint!*

Here, though, is a more reasonable way to bring some of the intensity and complexity of the greatest balsamic vinegar to everyday dishes: reduce a bottle of the affordable commerciale *grade of balsamic to a thick syrup. Don't look for the cheapest "balsamic" on supermarket shelves; look for a vinegar from a reputable company, produced in Italy—and expect to pay $8 to $10 for a pint.*

I use this condiment on a range of dishes (and in numerous recipes throughout the book), as a thick sauce to drizzle on meats and vegetables and, in a somewhat thinner state, as a glaze on roasts. As you'll see in the recipe, the vinegar reduces with added honey and bay leaf, but you can give it other flavor notes. I vary these with the dish I intend to dress: for vegeta-

bles I add whole cloves; for meat and poultry I add rosemary; for fish I add thyme. The basic formula will provide you with syrup for drizzling on a half-dozen dishes, maybe more. It will keep forever in the refrigerator, but I'm sure you'll use it up quicker than that!

MAKES ⅔ CUP OF THIN SYRUP FOR GLAZING,
OR ½ CUP THICK SYRUP TO DRIZZLE OR FOR DIPPING

I pint (or a 500-milliliter bottle) good-quality balsamic vinegar (*commerciale* grade)

I tablespoon honey

I bay leaf

One of the following (optional):

    4 whole cloves

    A tender branch fresh rosemary with lots of needles

    Several small sprigs fresh thyme with lots of leaves

Pour the balsamic vinegar into a heavy-bottomed saucepan, and place over moderate heat. Stir in the honey, drop in the bay leaf and optional cloves or herbs, and bring to a low boil. Adjust the heat to maintain a steady simmer, and allow the vinegar to reduce *slowly*. After ½ hour or so, when it has lost more than half of its original volume, the vinegar will start to appear syrupy, and you should watch it closely.

To Use as a Glaze

Cook the sauce to a third of its original volume (when it will measure ⅔ cup). It should be the consistency of molasses, thick but still spreadable. Pour the syrup through a small strainer into a heat-proof bowl or measuring cup. Discard the bay leaf and seasonings. Brush on the glaze while warm.

For Use as a Condiment and an Elixir to Drizzle over Vegetables

Reduce the vinegar even more, until it approaches a quarter of its original volume. Slow bubbles will rise from the syrup, and it will take on the consistency of honey, leaving a thick coating on a spoon. Pour it through a small strainer into a heat-proof bowl or measuring cup. Use a heat-proof spatula or spoon to clean out the saucepan before the reduction sticks to the pot for good! Drizzle on the syrup while it is still warm.

Store in the refrigerator, in a sealed container. It will congeal but keep indefinitely. To use, spoon the hard sauce into a bowl or heat-proof measuring cup, and heat it slowly in a pan of hot water or at low level in the microwave. For a thinner consistency, stir in drops of hot water.

Roasted Eggplant and Tomato Salad

*S*erve *this colorful and delicious salad as a first course by itself, with other an-
tipasti, or with grilled foods. You can use this low-fat method of preparing eggplant in other dishes too. I top it with shavings of* ricotta salata *(ricotta that has been
salted and dried in a small round cheese form for about 4 weeks).*

SERVES 6 AS A FIRST COURSE, OR MORE AS AN ANTIPASTO

Preheat oven to 450°. Trim the ends of the eggplant and slice crosswise into 1-inch-thick rounds; cut each round into halves or quarters, to make roughly equal pieces no bigger than 2 inches on a side.
Put the chunks on a baking sheet lined with parchment, or a silicone
baking mat, and sprinkle a tablespoon of the oil and ¼ teaspoon salt
over them. Toss to distribute the oil, and spread the pieces apart so
they'll brown quickly.

Put the tomatoes on another parchment-lined sheet, sprinkle 1
tablespoon oil and a pinch of salt over them, roll them around, and
spread them out. Put both sheets in the oven, and roast until both
the eggplant and the tomatoes are soft, shriveled, and nicely
caramelized on the edges, 30 minutes or more. While roasting, turn
the eggplant chunks a couple of times, roll the tomatoes over, and
shift the sheets around in the oven for even heating.

Let the vegetables cool on the sheets completely, then transfer
them to a large mixing bowl. Toss gently with the remaining olive oil
and salt, ground pepper, vinegar, and basil. Taste, and adjust the seasonings. Arrange the salad on a serving platter, or portion on salad
plates, and sprinkle the shredded cheese on top.

2 medium-size firm eggplants
(about 1 ¼ pounds), rinsed

4 tablespoons extra-virgin olive oil

½ teaspoon salt, plus more to taste

3 cups ripe grape or small cherry
tomatoes, rinsed

¼ teaspoon freshly ground black pepper

¼ cup red wine vinegar

12 small fresh basil leaves,
or 2 tablespoons shredded large
basil leaves

⅓ cup shredded fresh mozzarella or
ricotta salata

IDEAS FOR ROASTED EGGPLANT SALADS

*This salad can be an antipasto or a meal in itself. Without the
cheese, it can be an accompaniment to grilled fish and meat. Or just
put it between two slices of grilled bread to make a sandwich.*

Celery and Artichoke Salad with Shavings of Parmigiano-Reggiano

*C*elery is often underappreciated as a principal salad ingredient. The inner stalks of the head have a wonderful freshness, flavor, and delicacy when thinly sliced. Here I've paired them with fresh baby artichoke slices in a salad with lots of bright, subtle flavors and all kinds of crunch. Shards of hard cheese—either Parmigiano-Reggiano or Grana Padano—lend even more complexity to the mix.

Use only firm and very small artichokes for this: they should feel tight and almost squeak when you squeeze them, and they should have no choke.

SERVES 6

Freshly squeezed juice of 1 lemon

6 firm small artichokes, no more than 3 inches wide

8 to 12 tender celery stalks with leaves, from the inner part of the head (about 10 ounces)

FOR THE DRESSING

1 ½ tablespoons freshly squeezed lemon juice, or more to taste

6 tablespoons extra-virgin olive oil

¾ teaspoon salt, or more to taste

A chunk of Parmigiano-Reggiano or Grana Padano*

Note: You'll need only about ¼ pound sliced but it is easier to shave off slices from a good-sized chunk of cheese

Trimming the Artichokes and Celery

Stir the lemon juice into a bowl with a quart of cold water. The acidulated water will keep the artichoke slices from discoloring after you cut them.

Work with one artichoke at a time: Trim off the thick outside leaves, until you reach the tender, pale inside leaves. Cut off the tough bottom of the stem, but leave most of it (an inch or so) attached to the globe. With a vegetable peeler or paring knife, peel off the outer skin of the short stem, exposing the fresh layer underneath. Next, cut straight across the pointed top of the artichoke, removing the tips of the leaves and the darker, coarser top part, retaining only the pale green lower two-thirds. Drop the trimmed artichoke into the acidulated water. Trim the rest of them in this way, submerging them all in the bowl.

To prepare the celery, trim off the wide end of the celery stalks and pick off any coarse outer leaves, reserving only the tender, pale leaves. Peel the stalks if they're dark, tough, or blemished. Slice each one on the diagonal, ⅛ inch thick, into delicate, translucent crescents. Chop the tender leaves, and put all the celery—about 2 cups—in a large mixing bowl.

Making and Dressing the Salad

When you're ready to serve the salad, remove a trimmed artichoke from the lemon water and cut, from stem to top, in ⅛-inch slices; add them to the bowl. Quickly slice all the artichokes this way, and toss the celery and artichoke slices together with the lemon juice, the olive oil, and the salt.

With a vegetable peeler or sharp knife, shave about two dozen delicate large flakes of Parmigiano-Reggiano or Grana Padano from the chunk of cheese; each shaving should be a couple of inches long and 1 or 2 inches wide.

Fold the shavings of cheese gently into the sliced vegetables. Taste, and adjust dressing. Arrange the salad on a serving platter, or portion on salad plates. Shave more flakes of cheese, and scatter a dozen or more over the platter, or place three or four on top of each individual serving.

A WORTHY ALTERNATIVE TO PARMIGIANO-REGGIANO: GRANA PADANO

In my kitchen I use two Italian hard cheeses almost interchangeably (and almost, but not quite, in every dish!): Parmigiano-Reggiano and Grana Padano. Now widely available in our markets, Grana Padano is a 100-percent cow's-milk cheese, like Parmigiano-Reggiano, with a DOC designation, meaning it is regulated by the methods and standards of a consortium of producers. It is generally of high quality and less expensive than Parmigiano-Reggiano. When making recipes throughout this book, I give you the choice of Grana Padano to finish your dishes in fine style.

Both cheeses are grana types, signifying that they have a granular texture, suitable for grating or shaving. This granularity comes from the milk and, originally, from the bacteria in the milk. The processes by which the cheeses are made are quite similar. The difference in price is because Parmigiano-Reggiano can only be made from milk from strictly limited regions in certain seasons, processed by exacting standards and aged for longer periods. Grana Padano production is less restricted. Overall, the flavor differences are subtle. To my taste, Grana Padano has more granularity and a milkier character. Parmigiano-Reggiano is less granular in texture and more complex in flavor.

Roasted Beet and Beet Greens Salad with Apple and Goat Cheese

This beautiful salad really depends on good ingredients: small firm beets with fresh unblemished greens still attached; a crisp tart apple or perhaps ripe fresh peaches or Black Mission figs; and aged goat cheese with a crumbly consistency. Roasting the beets to intensify the sweetness is also a key to the best salad.

SERVES 6

10 to 12 small red and yellow (if available) beets with greens attached (about 3 pounds total)

½ teaspoon salt

⅓ cup extra-virgin olive oil

⅓ cup good-quality balsamic vinegar

Freshly ground black pepper to taste

1 medium-size tart crisp apple

4 ounces or so slightly aged goat cheese

Preheat the oven to 400°.

Slice the greens off right at the top of the beets, reserving the stems and greens, then scrub the beets and poke each of them with a fork a few times. Put them all in a shallow baking dish, uncrowded, with ⅛ inch of water covering the bottom. Place the dish in the oven, uncovered. Roast the beets—the water will actually steam them a bit first—until they are shriveled, dark, and caramelized outside, and tender all the way through (when poked with a knife), 45 minutes to 1½ hours, depending on size. Let them cool.

Meanwhile, rinse the beet greens well, trim off the tough parts of the stems, and cut the usable stem pieces from the leaves. Bring a big pan of water to the boil, drop in the stems, cook for about 10 minutes, then add the leaves. Cook for 20 minutes more, or until the stems are quite soft. Drain in a sieve; sprinkle ¼ teaspoon of salt over the hot greens, and let them cool.

Peel the beets well, removing all the skin, the stem base, and the root tip, exposing the gleaming flesh. Cut in wedges, and place in a big mixing bowl. Cut the greens (both leaves and stems) in 2-inch lengths, and toss with the beet wedges.

Whisk together the oil and vinegar, with the remaining salt and pepper. Drizzle the dressing over the beets, and toss.

Cut the apple in half, remove the core, then slice the apple halves into thin matchstick pieces. Arrange the dressed beets on a serving platter, or portion on salad plates; fold in the apple pieces, then crumble goat cheese on top just before serving.

Note: If the weather is hot and you do not want to roast the beets, boiling them will yield good results, but not as good as roasting.

Cooked Carrot Salad with Pine Nuts and Golden Raisins

*C*arrots are an unappreciated standby. We tend to use them for everything but rarely highlight them. This dish brings out their sparkle.

SERVES 6 OR MORE

Peel and trim the carrots, and cut them into 3-inch lengths. Slice these lengthwise into wedges, all about ⅓ inch thick.

Pour 3½ cups water and the vinegar into a 3- or 4-quart saucepan, and set over high heat. Stir in the honey. When the water's boiling, drop in the carrot wedges and cook, uncovered, at a good bubbling boil for 25 minutes, until cooked through but with some texture to the bite. Don't let them get mushy.

Meanwhile, toast the pine nuts in a dry skillet over medium heat, tossing them frequently until light gold; spill them onto a plate to cool.

When the carrots are cooked, lift them out of the pan with a spider; let them cool and drain in a colander. Keep the carrot-cooking liquid at the boil, and drop in the raisins; poach for about 5 minutes, until plump, then lift them out and let them cool and drain.

Boil the vinegar liquid vigorously now to reduce quickly—it will take 5 minutes or more—until only ¼ cup or so of thick syrup remains in the pan. Lower the heat as the liquid level nears the pan bottom, and pour it into a cup or small bowl before it burns.

Put the carrots in a mixing bowl, and toss with 2 tablespoons of the syrup and several pinches of salt. Let them marinate briefly. Before serving, toss the carrots with a tablespoon of olive oil, the pine nuts, the raisins, and the shredded mint leaves. Taste, and season with more salt if needed; if you want more dressing, add more oil or any remaining syrup. Arrange on a serving platter, or portion on salad plates.

1 ½ pounds carrots

1 ½ cups white vinegar

2 tablespoons honey

¼ cup pine nuts

¼ cup golden raisins

¼ teaspoon salt

1 to 2 tablespoons extra-virgin olive oil

1 ½ tablespoons finely shredded fresh mint leaves

Good as . . .

An appetizer, or as part of an antipasto

A fine alternative to greens as a salad course

A side dish to grilled fowl or fish

Warm *Broccoli di Rape* and Yukon Gold Potato Salad

I am delighted to see broccoli di rape *in the supermarket almost year-round and of excellent quality: fresh, bright-green stems and leaves, with tight heads of pale-green florets (don't buy any with yellowed, open flowers). I hope you are familiar with this versatile vegetable—related to both turnips and broccoli—and love its unique bitter-almond taste as much as I do. This warm salad is a particularly easy way to prepare* broccoli di rape, *and its mild flavor and comforting texture will please even those family members who are wary of new vegetables!*

SERVES 6

1 ½ to 2 pounds *broccoli di rape*

1 pound Yukon Gold potatoes, any size

¼ teaspoon or more salt

4 tablespoons extra-virgin olive oil

A pinch of dried *peperoncino* (hot red pepper flakes), or much more to taste!

Good as . .

An excellent appetizer

A delightful side course to meats and fish

A lunch or supper meal in itself, topped with a poached egg or a slice of gorgonzola

Rinse and trim the *broccoli di rape* as described in the box; cut the peeled stems into 4- or 5-inch lengths. Peel the potatoes, and cut into 1-inch cubes. Put the cubes in a pot with cold water to cover by several inches, and heat to a boil. Cook uncovered for about 5 minutes, then lay the greens and peeled stems on top of the potatoes, cover the pot, and cook for 5 minutes more.

Lift out the *broccoli di rape* and potatoes with a spider or other strainer, and lay them in a colander. Sprinkle about half the salt over the hot vegetables, let them drain and cool for a minute or two, then turn them into a mixing bowl. Drizzle the olive oil all over the pieces, and toss gently. Sprinkle on more salt and *peperoncino* to taste (I use ¼ teaspoon pepper flakes, or even more, when I'm making this at home). Toss, taste, and adjust the seasoning.

Serve on a big warm platter, or put portions on warm salad plates.

Removing the tough stem and peeling the base

Peeling the thinner stems

HOW TO TRIM BROCCOLI DI RAPE *FOR COOKING*

Broccoli di rape, *unlike conventional broccoli, is supposed to be mostly stems, not just florets. So don't cut off the stems and throw them away. They are full of flavor and become tender with quick cooking. But they need to be trimmed in this way:*

Separate any long stems that are joined together, and slice off the thick bottom end of each with a paring knife. Peel off the tough outer layer of the stems, as shown in the photo, and remove the large outer leaves attached to the lower parts of the stems.

Cook the peeled stems with florets intact, as for the salad here, or slice them crosswise into shorter lengths for dishes like the pasta sauces on pages 114 and 115.

Cooked Spinach Salad

R aw spinach salad can be delicious, but, in my opinion, a brief cooking—really just a dip in boiling water—brings out the vegetable's best qualities. Use really young, tender spinach for this salad. It's easy to find baby spinach in plastic packs these days, but whenever you can—especially in springtime—buy clusters of tender leaves with tiny reddish stems joined at the roots, as they were plucked from the earth. Trim only the hairy tip of the roots, and cook the leaves and stems still together. Make sure you wash them several times, since dirt lodges between the stems.

SERVES 6

2 pounds tender leaf spinach or baby spinach leaves, washed well and trimmed

FOR DRESSING

2 tablespoons lemon juice, or to taste

3 tablespoons extra-virgin olive oil, or to taste

¼ teaspoon salt, or to taste

Freshly ground black pepper to taste

Bring 4 quarts of water or more to the boil in a large pot. Pile the washed spinach into a colander, and dump it all at once into the boiling water. With a spider, turn the leaves over once or twice, then lift them all out quickly after 3 or 4 seconds total in the boiling water. Drop the spinach back into the colander; let it cool and drain for a minute or two, *but do not squeeze it.*

While it is still warm, turn the spinach into a mixing bowl; after a few moments, pour off all but a spoonful of the liquid that's accumulated in the bottom. Dress and toss with the lemon juice and olive oil, salt, freshly ground pepper—tasting and adding more as you like. Serve still slightly warm or at room temperature.

IDEAS FOR SPINACH AND OTHER SALADS WITH COOKED GREENS

- Additions to cooked spinach salad: fold in hard-cooked eggs, roughly chopped, after dressing.

- Instead of spinach, use 2 pounds of fresh dandelion greens, washed and cooked in boiling water for 10 to 20 minutes or until tender. Drain without squeezing and cool slightly; pour all but a spoonful of the liquid out of the bowl before dressing. Try adding 1 cup of cooked dried beans to either of these salads.

Cauliflower and Egg Salad

t my grandma's house, we used to have this kind of salad many a time, with a slice of homemade bread and some good cheese, for supper.

SERVES 6 OR MORE

Tear off all the outer leaves attached to the base of the cauliflower; reserve any tender green leaves. Cut out the bottom core, and snap or slice off all the big florets from the inner stem. Cut the florets into 1-inch chunks or thick slices (don't break them up into tiny florets).

Bring 3 or 4 quarts of water in a large pot to the boil, drop in the florets and reserved leaves, and cook, uncovered, at a steady boil for 5 minutes, or until cooked through but not soft. Lift out the cauliflower, spread the pieces out in a colander, and sprinkle with ¼ teaspoon of the salt. Cool to room temperature.

Before serving, slice the eggs in wedges, and cut the wedges into 2 or 3 pieces each. In the bottom of a large mixing bowl, whisk together the vinegar, oil, another ¼ teaspoon salt, and grinds of pepper. Put all the cauliflower in the bowl, and tumble to dress all the pieces. Scatter the egg pieces over the top, and fold them in. Taste, and adjust the seasonings.

Arrange the salad on a serving platter, or portion on salad plates.

1 large head cauliflower
(1 ½ to 2 pounds)

½ teaspoon or more salt

3 hard-boiled eggs (see box on
page 36)

3 tablespoons or more white wine
vinegar

¼ cup or more extra-virgin olive oil

Freshly ground pepper to taste

Good as . . .

A first course

A side dish

A partner with broccoli for a
supper dish

Long-Cooked Celery Root Salad

I t is so simple to transform a hard, homely celery root into a lovely salad with delicate taste and texture. Just drop the big root—a softball-sized unpeeled round—into a big pot of water, and let it cook for an hour or more. This technique retains and mellows the root's wonderful flavor, and makes it easy to peel and cut it up too. Dress this simply, or take the salad in a different direction (see variations).

SERVES 4 TO 6

1 large celery root, 2 to 2½ pounds

¼ to ½ teaspoon salt, or to taste

Two ¼-pound bunches scallions finely chopped (about 1 cup)

2 to 3 tablespoons olive oil, or to taste

2 to 3 teaspoons red wine vinegar, or to taste

¼ teaspoon freshly ground black pepper, or to taste

2 tablespoons chopped fresh Italian parsley

To cook whole celery root, rinse it briefly to remove any soil, then put it into a large saucepan with cold water to cover. Since it floats, you can weight it with a pot cover or dish on the root to keep it under the surface, or just turn it over in the water now and then to cook evenly. Bring the water to a boil, and cook for about an hour, until tender, when you can pierce the whole root with a skewer.

Set the root in a colander or on a wire rack, and let it cool for 10 minutes or so, until you can handle it. Use the back of a thin knife blade (the dull edge) to scrape off the soft brown skin; use the knife tip to cut out the bits of skin in the folds and knobby parts of the root. When it is completely clear, cut the round root into wedges, chunks, slices, cubes, sticks, or any shape you like, and sprinkle with about ¼ teaspoon of salt while still warm. Toss the pieces with the scallions, and dress with oil, vinegar, more salt, and pepper. Let the salad cool completely, or refrigerate it.

Serve at room temperature or chilled. Before serving, taste a piece of celery root and adjust the dressing if you like. Toss with the chopped parsley, and arrange the salad on a serving platter or in portions on salad plates.

VARIATIONS FOR CELERY ROOT SALAD

- For milder flavor, poach the scallions with the celery root for 10 minutes before slicing them.

- Garnish the salad with shavings of Parmigiano-Reggiano or Grana Padano.

- For a lovely and unusual first-course salad, fold in sliced fresh pears (but omit the scallions).

- For a heartier main-course salad, fold in hard-boiled eggs, tuna, or cooked meats.

- For an interesting twist on celery root, roast the whole unpeeled root in a 350° oven for an hour or more, until tender all the way through. Cool, peel, and make your favorite salad.

A Bowlful of Goodness—Soups

I love cooking soups, and whenever I am at home and the family is coming over, I put a pot of soup on the stove with the coffeepot first thing in the morning. I know I will find something in the refrigerator and cupboard that will yield a delicious soup. If pasta is not on the menu, then soup surely is. Everyone in our family loves soup, from the little ones to Grandma and Giovanni, the seniors. Soup is good, nutritional, even claimed to be medicinal. If nothing else appeals to the little ones, I take a few cups of the finished soup and pass them through the blender—the velvety texture is accepted even by the toothless ones.

Here I give you some of my family's favorite master recipes for *minestre* and *brodi*, but what will make me truly happy is when you navigate my world of *minestre* and *brodi* on your own.

Simple Soups from Garlicky White Beans and Broth

This is as simple as soup-making can be. It is nothing more than a pot of beans with cooking broth. But it has everything you need in a soup base: good body and texture and a mellow, sturdy flavor foundation. A bit of excitement gets blended in at the end with a *soffritto* of garlic lightly caramelized in olive oil. The result is not an ordinary pot of beans, but one in which you can simmer any vegetable or pasta and end up with a great soup.

Soup Base of Garlicky White Beans and Broth

Cooking the Beans

Drain the soaked beans and put them in the pot with the water, bay leaves, and olive oil. Cover the pot, and bring it to a boil over high heat, stirring occasionally. When the water is at a full boil, set the cover ajar, adjust the heat to maintain a steady gentle boiling, and cook for an hour more, until the beans are tender.

Stir in the salt, uncover, and continue cooking at a bubbling boil for another hour or more, until the beans and broth have reduced to 3 quarts. Lower the heat as the liquid evaporates and the soup base thickens, stirring now and then to prevent scorching.

Flavoring the Base with the *Soffritto*

When the soup base is sufficiently reduced, make the *soffritto*. Heat the olive oil and the sliced garlic in a skillet over medium heat for 2 minutes or so, shaking the pan now and then, until the slices are sizzling. Drop in the *peperoncino*, stir with the garlic, and cook another minute, or until the garlic is just starting to color.

From the soup pot, ladle out a cup of the simmering bean broth and pour it into the skillet. Let it sizzle and start to boil, shake and stir up the *soffritto*, and cook it for a couple of minutes in the broth. Then pour it all back into the bean pot, scraping in every bit of the *soffritto*, or just rinse the skillet out with more broth. Simmer the soup base for another 5 minutes with the *soffritto*, then remove from the heat.

The base is ready for a finished soup now; or let the whole pot cool, pick out and discard the bay leaves, and keep the soup refrigerated for 3 or 4 days or freeze, in filled and tightly sealed containers, for 4 to 6 months.

FOR COOKING THE BEANS

1 pound (about 2½ cups) dry cannellini or other small dried white beans, soaked overnight or quick-soaked (see box, page 59)

4 quarts cold water, plus more if needed

3 bay leaves

¼ cup extra-virgin olive oil

1½ teaspoons salt, plus more if needed

FOR THE GARLICKY *SOFFRITTO*

3 tablespoons extra-virgin olive oil

6 big garlic cloves, sliced

¼ to ½ teaspoon dried *peperoncino* (hot red pepper flakes)

RECOMMENDED EQUIPMENT

A heavy-bottomed soup pot, 6- or 8-quart capacity, with a cover

Peg-Pérego

A CULINARY VOCABULARY FOR SOUPS

It is hard to find exact translations for soup terms like minestra, brodo, zuppa, pestata, *and* soffritto. *I use them all the time because I grew up with them but I owe you some explanations.*

Minestra—*a soup of vegetables, legumes, fish, or meat to which pasta or rice is added*

Brodo—*a clear soup made with meat, fish, and vegetables to which rice, pasta, egg, cheese, and/or croutons are added as flavorings*

Zuppa—*a soup made of vegetables, legumes, fish, or meat to which bread is added as a thickener*

Pestata—*local vernacular for a paste of lard, bacon, or pork fat chopped with garlic and aromatics*

Soffritto—*vegetables and aromatics cooked in a fat over low heat, used in soups, braising, roasting, and sauce-making*

Of all the dishes we make, soups are the most forgiving when we deviate from the original recipe. Soups can be made of almost any legume, vegetable, meat, or fish you have in your refrigerator and/or cupboard, and the way you put them together is inconsequential as long as you cook the soup long enough.

So please use the recipes here—in particular the finished soups—as procedural guides and proportional models, not as fixed formulas. The amounts called for in the base soups are big on purpose, to give you some to store up and, at the same time, have plenty to play around with. The fun is in creating different soups from your base. Of course you can make smaller quantities if you like—you'll have just as good a soup. But making a big batch and freezing it provides you with a delicious meal to serve to an unexpected guest, and/or a pint of love to send home with family and friends.

Chicory and White Bean Soup

*M*ake soup with any of the greens (and reds) in the chicory-endive family, including the various kinds of radicchio now in the markets, escarole, curly
endive (or frisée), or Belgian endive, as well as unrelated leafy vegetables such as
Swiss chard, spinach, or arugula. The procedure is the same, though cooking times
will vary.

FOR 7 CUPS OF FINISHED SOUP, SERVING 4 OR MORE

Heat the broth to a boil, stir in the chopped greens, the salt, and
grinds of pepper, and return to a gentle boil. Cook covered for 30 to
40 minutes, or until the leaves are tender and wilted. If you want,
cook uncovered for some or all of the time to produce a thicker consistency. Taste and adjust the seasonings; serve hot in warm bowls,
with freshly grated cheese, extra-virgin olive oil, and other garnishes
(page 60).

6 cups (½ recipe)
Garlicky White Beans and Broth
(preceding recipe)

About ½ pound trimmed chicory
leaves, rinsed well, drained, and
chopped in 2- or 3-inch pieces
(10 cups)

½ teaspoon or more salt, to taste

Freshly ground black pepper to taste

SERVING SOUP IN MY HOUSE

To me, sharing soup is a wonderful ritual of our family meals.
Though the soup itself may be simple, or just one of many courses,
I like to give it the attention (and the garnishes) it deserves.

I have one rule for serving soup, whether it's for a formal
occasion or an everyday supper—hot soup and warm bowls. If
possible, I like to bring the soup in a terrine or in the pot to the table,
have the warm bowls stacked up, and ladle out and garnish each
serving when everyone is seated. I love the moment when there's a
steaming bowl of hot soup in front of us, and we're all enjoying its
warmth, aromas—and one another's company.

Zucchini and White Bean Soup

*Y*ou *can turn this soup into a main course by adding pieces of cooked chicken.*
Small shrimp are another delicious enhancement: cut about ½ pound of
shelled, cleaned shrimp into 1-inch pieces, and stir them into the pot when the zucchini is
tender. Remove from the stove and let the shrimp cook in the residual heat.

FOR 6 OR 7 CUPS OF FINISHED SOUP, SERVING 5 OR 6

6 cups (½ recipe) Garlicky White
Beans and Broth (page 55)

2 medium zucchini, cut in matchsticks
or small pieces (about 3 cups)

¼ teaspoon or more salt, to taste

Freshly ground black pepper

Heat the broth to a boil, stir in the zucchini, the salt, and grinds of pepper, and return to a gentle boil. Cook covered for about 15 minutes, or until the zucchini is tender. If you want, cook uncovered for some or all of the time to produce a thicker consistency. Taste and adjust the seasonings; serve hot in warm bowls, with freshly grated cheese, extra-virgin olive oil, and other garnishes (page 60). (If you've added shrimp, garnishing with olive oil and cheese is optional.)

BEAN BASICS

Best Bean Types

Imported cannellini beans from Tuscany, in particular the hard-to-find Sorana variety, are the ones to use for white-bean soups and any dishes with cannellini. If you can't find them, substitute any of the small white bean varieties, such as Great Northern, pea beans, or navy beans.

The borlotti bean is the Italian red kidney bean and one of my preferred varieties for the hearty bean-and-potato soup base. A close relative is our cranberry bean, a smallish bean with mottled pink skin; it's a good substitute for the borlotti.

Long-Soaking Beans

An overnight soak is the easiest way to rehydrate dried beans before cooking. First pick out any bits of dirt or stones from the beans, then rinse them. Put the beans in a large bowl or pot with cold water covering them by 4 inches or more. Most beans are sufficiently soaked in 8 hours; old beans (from the back of the cupboard, perhaps) take longer. Soak them up to 24 hours, until plump and not wrinkled. Skim off any floating particles, then drain well before cooking—don't cook beans in the soaking water.

Quick-Soaking Beans

If you don't have time for long-soaking, put the rinsed beans in a large pot with hot water to cover by several inches, and set over high heat. When boiling, cook for 1 minute; remove from the heat, and let the beans sit in the water, uncovered, for 1 hour. Drain, and proceed to cook the beans.

Cooking Beans

Start beans well covered with fresh cold water (as liquid reduces, make sure it always covers the beans). Cook until beans are tender but not falling apart; the time needed varies with age, variety, and size. Cook at a steady but not violent boil, partially covered.

Flavoring and Seasoning Beans

Salt and acidic ingredients like tomatoes toughen beans and therefore should not be added to the pot until after the beans are tender; let the beans cook longer or steep with the added ingredients to take in these flavors.

Simple flavorings to add to the pot (at the start or at any time during cooking): bay leaves, rosemary, garlic, onions, carrots, and, always, extra-virgin olive oil.

In Italy it is traditional to garnish each bowl of soup with swirl of extra-virgin olive oil and freshly grated top-quality Parmigiano-Reggiano, Grana Padano, or Pecorino Romano.

I dress each bowl with about a teaspoon of extra-virgin oil and a tablespoon of grated cheese. These small additions complete the seasoning and texture of the soup, in the same way that oil and cheese are the critical last step in finishing a skillet of pasta.

Other garnishes can add flavor, crunch, and a festive touch to any bowl of soup. Here are a few of my favorites:

Condimento di Parmigiano-Reggiano
By spinning grated Parmigiano-Reggiano and olive oil together in the food processor, you can create a glistening, lighter-than-mayonnaise dressing; you can also whiz in fresh basil leaves for color and a delicate herb flavor. I like to make both plain and basil dressings at the same time (a half recipe of each) and set them on the table in pretty bowls.

Stir 1 cup packed freshly grated Parmigiano-Reggiano or Grana Padano together with ½ cup olive oil into the bowl of the food processor, and let the cheese soak for 30 minutes, then blend for ½ minute or so, into a light and smooth emulsion.

For basil *condimento* (dressing), whiz in twelve fresh basil leaves (⅓ cup packed) along with the cheese and oil.

For a half recipe of plain and basil dressing, process all the cheese and oil to the emulsion, and remove half to a small serving bowl. Drop in six basil leaves and process with the remaining sauce.

Cover the dressing well, and store in the refrigerator for up to a week.

A Soup Garnish with Substance—Cheesy Crostini
Thick, toasted, cheesy slices of yesterday's country bread make a great addition to light-textured and creamy soups.

Film a large cast-iron pan with several tablespoons of extra-virgin olive oil, toss in 2-inch-wide chunks of bread in one layer, and heat the pan slowly, turning the bread in the oil and letting it toast on all surfaces for about 5 to 10 minutes. Be patient, and keep the heat low.

When the bread is nicely colored all over, sprinkle spoonfuls of freshly grated Parmigiano-Reggiano or Grana Padano on top. Remove from the heat, and tumble the bread chunks over and over: the cheese will immediately start to toast, but keep tossing, so the bread picks up all the cheese bits from the pan bottom before they burn.

Allow the *crostini* to cool and get crunchy. Float a few in every bowl of soup, with more cheese heaped on top.

Bacon Chips for Soup

Bacon chips are great for soup garnish, adding flavor and texture. I remember that my grandmother would use pork cracklings to dress soup (bacon was not always available).

Cut bacon (about one slice per serving or a little less) crosswise into ¼-inch-wide strips. Cook in a heavy skillet over medium heat, turning frequently, until all the fat has rendered out and the strips are dark brown and crisp. Remove with a slotted spoon; spread them out and cover with paper towels to blot off the fat.

Drop a few chips into each soup bowl, and put more in a bowl on the table.

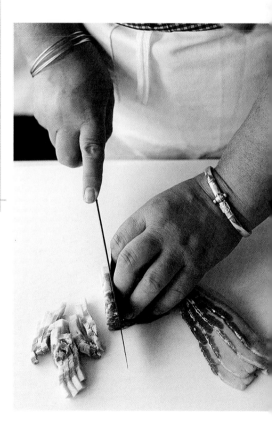

Frantoiana—White Bean and Dried Bread Soup

This is a traditional Tuscan soup from the area of Arezzo, made with bread grilled over an open fire and virgin olive oil, unfiltered, straight from the press—the frantoio. Believe me, a pot of beans never tasted this good.

As bread is a principal ingredient here, use one with fine flavor, preferably an artisan-baked loaf that has great crust and an airy crumb with lots of holes. Old bread—pane vecchio—is best, because it is already dry, but day-old or even fresh bread can be used.

FOR 6 TO 7 CUPS OF FINISHED SOUP, SERVING 5 OR 6

4 cups or more 2-inch chunks country bread

6 cups (½ recipe) Garlicky White Beans and Broth (page 55)

Salt to taste (optional)

Freshly ground black pepper

Toast 5 or 6 bread chunks slowly in a dry heavy skillet, such as cast iron, until completely crisp all the way through and deeply browned on both sides. If you happen to have a fire going, grill the bread, so the grill flavor can permeate the soup.

Heat the broth to an active simmer in a sturdy 4-quart pot. Stir in the grilled bread chunks. If they're floating in a lot of liquid, leave the pot uncovered; cover it if the broth just covers the bread. Cook slowly and steadily, anywhere from 10 to 20 minutes, until the soup is thick and soft but the bread chunks still have shape and integrity. Turn the bread in the broth frequently, so it doesn't stick to the bottom, but don't mash it up.

Taste and add salt, if necessary, and pepper. Serve right away in warm bowls, with generous amounts of fruity extra-virgin olive oil and freshly grated cheese.

Vegetable Soups from Savory Potato Broth

Savory Potato Broth

This versatile soup base is not really a broth, in the way my turkey broth is—that is, a clear liquid strained of all the ingredients that gave it flavor. In truth, the base starts cooking with several pounds of potatoes, carrots, and celery, and they stay in there. Yet, remarkably, it ends up light, clear, and clean-tasting, like a broth.

To enjoy the clarity and consistency of the base, often I'll add nothing more than rice, for texture and flavor. Onion and poached garlic make a flavorful yet light cream soup. On the other hand, I might fill the base with lots of textured ingredients, like mushrooms and barley, or lentils and ditalini pasta. And vegetables that break down during cooking and melt away, such as parsnip or winter squash and chestnut, utterly transform the texture.

ABOUT 4 QUARTS OF SOUP BASE, ENOUGH FOR
2 BATCHES OR MORE OF FINISHED SOUPS

Pour the oil into the pot, and set over medium-high heat. Let the oil get quite hot, but not smoking.

Dump in the potatoes, sprinkle on 1 teaspoon of the salt, and toss them in the oil until well coated. Cook them for 6 minutes or more, until lightly crusted and caramelized without taking on any color. Lower the heat to prevent burning and alternately stir the potatoes.

When the potatoes are leaving a crust on the pan bottom (about 3 to 5 minutes), toss in the celery and carrots. Stir up everything well, scraping up any potato crust, raise the heat a bit, and cook for 2 or 3 minutes, until all the vegetables are hot and steaming. Push them aside to clear the pan bottom in the center, and drop in the tomato paste. Toast it in the hot spot for a minute or two, stirring, then work the paste into the vegetables.

Pour the gallon of hot water into the pan, drop in the bay leaves and pieces of cheese rind, grind in ¼ teaspoon or more of black pepper, add the remaining teaspoon of salt, and stir well. Cover the pot

- ¼ cup extra-virgin olive oil
- 2½ pounds russet potatoes, peeled and diced into ½-inch cubes (6 cups)
- 2 teaspoons salt
- 2 stalks celery, finely chopped (about 1½ cups)
- 2 medium carrots, peeled and grated (about 1½ cups)
- 3 tablespoons tomato paste
- 4 quarts water, heated to boiling
- 3 bay leaves
- 1 or 2 pieces outer rind of Parmigiano-Reggiano or Grana Padano (2 or 3 inches square), rinsed (see box, page 66)

¼ teaspoon freshly ground black
pepper, or more to taste

RECOMMENDED EQUIPMENT

A heavy-bottomed soup pot, saucepan,
or Dutch oven, minimum 6-quart
capacity, 8-quart preferable,
with a cover

Savory Potato Broth (cont.)

and bring the broth to a boil, adjusting the heat to keep a steady but
not violent bubbling, and let cook for an hour, covered. Stir occasionally.

Uncover the pot and cook the broth for another hour or so, still at
a low bubbling boil, until it has reduced to 4 quarts. (If you're in a
hurry, raise the heat and concentrate the broth quickly; stir now and
then to prevent burning.)

Remove the bay leaves but leave the cheese rind, whole or
chopped up, for those who like it.

You can use the broth right away, or any part of it, for the finished
soups that follow. Or let it cool and pack it in measured containers.
Keep it refrigerated for 3 or 4 days, or frozen, in filled and tightly
sealed containers, for 4 to 6 months.

TIPS ON TOMATO PASTE

*Tomato paste, so important to the cooking of the north of Italy, where
my roots are, is always a staple in my kitchen. I use it in many dishes,
as here in the potato soup base, to introduce the sweetness and intensity of tomato flavor in a convenient and controlled way. Notice that I
drop the tomato paste directly onto the pan bottom—in what I call a
hot spot—and cook it for a minute before stirring it in with the other
ingredients. This brief toasting, or caramelizing, deepens and layers
additional flavor into the paste. It is a technique I use whenever I add
tomato paste to a hot pot.*

*About buying and storing tomato paste: Genuine Italian tomato
paste, packed in tubes, is available in most supermarkets. I encourage
you to buy it in that form, even if it is slightly more expensive. It is
usually of good quality and will keep indefinitely; hand-squeeze,
flatten, and fold the tube (just like toothpaste) to get out every drop,
and store in the refrigerator. Tomato paste in cans, on the other hand,
will go bad quickly once it's been opened. Transfer any unused
canned paste to a jar, cover it with a film of olive oil, and refrigerate.
Use it up quickly, and discard it if mold starts to appear.*

Simple Vegetable Soup with Rice

*Y*ou can make a cup or a gallon of delicious soup by cooking rice in the soup base: multiply or divide this formula as needed. If you like the lighter consistency, use ¼ cup of uncooked rice per quart of base; for a denser soup, use ⅓ cup. Don't start cooking the rice more than 15 minutes before serving, though, since the grains continue to expand and absorb broth even off the heat. Serve immediately after the rice is cooked.

FOR I QUART OF SOUP

Heat the broth to a low boil; stir in the salt as needed, the pepper, and the rice. Return to a boil, stir, and cover tightly. Cook over low heat for 12 to 15 minutes, until the rice is tender. Adjust the seasoning, and serve right away in warm bowls, with freshly grated cheese, extra-virgin olive oil, and other garnishes (see page 60).

4 cups of Savory Potato Broth (preceding recipe)

⅓ to ½ teaspoon salt, or more if needed

Freshly ground black pepper to taste

¼ to ⅓ cup long-grain white rice

GIVING SUBSTANCE TO A SOUP WITH RICE AND OTHER BODY BUILDERS

You can always give substance to a soup base quickly by adding rice. If you don't have the exact amount of parsnips in my recipe, for instance, or if you've added all the vegetables called for and the soup looks thinner than you like, add a little long-grain rice—a tablespoon or so for a quart batch—along with a few pinches of salt. Wait until the last 12 to 15 minutes of cooking before adding rice, and serve the soup when the rice is cooked al dente. Barley, small pasta like ditalini or pastina, lentils, and split peas are other body- and flavor-builders that go with most soups. You can use leftover rice or cooked grains and pasta, but they will not give the same texture to the soup.

Cauliflower Soup with Poached Garlic Purée

*T*his soup is nice without the addition of garlic purée, marvelous with it. If you like, add short shreds of Savoy cabbage in place of some of the cauliflower, or make Savoy-cabbage soup with poached garlic purée instead.

FOR 8 CUPS OF FINISHED SOUP, SERVING 6 OR MORE

8 cups Savory Potato Broth
    (page 63)

½ teaspoon salt, plus more to taste

½ head cauliflower florets on short
    tender stems, sliced lengthwise into
    ½-inch-thick pieces (about 3 cups)

4 bunches scallions, finely chopped
    (2 cups)

¾ cup Poached Garlic Purée,
    from 1 ½ cups peeled cloves
    (page 67)

Freshly ground black pepper to taste

Heat the broth to a boil, and add salt to taste. Stir in cauliflower and scallion pieces, and return to a steady perking boil. Cover and cook for about 30 minutes, until the cauliflower is tender. Stir in the poached garlic purée and cook for another 4 to 5 minutes. Add pepper, taste, and adjust the seasonings. Serve right away in warm bowls, with freshly grated cheese, extra-virgin olive oil, and other garnishes (see page 60).

CHEESE RINDS: A REWARD FOR THE THRIFTY

Don't ever throw away the rinds of your Parmigiano-Reggiano or Grana Padano. Those rinds, Italian know well, add a subtle richness to long-cooking soups and sauces.

In my kitchen, I keep a zippered freezer bag in a drawer in the refrigerator where I stow any sizable piece of rind with a good layer of cheese. Stored airtight, they will last indefinitely.

Before adding them to a dish, rinse rind pieces well; scrub or scrape off any mold or residue.

When the soup or sauce is finished, remove the rind piece (it will be soft and chewy), or leave it in the soup as a surprise for some lucky person at your table.

A KINDER, GENTLER GARLIC:
POACHED GARLIC PURÉE

When garlic cloves are poached in water, the enzymes responsible for their harsh bite are neutralized, leaving them soft and mildly flavored. As a purée, they melt into a hot soup, lending it a lovely undertone of garlic and a velvet texture. Add this purée to any soup you like; I suggest the Cauliflower (page 66), the Parsnip (page 72), and the *Frantoiana* (page 62) in particular. And if you, or someone you cook for, find sautéed garlic too strong, use this poached purée to flavor sauces, dressings, roasts, and braises too.

FOR ¾ CUP OF GARLIC PURÉE, TO FLAVOR 2 QUARTS OF SOUP

Peel 1½ cups of whole garlic cloves (about ½ pound of whole garlic heads). Put them in a small saucepan with 2½ cups of water or more, to cover them well. Bring the water to a steady boil, and cook, uncovered, for about 40 minutes, until the cloves are completely soft but still whole, with only a few spoonfuls of liquid left in the pot. Reduce the heat as the water evaporates so nothing burns.

Purée the cloves and the bit of cooking liquid in a food processor or blender. You'll get about ¾ cup purée; stir it into the simmering soup, and cook for at least 5 minutes—or longer, if the soup needs more cooking.

Creamy Poached Garlic and Onion Soup

*P*oached garlic lends its lovely flavor to the soup, and then everything gets a quick whirl in the food processor, producing a light, creamy soup—without cream. Add some crunch to this with Cheesy Crostini (page 60).

12 large whole garlic cloves, peeled
(about ¾ cup)

4 cups Savory Potato Broth
(page 63)

1 medium onion, finely chopped
(about 1 cup)

¼ teaspoon salt, or more to taste

Freshly ground black pepper

Poach the garlic in water, as for the purée on page 67, until the cloves are soft and the water is nearly evaporated. Heat the savory soup base to a gentle boil, add the garlic and any drops of poaching water; stir in the onion, salt, and pepper. Return to the boil, and cook covered for about 30 minutes—or uncovered, if you want it thicker.

Let the soup cool at room temperature, then purée it in a food processor or blender, in batches if necessary. Taste, and adjust the seasonings. Reheat the soup, and serve right away in warm bowls, with freshly grated cheese and extra-virgin olive oil. If you've made *crostini*, float two or three in each bowl; top with spoonfuls of cheese and a swirl of olive oil.

Mushroom and Barley Soup

FOR 8 CUPS OF FINISHED SOUP, SERVING 6 OR MORE

Lift the porcini out of the soaking water, squeeze dry (saving the water), and chop into small pieces. Strain the soaking water and pour it into the broth. Bring to a boil. Stir in salt and several grinds of pepper, the barley, chopped porcini, and sliced mushrooms, and return to a steady perking boil. Cover, and cook for about 40 minutes or longer, until the barley and the mushrooms are tender to the bite—uncover the pot near the end of cooking to thicken the soup if you want. Taste, and adjust the seasonings. Serve hot in warm bowls, with freshly grated cheese, extra-virgin olive oil, and other garnishes (see page 60).

½ ounce dried porcini
(about ½ cup loosely packed),
soaked in 2 cups warm water
(see box on page 140 for tips)

8 cups Savory Potato Broth
(page 63)

½ teaspoon salt, or more to taste

Freshly ground black pepper to taste

1 cup barley, rinsed

12 ounces firm mushrooms, button
or cremini, sliced (about 4½ cups)

Fresh Chestnut and Winter Squash Soup

*W*inter *squash and chestnuts are a wonderful combination with this base, adding nutty and sweet flavors and hearty texture. Any firm winter squash is suitable. Use fresh chestnuts or packaged peeled chestnuts (sold frozen or freeze-dried). If using fresh chestnuts, see my peeling method below.*

8 cups Savory Potato Broth
   (page 63)

½ teaspoon salt, plus more to taste

Freshly ground black pepper to taste

½ pound chestnuts, peeled, cut into
   bits and chunks (1½ cups)

½ pound winter squash, peeled,
   sliced into ⅓-inch pieces
   (about 1½ cups)

1 medium leek, sliced and chopped fine

Heat the broth to a boil. Stir in the ½ teaspoon salt, or more if the broth is bland, and a few grinds of black pepper. Stir in all the chestnut, squash, and leek pieces; return to a steady perking boil. Cover, and cook for 45 minutes to an hour, until the vegetables have softened, melted, and thickened the soup. Stir frequently, and lower the heat as the soup thickens. Cook uncovered if you want a thicker soup; add water to thin it. Taste, and adjust the seasonings. Serve hot in warm bowls, with freshly grated cheese, extra-virgin olive oil, and other garnishes (see page 60).

A SEASONAL CHORE: PEELING FRESH CHESTNUTS

I love fresh chestnuts. Though it's easy to take off the outer shell, the frustrating part is the skin-tight brown peel around the nut meat. With the blanching-and-chilling method here—and a cooperative batch of nuts—the shell and skin should come off together.

I always buy a few pounds of nuts when they're fresh, and enjoy most of them as Skillet Roasted Chestnuts (page 407). Be sure to try it—you won't have to peel those nuts; your guests will!

To peel chestnuts, cut a slit about ½ inch long in the outer shell of each nut. Bring a quart or so of water to the boil, drop in the nuts, and boil them for 5 minutes. Drain, and spread them on a tray or baking sheet; while the nuts are still hot, set the tray in the freezer (or outside, if it's cold enough), and freeze for 30 minutes to an hour, maximum. To peel a nut, break open the shell at the slit and tear apart the inner skin—it's helpful to use the tip of a paring knife. Loosen the skin with the knife, and pry off the shell and skin at one time. If necessary, break the nut meat to get the skin out of the wrinkles—the nuts will be chopped up for cooking anyway.

When you come upon a really unpeelable nut, just pare the peel, losing some nut meat, or try the technique suggested by Judith Jones, my editor and an expert cook. Put up to a dozen slit chestnuts in a microwave oven and cook them for about 30 seconds. The skin should come off easily, she says. If not, microwave for another few seconds.

Foraging in the Vermont woods

Parsnip and Scallion Soup

Try this with poached garlic purée too.

FOR 8 CUPS OF FINISHED SOUP, SERVING 6 OR MORE

8 cups Savory Potato Broth
(page 63)

½ teaspoon salt, plus more to taste

Freshly ground black pepper

3 medium parsnips, peeled, trimmed,
and cut into ⅓-inch pieces
(about 3 cups)

Six ¼-pound bunches finely chopped
scallions (about 3 cups)

Heat the broth to a boil. Stir in the ½ teaspoon salt, a few grinds of black pepper, the parsnips, and the scallions. Return to a steady perking boil and cook, covered, for 45 minutes, or until the parsnips have softened completely and broken up in the soup. Add poached garlic purée (see page 67) at this time, if you like, and cook a few minutes more. Taste, and adjust the seasonings. Serve hot in warm bowls, with freshly grated cheese, extra-virgin olive oil, and other garnishes (see page 60).

Soup with Lentils and Ditalini Pasta

Both lentils and pasta absorb liquid from the soup base, so add water from the beginning and more during cooking to get the consistency you like.

FOR 8 CUPS OF FINISHED SOUP, SERVING 6 OR MORE

8 cups Savory Potato Broth
(page 63)

2 cups water, or more if needed

½ teaspoon salt, plus more to taste

Freshly ground black pepper

1 cup lentils, rinsed and picked over

1 cup ditalini or other short tubular
pasta

Heat the broth with the additional 2 cups of water to a boil. Stir in the salt, several grinds of pepper, and the rinsed lentils. Return to a gentle boil, and cook, covered, for 35 to 40 minutes, until the lentils are tender—add more *hot* water as needed.

Taste, and add more salt to balance the pasta: stir in the ditalini and cook for 12 minutes or more, until the pasta is to your liking. Add hot water to thin the soup too, if necessary. Adjust the seasoning one last time, and serve right away in warm bowls, with freshly grated cheese, extra-virgin olive oil, and other garnishes (see page 60).

Hearty Minestre *from a Base of Pork, Beans, and Potato*

Hearty *Minestra* Base with Cranberry Beans, Potatoes, and Pork

I can still hear the staccato clack-clack-clack of my grandmother's cleaver on a wooden board as she chopped the pestata, *the fine paste of pork fat, garlic, and rosemary, that gave so much flavor to her rich* minestra. *Occasionally, she would pause and hand me the cleaver: I'd dip it in the boiling soup pot, already full of beans and potatoes, and watch the tiny specks of fat whirl into the broth. After a few moments I'd hand the cleaver back to my nonna, and instantly she'd be chopping again, the hot blade literally melting the thick fat, while the aroma of garlic and pork and beans and rosemary filled the kitchen. . . .*

Precious memories! But today I make pestata *in the food processor in about 10 seconds!*

In most ways, however, this minestra *is just like my grandmother's. It cooks for a long time—give it 3 full hours if you can—steadily drawing flavor from pork bones and a soffritto of onion and tomato, and slowly reducing in the soup pot.*

You'll have 4 quarts of minestra *base, to finish with any of the additions I suggest here, or with other vegetables or grains. Long-grain white rice or small pasta can be added to almost any variation for a denser* minestra. *For a thicker, smooth consistency, remove some of the beans (a third to a half) before adding the finishing vegetables; purée them, and stir back into the pot for the final cooking.*

ABOUT 4 QUARTS OF BASE, ENOUGH FOR 2 OR MORE
FINISHED *MINESTRE*

Drain the soaked beans and put them in the pot with the water, potatoes, bay leaves, and *peperoncino*. Cover, and bring to a boil over high heat, stirring occasionally so nothing scorches on the bottom of the pot.

While the water is heating, make the *pestata* in the food processor,

1 ½ cups dried cranberry beans, soaked overnight or quick-soaked (see box, page 59)

5 quarts cold water

2 pounds russet potatoes, peeled and
diced into ½-inch cubes
(about 5 cups)

3 bay leaves

½ teaspoon to 1 tablespoon dried
peperoncino (hot red pepper flakes),
or to taste

FOR THE *PESTATA*

3 ounces smoked bacon, cut in 1-inch
pieces (about ½ cup packed)

1 tablespoon (packed) fresh rosemary
leaves, stripped from the stem

8 plump garlic cloves, peeled
(about ¼ cup)

MEAT FOR FLAVORING

1 pound bony fresh pork: a small slab
of spare ribs, pork hock, or pork
neck (for more meat to eat,
see page 76)

FOR THE *SOFFRITTO*

2 tablespoons extra-virgin olive oil

1 medium onion, chopped
(about 1 cup)

1 cup canned San Marzano tomatoes
and juices (see box, page 124)

2 teaspoons salt, plus more to taste

RECOMMENDED EQUIPMENT

A heavy-bottomed soup pot, 8-quart
capacity, with a cover

A food processor for the *pestata*

Hearty Minestra *Base with Cranberry Beans, Potatoes, and Pork (cont.)*

chopping the bacon, rosemary, and garlic to a fine paste. Scrape every bit into the soup pot. Rinse in hot water the spare ribs, pork hock, or other bony pork, and add it to the pot too.

When the water is at a full boil, set the cover on ajar; adjust the heat to maintain a steady gentle boiling, and cook for an hour to 1½ hours, until the beans and the potatoes are tender and are beginning to break apart. Skim the fat or residue from the pork now and then, as it collects on the surface.

Meanwhile, prepare the *soffritto*. Pour the oil into a small skillet, stir in the onion, and set over medium heat. Cook the onion, stirring, until wilted, about 6 minutes. Crush the tomatoes into bits with your hands, and pour them with all the juices into the skillet. Stir in the 2 teaspoons salt, and simmer rapidly for about 5 minutes, until the juices have reduced a bit. When the beans are tender, pour the tomato mixture into them, dipping the skillet into the soup pot to slosh out every bit, and keep the *minestra* boiling.

Cook the *minestra* for another hour or more, 2½ to 3 hours total, until the volume has reduced to about 4 quarts (about midway up an 8-quart pot, when you take out any bones and meat). If there's too much broth, raise the heat and cook uncovered, but stir frequently to prevent burning. Taste the soup when reduced, and correct seasoning.

Take some of the base for a finished soup now if you want, or let the whole pot cool. Before using or storing, lift out the pork bones, pick off all the meat, shred it, and stir into the base; pick out the bay leaves and discard. Keep the soup refrigerated for 3 or 4 days, or freeze, in filled and tightly sealed containers, for 4 to 6 months.

FOR MEAT LOVERS: A MEATY MAIN COURSE
FROM THE *MINESTRA*

I will often add extra pork pieces to the big *minestra* pot for an hour of so of cooking, then serve the meat as a separate course. If your pot is big enough, you should be able to drop in a pound or more of meat, either bony spare ribs or hocks, or meatier cuts, such as pork butt or country-style ribs, in addition to the ones already cooking with the soup. Italian sausages and kielbasa are also great cooked this way. Wash meat well with hot water before, or you might give it a quick boil before adding to the pot.

You can cook such main-course meat anytime the *minestra* is perking away, though it will take on the best flavor after you've added the tomato-onion *soffritto* and salt. Remove the meat when tender, keep warm until ready, slice, and serve on a platter—moistened with a ladle of delicious *minestra* broth.

FOR A HEARTY NO-MEAT *MINESTRA*

If you prefer a vegetarian *minestra*, flavor it during the long cooking with an herb pesto instead of the bacon *pestata*: in the food processor, chop the garlic and rosemary in ¼ cup of extra-virgin olive oil, and scrape this into the soup pot as it comes to the boil. Then just follow the recipes for the base and any of the finished *minestre*.

Hearty Minestra *with* Rice

*C*ook rice just before serving to get the consistency of soup you like: ¼ cup of rice per quart of base for a lighter minestra, and up to ½ cup of rice for a hefty and hearty minestra.

4 cups *Minestra* Base (preceding recipe)

¼ to ½ cup long-grain white rice

½ to I teaspoon salt, or more to taste

Freshly ground black pepper to taste

Heat the base to a gentle boil; stir in rice and salt (more salt for more rice) and grinds of pepper. Return to a boil, stir, and cover tightly. Cook over low heat for 12 minutes or so, until the rice is tender. Add the pepper, and more salt if needed, and serve right away in warm bowls, with freshly grated cheese, extra-virgin olive oil, and other garnishes (see page 60).

My daughter, Tanya Bastianich Manuali, and my daughter-in-law, Deanna Damiano Bastianich

Hearty Minestra *with Corn*

*C*orn is a nice addition to minestra—*it adds texture and sweetness. It is also a good addition to other vegetable soups, such as fresh fennel, zucchini, or chicory and white bean.*

FOR 2 QUARTS OF SOUP, SERVING 6 OR MORE

Heat the broth to a boil, stir in the salt, corn kernels, and grinds of pepper, and return to a steady gentle boil. Cook, covered, for 10 to 15 minutes, until the corn is tender to the bite. Taste, and adjust the seasonings. Serve hot in warm bowls with freshly grated cheese, extra-virgin olive oil, and other garnishes (see page 60)

8 cups of *Minestra* Base (page 73)

I teaspoon salt, or more to taste

4 cups frozen or fresh corn kernels

Freshly ground black pepper to taste

Hearty Minestra *with Butternut Squash*

FOR 2 QUARTS OF SOUP, SERVING 6 OR MORE

Heat the broth to a boil, stir in the salt, squash pieces, and grinds of pepper, and return to a steady gentle boil. Cook, covered, for 35 to 40 minutes, until the squash is tender and breaking apart in the soup. Taste, and adjust the seasonings. Serve hot in warm bowls, with freshly grated cheese, extra-virgin olive oil, and other garnishes (see page 60).

8 cups of *Minestra* Base (page 73)

I teaspoon salt, or more to taste

I pound butternut or other winter
squash, peeled and cut in
$\frac{1}{3}$-inch pieces (about 3 cups)
Freshly ground black pepper to taste

Hearty *Minestra* with Fennel

8 cups *Minestra* Base (page 73)

1 teaspoon salt, or more to taste

2 pounds or more fresh fennel, chopped in ¼-inch pieces, both bulb and tender stalks (about 4 cups)

2 tablespoons minced fresh fennel fronds, for garnishing

Heat the broth to a boil, stir in the salt and chopped fennel, and return to a steady gentle boil. Cook covered for 15 to 20 minutes, until the fennel is tender. If you want, cook uncovered for a thicker consistency. Stir in the fennel fronds just before serving in warm bowls, with freshly grated cheese, extra-virgin olive oil, and other garnishes (see page 60).

The whole fennel

The outer layer of the bulb and the hollow stalks removed

Chopping off the remaining stalks and fronds

Slicing the bulb in half

TRIMMING FRESH FENNEL

Wild fennel is best for this soup. I recall foraging in the spring for wild fennel for my grandmother. "Pick only the tender center shoots," she would instruct me. I knew the light-green feathery fronds were the ones she wanted, and on my way home would lightly chew them and suck out their sweet licorice center.

Fresh fennel is now available year-round. Buy the whole bulb with stalks; look for the freshest fronds and firm white bulbs without bruises. An untrimmed bulb with attached stalks weighing 1 ¼ to 1 ½ pounds will yield about 2 cups of chopped fennel; a single 2-pound bulb will yield 3 to 4 cups chopped.

Slice off the tough bottom of the bulb, as shown in the photos. Break off the thick outer layers of the bulb and the big hollow stalks attached to them. Slice off the remaining stems and fronds. Save the short, tender inner stalks—they are flavorful and fresh and add a bit of color to sauces, soups, and other dishes.

Slice the trimmed fennel bulb lengthwise (through the root end and top). For long slivers to use in salads, lay the bulb half on the flat, cut side and slice thinly, lengthwise (separate the slivers if they're joined at the core).

For cubed or diced fennel, slice each bulb half in thin crosswise slices, and cut again to get cubes of any size (just as you would an onion). Be sure to chop up the tender inner stalks you saved.

For a garnish, pick off the freshest and most delicate fronds from the stalks. Leave them long and lacy, or mince.

The Delights and Diversity of the Big Bird Soup

All-Purpose Turkey Broth

C apon soup in Italy is the soup of the holidays. Rich and full of flavor, it is a soup base for tortellini, straciatella, and passatelli. Here it is difficult to get capon as readily as it is in Italy, but if you can find one, by all means make a big pot of capon soup following the recipe below.

It was my mother who started using turkey, especially the wings, in her basic poultry and vegetable broth. She and Giovanni enjoy the meaty pieces—a couple of wings is plenty for them for dinner. Everyone loves the broth, which is sweet, flavorful, and not too strong. And Lorenzo is always ready to have a bowl of broth with noodles after school—proof of its goodness. Not least important to Grandma is that turkey wings are readily available, inexpensive, and, at our big neighborhood market, often on sale. So turkey wings and turkey broth have become staple items in our freezer.

I use the broth as I would chicken or vegetable stock, in sauces, roasts, risotti, and lots of skillet dishes. I've found it extremely versatile and tasty—but not so much so that it overwhelms other flavors.

Here then is our All-Purpose Turkey Broth—my mother's original with my adjustments. You can use it in many recipes throughout this book, especially in the long-cooking pasta sauces and main course roasts and braises, as well as for all kinds of satisfying soups. Adjust the broth to suit you: either clear and light or with more body, with the vegetables mashed in.

This is a large recipe, giving you plenty to freeze and have on hand whenever you need it.

MAKES 6 QUARTS OF BROTH

8 quarts cold water

3 pounds turkey wings
   (or turkey legs or chicken backs
   and wings)

Heating, Skimming, and Cooking

Pour the cold water into the stockpot and set it over high heat. Rinse the turkey wings and drop them in the water, followed by all the other ingredients as you prepare them. Bring the water to a full active boil, then lower the heat slightly to maintain a gentle rolling boil. For the next 15 minutes, cook uncovered, frequently skimming off the residue and scum as it accumulates. Once there is no more or very little residue rising, set a cover ajar over the pot—I prop it up with a long wooden spoon resting on the pot rim—leaving a space for evaporation. Adjust the heat to keep the broth reducing slowly at a gentle boil. (Note the level of liquid in the pot when you put the cover in place, so you can tell how much it has reduced.)

After an hour or more, mash the softened vegetables (if you want) against the side of the pan, especially the carrots and tomatoes. A good smush with a spoon or spatula is enough. Or (another choice) leave a few of the nicest carrot pieces intact to enjoy as a soup vegetable later on. *But*—a major decision—if you want to end up with an especially clear broth, do not mash any vegetables at all.

At this time, the liquid level should be noticeably lower—1 or 2 inches in most pots. If not, make sure the broth is boiling actively and leave the cover off.

After 2 hours or so, when the broth is reduced by approximately ¼ of its original volume, check its consistency and flavor. If you want it for sauces, roasts, or other dishes, and it is light bodied with distinct brothy flavor—though not strong enough to call soup—*stop cooking now.*

If you want it to have a stronger flavor and more body—to serve as soup or use for more intense sauces—*keep cooking uncovered,* until it has concentrated to the degree you like. (Or divide the broth: remove and reserve some of the lighter broth and cook the rest to intensify it.)

Straining, Cooling, and Storing the Broth

When the broth is cooked to your taste, turn off the heat. Lift out the turkey wings with a spider or slotted spatula, and put them in a bowl to cool; extract any whole, attractive carrot pieces for later eating, too. Set a sieve (either coarse, if you want body and color, or fine-meshed for clearer broth) or a colander into the empty pot and strain the broth through it. Ladle out in stages if the pot is too heavy to pour from.

After the broth has drained through, press and scrape the vegetables against the sieve, mashing them well, then scrape the soft veg-

4 large carrots, peeled, trimmed, cut in 1-inch lengths (about 5 cups)

4 big celery stalks with leaves washed, trimmed, and cut in 1-inch lengths (about 4 cups)

1 large onion (or several smaller ones) peeled and cut in big chunks (3 cups or more)

1 medium leek, rinsed thoroughly, trimmed, cut in 1-inch lengths (about 2 cups)

2 fat garlic cloves, peeled

3 fresh plum tomatoes (about ¾ pound), rinsed but left whole

A handful of fresh Italian parsley (6 to 8 long stems with lots of leaves, left whole)

1 or 2 pieces (about 2 ounces) rind of Parmigiano-Reggiano or Grana Padano, if available, scraped and rinsed (page 66)

1 teaspoon whole black peppercorns

1 scant tablespoon kosher salt

RECOMMENDED EQUIPMENT

A 12-quart stockpot with a cover for cooking

A sturdy wire sieve for straining, or a colander

An 8-quart pot or a couple of smaller pots to collect the strained finished broth

etable purée from the bottom of the sieve and blend it into the broth. But if you want clear broth, *don't* press the vegetables at all.

If you are using the broth right away, skim the surface with a spoon or ladle, scooping up as much fat as possible; soak up the last floating slicks of fat by touching them with the edge of a paper towel. Otherwise chill the broth (either in the pot or in smaller freezer containers) and pry off the fat layer after it has solidified.

Store unused broth in the refrigerator for 4 or 5 days; freeze for use within 4 or 5 months. Bring it back to the boil before using in other dishes or serving as a soup.

Don't forget the turkey wings: separate and shred all the meat—discard the bones, skin, and cartilage. Enjoy the meat (and any carrots or other vegetables that you've saved).

SIMPLE SOUPS WITH TURKEY BROTH

Turkey broth makes a delicious soup and soup base, whether you've made it Nonna Erminia–style (substantial with mashed vegetables) or ultra-clear from careful straining. The important factor is concentrating the broth to the intensity of flavor you want. If you take some broth out of the freezer, for example, and find that it's too light for soup, you can still reduce it to strengthen the flavor. And always taste and salt the broth as needed before serving it or adding additional ingredients.

A bowl of plain turkey broth can sometimes be the right soup for the moment, delicious, nourishing, and comforting without any embellishment. But there are countless good things to cook, and float in the broth, too. Here are some of my family's favorites:

● Stockpot special broth: Heat freshly made broth to the simmer, adjust the seasonings, and drop in shredded turkey wing meat and carrots saved from the stockpot. Turn off the heat and serve immediately, dusted with freshly grated cheese. Cooked turkey or chicken meat should always be shredded and dropped into simmering broth after other ingredients are cooked, just to heat it up, before serving.

- Lorenzo's After-School Special: For that matter all the grandchildren love *pastina in brodo,* little star pasta cooked in the broth with a speck of the vegetables and grated Parmigiano-Reggiano or Grana Padano.

- The adults love rice in turkey broth with grated cheese. Cook the rice directly in the soup or precook the rice in salted water, drain, and combine just before serving.

- Broth with fresh tagliolini: For 2 servings, add ½ cup Rich Man's Golden Pasta tagliolini (see page 158) to 3 cups seasoned boiling broth and cook for about 2 minutes until the pasta is tender. Ladle into bowls and top with freshly grated cheese. (Make a note! The next time you make pasta, put a *nidodi fidelini,* a little nest of noodles [photo, page 167], in the freezer and save it for soup.)

- Broth with *passatelli:* For 2 servings, add ½ cup cut *passatelli* (see page 84) to 3 cups seasoned boiling broth and cook for 4 or 5 minutes until the pasta is tender. Ladle into bowls and top with freshly grated cheese.

- Broth with spinach: For every 3 cups broth, clean and trim 1½ cups tender spinach leaves, cut in shreds (or left whole if small). Drop into the boiling, seasoned broth and cook for about 3 minutes. You may also drop the spinach into broth while tagliolini or *passatelli* are cooking.

- Serve with Cheesy *Crostini* on the side, or float a *crostini* slice and top with a poached egg—Zuppa Pavese, as it is called. Pavia is a city in Lombardy.

- Shred finely some leftover Herb Frittata or make one to order (see page 24).

- Another good garnish would be any small piece of pasta dough you might have left, rolled very thin, and then sliced in strips from extra fine to fettucine. Or make quadrucci—little squares cut out from small pieces of dough or simply pieces of broken thumb-size dough.

VEGETABLE BROTH

For a simple vegetable broth to use as a moistening agent in preparing other dishes, see page 288.

A potful of broth with round *passatelli*

SHAPING ROUND PASSATELLI

In Italy, traditional round strands of passatelli *are shaped with a special tool somewhat like a potato masher, with a heavy-duty perforated sheet that is pressed into the dough. With enough pressure, the dough is forced up through the holes, forming spaghetti-like pieces. I have one of these, a handheld cylindrical extruder, at home and it works well most of the time. But you have to be careful about the density of the dough; it must be neither too hard nor too soft.*

A good alternative—and one that I hope many of you can try—is to use an electric meat grinder or the meat grinder attachment for a food processor. You set it up as usual with a disk of medium or large holes, but without the rotary cutting blade. The machine will now act as an extruder rather than a grinder: you drop the dough into the hopper and the auger will do the work, pushing it out the holes in a continuous stream of perfect passatelli. *Let them fall onto a tray or plate and break naturally into pieces (or cut them shorter). Cook them as in the recipe below.*

The finished dough

Passatelli

Passatelli *are a traditional soup garnish that resemble fat round noodles (see the photo, above) but they're made with dried bread crumbs rather than flour. This gives them lots of flavor and a pleasant crumbly texture; in fact, they may remind you of matzoh balls, the Jewish soup dumplings that are also made from dried crumbs and eggs.*

Passatelli *are a snap to make—well ahead if you want—and they cook in less than 5 minutes, right in the soup pot, just before you serve the soup. They are a splendid addition to plain broths, either All-Purpose Turkey Broth (see page 80) or chicken poaching broth (see page 328), and they'd be a nice addition to Savory Potato Broth as well (see page 63).*

For this small amount of passatelli, *I suggest using the simple method of rolling and cutting in the recipe. The shape is not traditional but the taste and texture are exactly as they should be. It doesn't seem like a lot but the* passatelli *swell up nicely in the soup. If you want a larger quantity, just multiply the formula here.*

To mix, beat the egg lightly, then stir in the bread crumbs, salt, and cheese. Blend thoroughly to form a dense and somewhat sticky paste (see illustrations). Cover the dough and refrigerate now if you want, for up to 2 days.

To make the *passatelli*, flatten the dough on a floured board and roll into a rough rectangular shape, ¼ inch thick or a bit less, if it will stretch without breaking. Cut the dough lengthwise every ¼ inch into long sticks; cut these into 3-inch pieces (on the bias for a decorative touch). Toss lightly in flour, then lay out on a tray or baking sheet, covered with a towel, until you're ready to cook them. They can be frozen at this point and dropped into the boiling soup to cook frozen.

Cook about ½ cup of cut pieces per serving. Bring seasoned broth to an active boil, drop in the *passatelli*, and boil for 4 to 5 minutes (or a bit longer if they are thick), until they are soft but still hold their shape.

1 large egg

1 cup fine dried bread crumbs

⅛ teaspoon salt (2 or 3 good pinches)

¼ cup freshly grated Parmigiano-Reggiano or Grana Padano

The rolled-out dough

Cutting the dough into 3-inch pieces

Tossing in flour

The Wonders of Pasta—
Plus Polentas and Risottos

I was gathering my recipes and instructions for the pasta chapter in this book with David Nussbaum and e-mailing them to my editor, Judith Jones, when I received a stern message from her: "Lidia, we must meet." Now, you have to understand, Judith is the best cookbook editor at large, a gentle woman, who in her more-than-45-year career has worked with the best, including Julia Child, Jacques Pépin, and James Beard. Clearly she wanted to tell me something. We met in my office, and as she sat down she plopped a pile of well over 300 pages on my desk. It was the pasta chapter. "Lidia," she said, "this could be a book in itself." Yes, I guess I did get carried away, but the subject of pasta is endless, delightfully endless.

I have since cut and condensed much from that pile (and saved it), but still I am very excited about what I am giving you here.

First of all, I am sharing my enthusiasm for and love of pasta-making, of cooking and enjoying it.

I explore with you various dry pastas and demonstrate how the different shapes marry with different sauces—with quick skillet sauces made while the pasta cooks, with slow-cooking, meaty sauces, and with tomato sauces for all seasons, the making of which has careful instructions here.

I work with you to help you better understand the simple art of mixing and rolling out egg-pasta doughs, and we experiment with different healthful flavors and textures—whole-wheat pasta, chestnut, semolina, buckwheat, flaxseed, barley, and cornmeal pastas, some enhanced with nuts and seeds.

I explain the secret of feathery light gnocchi, and again we play with interesting variations in the dough. The smooth art of polenta is explored, as well as the rolling and filling of large pillowy ravioli. And I particularly enjoy walking you through all the steps of risotto-making so you can understand exactly what you are doing. I am sharing the baking of pasta and the simple art of making fresh pasta. Properly made and sauced, pasta is the perfect meal. It is gratifying and nutritionally sound; it contains complex carbohydrates, and when properly prepared it is balanced with vegetables and proteins.

Pasta is the perfect food for large buffets, particularly for budget-conscious households. It is perfect when unexpected guests arrive at the door, and for children's parties or family gatherings.

Pasta makes leftovers into a new dish. When you have some pot roast left, turn it into a risotto; some meatballs left, turn them into ravioli; some chicken and/or vegetables left, create a plate of pasta.

The only family image better than the picture of a family making pasta together is of a family eating pasta together. This happens at our house all the time.

A Sauce from Scratch While the Pasta Boils

When I cook a simple pasta dish at home, I do two things automatically. First I get out my 10-quart pot and start filling it with cold water. Next I take down one of the well-worn large skillets hanging over the brick fireplace and set it on the stove.

After years of making fast pastas for hungry people, I know that, whatever pasta I choose from the cupboard or whatever sauce ingredients I find in the refrigerator, I will need those two pans. When the water in the big pot boils, I will start cooking the pasta. In the big skillet, I will create a sauce from scratch while the pasta is cooking. Such spur-of-the-moment sauces are fairly simple, sometimes just garlic and oil, or butter and fresh herbs, and a splash of pasta-cooking water to moisten them. These are small sauces, just filling the wide bottom of the pan.

I like a big skillet because it provides the room and the heat that I need to finish the pasta the way I like it. After the pasta has boiled for a few minutes, I scoop it out of the pot and drop it into the skillet on top of the simmering sauce. Then I toss them together for a couple of minutes, while they finish cooking and merge together. When the pasta is done *al dente*, it is coated with just enough sauce so that it glides, not splashes around, in the pan.

I've devoted the first part of this chapter to such simple skillet pastas. These are dishes for every day made with ingredients you probably have in your cupboard and refrigerator right now: dry pastas, savory condiments, fresh vegetables, and cheese.

If you've never made pasta this way, you'll find all it takes is a little preparation and planning. Have everything ready and near at hand, warm the serving bowls, and alert the children the moment you plop the pasta into the boiling water. I love the fast pace of cooking this way, and I'm sure you'll find it fun.

In the first three recipes that follow, I pair a skillet sauce with a particular pasta and detail the preparation of both, with coordinated timing. Following these three are a large group of recipes for quick skillet sauces to match with any pasta you like. In boxes, sidebars, and notes you'll find tips and explanations about sauce and pasta cookery, which I hope will add to your understanding and confidence in creating your own everyday pasta dishes.

Capellini with a Sauce of Anchovies, Capers, and Fresh Tomatoes

*T*his recipe provides a good introduction to the quick skillet sauces and pastas in this section. Typical of these dishes, it's quick: the sauce itself cooks in 5 minutes in the skillet, and the capellini I've paired it with needs barely 2 minutes in the pot; when all is tossed and garnished, the pasta is on the table in 10 minutes. And it demonstrates how well a pasta dish can be created from common pantry ingredients when they are cooked and combined thoughtfully.

With its generous amounts of anchovies, capers, peperoncino flakes, garlic, and tomato, I can honestly tell you that this is the kind of pasta I love to eat. The flavors are strong and sharp yet balanced—staccato notes in harmony, to use a musical metaphor.

In the recipe, I've given a range of amounts for the bold ingredients. If you use the lesser measures of anchovies, capers, peperoncino, and garlic, you will enjoy a distinctive dish suited for most people's tastes, what I call "middle of the road" at my restaurants. If you use the greater measure, you'll have the same dish I make for myself at home.

Incidentally, you don't need to use perfect summer tomatoes for this sauce. Even in winter, decent market tomatoes will work as long as they're not too soft. If none are available, you can make a fine sauce without tomato at all (just don't substitute canned tomatoes). You'll need more pasta water for moisture, but otherwise follow the recipe.

Like all sauces, this one goes with many pastas. In addition to thin varieties like the capellini, presented here, I suggest linguine, spaghettini, or just regular spaghetti.

Remember to coordinate the cooking of the sauce with the cooking time of each kind of pasta. If I was cooking linguine that takes 9 or 10 minutes in the pot, I would put the pasta in first and then start cooking my sauce, reversing the sequence given in the recipe.

SERVES 6

Prepping

Start heating 6 quarts of water, with the tablespoon kosher salt, in the pasta pot.

Rinse the tomatoes, cut out the cores, and slice them in half. Squeeze each half over a sieve set in a bowl, forcing out the seeds and juice; clean reluctant seeds out of the halves with your finger. Scrape the seeds against the sieve to extract any remaining juice. Dice the tomatoes into ½-inch pieces—you should have about 1½ cups total—and put them in the bowl with the strained juice.

FOR THE SAUCE

2 or 3 fresh medium-size tomatoes (about 1 pound)

2 to 3 ounces anchovy fillets, chopped (¼ to ⅓ cup)

½ to ⅔ cup tiny "nonpareil" capers, drained

½ to 1 teaspoon dried *peperoncino* (hot red pepper flakes)

4–5 garlic cloves, sliced (¼ to ⅓ cup)

½ cup extra-virgin olive oil

Hot water from the pasta-cooking pot

FOR THE PASTA AND FINISHING

1 tablespoon kosher or coarse sea salt, for the pasta-cooking water

1 pound thin capellini, vermicelli, or other thin dry pasta

½ cup chopped fresh Italian parsley

½ cup Dry Toasted Bread Crumbs (see box)

RECOMMENDED EQUIPMENT

8-quart pasta-cooking pot

A 12-inch or larger skillet for the sauce and the pasta

Warm bowls for individual servings of pasta

Capellini with a Sauce of Anchovies, Capers, and Fresh Tomatoes (cont.)

Cut the anchovies into 1-inch lengths.

Prep and measure the remaining ingredients (vary capers, *peperoncino*, or even garlic amounts to taste) and have them handy to the stove.

Making the Sauce and Cooking the Pasta Simultaneously

• Pour ⅓ cup of the olive oil into the big skillet, scatter the garlic slices in the oil, and set over medium-high heat. Cook for 1½ minutes or so, shaking the pan now and then, until the garlic is sizzling; push the slices to one side of the pan.

• Scatter the anchovy pieces in the clear side of the skillet, and drop the *peperoncino* into another open "hot spot." Cook for a minute or more, as the anchovies start sizzling and melting and the dried *peperoncino* toasts, then stir and shake everything together.

• Clear space in the skillet and dump in the capers. Spread them out, and cook for about 1½ minutes, as they dry and start sizzling. Stir the garlic, pepper, and anchovies too, on their side of the pan, for even cooking.

• Ladle 2 cups of water out of the pasta-cooking pot (it should be boiling by now) and into the skillet. Stir up all the seasonings and get the liquid boiling; turn up the heat if necessary. The sauce should fill the pan to a depth of nearly ¼ inch (add more water if your skillet is huge). Boil for a minute or so.

• Pour in the tomato pieces and juice, stir and bring to a boil.

• Start cooking the capellini. Push the long pasta strands gradually into the boiling water, letting them soften. Stir, return to the boil, and cook 1½ to 2 minutes.

• Meanwhile, continue to cook the sauce at a rapid boil for 1½ to 2 minutes, then stir in 2 tablespoons olive oil.

Finishing the Pasta in the Sauce

• When the pasta is almost done—still a little hard to the touch and bite—lift it out of the pot with tongs or a spider. Let excess water drip off a moment, and drop the wet pasta into the simmering sauce.

- Ladle in another cup of pasta water, raise the heat slightly, and start tossing pasta and sauce together.

- Sprinkle on the parsley, toss it in, and cook, still tossing almost continuously, for 2 to 3 minutes, until the capellini is perfectly *al dente* and coated with sauce. If the pasta appears dry, ladle in more hot pasta water. If the pasta appears soupy, cook rapidly to thicken the sauce.

Serving the Pasta

- As soon as it is finished, put portions of pasta in the individual warm bowls.

- Sprinkle approximately 1 tablespoon of toasted bread crumbs over each serving—most of it on top and some around the edges of the bowl.

- Serve immediately in individual warm bowls.

DRY TOASTED BREAD CRUMBS

Golden-brown bread crumbs make a nice finishing touch for pasta dishes like this one—a light counterpoint of texture, taste, and color. Start with ordinary dried crumbs (see page 19) that have some larger bits in them, rather than crumbs that have been ground and sieved into a fine powder.

To toast, put the crumbs you need (½ cup or so for most pasta dishes) in a small dry skillet and set over medium heat. Keep tossing or stirring the crumbs—in a minute or so, they will start to color. Lower the heat if they're browning fast, and keep tossing until the crumbs are getting fairly close to the color you like. Remove the skillet from the heat now, and toss while the residual heat colors the crumbs the deep-golden shade you like, then turn them out of the pan.

If you toast them completely and leave them in the skillet, they will get too dark or even burn. I know from experience.

HELPFUL EQUIPMENT FOR PASTA-MAKING

- A large, sturdy, not-too-heavy skillet for "sauce and toss":

  For dishes using 1 pound of pasta—the amount in my recipes—you need at least a 12-inch-diameter skillet. Whether it has curving or straight sides (usually called a sauté pan), it should be 2½ to 3 inches deep, with a 4-quart capacity. A tight-fitting cover is useful, a non-stick surface preferable.

  A 14-inch-diameter skillet gives more room for tossing pasta. In a high-sided sauté pan you can toss as much as 2 pounds of cooked pasta with sauce.

  If you only have a smaller sauté pan, use two. You can also make half-batches of all these recipes, which provide a generous dinner for two.

- A pasta-cooking pot—at least 8-quart capacity to cook 1 pound of pasta. A wide pot in which the pasta has lots of room to turn and tumble is best.

- Pasta "picker-uppers": for skillet pastas, don't drain the pasta into a colander; use straining tools to scoop the pasta up and out of the boiling water, drain it briefly (not too much), and transfer it to the skillet. A variety of implements will work, but I recommend the following:

  A "spider": the Asian-style long-handled strainer, with a flat wire basket, usually with a bamboo handle. I have several, and suggest that you have at least one, with a 7- or 8-inch-wide basket for moving and draining pasta. A smaller one is handy to use as a "tosser."

  Tongs: hinged stainless-steel tongs are excellent both for lifting up clumps of long pastas like capellini or spaghetti and for tossing them.

Ziti with Sausage, Onions, and Fennel

*H*ere the meaty skillet sauce and the ziti cook at a leisurely pace compared to the rapidity of the preceding capellini with caper sauce. But the cooking principles are the same. In the first few minutes you want to caramelize each ingredient as it is introduced to the pan—this is especially important with the tomato paste, to give it a good toasting before it is liquefied in the pasta water. The sauce needs 6 minutes or more at a good bubbling simmer after adding the water in order to draw out and meld the flavors of the meat and vegetables as well as to soften the pieces of fresh fennel. At that time the ziti will be ready to finish cooking in the sauce.

SERVES 6

Prepping

Heat 6 quarts of water with the tablespoon of kosher salt to boiling in the pasta-cooking pot.

Remove the sausage from its casing and break the meat up a bit with your fingers.

Trim the fennel bulb (see box and photos, pages 78–79). Slice the bulb in half lengthwise, then slice each half in ¼-inch-thick lengthwise slices. Separate the slivers of fennel if they are attached at the bottom; cut the long slivers in half so you have about 3 cups of 2-inch-long matchsticks of fennel. Chop and reserve ⅓ cup fronds for garnish.

Have the remaining sauce ingredients ready and nearby.

Making the Sauce and Cooking the Pasta Simultaneously

• Pour the olive oil into the skillet and set it over medium-high heat. Add the sausage meat and cook, stirring and breaking it up more with a wooden spoon, until it is sizzling and beginning to brown, about 1½ minutes.

• Push the sausage a bit aside and drop the onion slices into a clear part of the pan; sauté, stirring, till they're sizzling and wilting, another 2 minutes or so, then stir them in with the meat.

FOR THE SAUCE

1 pound sweet Italian sausage (without fennel seeds)

1 large fennel bulb with stem and fronds (about 1 pound)

⅓ cup extra-virgin olive oil

2 medium onions, cut in half-moon slices (2 cups)

½ teaspoon salt

½ teaspoon dried *peperoncino* (hot red pepper flakes)

½ cup tomato paste

Boiling water from the pasta-cooking pot

FOR THE PASTA AND FINISHING

1 tablespoon kosher salt, for the pasta-cooking water

1 pound ziti

⅓ cup finely chopped fennel fronds

1 cup freshly grated Pecorino Romano
(or Parmigiano-Reggiano or
Grana Padano)

8-quart pasta-cooking pot

A 12-inch or larger skillet for the sauce
and the pasta

Clearing a space in the pan and
sautéing the fennel

Pushing aside the fennel and sausage
and creating a hot spot to toast the
peperoncino

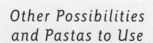

Other Possibilities
and Pastas to Use

Shells, rigatoni, radiatori,
fettuccine

• Following the illustrations, clear a space and drop in the fennel; let it heat up and wilt for 1 minute or more, then stir it around with the sausage and onions.

• Sprinkle on ¼ teaspoon salt; drop the *peperoncino* in a hot spot and toast the flakes for ½ minute, then stir them in.

• Clear a good-sized hot spot in the center of the pan, plop in the tomato paste, and cook, stirring it in the spot for a good minute or more, until it is sizzling and caramelizing; then stir it in with everything else.

• Ladle 3 cups of boiling pasta water from the pot into the skillet, stir well, and bring the liquid to a boil. Adjust the heat to maintain an active simmer all over the pan.

• Drop the ziti in the boiling water in the pasta pot. Stir and bring back to the boil. Cook about 8 minutes (a minute less than what is recommended on the package), until the ziti are not quite *al dente*.

• Continue to simmer the sauce until the flavors have developed and the fennel is soft but not mushy, 6 minutes or more. The sauce should not get too thick: stir in another cup or two of boiling pasta

Creating another hot spot to toast the tomato paste

Mixing all the elements together

water if it reduces rapidly. When the sauce is done, taste it and add more salt if you want. If the pasta is not ready, turn down the heat to keep the sauce at a very low simmer until the ziti are on their way—then turn the heat up.

- As soon as the ziti are ready by your timing, lift them out of the pot with a spider. Let excess water drip off only for an instant, and drop the wet cylinders into the simmering sauce.

- Start tossing pasta and sauce together; ladle in more water if the sauce seems too thick.

- Sprinkle over all the chopped fennel fronds, and continue to cook and toss the ziti in the skillet for 2 minutes, or until they are perfectly *al dente* and coated with sauce. If the pasta appears dry, ladle in more hot pasta water; if it is soupy, cook rapidly to thicken the sauce.

Finishing the Pasta

- Remove the skillet from the heat, sprinkle the grated cheese over the ziti, and toss it in. Serve the hot pasta right from the skillet into warm pasta bowls.

CONDIRE LA PASTA! HOW MUCH SAUCE DOES PASTA NEED?

In Italian, the verb we use to describe the final dressing of the pasta with sauce is condire—*translated, "to season, to flavor." And the phrase* condire la pasta *reminds us that the sauce should be considered a condiment, an enhancement to the pasta.*

I like to think of pasta, especially fresh egg pastas, as playing the leading role in the pasta dish. So why drown the chief protagonist before the drama has started?

Keep these ideas in mind when you bring your pasta and sauce together in a skillet. If you see that the quantity of sauce is disproportionate to the pasta, spoon some out (and save it, of course) before tossing and finishing the dish. And if you see that the sauce is soupy and collects in the bottom of the skillet, raise the heat while tossing the pasta actively, evaporating the excess water and thickening the sauce so it adheres to the pasta.

TIPS ON BOILING THE PASTA

- For 1 pound of pasta, bring 6 quarts of water to a full boil (too little water produces a gummy pasta; too much water washes away too much starch).

- Stir 1 tablespoon kosher or coarse sea salt into the water anytime before adding pasta.

- Adding pasta to the pot: Drop shaped and tubular pasta into the boiling water and stir well. Slip long pasta into the water and push the strands under gradually as they soften, bending them into the water, then stirring well to make sure the strands are separated.

- After adding pasta, cover the pot and return water to the boil over high heat.

- Be prepared to uncover the pot before the water boils over.

- Tip: if the water is boiling up and over, blow on it to settle it down.

- Start timing the pasta when the boil resumes.

- For dry pastas that will finish in the skillet, cook in the pot for 2 minutes less than the minimum time given on the package.

- Cook pasta at a rolling boil, either partly covered (you can reduce the heat and save energy) or uncovered. Stir the pasta now and then.

- Did you forget to salt the water? Better to check before the pasta is done: sip water from a wooden spoon; it should be "comfortably" salty at least.

- If you forgot to salt, add it right away: saltless pasta is redeemable while it's in the water; it will absorb some salt even in a brief boil.

- Test pasta by extracting a piece and tasting it 1 to 2 minutes before the designated time for doneness. When it is not quite done al dente, lift out with a spider, tongs, or other tool, let excess water drain into the pot, and drop the pasta with clinging water into the skillet.

- Don't discard pasta water until the dish is finished!

Spaghetti with Asparagus Frittata

*A*sparagus frittata and pasta . . . If you think you have seen a recipe of mine that sounds like this one, you are right. In an earlier book I gave a recipe for an "Asparagus Frittata with Capellini." And here's "Spaghetti with Asparagus Frittata." But they are not at all the same, even though the ingredients are nearly identical.

In the earlier recipe, a bit of leftover cooked pasta is stirred into a frittata as it cooks and bakes into a tender cake, which is then served in wedges.

Here you have a quick skillet pasta. In fact, it is a "two-skillet" pasta. In the big skillet you make a very simple sauce with oil, scallions, and pasta water. In another skillet, you scramble up a soft frittata with sautéed asparagus. You also cook a pot of spaghetti. When everything is tossed together—in the big skillet—the textures, tastes, and colors blend beautifully. Follow the recipe instructions for coordinating the cooking the first time you make this. Once you see and sense how everything goes together, you'll have added a truly wonderful dish to your repertoire of family recipes.

This is a good dish to make with fresh homemade egg pastas, such as fettuccine, garganelli, pappardelle, capellini, spaghettini.

Instead of asparagus, you could use another vegetable in your frittata, such as zucchini, broccoli, or just onions; or ham, prosciutto, or bacon. Or have a plain frittata.

SERVES 6 OR MORE

Prepping

Start heating 6 quarts of water with 1½ tablespoons kosher salt in the pasta-cooking pot.

Have all the ingredients for the simple sauce measured and at hand. Have both skillets on the stove, ready to start cooking.

For the frittata, snap off the tough bottom stubs of the asparagus and peel the thick skin from the lower 4 inches of each spear. Slice the spears, including the tips, crosswise or slightly on the diagonal, into ⅛-inch-thick rounds or ovals. You should have 2 cups of small asparagus pieces.

Crack the eggs into a bowl and whisk them well with the milk, ½ teaspoon of salt, and several grinds of black pepper.

FOR THE SIMPLE SAUCE

⅓ cup extra-virgin olive oil

4 garlic cloves, sliced (¼ cup)

2 cups thinly sliced scallions, white and green

½ teaspoon salt, plus more if needed

Freshly ground black pepper

Boiling water from the pasta-cooking pot

FOR THE FRITTATA

4 to 6 asparagus stalks
(medium thickness)

6 large eggs

¼ cup milk

½ teaspoon salt

Freshly ground black pepper

¼ cup extra-virgin olive oil

FOR THE PASTA AND FINISHING

1 ½ tablespoons kosher salt,
for the pasta-cooking water

1 pound spaghetti

1 to 2 tablespoons extra-virgin olive oil

1 cup freshly grated Parmigiano-
Reggiano or Grana Padano

RECOMMENDED EQUIPMENT

8-quart pasta-cooking pot

A 12-inch or larger skillet for the sauce
and the pasta

A 10-inch or larger non-stick skillet for
the frittata

Making the Sauce

● Pour the ⅓ cup olive oil into the big pasta skillet, scatter the garlic slices in the oil, and set over medium heat. Cook for 2 or 3 minutes or so, shaking the pan now and then, until the garlic is sizzling and starting to color.

● Toss the scallions into the skillet, stir with the garlic and oil, and cook for 2½ to 3 minutes, over medium heat, until the scallions are very soft and wilted and the garlic is golden. While the scallions are cooking, stir in ½ teaspoon of salt and a generous amount of freshly ground black pepper.

● Take 2 cups of boiling water from the pasta pot and pour it into the skillet. Stir up the scallions and garlic, and adjust the heat so the liquid is simmering gently.

Cooking the Frittata and the Spaghetti (and the Sauce) Simultaneously*

● Pour the ¼ cup of olive oil into the empty non-stick skillet, scatter in the sliced asparagus, and turn on medium heat. Let the pieces heat and start to sizzle, about 2 minutes; stir and toss now and then.

● As soon as you've started the asparagus, push the spaghetti into the boiling water. Stir as it softens, and bring the water back to the boil as rapidly as possible. Start timing the pasta to *undercook as required*, about 8 minutes.

● Now take ¼ cup or so of water from the pasta pot and pour it in with the sizzling asparagus. Season with grinds of black pepper and ¼ teaspoon of salt. Stir, toss, and cook the slices until they're cooked through but still bright green, about 4 minutes. Moisten with more pasta water if the slices seem dry.

*__Note:__ You can cook the frittata ahead. But it will solidify when it cools, so you will have to cut it into small pieces before adding it to the pasta.

- While the spaghetti and the asparagus cook, make sure there's a good layer of simmering liquid in the scallion-sauce skillet; add more pasta water if needed.

- When the asparagus slices are tender, turn down the heat a bit and pour in the eggs. Let set for about ½ minute, then stir the thickening eggs and the asparagus with a wooden spoon. Continue turning the curds over for a minute, so they are evenly heated but still quite wet and soft. Remove from the heat.

- Check the spaghetti; when it is almost but not quite *al dente*, lift the pasta from the pot and drop it into the simmering simple sauce.

- Raise the heat if it was very low, and add more hot pasta water if the pasta seems dry. Toss and cook the spaghetti and scallion sauce together for ½ minute, mixing well.

- Scrape the frittata on top of the pasta and toss it in, breaking the frittata into small pieces. If any eggs are stuck in the pan, loosen them with a slosh of pasta water and toss that into the pasta skillet too.

- Toss for a minute or more, still over heat, until the pasta is perfectly cooked and the frittata is well distributed.

- Remove the skillet from the heat, drizzle 1 or 2 tablespoons of olive oil over, and toss. Sprinkle on the grated cheese and toss. Grind black pepper on abundantly.

- Serve right away.

ANOTHER SKILLET PASTA LESSON: TOSSING IN GRATED CHEESE

When adding cheese, take the pan off the heat before you toss it in. Otherwise, the cheese can overheat and separate into oily and stringy components.

I always recommend either Parmigiano-Reggiano or Grana Padano for finishing a pasta with cheese. Keep either or both as staples in your refrigerator.

Serving Skillet Pastas

Pasta dishes should always be served hot, as soon as the dish is finished.

For family meals, I bring the skillet to the table and serve portions directly into warm bowls.

For more formal occasions, I dish it up into warm bowls in the kitchen and bring them quickly to the table. The shorter the trek from the hot skillet to the individual bowl, the better.

Be sure to pass a bowl of freshly grated cheese around the table.

More Skillet Sauces for Everyday Pastas

The sauce recipes on the next pages are all quick skillet creations. The choice of pasta is up to you. Of course, some pastas take longer to cook, so you may have to adjust the timing a little. But don't worry—in most cases you can complete the cooking of the sauce and keep it hot until the pasta is cooked.

You finish all the sauces and pastas in essentially the same way, whether you use dry or fresh pasta, or whatever the shape. The idea, again, is to undercook the pasta slightly, transfer it to the skillet dripping wet, and finish cooking it with the sauce. Cheese is tossed in off heat, and perhaps a final spoonful of olive oil.

The opening sauces are made with a base of olive oil and garlic—the first one is *just* oil and garlic, for traditional pasta *all'aglio e olio*. Following them are butter-based sauces. Although I give suggestions for pastas that go best with each recipe—both dry pastas and different homemade fresh pastas from the recipes on pages 156 to 193—be flexible and use what you have, and bring the sauce and pasta together as if they were meant for each other from the start.

FAST LESSONS FROM A QUICK SAUCE

As you make the sauce, keep in mind these brief explanations of what is happening in the step-by-step cooking process:

- *Start cooking oil and garlic together. As the garlic heats and caramelizes gradually, it releases more flavor and cooks all the way through. If it was thrown into hot oil, it would get crisp and bitter on the outside but uncooked inside, and the flavor would be sealed in too.*

- *"Toast" peperoncino (hot red pepper flakes) and other ingredients in a skillet "hot spot." The brief, concentrated sauté time given peperoncino, capers, onions, and many other foods in these recipes starts caramelization. Though you can't always see it, the caramelized surfaces are adding a "layer" of flavor on the food that will ultimately meld into the sauce. If you skipped the hot spot and just stirred the food in with other ingredients, this depth of flavor would not develop.*

- *"Melt" anchovies in the sauce. When heated in the skillet, anchovy fillets naturally disintegrate to some degree. For people who don't like anchovies (or think they don't), add chopped-up anchovies rather than whole fillets or pieces. The bits will totally disappear, and only you will know they contributed their wonderful flavor.*

- *Remember that the pasta should be still slightly hard when you extract it from the water and drop it into the skillet. That is as you want it, because the pasta will finish its cooking for about 2 minutes in the sauce.*

- *Adding a finish of olive oil as you toss sauce and pasta contributes a layer of taste and brings a gloss to the final dish. I think of this as making your pasta "smile."*

- *If using bread crumbs, keep them crunchy. In pastas where toasted bread crumbs replace cheese as a garnish, sprinkle the crumbs over the individual servings at the last moment, so they don't get wet and mushy. And, to give every bite of pasta the nice textural contrast, also sprinkle crumbs on the plate or around the bowl.*

- *Serve your pasta right away. Long, skinny pastas particularly continue to absorb liquid after they've stopped cooking. If you delay serving them, you'll lose the balanced texture that you have achieved.*

Basic *Aglio e Olio*—Oil and Garlic Sauce

(a 5-minute sauce)

¼ cup extra-virgin olive oil, plus more
  if you want

5 plump garlic cloves, sliced (about
  ⅓ cup)

¼ teaspoon dried *peperoncino* (hot red
  pepper flakes), or more to taste

Hot water from the pasta-cooking pot

¼ teaspoon salt, or more to taste

⅓ cup chopped fresh Italian parsley

I cup freshly grated Parmigiano-
  Reggiano or Grana Padano

Put a large pot of salted water on to boil.

• If using dry pasta, plunge it into the boiling water 5 minutes before starting the sauce; fresh pasta is added at the same time you start the sauce.

• Pour 3 tablespoons of the oil into the big skillet, scatter the garlic slices in the oil, and set over medium heat.

• Cook for a minute, add the *peperoncino*, and cook another minute, shaking the pan now and then, until the garlic slices are an even light gold.

• Ladle in 2 cups of boiling pasta water (watch out for sizzling spatters) and cook rapidly for 2 to 3 minutes, reducing the liquid by a third or so. Taste the sauce; add salt as needed. Keep at low simmer until the pasta is ready.

• When the pasta is not quite done *al dente*, bring the sauce to an active simmer, and then dump the pasta in.

Finish the sauce and pasta by tossing them together in the skillet over low to moderate heat until the pasta is tender to the bite. If the dish is dry, incorporate more hot pasta water; if soupy, reduce with higher heat and a bit more cooking. Add the parsley during the initial tossing; off the heat, toss in the cheese and the final tablespoon of olive oil just before serving.

Good With . . .

Capellini

Linguine

Spaghetti

I also like a fresh pasta, especially
  whole-wheat-and-flaxseed.

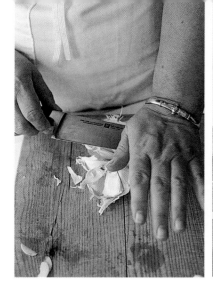

Smashing the whole head with a flat knife to separate the cloves

The separate cloves

Slicing the peeled garlic

FINISHING PASTA DISHES IN THE SKILLET

- *Just before adding the pasta, bring the sauce to an active simmer. Stir in extra-virgin olive oil if indicated in the recipe.*

- *Lift dry pastas from the cooking pot when done almost al dente. Drain excess water briefly, then drop moist pasta onto simmering sauce.*

- *Lift fresh egg pastas from the pot when they float and are tender to the bite. Fresh pastas with whole grains will need longer cooking after floating. Drain excess water and drop into sauce.*

- *Toss pasta and sauce together—sprinkle on chopped parsley, if using—and keep tossing over low to moderate heat, until the pasta is perfectly cooked and nicely sauced.*

- *If the dish is dry, incorporate more hot pasta water. If the dish is soupy, reduce the moisture with higher heat and a bit more cooking.*

- *Remove the skillet from the heat and toss in grated cheese, if using. Toss with additional olive oil, if called for in the recipe or if you want to give your pasta a "smile."*

Sauce of Black Olives, Orange, Pine Nuts, and Golden Raisins

(a 7-minute sauce)

The flavors of oranges and black olives are quite harmonious and make an unusual and interesting sauce.

½ cup extra-virgin olive oil

5 plump garlic cloves, sliced (about ⅓ cup)

1½ cups oil-cured black olives, pitted and chopped into ⅓-inch pieces

½ cup golden raisins

3 tablespoons fine long threads of orange zest

⅔ cup fresh-squeezed orange juice

1 cup pine nuts, toasted in a dry pan

Hot water from the pasta-cooking pot

½ teaspoon salt, plus more if needed

1 tablespoon chopped fresh Italian parsley

FOR 1 POUND OF PASTA

Put a large pot of salted water on to boil.

Plunge the pasta into the boiling water 5 minutes before you start the sauce.

• Pour ⅓ cup of the olive oil into a big skillet, scatter the garlic slices in the oil, and set over medium-high heat. Cook for about 1½ minutes, shaking the pan, until the garlic is starting to color.

• Drop the chopped olives into the skillet, and stir with the garlic. Cook for another 1½ minutes, shaking the pan occasionally, as the olives sizzle and caramelize.

• Scatter the raisins in the skillet and cook, stirring, for ½ minute.

• Scatter the threads of orange zest in, and cook, stirring, another 30 seconds or more, until they're sizzling.

• Pour in the orange juice, taking care as it will sizzle right away. Stir to moisten everything as the juice bubbles and starts to thicken.

• After 20 seconds or so, toss in the toasted pine nuts; stir to moisten and mix with the other ingredients.

• When the orange juice has nearly evaporated, ladle in 2 cups of boiling pasta water. Boil and stir the sauce for 3 minutes or more (while the pasta is cooking).

• When it's reduced by half, stir in ¼ teaspoon of the salt. Taste and add more salt if you want. Stir in another tablespoon of the olive oil. Reduce the heat to keep the sauce hot until the pasta is ready.

Finish the sauce and pasta together in the skillet, adding a little more pasta water or reducing it as necessary. Add the parsley during the initial tossing; off the heat, toss in a final tablespoon of olive oil just before serving.

Good With . . .

Capellini

Other thin dry pastas, such as
   spaghettini or linguine

NO SKILLET NEEDED: RAW OLIVE OIL, PARMIGIANO-REGGIANO, AND PASTA (AND MAYBE PARSLEY)

On occasion, I cook a pasta that I want to dress so simply that I do not even take down a skillet, especially if the pasta is a fresh pasta rich in flavor, such as all-egg pasta, chestnut pasta, walnut pasta, or whole-wheat pasta. For those days when you need simplicity in your life but still want flavor and elegance, this approach is perfect.

I drain the pasta quickly, turn it into a big warm bowl, and immediately drizzle over it "raw" extra-virgin olive oil, a gentle olive oil from Liguria or Lago di Garda, and toss well. Just enough oil to coat it, about ½ cup for a pound of pasta. And then I toss again with a cup of freshly grated Parmigiano-Reggiano or Grana Padano.

That's it. Although, if it's spring and there's fresh parsley growing, I'll chop some up and toss that in too.

Sauce of Green Olives and Roasted Red Peppers

(a 10-minute sauce)

1 pound jar roasted red peppers in brine or fresh roasted peppers

1½ cups flavorful green or black olives, pitted

¾ cup extra-virgin olive oil, plus more for finishing

7 or 8 plump garlic cloves, sliced (about ½ cup)

½ teaspoon dried *peperoncino* (hot red pepper flakes)

Hot water from the pasta-cooking pot

½ teaspoon salt, or more to taste

2 tablespoons chopped fresh Italian parsley

1 cup freshly grated Parmigiano-Reggiano or Grana Padano

Good With . . .

Campanelle

Lumache

Rigatini

Radiatori

Put a large pot of salted water on to boil.

Drain the roasted peppers, reserving ⅓ cup of the brine. Slice them crosswise into thin strips, about ⅛ inch wide and 3 inches long.

Purée the olives in a food processor with ½ cup of the olive oil, pulsing them to a paste; scrape into a small dish.

Plunge the pasta into the boiling water 5 minutes before you start the sauce.

Pour ¼ cup of the olive oil into a big skillet, scatter the garlic slices in the oil, and set over medium heat. Cook for 1½ to 2 minutes, shaking the pan now and then, until the garlic is just sizzling.

- Drop the *peperoncino* into a hot spot; let it toast for a minute, then stir it in with the garlic.

- Scrape the olive paste onto a hot spot. Spread it out, let it cook for a minute to caramelize lightly, then stir in with the garlic around the pan.

- Drop the roasted pepper strips in the center, spread them out, and let them start to sizzle and fry, about a minute.

- Spill the reserved pepper brine into the skillet, stir everything together, raise the heat slightly, and bring the brine to boiling. Let it bubble and evaporate, shaking the pan and stirring until the brine is gone and the vegetables start to sizzle and caramelize once again.

- Ladle in 3 cups of boiling pasta water. Stir and cook the skillet sauce rapidly for 3 or 4 minutes (while the pasta is cooking). Reduce the liquid by a third or so, then taste the sauce and add salt as needed. Keep at a low simmer until the pasta is ready.

When the pasta is done almost *al dente*, scoop it up and into the skillet to finish cooking, adjusting with more pasta water or reducing the liquid as necessary. Add the parsley during the initial tossing; off the heat, toss in the cheese and a tablespoon of olive oil just before serving.

TOASTING INDIVIDUAL INGREDIENTS IN A HOT SPOT

By now you are probably quite used to my instructions to "toast" each new sauce ingredient in a hot spot. Even if you can't see a change in its color, the short period of concentrated heat is creating particles of caramelization on the outside of the food.

In this recipe, the process of caramelization is made visible, briefly, by the addition of the brine from the roasted peppers. When this small amount of liquid moistens the peppers and olives and starts boiling, these particles are released in the liquid. If you look closely in the pan during the moments of "deglazing," you'll see them!

However, as the brine evaporates, the particles reattach to the solid foods, then deepen in flavor as the sizzling and caramelization start again. Moreover, the taste components, once they have dissolved in the brine, are left behind to heat and become caramelized particles too. In effect, you have "toasted" a liquid ingredient to create a new layer of flavor. Finally, all these layers are homogenized and blended into a sauce by the pasta water (which contributes additional salt and starch).

Each of these recipes utilizes the skillet in this way, to maximize the flavors available from a handful of ingredients and produce a dish with a depth and complexity that belie how quickly it was made.

Sauce of Small Shrimp and Scallions

(a 5-minute sauce)

*S*mall shrimp make a lovely addition to skillet sauces, because they cook so quickly, barely 2 minutes in the skillet. The trick is to make sure that you don't overcook the shrimp. If you can, start your pasta before the sauce, so they finish at the same time. But if your pasta isn't ready when the shrimp and sauce are, take the skillet off the heat.

FOR I POUND OF PASTA

½ cup extra-virgin olive oil

7 or 8 fat garlic cloves, sliced (about ½ cup)

About 12 whole Tuscan-style *peperoncini* in vinegar, drained, seeded, and thinly sliced (¼ cup)

I pound (about 2 dozen) small shrimp, washed, peeled, and deveined

½ teaspoon salt

½ cup of scallions cut into thin rounds

4 tablespoons (½ stick) soft butter, plus 2 tablespoons for finishing

Hot water from the pasta-cooking pot

⅓ cup chopped fresh Italian parsley

Good With . . .

Linguine

Cappellini

Tagliatelle

Bring a large pot of salted water to boil. If you are using dry pasta, start cooking the pasta 5 minutes before you start sauce; if you are using fresh, start the sauce and then put on the pasta to cook at the same time.

• Pour the olive oil into a big skillet, scatter the garlic slices in, and set over medium-high heat. Cook for 1 minute, until the garlic is sizzling.

• Scatter the slices of *peperoncino* in a hot spot; cook for 1 minute; shake the pan now and then.

• Push the garlic and peppers to the side; turn the heat to high. Drop the shrimp in the center of the skillet and spread them so they're not crowded. Sprinkle on the salt, and let them sizzle for ½ minute.

• Flip the shrimp over, giving the skillet a good toss or stirring and turning them; cook another ½ minute or so, until the flesh is just turning opaque.

• Scatter the scallions into the skillet; toss and stir in with the shrimp, for 20 to 30 seconds, just until they're sizzling.

• Stir in 2 tablespoons butter and cook until it is melted and starts to simmer, 10 to 20 seconds.

• Ladle in 2 cups of boiling pasta water. Stir up everything in the skillet, *and let the sauce boil for only a moment.* If the pasta is ready to add, turn *down* the heat to very low. If the pasta is *not* ready, remove the skillet from the heat immediately; set it back over low heat when you do add the pasta.

When the pasta is done *al dente*, scoop it up and drop into the shrimp pan. Toss briefly, sprinkle on the parsley, and toss again. Remove from the heat, drop the remaining 2 tablespoons butter on top of the pasta, and toss in. Serve right away.

USING "PASTA WATER" TO MAKE A QUICK SAUCE

Boiling, salted pasta water is an essential component of skillet pastas, both in the sauce-making stage and in finishing the dish. Here are tips for when to add pasta water:

- *After you've caramelized all your seasonings and sauce ingredients, add water from the pasta pot as a medium to extract and blend their flavors.*

- *Add water to prevent scorching if something is browning too fast!*

- *In a large skillet, liquid will evaporate quickly. Replenish the moisture with pasta water whenever needed.*

- *If your sauce is complete but must wait a while for the pasta to cook, it may thicken. Add more water (and bring it to a good simmer) before dropping in the pasta.*

- *If there's not enough sauce to coat the pasta when you're tossing them together in the skillet, add more water.*

- *A thin pasta, like capellini or spaghetti, will absorb more liquid than a tubular pasta, so be prepared to add more water as you toss the strands with sauce.*

- *Remember that the cooking water is salty and starchy—qualities that can add seasoning and body during the final cooking of pasta and sauce.*

Sauce of Sun-Dried Tomatoes and Cannellini Beans

(a 7-minute sauce)

3 tablespoons extra-virgin olive oil

2 tablespoons olive oil from sun-dried tomato container

4 fat cloves garlic, sliced (about ¼ cup)

½ teaspoon dried *peperoncino* (hot red pepper flakes), or more or less to taste

I cup sun-dried tomatoes packed in olive oil, drained and sliced in ¼-inch strips

Hot water from the pasta-cooking pot

I ½ cups cooked cannellini beans, or I pound canned beans, drained and rinsed

¼ teaspoon salt, or more to taste

I tablespoon chopped fresh Italian parsley

½ cup grated Parmigiano-Reggiano or Grana Padano

Good With . . .

A short tubular dry pasta such as ziti, rigatoni, gomiti (elbows), or radiatori

Start cooking the pasta in a large pot of boiling salted water 5 minutes before you start the sauce.

- Pour 2 tablespoons of the olive oil and the tomato-packing oil, ¼ cup total, into a big skillet, scatter the garlic slices in the oil, and set over medium-high heat. Cook for 1 minute or so, until the slices are sizzling.

- Drop the dried *peperoncino* in a hot spot, toast for ½ minute, and stir in with the garlic.

- Drop the strips of sun-dried tomato into a clear part of the skillet, stir, and spread them out. Let them sizzle and toast for a minute or so.

- Ladle 1 cup of boiling pasta water into the skillet and stir up everything well. Keep the liquid simmering actively so the tomatoes soften and release their flavor. Cook for 2 minutes or so, until the liquid has reduced by half.

- Stir in the cannellini beans, the ¼ teaspoon salt, and about 1½ more cups of pasta water. Bring the sauce rapidly to the boil, stirring, and cook at an active simmer for 4 minutes, thickening slightly. Keep hot until the pasta is ready.

When the pasta is almost done *al dente*, scoop it up and into the skillet to finish cooking, adding a little more or reducing the pasta water as necessary. Add the parsley during the initial tossing; off the heat, toss in the cheese and a final tablespoon of olive oil just before serving.

Sauce of Cannellini, Sun-Dried Tomatoes, and Spinach

Wash, dry, and stem about 4 ounces tender fresh spinach; use small whole leaves, or cut larger leaves in pieces.

Make the sauce as detailed in the main recipe. When the cannellini beans have been simmering in the skillet for a couple minutes, drop the spinach leaves on top. Let them steam until they wilt, then stir them into the sauce, with another cup or more of pasta water. Cook at an active simmer for 2 to 3 minutes, until the spinach and the beans are cooked, and the sauce has reduced. Finish with pasta as in main recipe, but omit the parsley.

Sauce of *Broccoli di Rape* with *Ceci* (Chickpeas) and Bacon

(a 15-minute sauce)

½ cup extra-virgin olive oil

7 or 8 fat garlic cloves, sliced (about ½ cup)

6 ounces bacon or prosciutto end in strips (I cup) (see photo, page 61)

½ teaspoon dried *peperoncino* (hot red pepper flakes), or to taste

1 ½ cups cooked *ceci* (chickpeas), or I pound canned, drained and rinsed

Hot water from the pasta-cooking pot

2 pounds *broccoli di rape*, trimmed, washed and cut into 1-inch lengths (about 6 cups) (see box, page 47)

½ teaspoon salt, or to taste

I cup grated Pecorino Romano, Parmigiano-Reggiano, or Grana Padano

Good With . . .

A tubular pasta such as gomiti or ziti. But if you have made some fresh pasta, such as whole-wheat or egg pasta, the combination will be sublime.

Start cooking the pasta in a large pot of boiling salted water 5 minutes before you begin the sauce if you are using dry pasta, or just after, if using fresh pasta.

Pour ⅓ cup of the olive oil into a big skillet.

• Toast the *peperoncino* for ½ minute; stir in with the garlic and bacon or prosciutto. Cook for another 2½ minutes or more, shaking the pan and stirring now and then, until the bacon has rendered its fat and is crisping.

• Pour the *ceci* into the skillet, and ladle in 2 cups of hot water from the pasta-cooking pot. Stir briefly, and bring the liquid to a boil.

• Dump the *broccoli di rape* pieces on top of the other ingredients, place a cover on the pan, and let the greens steam and wilt for a minute or so.

• Uncover, and stir in the *broccoli di rape* and another 1½ tablespoons of the olive oil. Lower the heat to maintain an active simmer, and cook the sauce, covered, for 6 to 8 minutes, until the beans and greens are quite tender. (You can start cooking dry pasta at this time too.)

• Uncover the pan and taste the sauce; add salt if you wish. If the sauce seems soupy, raise the heat and cook until there's only a shallow layer of liquid around the vegetables. Keep the sauce barely simmering until the pasta is ready.

When the pasta is done almost *al dente*, scoop it up and into the skillet to finish cooking. Add the parsley during the initial tossing; off the heat, toss in the cheese and the remaining olive oil just before serving.

Sauce of Broccoli di Rape with Anchovies

(a 12-minute sauce)

½ cup extra-virgin olive oil
7 or 8 fat garlic cloves, sliced (about ½ cup)
½ teaspoon dried *peperoncino* (hot red pepper flakes), or to taste
2 to 3 ounces anchovy fillets, or even more to taste!
2 pounds *broccoli di rape*, trimmed, washed, and cut into 1-inch lengths (about 6 cups)
Hot water from the pasta-cooking pot
½ teaspoon salt, or to taste
⅓ cup Dry Toasted Bread Crumbs (see page 93)

Start cooking the pasta in a large pot of boiling salted water 5 minutes before you start the sauce if you are using dry pasta, or just after you have started the sauce if using fresh pasta.

Pour ⅓ cup of the olive oil into a big skillet, scatter the garlic slices in, and set the pan over medium-high heat. Cook for 1 minute, until the sizzling starts.

• Toast the *peperoncino* in a hot spot for ½ minute; stir in with the garlic.

• Drop the anchovies into the pan, and spread them out. Cook for a minute or so, stirring once or twice, until they've started to melt into the oil.

• Dump the *broccoli di rape* pieces in the skillet, place a cover on the pan, and let the greens steam and wilt for a minute or so. Uncover, and stir the greens around the pan. If the greens were wet from washing, there should be a good layer of liquid in the pan. If there's not, ladle in a cup or so of hot water from the pasta-cooking pot.

• Stir in another 1½ tablespoons of the olive oil and cover the pan. Lower the heat, and simmer the greens for 5 minutes or longer, until they're quite tender. Add more pasta water if necessary to keep the greens steaming.

• Uncover the pan and reduce the liquid (or add water) so there's just a cup or so surrounding the greens. Keep the sauce hot until the pasta is ready.

When the pasta is done almost *al dente*, scoop it up and into the skillet to finish cooking. Off the heat, toss in the remaining olive oil. Put individual portions of pasta into warm bowls. Sprinkle 2 teaspoons of toasted crumbs on top of each serving and around the rim of the bowl as well.

Sauce of Marinated Artichoke Hearts and Sun-Dried Tomatoes

(a 10-minute sauce)

6 tablespoons extra-virgin olive oil

5 plump garlic cloves, sliced (about ⅓ cup)

½ teaspoon dried *peperoncino* (hot red pepper flakes)

Two 6-ounce jars (1¾ cups) marinated artichoke hearts, drained, sliced thin

⅔ cup sun-dried tomatoes packed in olive oil, drained and sliced in ½-inch strips

½ teaspoon salt

1 teaspoon grated lemon zest

Hot water from the pasta-cooking pot

2 tablespoons chopped fresh Italian parsley

½ cup freshly grated Parmigiano-Reggiano or Grana Padano

Start cooking the pasta in a large pot of boiling salted water 5 minutes before you begin the sauce if you are using dry pasta, or just after if using fresh pasta.

• Pour 4 tablespoons of the olive oil into the big skillet, scatter the garlic slices in, and set the pan over medium-high heat. Cook for 1 minute, until the garlic is sizzling.

• Toast the *peperoncino* in a hot spot for ½ minute; stir in with the garlic.

• Add the sliced artichokes and tomatoes, salt, and lemon zest; stir well. Cook for about 4 minutes, shaking the pan and tossing the vegetables occasionally, as everything sizzles and the juices in the pan thicken.

• Ladle 2 cups of boiling pasta water into the skillet, stir up the sauce, and cook at a perking boil for about 5 minutes, until the liquid is reduced by half.

• Stir the remaining 2 tablespoons of olive oil into the sauce. Keep it at a low simmer until the pasta is ready.

When the pasta is done almost *al dente*, scoop it up and into the skillet to finish cooking, adding more pasta water or reducing it as necessary. Add the parsley during the initial tossing; off the heat, toss in the cheese just before serving.

Simple Sauces with Butter

These butter-based sauces are made in the big skillet and tossed with the pasta the same way as the previous, oil-and-garlic sauces. But they are considerably quicker, making them especially convenient for everyday fast-cooking pastas for hungry families. They are less demanding as well, without the careful timing and caramelizing of sauce ingredients in sequence. That doesn't mean they are boring. You can toast nuts and herbs in the butter to great advantage. Sometimes I caramelize the butter itself—producing "brown butter," with its distinctive flavor.

Such sauces are customarily used to dress fresh pastas, but they go well with dry pastas too. If you have a nest of fresh pasta pappardelle or lacce in the freezer (page 168), you can make a wonderful butter sauce in any amount you like—just reduce the ingredients proportionally.

Butter and Fresh Sage Sauce

(a 3-minute sauce)

8 to 12 tablespoons (1 to 1½ sticks) butter, to taste!

10 whole fresh sage leaves

Hot water from the pasta-cooking pot

¼ teaspoon freshly ground black pepper, or to taste

1 cup grated Parmigiano-Reggiano or Grana Padano

- Melt the butter in the pan over medium heat, lay in the sage leaves, and heat until the butter is sizzling gently. Toast the leaves for 1 minute or so.

- Ladle in 1 cup boiling pasta water; stir the sauce, and simmer for about 2 minutes, reducing liquid by half, before adding pasta. Grind the black pepper directly into the sauce.

- Keep the sauce hot over very low heat; return to a simmer just before adding pasta.

Finish cooked pasta and sauce in the skillet. Off the heat, toss in the cheese just before serving.

Good With . . .

Fresh pastas

Gnocchi

Gnudi

Ravioli

Or a box of ziti, if that's all you have

Butter and Fresh Basil Sauce

Substitute about twenty shredded leaves of basil (½ cup packed) for the sage leaves. Long thin dry pastas like capellini or long flat-cut fresh pastas are good with this.

NO SKILLET NEEDED:
BUTTER AND CHEESE AND PASTA IN A BOWL

This is the butter version of the Raw Olive Oil dressing for pasta on page 107. I make it at least four times a week, whenever Lorenzo and perhaps some of his cousins want "cheesy pasta" or gnocchi. To make them happy I just toss hot pasta—dry tubettini, fettuccine, or gnocchi—in a warm bowl with soft butter and grated Parmigiano-Reggiano in about the same proportions as in the Butter and Fresh Sage Sauce. Yet this is not just kid food: butter and cheese are time-honored condiments for pasta with a twist of freshly ground black pepper.

BROWN BUTTER AND FRESH ROSEMARY SAUCE

In its usual state—with cream and fat in a stable suspension—butter has a creamy taste. But this changes dramatically when it is heated quickly and starts to brown. The cream solids and fat separate; the particles caramelize and take on a nutty flavor as they toast. I like butter both ways, and I use either as a base for pasta sauce. Try making brown-butter sauces with other herbs and seasonings to use with the pastas suggested on the preceding page.

FOR 1 POUND OF PASTA

- In a big skillet, melt a stick of butter over medium heat, swirling the pan so it starts to sizzle evenly.

- Let the butter sizzle until it turns pale brown, lower the heat, and toss in 1 teaspoon fresh rosemary needles and a twist of freshly ground black pepper. Shake the pan and toast the rosemary for ½ minute.

- Ladle in ½ cup of pasta-cooking water and simmer for a couple of minutes, until the sauce is reduced.

Finish sauce with cooked pasta as usual, tossing and cooking together over low heat (for details, see page 105). Off the heat, toss pasta with 1 cup freshly grated cheese.

Butter, Fresh Sage, and Walnut Sauce

(a 5-minute sauce)

FOR 1 POUND OF PASTA

8 tablespoons (1 stick) butter, or more to taste!

6 fresh sage leaves

1 cup chopped walnuts, ⅛-to-¼-inch bits

Hot water from pasta-cooking pot

1 cup freshly grated Parmigiano-Reggiano or Grana Padano

- Melt the butter over medium-high heat in the skillet, and scatter the sage leaves around the pan.

- When the butter begins to sizzle, drop the chopped walnuts in a hot spot. Toast them, stirring them in the butter for a minute or so, until they start to turn light brown.

- Ladle in 1 cup of pasta-cooking water. Cook at an active simmer for about 3 minutes, to develop flavor and thicken the sauce.

Finish sauce with cooked pasta, tossing and cooking together over low heat (for details, see page 105). Off the heat, toss pasta with the freshly grated cheese just before serving.

Good With . . .

My favorite—fresh Buckwheat Pasta with Walnuts (page 173), cut in lacce (shoestrings). Also, whole-wheat, flaxseed, corn-meal, and barley pasta. Yes, and dry spaghetti is good when no fresh pasta is around.

Butter, Dried Chestnut, and Fresh Rosemary Sauce

(a 5-minute sauce)

- Heat the butter and 1 tablespoon of the olive oil in the skillet set over medium-high heat until sizzling; drop in the chopped chestnuts; toast and stir for a minute.

- Scatter in the rosemary needles and cook another minute or so, until the nuts are lightly colored.

- Ladle in 1½ cups of pasta-cooking water; cook rapidly for 2 to 3 minutes, reducing the liquid by half; keep at low simmer until the pasta is ready.

Finish the sauce and pasta together in the skillet (for details see page 105). Add the parsley during the initial tossing; off the heat, toss in the cheese and a final tablespoon of olive oil just before serving.

8 tablespoons (1 stick) butter

2 tablespoons extra-virgin olive oil

½ cup finely chopped dried chestnuts, reconstituted and cooked in boiling water, then chopped or pulsed to small bits in the food processor

1 teaspoon fresh rosemary needles

Hot water from the pasta-cooking pot

3 tablespoons chopped fresh Italian parsley

1 cup freshly grated Parmigiano-Reggiano or Grana Padano

Good With . . .

Pappardelle of fresh Chestnut Pasta (page 177)

Rich egg pasta

A thin dry pasta such as capellini, spaghettini

Toasted Bread Crumb and Butter Sauce

(a 5-minute sauce)

2 tablespoons dry bread crumbs

8 tablespoons (1 stick) butter

Freshly ground black pepper

Hot water from the pasta-cooking pot

1 cup freshly grated Parmigiano-Reggiano or Grana Padano

Toast the bread crumbs in a small skillet (see page 93), tossing and stirring them, until they start to color. When they are almost completely browned, drop in 2 tablespoons of butter. Take the pan off the heat, and swirl it to melt the butter and stop the crumbs from darkening further.

Melt the remaining butter in a big skillet over medium heat; grind pepper in generously.

Ladle in 1 cup hot pasta water and cook actively for a couple of minutes, reducing the sauce slightly. Keep at low simmer until the pasta is ready.

Toss cooked pasta and sauce together in the skillet. Off the heat, toss in the cheese and sprinkle the toasted bread crumbs on top of the pasta, just before serving.

Good With . . .

Egg pasta—tagliatelle

Cornmeal pasta

Ricotta Ravioli (page 181)

Potato, Leek, and Bacon Ravioli (page 186)

A simple pasta such as rigatoni or linguine

Toasted Poppy Seed and Butter Sauce

Follow the recipe for Toasted Bread Crumb and Butter Sauce above, but substitute 2 tablespoons poppy seeds for the crumbs. Toast them in the dry pan until they are fragrant, reserve some for topping if you like, then add the butter and swirl them together.

Toss cooked pasta and sauce together in the skillet. Off the heat, toss in grated cheese and sprinkle the reserved toasted poppy seeds on top, just before serving. This sauce is especially good with Ricotta Ravioli.

Can Canned Tomatoes Make a Great Sauce?

From talking with hundreds of cooks every year, I sometimes feel that Americans are obsessed with fresh tomatoes. I agree that a garden-grown ripe tomato, *in its season*, is one of the most wonderful foods on earth. They are essential to my life and to some of my favorite summer dishes, including several wonderful Summer Tomato Sauces, which you will find in the vegetable chapter. But I don't share the opinion that fresh tomatoes *always* make the best sauces. In fact, most of the year I make my basic sauces with canned San Marzano tomatoes from Italy (see box, page 124). Even with brief cooking, these lend a sweetness and juiciness to sauces that I cannot get from a typical "fresh" tomato out of season.

The sauces here, all made with canned tomatoes, provide you with many choices for pasta dishes throughout the year. Two are skillet sauces of the quick, last-minute sort, which you prepare at the same time that you cook your pasta. Tasty and versatile marinara sauce can be both a last-minute and a do-ahead, making it a sauce I depend upon constantly. Last in this group is Simple Tomato Sauce, an uncomplicated "long-cooking" sauce that is complex in flavor, essential for dressing pasta and as a component for many baked and braised dishes. It takes about 2 hours to develop its fine flavor, but the basic recipe yields enough for several enjoyable meals.

SAN MARZANO: THE BEST CANNED TOMATOES FOR THE BEST SAUCES

For a really good tomato sauce, you should use the best: San Marzano tomatoes. These distinctive plum tomatoes (known for their womanly shape as well as their sweetness) are deservedly the most celebrated of the many kinds of canned tomatoes imported from Italy. Fortunately, these days they are available in the United States at most supermarkets; if you can't find them, try the Internet or an Italian deli.

San Marzano is a town outside of Naples and the center of the growing region where a particular variety of tomato got its reputation. The volcanic soil of the area is extremely fertile, and the intense sun of Campagna reflects off the metallic particles in the volcanic soil, bathing the tomatoes in sunshine from all sides, making them wonderfully sweet. Tomatoes of the San Marzano variety can be grown elsewhere, of course—we grow them at home in Queens—but the only canned tomatoes that can be labeled as "San Marzano" must have been grown in the designated district. And only the very finest of these can carry a special DOP seal, guaranteeing that they have been produced to the standards of the San Marzano growers' consortium—just like a vintage wine!

I encourage you to use San Marzano tomatoes (with or without the DOP symbol), or other tomatoes that are truly grown in Italy, for these recipes. Read the labels of cans carefully: many brands will process tomatoes from other countries but proclaim they are "Packed in Italy." Others are just "Italian-style," which likely means they have some basil in the can. When you cook with real Italian tomatoes, you will taste the difference.

There are also good plum tomatoes that are grown and packed in the United States. Buy whole plum tomatoes packed in their juice. When of good quality and ripened on the vine, they make an excellent sauce.

Anytime Tomato Primavera Sauce

*Y*ou don't have to wait for primavera—*springtime*—to make this quick skillet sauce. You probably have most of the ingredients in your pantry and refrigerator all year: canned tomatoes, onions, garlic, a few perennially fresh vegetables like broccoli, mushrooms, and zucchini, and sweet peas from the freezer. (The recipe lists the vegetables I prefer, but don't be afraid to use others, if that's what you have on hand.)

A key step here is parboiling the firm green vegetables and shocking them in ice water. Then they will only need to heat briefly in the tomato sauce and will keep their own colors, flavors, and textures.

This recipe yields about 5 cups or more of sauce, depending on the vegetables. If that looks like more than you need for the amount of pasta you are cooking, take the extra sauce out of the skillet before you toss in the pasta. (See box, page 97.) Refrigerate the reserved sauce and use within 2 or 3 days, or freeze it for a few weeks (it will still taste good, although the color of the vegetables changes a bit in reheating it).

ABOUT 5 CUPS, ENOUGH TO DRESS 1½ POUNDS OF PASTA

Blanching the Vegetables

Fill the pasta pot with salted water (1 tablespoon kosher salt to 6 quarts of water) and bring to a boil. Fill the large bowl with ice water.

When the pasta water is boiling vigorously, dump in the cut vegetables and peas, bring the water back to the boil, and cook, uncovered, for 2 minutes. Scoop out the pieces with a spider or strainer, drain briefly, and drop into the ice water to shock them. When they're thoroughly chilled, let them drain and dry in a colander. Keep the water in the pot boiling so you can cook the pasta as you make the sauce.

Making the Skillet Sauce

● Pour the olive oil into the skillet, scatter the onion slices in the oil, and set over medium-high heat. Cook for 1 minute, tossing to coat the onions with oil.

VEGETABLES FOR BLANCHING

3 cups or so *total* of the following in any colorful combination:

Zucchini, sliced crosswise into ½-inch pieces

Small broccoli florets on short stems, about 1 inch wide (slice if necessary)

Asparagus stalks, trimmed and sliced on the bias into ¾-inch pieces

Green beans, trimmed and sliced on the bias into ¾-inch lengths

1 cup frozen peas

Or equivalent amounts of cut-up cauliflower, peppers, leeks

⅓ cup extra-virgin olive oil

1 small onion, cut in ¼-inch-thick
    half-moon slices (about ½ cup)

4 fat garlic cloves, sliced
    (about ¼ cup)

¼ teaspoon dried *peperoncino*
    (hot red pepper flakes)

2 cups fresh mushrooms, stems
    trimmed, sliced ¼ inch thick,
    or a mixture of cremini, common
    mushrooms, and shiitake
    (caps only)

½ teaspoon salt

2 cups (half of a 35-ounce can) canned
    San Marzano or other Italian plum
    tomatoes, with juices, crushed by
    hand into small chunks

Boiling salted pasta-cooking water

FOR DRESSING PASTA

2 tablespoons extra-virgin olive oil
    (optional)

¾ cup freshly grated Parmigiano-
    Reggiano or Grana Padano

RECOMMENDED EQUIPMENT

8-quart pasta-cooking pot

A large bowl with ice water

A 12-inch or larger skillet for the sauce
    and the pasta

Anytime Tomato Primavera Sauce (cont.)

• Strew the garlic slices and *peperoncino* in clear hot spots of oil,
and cook them until they're sizzling, another minute or so, then stir
in with the onions. Don't let them darken; lower the heat if they
start to color.

• Scatter the mushroom slices in a clear part of the skillet, and
sprinkle on the ½ teaspoon salt. Cook and stir them separately for 1
minute or so, until sizzling, then stir them in with the onions.

• Pour all the crushed tomatoes and juices into the skillet, and
stir in with the sautéed vegetables. Slosh 1 cup of hot pasta water
around the tomato container, then stir that into the skillet. Heat the
sauce so that it's actively bubbling all over, and cook at a gentle boil
for 5 minutes, stirring occasionally. Add pasta water if the sauce is
thickening or sticking.

• Drop all the cut, blanched vegetable pieces into the skillet,
and stir them into the sauce. Bring to a simmer, and cook for about
2 or 3 minutes or more, until the blanched vegetables are cooked
thoroughly but still *al dente*. If the pasta is not ready, turn off the heat
so the vegetables don't get soft. Just before adding the pasta, stir in
some hot pasta water to loosen the sauce if it has thickened, and return it to a simmer.

To dress any pasta with tomato primavera, toss and cook them together, following the procedure on page 105. Remove the skillet
from the heat, and toss in the 2 tablespoons olive oil and the cheese
just before serving.

Good With . . .

Fresh whole-wheat pasta is particularly good with this all-vegetable
sauce. Or any of the whole-wheat dry pastas (or regular dry pastas) in
short tubular shapes, such as ziti or campanelle.

A TWO-MINUTE SAUCE WITH A "WINTER" TOMATO

Though I'm reluctant to use out-of-season, commercially produced fresh tomatoes in a sauce, tomatoes from hothouses are a decent alternative. I sometimes dice up such a tomato for a quick skillet sauce, where the texture and color of the flesh are enjoyable, giving a dish acidity and freshness. A good example is the Sauce of Anchovies, Capers, and Fresh Tomatoes on page 91. Here is an even simpler one, for which a ripe market tomato will do, even in winter. Try this simple sauce with Shrimp and Tomato Ravioli (page 182), or tagliatelle, or capellini.

For 1½ pound of pasta, dice up a cup or so of tomato pieces (without seeds—or skin, if you are willing to peel the tomatoes). Slice 3 plump garlic cloves. Shred 2 tablespoons of fresh basil.

Toast the garlic slices in 2 tablespoons of extra-virgin olive oil for 1 minute in a fairly large skillet. Scatter in the diced tomato, sprinkle on a pinch of salt and a pinch of *peperoncino,* and toss the pieces for 1 more minute, just barely cooking them. Turn off the heat and stir in the basil leaves and the cooked pasta with 3 or 4 tablespoons of the pasta water. Toss all, then add grated cheese— Parmigiano-Reggiano, Grana Padano, or Pecorino Romano.

Spicy Tomato Sauce—*Salsa Arrabbiata*

Salsa arrabbiata—*literally, "angry" sauce—is a tomato-based pasta sauce made in countless versions in Italy, sometimes with meat, sometimes without, but always with some kind of hot pepper. I like bits of meat in my sauce, either thick bacon or, even better, prosciutto "end" (see box on the facing page). The heat here comes from small whole pickled peppers, packed in jars of vinegar, labeled* peperoncini *or* peperoncino *(the same term I use for red pepper flakes). Though these are milder than pickled "cherry" peppers, they provide plenty of spice—especially* peperoncini Toscano, *which I hope you can find.*

The sauce should have a pleasing play of textures as well as tastes, providing nice and distinctive bites of all the ingredients. Cut the onions, peperoncini, *and prosciutto (or bacon) thick enough so that they don't get lost, or lose their shape in the tomato sauce.*

---

3 TO 4 CUPS OF SAUCE, ENOUGH TO DRESS I POUND OF PASTA

3 cups (one 28-ounce can) canned San Marzano or other Italian plum tomatoes, with juices

2 to 3 tablespoons extra-virgin olive oil

2 medium onions sliced in ¼-inch-thick "half-moons" (about 1½ cups)

About 6 ounces (1 cup) prosciutto end or thick bacon cut in ½-inch strips (see box, page 129)

3 bay leaves

8 to 10 whole Tuscan-style *peperoncini* in vinegar, drained, seeded, and sliced in strips (½ cup), or more to taste

Hot water from the pasta-cooking pot

½ teaspoon salt, or more to taste

Dump the tomatoes and juices into a large bowl, and squeeze the tomatoes into small chunks with your hands.

Pour the olive oil into the skillet, toss in the onion slices and the prosciutto or bacon strips, and set over medium-high heat. Stir well, toss in the bay leaves, and cook, stirring and shaking the pan occasionally. If using bacon, start over medium heat and turn it up as the bacon releases its fat.

After 5 minutes or so, when the onions have softened, drop the *peperoncino* strips into a clear part of the skillet, and toast them in the hot spot for a minute. Pour the crushed tomatoes into the pan; rinse out the tomato can and bowl with 1 cup of pasta-cooking water, and pour it into the skillet too. Add the salt, stir well, and rapidly bring the sauce to a boil, then lower the heat so it is bubbling steadily.

Cook at a gentle boil for 8 to 10 minutes, until the sauce has thickened and reduced by a third or so. The onions and peppers should be cooked through but still retain their shape and texture to the bite.

Remove bay leaves, then toss and cook the pasta together with *salsa arrabbiata*, following the procedure on page 105. Remove the skillet from the heat, and toss in the cheese just before serving.

FOR DRESSING PASTA

I cup grated Parmigiano-Reggiano or
  Grana Padano

RECOMMENDED EQUIPMENT

A 12-inch or larger skillet

Good With . . .

I like a dry pasta here—linguine, ziti, campanelle, radiatori, or capellini.

A FLAVORFUL STAPLE: PROSCIUTTO END PIECES

A fine substitute for bacon in this recipe and others is small pieces cut from the end of a prosciutto. This is a chunk of dense and flavorful meat (with a layer of flavorful fat) at the shank end of a prosciutto, all that's left after the rest of the ham has been sliced paper-thin, in the traditional manner.

The next time you are in an Italian deli or grocery, ask if they have one to sell you; it's a useful piece of meat to have on hand (and much less expensive than regular prosciutto). With the skin on, it will keep for a long time in your refrigerator or freezer, and you can use small amounts of the salt-cured meat to add flavor to sauces, soups, and pasta, wherever you would use bacon. Remove skin before cutting the prosciutto. You can also slice off a piece of the skin and use the layer of fat underneath to lend flavor to dishes. Just rub the fat over a frying pan, or the surface of a grill, to apply a thin film of grease.

Twenty-Minute Marinara Sauce with Fresh Basil

*M*arinara is my quintessential anytime tomato sauce. I can start it when the pasta water goes on the stove and it will be ready when the pasta is just cooked. Yet, in its short cooking time, it develops such fine flavor and pleasing consistency that you may well want to make a double batch—using some right away and freezing the rest for suppers to come. The beauty of this marinara sauce is that it has a freshness, acidity, and simplicity of taste, in contrast to the complexity and mellowness of the long-cooking tomato sauce that follows.

This recipe for marinara includes lots of fresh basil, which I keep in the house at all times, now that it is available in local supermarkets year-round. I cook a whole basil stalk (or a handful of big sprigs with many leaves attached) submerged in the tomatoes to get all the herb flavor. Then I remove these and finish the sauce and pasta with fresh shredded leaves, giving it another layer of fresh-basil taste. (If you are freezing some of the sauce, by the way, you can wait until you're cooking with it to add the fresh-basil garnish.)

This sauce can be your base for cooking any fish fillet, chicken breast, pork filet, or veal scaloppini. Sear any of these in a pan, add some marinara sauce, season with your favorite herbs, and let it perk for a few minutes—you'll have yourself a good dish.

4 CUPS OF SAUCE, ENOUGH TO DRESS 1 POUND OF PASTA (OR A BIT MORE)

4 cups (one 35-ounce can) canned San Marzano or other Italian plum tomatoes, with juices

⅓ cup extra-virgin olive oil

7 or 8 fat garlic cloves, sliced (about ½ cup)

¼ teaspoon dried *peperoncino* (hot red pepper flakes), or more to taste

Hot water from the pasta-cooking pot

1 teaspoon salt, or more to taste

1 stalk or big sprigs of basil, with 20 or so whole leaves

Pour the tomatoes and juice into a big mixing bowl. Using both hands, crush the tomatoes and break them up into small pieces. (You don't have to mash them to bits; I like chunkiness in my marinara, with the tomatoes in 1-inch pieces.)

Pour the oil into the big skillet, scatter the garlic slices in the oil, and set over medium-high heat. Cook for 1½ minutes or so, until the slices are sizzling, then add and toast the *peperoncino* in a hot spot for another ½ minute.

Shake and stir the pan until the garlic slices are light gold and starting to darken. Immediately pour in the crushed tomatoes and stir in with the garlic. Rinse out the tomato can and bowl with 1 cup of pasta-cooking water, and dump it into the skillet too.

Raise the heat; sprinkle in the salt and stir. Push the stalk or sprigs of basil into the sauce until completely covered. When the sauce is boiling, cover the pan, reduce the heat slightly, and cook for 10 minutes at an actively bubbling simmer.

Uncover the pan and cook another 5 minutes or so. The sauce should be only slightly reduced from the original volume—still loose and juicy. Remove the poached basil stalk or sprigs from the skillet and discard (but save the sauce that's clinging to it), and keep at a low simmer until the pasta is ready.

To dress pasta with marinara sauce, toss and cook them together (for details, see page 105), incorporating the shredded basil. Remove the skillet from the heat and toss in the cheese just before serving.

(for details, see page 105)

FOR DRESSING PASTA

⅓ cup shredded fresh basil leaves,
    packed (about 12 whole leaves)

¾ cup freshly grated Parmigiano-
    Reggiano or Grana Padano

RECOMMENDED EQUIPMENT

A 12-inch or larger skillet for the sauce,
    with a cover

QUICK PANTRY PASTAS WITH MARINARA

With Tuna
Marinara with the addition of canned tuna and capers makes a great pasta sauce.

> *4 cups marinara*
>
> *One 6-ounce can tuna, drained*
>
> *¼ cup drained capers, washed*

Bring the marinara to a boil, then add the tuna chunks (do not break them up) and the capers. Simmer for 5 to 7 minutes while the pasta cooks. I like dry tubular pasta, such as rigatoni or ziti, with this sauce.

Olives and Capers
Marinara with olives and capers makes a tasty pasta dish. Use 1½ cups pitted green or black olives to 4 cups of marinara plus ¼ cup of capers.

Mozzarella
A quick and delicious option is to toss 2 cups of cubed mozzarella when you're tossing the cooked pasta in your marinara sauce. For a finish, top with 8 shredded basil leaves.

Good With . . .

Dry and fresh pastas and raviolis.

Wonderful for baked pastas.

Simple Tomato Sauce

I don't call this sauce "simple" because it is dull in any way. It is a wonderful sauce, lightly textured but richly flavored, sweet and tangy like good tomatoes, and so versatile that I consider it a kitchen staple, one of the sauces that I always have in the freezer. All you need are canned tomatoes; a small amount of onion, carrot, and celery; and salt, peperoncino flakes, and two bay leaves. Then the sauce should mellow for a few hours if possible before using.

7 TO 8 CUPS OF SAUCE

8 cups (two 35-ounce cans) canned San Marzano or other Italian plum tomatoes, with juices

1 large onion, chopped in small pieces

1 medium carrot, chopped in small pieces

1 inner rib celery, chopped in small pieces

6 tablespoons extra-virgin olive oil

1 teaspoon salt, plus more to taste

2 cups water

2 bay leaves

1 teaspoon dried *peperoncino* (hot red pepper flakes)

½ teaspoon honey (optional, after tasting)

RECOMMENDED EQUIPMENT

A rotary food mill with a medium puréeing disk

A heavy-bottomed saucepan, 6 quarts or larger, with cover

Put the tomatoes through a food mill, using the medium blade, or a colander or sieve, set over a bowl. If you're sieving the tomatoes through a sieve or colander, push the flesh through, scraping against the sieve to extract all the pulp and juice.

Put chopped onion, carrot, and celery pieces in the food processor and pulse several times, until you have very finely chopped small shreds. Or chop the pieces by hand into tiny bits.

Pour the oil into the sauce pot, stir in the chopped vegetables, and set over medium-high heat. Sprinkle on the salt. Cook for 3 minutes or so, stirring frequently, as the vegetables start to sizzle and soften; don't let them brown.

Pour the milled tomatoes and juices into the pan, and stir with the vegetables. Rinse out the bowl and the tomato cans with the water, and pour this into the saucepan as well. Stir in the bay leaves, honey, and *peperoncino*, turn up the heat, cover, and bring the sauce to a boil, stirring and checking it frequently.

Adjust the heat to maintain an active simmer, with lots of small bubbles all over the sauce. Cover, and cook for about 45 minutes, stirring occasionally.

Remove the cover; raise the heat so the sauce is still bubbling energetically and gradually reducing. Cook for another hour or so, stirring frequently to make sure nothing's sticking to the bottom of the pot. Turn down the heat as the sauce thickens (and if the bubbles are bursting out of the pot). Taste for salt near the end of cooking, and add more if needed. When the sauce has reduced by about a quarter and is concentrated but still pourable, remove from the heat.

Let the sauce cool; remove the bay leaves. Allow the flavors to mellow for an hour or two. Use however much sauce you need immediately; refrigerate or freeze the rest.

Good With . . .

Pastas

Gnocchi

Baked pastas

Non-pasta dishes (such as the skillet meat *gratinati,* pages 281 to 287)

Long-Cooking Sauces

There are some flavors and textures in cooking that can only be obtained through long, slow cooking. The technique for making these long-cooking sauces entails cooking meats slowly with seasonings and herbs in a limited amount of flavored liquid, then, as it evaporates, adding more liquid, until the meat is completely cooked and begins to break down. The flavors of the meat, as it cooks slowly, seep out and combine with the flavors of the herbs and spices in the liquid. That liquid, as it evaporates with heat, is slowly reabsorbed by the meat, and is released again as more liquid is added. And so the exchange of flavors goes on until the sauce is syrupy with flavors and the meat is tender and impregnated with the sauce.

In contrast, just simmer the same meat, herbs, seasonings, and vegetables in a large pot filled with water and you've got yourself a tasty soup, with most of the flavors seeped out of the ingredients to create a strong broth.

Asparagus, Green Pea, and Scallion Sauce

Here's a fitting sauce for springtime, full of seasonal treasures: asparagus, sweet peas, scallions, leeks, and fresh mint. And the color? Springtime green!

Of course, since all of the ingredients are available year-round, you can enjoy this anytime. But it is truly splendid when made with produce in season. Fresh asparagus—locally grown if you can get it—is the foundation of this sauce, both its sweet flavor and the pleasing texture of the finely sliced vegetable.

Use skinny asparagus spears for uniform appearance and easy slicing (and don't throw away the stubs; see recipe that follows). If available, fresh sweet peas are wonderful in the sauce. If not, frozen peas are always acceptable.

ABOUT 4 CUPS OF SAUCE, ENOUGH
FOR 1 POUND OF PASTA AND OTHER DISHES

Rinse the asparagus, snap off the tough bottom stub of each spear (and save; see the recipe that follows). Slice each spear crosswise into ¼-inch pieces; if the spear is fatter than ½ inch, slice it lengthwise in half or quarters. You want the asparagus pieces to be approximately pea-size. Slice the spears to make 4 cupfuls.

Pour ¼ cup of the oil into the skillet, set over medium-high heat, and stir in the onions. After a minute or two, when the onions are gently sizzling, stir in the leek pieces and ½ teaspoon of the salt. Cook for a minute, drop the *peperoncino* into a hot spot to toast briefly, then stir and cook until the leeks are hot and starting to wilt, 3 minutes or so.

Dump in the green peas and stir with the other vegetables. Cover the pan, lower the heat, and let the vegetables cook, sizzling gently. Shake the pan frequently, uncover it occasionally, and adjust the heat as needed to make sure the onions aren't in danger of burning.

After 6 minutes or more, when the onions are pale gold and the peas are softening, stir in the asparagus pieces and the scallions, then the butter and another ½ teaspoon salt. Pour in ⅓ cup of water, and stir well to moisten everything.

Bring the sauce to a slow simmer and keep it cooking, very slowly, over low heat, for about 30 minutes. Stir occasionally, and add

1 to 1½ pounds asparagus spears, preferably ½ inch wide or less

6 tablespoons extra-virgin olive oil

1 medium onion, finely chopped (about 1 cup)

1 large leek, both green and white parts, sliced into ½-inch pieces (about 1 cup)

1 teaspoon salt

¼ to ½ teaspoon dried *peperoncino* (hot red pepper flakes), or to taste

10 ounces frozen peas, thawed, or 1 pound fresh peas, shelled

2 cups finely chopped scallions

2 tablespoons butter, cut up

⅓ cup water, plus more if needed

½ teaspoon shredded fresh mint leaves

RECOMMENDED EQUIPMENT

A 12-inch heavy skillet with a cover

Asparagus, Green Pea, and Scallion Sauce (cont.)

spoonfuls of water to the sauce if it seems to be getting dry. The vegetables should become very soft but still retain their shape and identity—the sauce as a whole should be moist and thick. When it's reached this stage, turn off the heat, and stir in the remaining 2 tablespoons of olive oil and the shredded mint leaves.

Use right away or let it cool. The sauce can be refrigerated for several days. If frozen, the texture will change but the flavor will be fine—it will keep for several weeks.

Good With . . .

Both dry and fresh pastas

Gnocchi

As a topping for polenta

As a base for risotto

Potato, Leek, and Bacon Ravioli
(page 186)

A Smooth Sauce from a Couple of Tough Veggies

Your family will love this fresh-flavored purée and won't guess that it was made from what some consider scraps—the stubs from asparagus stalks and the thick green tops of leeks. And if you hate to throw away tasty, usable food, as I do, you will feel virtuous.

The stubs of fresh, tender, skinny asparagus are best for this—don't even bother if the stubs are dry, white, and woody. Likewise, use only fresh, flexible leek greens here—it's OK if the leaves are firm and thick but not if they're wilted, old, or hard as leather.

Good For . . .

Dressing and filling ravioli

A base to a vegetable risotto

A sauce for poached zucchini or asparagus

FOR ABOUT 2 CUPS OF SAUCE

Rinse the asparagus stubs and the leek and scallion tops well. Cut off any wilted or bruised parts. Rap each asparagus stub with a heavy knife handle or a small skillet to crush it a bit and open the inner layers. If a good whack doesn't mash it, throw that one away!

Put the stubs, greens, garlic, and onion in a 2-quart saucepan and pour in 2 cups of water. There should be plenty to cover the vegetables; add more if necessary. Add the oil, salt, and peppercorns and bring the water to a boil. Cover the pot, adjust the heat to maintain a low bubbling boil, and cook for an hour. Lower the heat if the water's evaporating too fast—the vegetables should cook in water the whole time.

Uncover after an hour, and boil off the water almost completely. Before there's absolutely none left, turn down the heat and stir as the last visible moisture evaporates, but don't let the soft vegetables stick to the pot or burn.

Turn all the vegetables into the food processor and purée them thoroughly, scraping down the sides as necessary. If there are vegetable fibers that haven't broken down that mar the texture of the sauce (there may *not* be any), strain through a sieve. Return the sauce to the processor bowl, drop in the parsley and basil, and purée again. Taste and adjust seasonings.

Reheat before using; thin with boiling pasta water to a consistency you like. Store for several days in the refrigerator, or freeze for several months in airtight containers.

1 cup asparagus stubs

Four 5-inch-long pieces of leek green, top and outer layers

4 or 5 scallion greens, top and outer leaves (fresh trimmings only)

4 large garlic cloves, peeled

1 large onion, cut into large chunks

2 to 3 cups water

2 tablespoons extra-virgin olive oil

½ teaspoon salt, plus more if needed

½ teaspoon whole black peppercorns

1 tablespoon coarsely chopped fresh Italian parsley

3 tablespoons (packed) coarsely chopped fresh basil leaves

Boiling pasta-cooking water

Long-Cooking Savoy Cabbage, Bacon, and Mushroom Sauce

*S*avoy cabbage is the base of this flavorful and hearty wintertime sauce. The cabbage, bacon, and mushrooms are simmered gently for several hours, until the cabbage attains an almost melting texture. The sauce will be thick—and delicious as is with polenta, or loosened in some pasta water to serve with pasta.

ABOUT 6 CUPS OF SAUCE

8 ounces thick-cut bacon or prosciutto end (including fat and lean)

1 pound firm mushrooms, mixed types (see box on facing page)

2-pound head of Savoy cabbage, or slightly larger

1/4 cup extra-virgin olive oil

7–8 fat garlic cloves, sliced (about 1/2 cup)

1/2 teaspoon dried *peperoncino* (hot red pepper flakes), or to taste

1 teaspoon salt

1 cup or more Simple Vegetable Broth (page 288) or water

RECOMMENDED EQUIPMENT

A 14-inch sauté pan with high sides, or a 14-inch Dutch oven

Cut the bacon rashers into 1-inch pieces, or cut prosciutto end into pieces of similar size. Slice the mushrooms 1/8 inch thick or slightly thicker—you should have 6 cups. Trim off tough, discolored, or loose leaves from the cabbage; slice it in half or quarters, and cut out the hard core. Slice the cabbage into shreds about 1/3 inch thick; you should have nearly 4 quarts!

Pour the oil into the pan, strew in the garlic and bacon pieces, and cook over medium heat for 10 to 12 minutes, stirring occasionally, as the bacon renders and the garlic sizzles and colors slightly. Don't let either get too crisp or brown. Add the *peperoncino* during this time, toasting it in a hot spot for a minute before stirring in.

Pile all the cabbage and mushrooms in the pan; sprinkle the salt all over. Stir just a bit, to begin mixing the vegetables with the oil, bacon, and garlic. Cover the pan, turn down the heat slightly, and let the vegetables heat and begin to sweat for 3 or 4 minutes, then stir again. Cook, covered, and stir every couple of minutes—it will get easier as the vegetables wilt—until everything is mixed together.

Continue to cook, covered, for an hour or so, as the cabbage and mushrooms continue to shrink and soften. Stir every now and then; adjust the heat so everything is sizzling and steaming but not darkening or sticking. Add 1/2 cup or so of broth or water to the pan whenever the vegetables seem too dry.

Uncover the pan and cook for 45 minutes or longer, stirring frequently and moistening the sauce with broth or water at intervals. Adjust the heat to maintain the slow and steady concentration of the cabbage. Taste for salt, and add more if you wish. When the cabbage shreds are completely soft and there's about 1½ quarts of sauce in the pan, remove it from the heat.

Use the sauce immediately if you want. Store it in the refrigerator for a week, or freeze for use within several months.

Good With . . .

Tubular dry pasta

Fresh mixed and whole-grain
    pasta

Gnocchi

As a topping for polenta
    or polenta *pasticciata*

Risotto

Grilled meats

MY FAVORITE FRESH MUSHROOM MIX

I have to be honest and tell you that my favorite fresh-mushroom mix is one that has some of the amazing wild mushrooms we usually serve at the restaurant: fresh porcini, chanterelles, morels, and even wilder varieties! If any of these are available, you should certainly include them with ordinary cultivated mushrooms in any of the recipes in this book—even a few will add a special flavor.

All of the recipes, however, will be delicious with the domestic cultivated mushroom types available in the supermarket: common (white) mushrooms and cremini are my standards. They must be firm and fresh, with caps tight to the stem. Size doesn't matter that much, though in some dishes I specify button mushrooms. Oyster mushrooms are good too but are often quite soft and will break up, so you don't get texture. Shiitake mushrooms are fine (use only the caps), though I generally will not use them for more than a quarter of my mushroom mix.

Preparing mushrooms is not complicated. Trim away any tough parts—with odd-shaped mushrooms, just feel to determine what needs trimming. And don't soak mushrooms: wipe them with a damp paper towel to remove any grit or dirt.

TIPS ON DRIED PORCINI

Make dried porcini a staple in your kitchen.

- *Buy in bulk, if possible, as the small packets in most markets give you only 1 ounce or so. That's the equivalent of 1 cup loosely packed pieces—and most recipes require at least ½ cup (½ ounce).*

- *Store dried porcini in an airtight plastic bag in the freezer—that's what my mother does!*

- *To rehydrate dried porcini, put the dried pieces in a bowl or—even more useful, I find—a heat-proof measuring cup with a spout. Pour over very warm water: use at least enough water to cover (1 cup water for 1 cup porcini), or as much as two times the volume, which will give you more flavored liquid to use in soups or long-cooking sauces where you need plenty.*

  Let the dried porcini soak for ½ hour to a couple of hours.

  When you are ready to use them, lift them out of the container with your hand so the residue falls off—if you pour everything through a strainer, the mushrooms will get gritty again. Squeeze the juices out of the wet mushrooms (back into the container), chop, and add them to the dish as called for in the recipe. To use the liquid, strain it through a coffee filter to remove any dirt, or just make sure the dirt's settled at the bottom and pour off the clean mushroom water carefully.

- *Porcini powder is a fantastic way to add flavor to foods quickly—to season meats before grilling, or to use in stuffing and breading. Make sure the porcini are crackling dry; sometimes they absorb moisture and are soft and hard to pulverize. If so, toast them lightly under the broiler, then let cool.*

  To make a tablespoon or so of the powder, break up ¼ cup of dried porcini into pieces, put them in a spice grinder, a clean coffee grinder, or a powerful mini-chopper and pulverize them as fine as possible. Sift the ground powder through a fine sieve. (Keep the larger pieces for another use; throw them into a sauce or stew without even hydrating, for loads of flavor.)

  Store for a few months sealed in a glass jar, in a dry place.

Mushroom Ragù

This is a great vegetarian sauce, very complex and satisfying. It's excellent for pasta, baked in a lasagna or polenta pasticciata, cooked into risotto—or as a condiment for grilled steak or fish. The mushrooms you can buy at the supermarket will make a fine sauce; if you have fresh wild mushrooms it will be even better. In either case, dried porcini provide a key element in this sauce (and many others). On using dried porcini, see box on facing page.

ABOUT 6 CUPS OF SAUCE, ENOUGH TO DRESS
3 POUNDS OF PASTA

Prepping the Ingredients

Squeeze out the soaked porcini, and slice them into pieces about ¼ inch wide. Strain the soaking water, and keep it in a warm spot.

Clean, trim, and slice the fresh mushrooms into moderately thin slices, barely ¼ inch wide.

Tie all the fresh herb sprigs together with a piece of kitchen twine, or enclose the leaves in cheesecloth.

Cooking the Sauce

Put the oil and butter in the big skillet (or other saucepan) and place over medium heat. When the butter has melted, dump in the shallots and onion and ¼ teaspoon of salt, and stir well. Heat the onions to a slow sizzle and cook for 6 minutes or more—stirring often—until they're soft, wilted, and shiny, without any browning.

Pour all the mushrooms into the pan—both the chopped porcini and the sliced mushrooms—spread, and toss them in the pan. Sprinkle another ¼ teaspoon salt, drop in the herb bouquet, toss briefly, raise the heat a bit, and cover the pan. Cook, covered, for about 3 minutes—shake the pan now and then—to sweat the mushrooms.

Uncover, and continue to cook over fairly high heat, stirring frequently, as the mushrooms shrink and the liquid evaporates, 5 minutes or more. When the pan is dry and the mushrooms begin to

½ ounce dried porcini
(about ½ cup loosely packed pieces), soaked in 1½ cups warm water

2½ pounds small, firm fresh mixed mushrooms
(see box on page 139 for suggestions)

3 sprigs fresh thyme

1 sprig fresh rosemary, a tender stem about 4 inches long

1 sprig fresh sage with 4 big leaves (or more smaller ones)

¼ cup extra-virgin olive oil

4 tablespoons butter

1 cup finely chopped shallots

1 medium onion, finely chopped (about 1 cup)

½ teaspoon salt, plus more to taste

⅓ cup tomato paste

1 cup dry Marsala

4 cups hot Turkey Broth (page 80)
    or Simple Vegetable Broth
    (page 288)
Freshly ground black pepper

RECOMMENDED EQUIPMENT

A 14-inch sauté pan with high sides,
    or a 14-inch-wide Dutch oven

Good With . . .

Dry and fresh pastas

Gnocchi

Polenta and polenta *pasticciata*

Risotto

Baked pastas and *pasticciate*

Ravioli

Mushroom Ragù (cont.)

brown, clear a hot spot, drop in the tomato paste, and toast it, stirring, for a minute or so, then stir it into the mushrooms.

When everything is sizzling and browning again, and just starting
to stick, pour the Marsala all over. Stir constantly as the wine thickens and evaporates. When the mushrooms again start sticking to the
bottom, pour in the warm mushroom water and 2 cups of the hot
broth. Bring to an active boil, stirring up any caramelization on the
pan bottom. Lower the heat to keep the sauce bubbling gently all
over the surface, and cover the pan. Cook for about 20 minutes, occasionally stirring and adding broth to keep the mushrooms nearly
covered in liquid; expect to add ½ cup or so. Adjust the heat to keep
the perking steady but not too rapid.

Uncover the pan, and cook for another 20 minutes, maintaining
the simmer and adding broth as needed. When mushrooms are thoroughly tender and the saucy liquid is thickened—but not too condensed—the sauce is done. Remove the herb bouquet and discard it
(after you scrape off all the good sauce). Taste and add salt, if needed,
and freshly ground black pepper to taste.

Use the sauce immediately, or let it cool. Store it in the refrigerator for a week, or freeze for use within several months.

Ragù alla Bolognese, *Ricetta Tradizionale* and *Ricetta Antica*

Everyone traveling to Bologna, Emilia Romagna, is bound to eat ragù Bolognese, ricetta tradizionale *and/or* ricetta antica. *Served with fresh tagliatelle, particularly spinach tagliatelle, it is the precursor to meat sauce as we know it, and still the main Sunday staple at a Bolognese Sunday meal. The* ricetta antica, *an old recipe, has milk added while the sauce simmers, to give it additional richness and velvety texture. Today it is mostly the* tradizionale, *without milk, that is cooked in Bologna.*

ABOUT 3 QUARTS OF SAUCE FROM EITHER FORMULA,

ENOUGH FOR 6 POUNDS OF PASTA

For Both Ragù Bolognese: Preparing the Meat and *Pestata*

Put all 4 pounds of ground meat in a large mixing bowl. With your fingers, crumble and loosen it all up; then toss and crumble the beef and pork together. Pour over it the white wine, and work all the meat through your fingers again so it's evenly moistened.

To make the *pestata*, cut the bacon or pancetta slices into 1-inch pieces and put them in the bowl of a food processor with the peeled garlic. Process them into a fine paste.

For Both Ragù Bolognese: Cooking the Sauce Base

Pour the olive oil into the heavy saucepan, and scrape in all of the *pestata*. Set the pan over medium-high heat, and break up the *pestata* and stir it around the pan bottom to start rendering the fat. Cook for 3 minutes or more, stirring often, until the bacon and garlic are sizzling and aromatic and there's a good deal of fat in the pan.

Stir the minced onions into the fat and cook for a couple of minutes, until sizzling and starting to sweat. Stir in the celery and carrot, and cook the vegetables until wilted and golden, stirring frequently and thoroughly over medium-high heat, about 5 minutes or more.

Turn the heat up a notch, push the vegetables off to the side, and plop all the meat into the pan; sprinkle the salt on. Give the meat on the pan bottom a few moments to brown, then stir, spread, and toss with a sturdy spoon, mixing the meat into the vegetables and mak-

FOR BOTH RAGÙ
BOLOGNESE — *PESTATA*,
VEGETABLES, AND MEAT

2 pounds ground beef (15-percent fat content)

2 pounds ground pork (15-percent fat content)

2 cups dry white wine

6 ounces bacon or pancetta

5 fat garlic cloves

2 tablespoons extra-virgin olive oil

2 medium onions, minced in a food processor or finely chopped

2 large stalks celery, minced in a food processor or chopped

1 carrot, shredded

1/2 teaspoon salt, plus more to taste

LONG-COOKING
INGREDIENTS FOR
THE *RICETTA ANTICA*

6 tablespoons tomato paste

8 cups very hot milk

Nutmeg for grating
(to make ½ teaspoon,
or more to taste)

2 cups or more hot Turkey Broth
(page 80), hot Simple Vegetable
Broth (page 288),
or plain hot water or a
combination of these

Freshly ground black pepper

LONG-COOKING
INGREDIENTS FOR THE
RICETTA TRADIZIONALE

2 cups dry red wine

2 tablespoons tomato paste

2 cups canned plum tomatoes and
juices, passed through a food mill
or crushed by hand

8 to 12 cups or more hot Turkey Broth
(page 80), Simple Vegetable Broth
(page 288), or plain hot water

1 teaspoon freshly ground black
pepper

RECOMMENDED EQUIPMENT

A 10-to-12-inch heavy-bottomed
saucepan, or Dutch oven with a
6-quart capacity

ing sure every bit of meat browns and begins releasing fat and juices. Soon the meat liquid will almost cover the meat itself. Cook at high heat, stirring often, until *all* that liquid has disappeared, even in the bottom of the pan. This will take 30 to 45 minutes, depending on the heat and the width of the pan. Stir occasionally, and as the liquid level diminishes, lower the heat too, so the meat doesn't burn.

Heat up slowly the cooking liquids for either the *ricetta antica* (milk) or the *ricetta tradizionale* (broth), whichever version you are making. The procedures for the two are different, so I am giving them in separate sections.

Long-Cooking Bolognese *Ricetta Antica* with Milk

When all the meat liquid has been cooked off, drop the 6 table-spoons of tomato paste into a clear space on the pan bottom. Toast it for a minute in the hot spot, then stir to blend it with the meat and cook for another 2 or 3 minutes.

Pour in 2 cups of the hot milk and stir into the meat; add more milk if needed to bring the level just over the top of the meat. Grate the nutmeg right above the pan, dropping in at least ½ teaspoon, or more if you love it. Stir it in well; also, carefully clear the pan bottom of any caramelized bits, meat or vegetable, as milk will stick in these spots and scorch.

Bring the sauce liquid to an active simmer, cover the pan, and adjust the heat to maintain slow, steady cooking, with small bubbles perking all over the surface of the sauce.

From this point, the Bolognese should cook for 3 hours. Check the pot every 20 minutes, and add hot milk as needed to cover the meat. The liquid level should be reducing by 1½ to 2 cups between additions, so you'll need to have warm broth or water ready to replenish the sauce after all the milk has been added.

If the sauce level is falling much faster, and it takes more than 2 cups to cover the meat, lower the heat to slow the evaporation. If the sauce level drops slowly or not at all, raise the heat and set the cover ajar to speed its concentration. Stir well at every addition (and in between), and make sure nothing's sticking to the bottom.

For the final stage, see below.

Long-Cooking Bolognese *Ricetta Tradizionale* with Wine, Tomatoes, and Broth

When all the meat liquid has been cooked off, pour in the 2 cups of red wine. Raise the heat if you've lowered it, and stir the meat as the wine comes to a boil. Cook until the wine has almost completely evaporated, about 5 minutes. Now drop the 2 tablespoons tomato paste into a clear space on the pan bottom. Toast a minute in the hot spot, then stir with the meat and let caramelize for 2 or 3 minutes.

Stire in the crushed tomatoes; slosh the tomato container out with a cup of hot broth and add. Bring the liquid to a boil, stirring the meat, and let the liquid almost boil off, 5 minutes more.

Pour in 2 cups of hot broth, stir well, and add more if needed to cover the meat. Bring it to an active simmer, cover the pan, and adjust the heat to maintain slow, steady cooking, with small bubbles perking all over the surface of the sauce.

From this point, the Bolognese should cook for 3 hours. Check the pot every 20 minutes, and add hot broth as needed to cover the meat. The liquid level should be reducing by 1½ to 2 cups between additions; if it's falling much faster, and it takes more than 2 cups to cover the meat, lower the heat to slow the evaporation. If the sauce level drops slowly or not at all, raise the heat and set the cover ajar to speed its concentration. Stir well at every addition.

For Both Ragù Bolognese: Finishing the Sauce and Final Steps

During the final interval of cooking, you want to reduce the level of the liquid—once milk or broth, but now a highly developed sauce. At the end, the meat should no longer be covered but appear suspended in a thick, flowing medium. If the meat is still submerged in a lot of liquid, remove the cover completely to cook off moisture quickly.

A few minutes before the end of cooking, taste a bit of meat and sauce, and add salt if you want. Grind 1 teaspoon of black pepper right into the sauce, stir it in, and cook about 5 minutes before removing the pan from the heat.

If you'll be using the sauce right away, spoon off the fat from the surface—or stir it in, as is done traditionally. Otherwise, let the sauce cool, then chill it thoroughly and lift off the solidified fat. Store the sauce for several days in the refrigerator, or freeze it (in measured amounts for different dishes) for use within a few months.

Good With . . .

Pasta, preferably

Gnocchi

As a topping for polenta or polenta *pasticciata*

In lasagna *pasticciata* (page 200)

To make risotto

To fill and sauce ravioli

Long-Cooked *Sugo* and Meatballs

ABOUT 2 QUARTS OF *SUGO*, TO COOK AND SERVE
WITH 3 DOZEN MEATBALLS (SEE PAGE 149 TO 150)

FOR THE *SOFFRITTO*

6 tablespoons extra-virgin olive oil

2 medium onions (¾ pound),
   minced in a food processor

3 or 4 plump shallots, minced in a food
   processor

2 or 3 fat garlic cloves, minced in a food
   processor (about 2 tablespoons)

1 large carrot, minced in a food
   processor (about 1 cup)

2 large stalks celery, minced in a food
   processor (about 1 cup)

5 or 6 fresh bay leaves

¼ cup tomato paste

FOR THE *SUGO*

One 35-ounce can San Marzano plum
   tomatoes and juices, passed
   through a food mill (4 cups)

8 to 12 cups or more hot Turkey Broth
   (page 80) or Simple Vegetable Broth
   (page 288) or plain hot water

½ teaspoon salt, plus more if needed

1 cinnamon stick

or 2 tablespoons finely grated orange
   zest

   1 tablespoon fresh thyme leaves,
   stripped from the stem

   ¼ teaspoon *peperoncino* (hot red
   pepper flakes), or to taste

Frying the *Soffritto* and Starting the *Sugo*

Pour the olive oil into the pan, drop in the onions and shallots, and set over medium-high heat. Stir for a minute or two, until the onions begin to sizzle.

Drop the garlic into a hot spot and spread it out to caramelize for a minute, then stir with the onions. Stir in the carrot and celery, and get them cooking; drop in the bay leaves and cook the *soffritto* for another 4 minutes, until it is starting to dry out. Lower the heat if necessary to prevent burning.

Push the vegetables to the side and drop the tomato paste into a hot spot. Toast it for a minute or more, then blend it into the *soffritto*. Pour in the milled tomatoes and juices, and stir; slosh the tomato container with a cup of hot broth or water and stir that in too. Bring the sauce to a boil quickly, and cook over medium-high heat for 5 minutes or more, stirring frequently, until it has just begun to thicken.

Pour in 4 cups of the hot broth, stir it in, and note now the level of the liquid in the pan: this is about the level that the *sugo* should be at the very end of cooking, after the meatballs have been removed. Stir in another quart of the broth, and bring to a lively boil.

For turkey meatballs, submerge the cinnamon stick in the sauce. For sausage meatballs, stir in the orange zest, fresh thyme leaves, and up to ½ teaspoon of *peperoncino*, to taste.

Cover the pot and adjust the heat to maintain a steady but gentle bubbling all over the surface of the *sugo*. Let it cook for at least an hour or longer, checking the pot every 20 minutes or so. It should be reducing steadily. If it's barely dropping, or not at all, raise the heat and set the cover ajar to speed its concentration. If it's dropping extremely fast, lower the heat to slow the evaporation. Add hot broth or water if needed to keep the sauce at the level you want.

Make either the turkey or sausage meatballs while the *sugo* cooks, following the directions at the end of this recipe.

Have the *sugo* at a gentle simmer over low heat when the meatballs are fried and ready to go into the saucepan. Have hot broth or water on hand if needed. Drop the meatballs in one at a time; fit as many as you can in the bottom of the pan in one layer, but leave enough space to roll them around. Drop the rest of the meatballs in to make a second layer. Add hot broth or water if necessary so the meatballs are all covered with liquid. Stir gently to mix the broth with the *sugo*—don't break the meatballs! Cover the pan and raise the heat slightly to bring the *sugo* back to a simmer. Set the cover ajar and adjust heat to maintain steady simmering (but no threat of burning the meat on the bottom), and cook the meatballs for 35 to 40 minutes.

Turn off the heat and let the meatballs cool in the *sugo* and absorb more of its flavor (unless you need them right away). When cool, remove them to a big bowl. If the sauce is thin (probably well above the 2-quart mark), return it to a boil gradually and cook it uncovered to thicken. Stir frequently as it thickens; reduce it to the 2-quart level, or to whatever consistency you like—that's the most important guideline. Taste the sauce during this final cooking, and add salt, if needed, or adjust the other seasonings.

Serve sauce and meatballs right away if you want. Otherwise, pack the meatballs in containers with enough *sugo* to cover and the rest of the sauce in separate containers. Portion them, for convenience, in the amounts you'll use in different dishes. Store in the refrigerator for 4 days, or for several months in the freezer.

A 12-inch heavy-bottomed saucepan or Dutch oven, 8-quart capacity. You will need this width and depth to braise the meatballs.

Good With . . .

As a topping for a big bowl of dressed pasta (ziti, rigatoni, spaghetti)

As a meat course with vegetables, following a first course of dressed pasta

With fresh pasta (tagliatelle, pappardelle)

In baked pasta, such as cavatappi-and-meatball torta (page 196; 2 cups of *sugo* and 6 meatballs needed)

As a topping for polenta

Gnocchi

In a risotto, using the sauce and broken-up meatballs

In a fresh-pasta Lasagna with Sausage Meatballs and *Sugo* (page 206; 4 cups of *sugo* and 12 meatballs needed)

As a filling and sauce for ravioli

In a sandwich

MUST MEATBALLS BE FRIED?

Frying meatballs before adding them to the sauce adds another layer of flavor and creates a crust that holds the meat together so the ball doesn't break apart in the sauce. But it is not essential, and unfried meatballs can be quite good providing they have lots of sauce to cook in, so increase the sauce by a third (or decrease the meatballs by a third) if you choose the unfried method.

SUGO—*THE GRAVY FOR MEATBALLS*

Sugo, or gravy, is a long-cooking sauce that has a big component of meat in it, which releases its flavors as it cooks and transforms the sauce into a more complex and flavorful gravy.

This is the base in which I cook meatballs. Here I give you two different recipes for meatballs, one made from turkey meat and the other made from sausage meat. Both are quite easy to make.

The common denominator in both is the sugo, and the base for a good sugo is a soffritto—that essential Italian technique of cooking vegetables and aromatics in fat or olive oil slowly over low heat. Italian cuisine uses a soffritto as the start of many dishes—soups, braised meats, and pasta sauces. For this sugo the soffritto is made of onions, garlic, carrots, celery, and shallots. It is the first thing that goes into the pot with the olive oil.

The sugo can be cooked to the halfway point (which it reaches after about 30 minutes of cooking) in advance. Then, when you are ready with the meatballs, add them to the unfinished sugo and continue to cook together until done. You can also make the meatballs in advance, freeze them, and when you are ready proceed with the final cooking in the sauce.

A platter of Long-Cooked *Sugo* and
Meatballs

Turkey Meatballs with Pine Nuts and Golden Raisins

Sausage Meatballs with Fresh Fennel and Orange

ABOUT 3 DOZEN 2-INCH MEATBALLS,
EITHER TURKEY OR SAUSAGE

Making Turkey Meatballs

Pour the olive oil into a medium skillet, drop in the minced onions, sprinkle with a pinch of salt, and set over medium-high heat, stirring until they begin to sizzle. Lower the heat and cook for 4 to 5 minutes, stirring occasionally, until the onion is wilted and slightly dry (but not colored). Scrape out of the pan and let cool.

Break up the dry bread slices into pieces roughly an inch or two across—you should have almost 4 cups—and put them in a shallow bowl or baking dish. Pour enough milk over to cover them, and soak for 4 to 5 minutes. When the pieces are completely soft, gather them in your hands and firmly squeeze out all the milk; you should have almost 1 cup of densely packed moist bread. (Give the milk to your cat.)

Loosen up the turkey meat if it's been compressed in packaging; spread it out in a large mixing bowl. Pour the beaten eggs on top, sprinkle on the parsley, porcini powder, salt, and freshly ground pepper. Scatter the drained raisins and the pine nuts on the meat, then spread the cooled wilted onions on top. Break up the clump of wet bread, spreading little bits over the meat. Now fold, toss, and squeeze the meat and seasonings together with your hands and fingers to distribute all the ingredients evenly.

Form, flour, and fry the meatballs following the instructions below.

Making Sausage Meatballs

Pour the olive oil into a medium skillet, drop in the minced onion and fennel, and set over medium-high heat. Stir them in the pan for a minute or two, until they begin to sizzle; clear a space for the garlic, and get it sizzling on the side for a minute or so. Sprinkle on half the salt, and stir all together. Turn down the heat and cook for 5 minutes,

FOR TURKEY MEATBALLS

1 ½ tablespoons extra-virgin olive oil

1 medium onion, finely chopped (about ¾ cup)

½ teaspoon salt, plus more as needed

4 slices dried white bread from a sandwich or big Italian loaf

1 to 2 cups milk

3 pounds ground turkey meat

3 large eggs, well beaten with a pinch of salt

2 tablespoons chopped fresh Italian parsley

1 ½ tablespoons porcini powder (page 140)

½ teaspoon freshly ground black pepper, or to taste

¾ cup golden raisins, plumped in warm water and drained

¾ cup pine nuts, toasted in a dry skillet

FOR SAUSAGE MEATBALLS

2 tablespoons extra-virgin olive oil

1 medium onion, minced in a food processor

⅓ of a small fennel, minced in a food processor (about ⅔ cup)

2 fat garlic cloves, minced in a food processor

¾ teaspoon salt

3 pounds sweet Italian sausage (without fennel seeds)

3 large eggs, well beaten with a pinch of salt

3 tablespoons chopped fresh Italian parsley

½ teaspoon freshly ground black pepper

2 tablespoons finely grated orange zest

1 teaspoon fresh thyme leaves, stripped from the stem

1 heaping cup fine dry bread crumbs

FOR COOKING BOTH KINDS OF MEATBALLS

1 cup or more all-purpose flour

2 cups or more vegetable oil

Salt for sprinkling

Spread the flour about ¼ inch deep in the center of a baking sheet.

Pine nuts, toasted and untoasted

stirring occasionally, until the vegetables are wilted and slightly dried, but don't let them color at all. Scrape them out of the pan to cool.

Meanwhile, take all the sausage meat out of the casing (if packed in links), crumble it up well, and spread it out in a large mixing bowl. Pour the beaten eggs on top of the meat. Add the parsley, remaining salt, pepper, orange zest, thyme leaves, and spread over all the cooled onions, fennel, garlic, and the bread crumbs. Now fold, toss, and squeeze the meat and seasonings together with your hands and fingers to distribute all the ingredients evenly.

Forming, Flouring, and Frying Meatballs

Spread the flour about ¼ inch deep in the center of a baking sheet.

Pour vegetable oil into a large, heavy skillet or sauté pan—12 inches in diameter if possible—to a depth of at least ⅓ inch.

Scoop up a portion of meat with a small ice-cream scoop, a large spoon, or your fingers. Lightly shape the meat between your palms into 2-inch balls, a bit larger than golf balls (or whatever size you like). Drop each ball onto the floured sheet, roll it around until coated, then place it on another baking sheet. Form and flour all the meat into balls in this manner.

Set the skillet over high heat until the oil is very hot. With tongs or a spatula, carefully transfer meatballs to the pan, as many as you can, leaving at least an inch or so between them. Cook for a minute or two, until they've started to brown on the bottom, then turn them continuously—watch out for oil spatters—until golden-crusted on all sides, about 6 minutes. As they are done, transfer the fried balls to a baking sheet. When all the meatballs are on the tray, sprinkle salt lightly over them (just a couple of pinches in all).

Note: The meatballs will finish cooking in the sauce; they are fried just until a golden crust forms. So, if you intend to eat them as is instead, be sure to fry them longer, until they are cooked through.

Before frying the next batch, turn off the heat and, with a fine-meshed skimmer or strainer, remove any browned bits from the oil. Add oil if needed to restore the ⅓-inch depth, and heat it up again.

When all the meatballs are fried, cook them with the *sugo*, following the instructions on page 146.

Pork Rib *Guazzetto*

*G*uazzetti *are sauces made by slowly simmering meat, game, or poultry in stock, creating a velvety texture that coats pasta wonderfully. Traditionally, a guazzetto got its great flavor from bones with little flesh, but it works with meaty cuts too. Country ribs can be so meaty you'll have more pork than you need for the sauce, so enjoy it in sandwiches or salads or as a ravioli stuffing.*

5 OR 6 CUPS OF MEATY *GUAZZETTO*,
ENOUGH FOR 2 ½ TO 3 POUNDS OF PASTA

Prepping and Cooking the Sauce Base

Trim the fat off the ribs—country ribs often have the fat cap from the loin—leaving only a thin layer on the meat.

Lift the soaked porcini out of the soaking liquid and squeeze the juices back into it. Chop the mushrooms into small pieces; strain the soaking liquid (see box, page 140) and keep it in a warm spot.

Film the pan bottom with the olive oil, and set over medium-high heat. When quite hot, lay the ribs in and let them sear for a couple of minutes in place. When they're colored and slightly crusted, turn them all to another side and brown well. Turn after 2 minutes and continue to brown evenly all over, about 8 to 10 minutes in all. Thick ribs should be seared on the narrow sides as well as the cut surfaces. Keep the pan as hot as possible without burning.

Remove the crusty ribs to a bowl or a platter and sprinkle ¼ teaspoon salt all over them. Immediately drop the minced bacon into the pan. Lower the heat and stir the bacon around the pan bottom, rendering the fat and scraping up some of the meat crust before it burns, for about 2 minutes.

When the bacon is rendered and sizzling, dump in the minced onions, stir well, and get them sizzling and starting to sweat. Stir in the celery, shredded carrots, and chopped porcini, and cook over medium-high heat until the vegetables are wilted and golden, stirring often, about 5 minutes. Clear a hot spot, plop in the tomato paste, toast it for a minute on the pan bottom, then blend it into the vegetables. Drop in the strips of orange rind and stir them in.

3 pounds country-style pork ribs, bone in

½ cup dried porcini, soaked in 1 ½ cups warm broth or water (see box, page 140)

¼ cup extra-virgin olive oil

¼ teaspoon salt, plus more to taste

¼ pound bacon, minced in a food processor or finely chopped (about ½ cup)

1 large onion, minced in a food processor or finely chopped (about 1 ¼ cups)

2 large stalks celery, minced in a food processor or chopped (about ½ cup)

1 medium carrot, shredded (about ½ cup)

2 tablespoons tomato paste

3 strips of orange rind, each the size of a standard Band-Aid

1 cup dry red wine

2 to 4 cups hot Turkey Broth (page 80), Simple Vegetable Broth (page 288), or water or combination

3 bay leaves

I sprig fresh rosemary about 4 inches long, with lots of needle clusters

Freshly ground black pepper

RECOMMENDED EQUIPMENT

A 10-to-12-inch heavy-bottomed saucepan or Dutch oven

Pork Rib Guazzetto *(cont.)*

Return the ribs to the pan (with the juices they've released) and toss them with the vegetables for a minute to heat them all over. Pour in the wine, raise the heat, and let it boil until almost completely evaporated, turning the ribs over and over in the pan.

Long-Cooking the Sauce

Pour in the mushroom-soaking water and enough hot broth just to cover the ribs. Drop in the bay leaves and the rosemary sprig, submerge them, and bring the liquids to a boil. Cover the pan and lower the heat slightly—check and adjust it to maintain steady perking of bubbles all over the surface of the sauce.

Cook for about 2½ hours or more, until the meat is so tender it's falling off the bone—almost falling apart. During that time, check the pot every 20 minutes or so, and add hot broth in small quantities (½ to 1 cup) just to keep the rib meat covered. If the level is falling much faster, lower the heat to slow the evaporation; if the sauce level isn't dropping at all, raise the heat and set the cover ajar to speed its concentration.

Finishing the *Guazzetto*

When the meat is sufficiently tender, turn off the heat. Taste the sauce and adjust the seasonings. If you'll be using the sauce right away, spoon off the fat from the surface. (Otherwise, wait until you've chilled the sauce and just lift off the solidified layer of fat.)

Let the ribs cool completely in the sauce, then with a wide spatula lift them out whole and set them on a platter. Pick out the bay leaves, herb stems, and strips of orange rind and discard; also retrieve any rib bones or meat pieces that may have broken off during the long cooking.

With your fingers, or a fork, tear or shred just enough pork into rough bite-size pieces, until you have a quantity that's equal to the volume of sauce in the pot—a one-to-one ratio of sauce to shredded meat. This is enough for a traditional *guazzetto*, which should have the character of a meat-laden sauce rather than a meat stew. Fold and stir the pork pieces into the sauce.

The traditional way to serve this *guazzetto* is to dress the pasta with the sauce and shredded meat for the first course, then serve the remaining whole ribs with vegetables for the second course.

If you have meaty ribs left, shred the meat to toss in salads, fill sandwiches, use for ravioli stuffing, or make a pork-rib hash for breakfast. Or reserve the whole ribs and meat and, when ready to eat, reheat under the broiler until crisp like spare ribs and serve with salad.

Use the *guazzetto* now or chill it thoroughly. Store for several days in the refrigerator, or freeze it, in measured amounts for different dishes, for use within a few months.

Good With . . .

Dry and fresh pastas

Gnocchi

Risotto

In baked pastas

To fill and dress ravioli

To top polenta and *pasticciata*

Duck Leg *Guazzetto*

I suggest you use duck legs to make this guazzetto, because they are juicier. But if you can't buy duck legs separately, you can cook the whole duck. Another way to skin this cat is to remove the duck's breasts, make the guazzetto with the rest of the duck, and sear the breasts to be served as a second course or a treat for another meal.

5 OR 6 CUPS OF MEATY *GUAZZETTO*,

ENOUGH FOR 2½ TO 3 POUNDS OF PASTA

3 ½ pounds duck legs (4 or 5 legs), or 1 whole duck, quartered

½ cup dried porcini, soaked in 1 ½ cups warm broth or water (see box, page 140)

¼ cup extra-virgin olive oil

¼ teaspoon salt, plus more to taste

¼ pound bacon, minced in a food processor or finely chopped (about ½ cup)

1 medium onion, minced in a food processor or finely chopped (about 1 cup)

2 tablespoons tomato paste

1 cup dry white wine

2 to 4 cups hot Turkey Broth (page 80), Simple Vegetable Broth (page 288), or water or some of each, as needed

3 bay leaves

1 sprig rosemary about 4 inches long, with lots of needle clusters

5 whole cloves

Freshly ground black pepper

Prepping and Cooking the Sauce Base

Trim the excess skin and all the visible clods of fat from the duck legs, then shave off the skin and the thick fat layer that covers the thigh, exposing the meat. Leave a strip of skin and fat covering about a third of the thigh (and the skin on the drumstick) to add flavor. Depending on how well the legs were trimmed by the butcher, you may remove a pound or more of fat (see box, page 327).

Lift the soaked porcini from the soaking liquid, then squeeze the juices back into it. Chop the mushrooms into small pieces; strain the soaking liquid (for details, see box, page 140) and keep in a warm spot.

Film the pan bottom with the olive oil, and set over medium-high heat. When quite hot, lay in the duck pieces, skin side down, and let them sear for a couple of minutes in place. When they're slightly crusted, turn them over and brown the other side; turn to brown all the surfaces a bit, 6 to 8 minutes in all.

Remove the duck to a bowl and sprinkle ¼ teaspoon salt all over. Scatter the minced bacon into the pan, and stir it around so the fat starts to render quickly. Cook for about 2 minutes, scraping up the crisp duck bits in the pan.

When the bacon is rendered and sizzling, dump in the minced onions and stir them in the fat. Cook for about 5 minutes as they sweat, sizzle, and wilt, then stir in the chopped porcini. Clear a hot spot in the pan bottom, drop in the tomato paste, toast it for a minute, then stir it in with the onions.

Return the duck legs to the pan, pour in any juices they've released, then toss them with the vegetables so they heat up on all sides. Pour in the wine, raise the heat, and let it boil until almost completely evaporated as you turn the duck several times in the pan.

Long-Cooking the Sauce

Pour in the mushroom-soaking water and enough hot broth just to cover the legs. Stir in the bay leaves, the rosemary sprig, and the cloves, and bring the liquid to a boil. Cover, and adjust the heat to maintain steady perking of bubbles all over the surface of the sauce.

Cook for about 2½ hours or more, checking every 20 minutes or so and adding just enough more broth to keep the meat covered. If the level of liquid is falling much faster, lower the heat to slow the evaporation; if the sauce level drops slowly or not at all, raise the heat and set the cover ajar to speed its concentration. When done, the duck meat should be falling off the bone.

Finishing the *Guazzetto*

Remove from the heat, add several grindings of black pepper, taste the sauce, and adjust the seasonings. If you'll be using the sauce right away, spoon or pour off the fat from the surface. (Otherwise, wait until you've chilled the sauce and lift off the solidified layer of fat.)

Let the legs cool completely in the sauce. Before refrigerating or serving, lift them onto a large platter or board; also pick out the bay leaves and herb stems and discard. Strip and trim all the edible duck meat from the legs; discard bones, skin, and cartilage.

Tear the tender meat into rough bite-size pieces. If you have much more meat than sauce—which you may well get from meaty legs— don't put it all into the pot. *Guazzetto* should have the character of a thick sauce chock-full of meat, not that of a stew of meat chunks, so you want a one-to-one ratio of sauce to shredded meat. Fold that amount of duck in, and what you don't use up now will be delicious in soups, salads, or pastas, or it will make an excellent hash.

Use the *guazzetto* now, or chill it thoroughly. Store for several days in the refrigerator, or freeze it, in measured amounts for different dishes, for use within a few months.

A 10-to-12-inch heavy-bottomed saucepan or Dutch oven

Good With . . .

Dry and fresh pasta

Gnocchi

Polenta

To make risotto

To stuff and dress ravioli

Homemade Pasta: Playing with the Dough

Making fresh pasta is a joy. I remember making it as a child with my grandmother, and today I do it with my grandchildren. It's one of the simple marvels of the kitchen. So roll up your sleeves and join us. I'm here to guide you.

In this book I am giving you formulas for small batches—three with white all-purpose flour, and a large group with mixed grains, beans, seeds, and nuts. The differences in the doughs are fascinating, and you'll be delighted with the range of flavors and textures they bring to pasta dishes.

Making any dough here—even the most unusual—is simple. I've kept the recipes short and uniform. Every dough consists of 2 cups of flour and barely a cup of eggs, oil, and water mixed together. You won't have to clear your kitchen to make them. With a mixing a bowl, a little space on the table, and 5 minutes to spare, you can put any dough together (or use a food processor and you will be done in 3 minutes). Rest the dough for ½ hour, then roll and shape it by hand, or use a pasta machine. You can have fresh pasta for supper almost anytime you want.

Once you get your hands into these recipes, I hope you have as much fun as my grandchildren and I do. The transformation of wet and dry ingredients into a dough, and dough into noodles, is one of the great delights of the kitchen, for cooks of all ages.

TIPS TO KEEP IN MIND ABOUT DOUGH CONSISTENCY

- *All the egg-pasta doughs in this section are made exactly the same way.*

- *You can use either the hand method or the machine method. However, if you are making a mixed-flour dough for the first time, I suggest you use the food processor. With non-wheat flours, some doughs will start out quite sticky (or quite dry), and the processor blade can knead them to a workable consistency in seconds.*

- *Remember that any dough (whether hand- or machine-mixed) has to rest for 30 minutes before you roll it. But then you can cut the pasta in shapes and cook it right away, without further delay.*

- *Every dough will soften as it rests. Some doughs that feel stiff after kneading will be quite malleable by the time you roll them.*

- *If a dough gets resistant and nervous when you start rolling, cover it and let it relax and rest for several minutes.*

- *If a dough is too moist and soft when you try to roll it—sticking to the rollers or spreading too thin—let it air-dry, rather than trying to dry it by working in more flour. Run pieces of dough through a wide opening of a pasta-making machine to form a strip, sprinkle each strip lightly with flour, and let it rest on a floured surface for a few minutes; then turn it over to expose the other side to air. Rest for a few more minutes before rolling again.*

Making Egg Dough Pastas

Those three pasta doughs look almost identical on paper—all-purpose flour, eggs, olive oil, water. So you may wonder: How do I know which one to make? Which is the best?

The truth is, I'd love to have you make all three so you can see and feel and taste the big differences that result from small variations. And you will realize there is no single "best." As Italian cooks know, you can mix flour into a fine pasta dough with whatever egg-oil-water mixture you like, whatever is available in the pantry, or whatever you can afford.

This last factor in particular reflects the way pasta has fit into Italian life for centuries: The rich man can have his cook make pasta moistened entirely with fat-laden, tasty egg yolks. A poor family might make their Sunday pasta with one precious egg (and have weekday pasta mixed only with water and a bit of oil). And families in between make pasta with the ingredients they have. But don't be fooled. The richest is not necessarily best. With two eggs and a goodly amount of extra-virgin olive oil, Poor Man's Pasta is quite rich and delicious (frankly, it's my favorite). Part of the fun is in mixing and matching the right pasta with the most compatible sauce, and you'll find guidance in the pages ahead as well as the challenge to try your own pairings.

Suggested Shapes and Sauces

This pasta should always be the star of the show: cut it in long flat shapes, either tagliatelle or pappardelle. It will not take much dressing, since it has lots of flavor. Dress simply with butter and cheese (page 119), and top with a shaved truffle if you have one. Or serve it with the juice of roast meat or poultry. One traditional way is to dress it with Bolognese sauce topped with grated Parmigiano-Reggiano or Grana Padano. Long-cooked savory sauces, such as *guazzetto*, make this a truly festive dish. But just remember not to oversauce and smother the pasta.

Rich Man's Golden Pasta

FOR I POUND OF PASTA

DRY

2 cups all-purpose flour

WET

9 egg yolks from large eggs (⅔ cup)

2 tablespoons extra-virgin olive oil

2 tablespoons water

The Rolls-Royce of noodles! It tastes rich (and it is rich) yet has such a delicate texture it melts in the mouth and hardly seems filling at all. For all its tenderness, the dough is resilient and easy to work, but it cooks very quickly.

Middle-Class Not-Quite-Golden Pasta

You will sense the difference in your mouth: this pasta has a bit more substance to the bite than the all-yolk pasta. Still, it is quite tender and rich.

Suggested Shapes and Sauces

Another pasta to savor in simple flat cuts—tagliatelle, tagliolini, or pappardelle. Sauce with Marinara (page 130); also good with long-cooking meat or vegetable sauces like Ragù alla Bolognese (page 143), either of the *guazzetti* (pages 151, 154), or Asparagus, Green Pea, and Scallion Sauce (page 135). Cheese sauces and game sauces are also good with this pasta.

DRY

2 cups all-purpose flour

WET

1 egg yolk (from a large egg)

3 large whole eggs

2 tablespoons extra-virgin olive oil

Poor Man's Two-Egg Pasta

Firmer than the preceding two, yet flavorful and light, this is a versatile pasta that serves as an excellent carrier for all flavorful sauces. It is the pasta I recommend for ravioli and lasagna.

Suggested Shapes and Sauces

Cut this pasta in any shape you like; sauce it with almost anything. Since it is not as rich as the first two, it goes very well with fish and vegetable sauces.

Here's a specific recommendation: practice making boccoli (Shirley Temple curls) with this pasta and dress with Simple Tomato Sauce (page 132), or with vegetable and pesto sauces.

DRY

2 cups all-purpose flour

WET

2 large whole eggs

1/4 cup extra-virgin olive oil

3 tablespoons water

Making the Dough by Hand

Measure the flour and shake it through a sieve into a medium-size mixing bowl (sifting aerates the flour). However, if you are making a mixed-flour pasta, don't try to sift; just stir or whisk the flours to blend them.

Following the illustrations, drop the eggs and/or egg yolks (in the specified amounts) into a small bowl or measuring cup; beat briefly with a fork to break them up. Pour in the measured amounts of oil and water and mix well with the eggs. (In a measuring cup, you should have 7 fluid ounces.)

Pour the wet ingredients into the flour. Toss and mix everything with a fork until all the flour is moistened and starts to clump together. Lightly flour your hands, then gather the clumps—or use a flexible plastic dough-scraper—and begin kneading right in the bowl, folding the raggedy mass over, pushing and turning it, then folding again. Use the kneading action to clean the sides of the bowl.

When you've formed a cohesive clump of dough, turn it out onto a small work surface *lightly dusted* with ½ teaspoon flour and continue kneading for 2 to 3 minutes, until the dough is smooth and shiny on the outside, soft throughout (no lumps), and stretchy. If your dough seems too sticky or too hard after it has been kneaded for a minute or two, adjust the consistency with very small amounts of flour or water and see box, page 157. If you are adding *nuts* to a dough, do it when you turn the dough out of the bowl (see page 172).

Form the dough into a disk, wrap it tightly in plastic wrap, and let it rest at room temperature for ½ hour. Store, very well wrapped, in the refrigerator for a day; or for a month or more in the freezer. Defrost frozen dough slowly in the refrigerator, and let it return to room temperature before rolling. Defrosted dough will need a bit more flour.

Making the Dough in the Food Processor

Fit the regular steel cutting blade in the bowl of the processor (these batches are too small for the dough blades of most machines).

Measure the flour or different flours into the bowl; process for a few seconds to blend and aerate.

Drop the eggs and/or egg yolks (in the specified amounts) into a

Beating the eggs with a fork

Adding the oil to the eggs and water

1. Pouring the wet ingredients into the flour

2. Mixing with a fork to moisten the flour

3. Kneading in a bowl

4. Starting to knead on a floured board

5. Continuing to knead

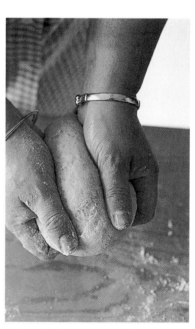

6. The dough—smooth, soft, and stretchy—ready to rest

spouted measuring cup or a small bowl; beat briefly with a fork to break them up. Mix in the measured amounts of oil and water (you should have 7 fluid ounces). To minimize the chance of overheating the dough, use eggs right from the refrigerator and cold water.

Start the machine running with the feed tube open. Pour the wet mixture into the bowl quickly; scrape all the egg drippings out of the cup into the processor too.

Let the machine run for about ½ minute. A dough should form quickly; most of it should clump or ball up on the blade—some may spread on the sides of the bowl—where it will twist and knead. Let the machine knead the dough for about 10 seconds (no more than 40 seconds total processing). Turn the dough out onto a very lightly floured surface, and knead by hand for another ½ minute or so, until it's smooth, soft, and stretchy. Wrap and rest the dough, or store it as described for making the dough by hand.

If you have problems in the food processor—if there's no apparent clumping after 30 seconds, or the dough stiffens up very quickly—

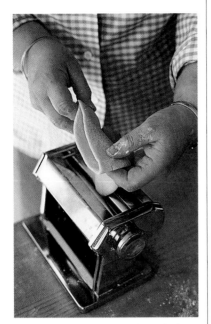

Putting the folded dough through the machine at its widest setting

Folding the rectangle in thirds

After turning the dough ninety degrees, putting it through the machine again at its widest setting

Putting the elongated dough through the third setting

stop the machine and feel the dough. Adjust for stickiness or dryness by working in either flour or water in small amounts (see box, page 157). You can continue to work the dough in the machine, but don't process for more than a total of 40 seconds—or turn the dough out to correct the consistency and finish kneading by hand.

Rolling the Dough by Machine

When I make pasta at home, I rarely take out my pasta machine to roll out the dough. Even though I've got a great machine (with a motor!), I find that it's still faster to cover the counter with a big wooden board, grab the thick wooden dowel I use as a pin, and start rolling.

For most people, though, I think a sturdy pasta machine is an important, even essential, kitchen tool. (I'm referring to the kind of machine with rollers—not the home pasta "extruders.") The machine itself is simple to operate; the part that takes practice and attention is handling the dough, as I detail below. Once you get the feel of it, you can use your machine to develop your dough and then stretch it into thin and tender pasta quite quickly. So, if you don't have a machine, try to get one—and if you do, keep it readily available (not on the top shelf of a cupboard!) and use it often.

Have your dough at room temperature for rolling.

Cut 1 pound of dough into four pieces. Work with one piece and keep the others covered. Have a large tray or baking sheet nearby (or two if you have them) lightly sprinkled with flour, on which to lay thin dough strips. Smooth kitchen towels are also useful as resting surfaces and to separate layers of strips. Have flour for sprinkling and a knife or sharp pastry cutter handy too.

Turn the knob to the widest setting—you'll work at this setting for a while. Following the photographs press the first piece of dough with your hands into a circle or a small rectangle, then fold it in half, and roll it through the machine two times. Fold the now elongated rectangle in thirds, turn the dough 90 degrees (so the fold is on the side), and roll it through.

Catch the dough; fold it and roll it through again with the fold on the side. Repeat the folding and rolling six more times (total of eight) to strengthen and smooth the dough. Like kneading, this will make it more resilient and workable. Lay the first piece down, sprinkle it with a tiny bit of flour on both sides, and cover it (with plastic

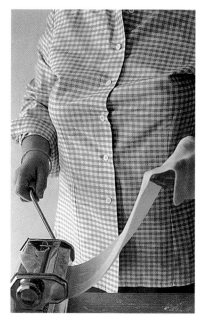
Catching the dough as it comes through the increasingly tightened rollers

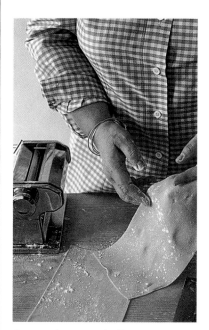
Cutting the strip in half

THE SECRET OF A WOODEN BOARD AND ROLLING PIN

Having urged you to use a pasta machine frequently, I also hope you will roll your pasta by hand now and then—the way I do, on a wooden table or board with a wooden rolling pin.

It is a satisfying skill to master (see the procedures, page 165), and a speedy way to roll out pasta in large pieces. Most important, you'll get a pasta with a quality that a stainless-steel machine can't produce. When you roll on a wooden board, with a wooden pin, the sheet of pasta, and any shapes you cut, are imprinted with the irregular textures of the wood surfaces. This roughness, though not apparent to the eye, gives the pasta a more pleasing texture in the mouth, and better ability to carry sauce. I used to wonder why my grandmother, who had a beautiful marble pastry table, always covered it with an old wooden board when rolling pasta. Now I find myself doing the same thing.

wrap or a towel). Put the remaining pieces of dough through the same steps of rolling and folding.

Either reset the rollers to the very next setting (slightly narrower) or skip to the third (even narrower)—I generally roll dough at *every other* setting, from wide to narrow. Roll your first strip through, short end in first (don't fold it again). Let the rollers grab and move the dough—don't push it or pull it through—and catch it in your hand as it comes out. Roll the strip again to stretch and widen it; lay the strip down (on the lightly floured tray) and stretch the others in the same way.

Reset the machine even narrower; you should be on the third or fifth setting by now. Pass the first strip through once; it will lengthen rapidly, and you will need to catch and support it as it comes through the rollers. Flour the strip lightly if it is sticking to the rollers. After the second pass, if the strip is 20 inches or longer, cut it crosswise in half, to get two shorter strips. Lay these down (not overlapping) and dust with flour; roll and cut the other strips in the same way.

You should have eight long strips at this point, each about 5 inches wide (nearly the width of the rollers). Because some doughs stretch more readily than others, the strips may be thin enough. If they are over 15 inches in length and you can nearly see through the

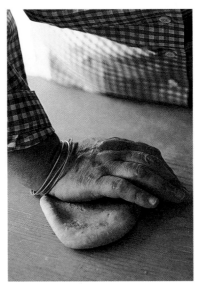

Pressing the dough flat

Dimpling the dough with your fingertips

dough, you can stop rolling—if you want to. But if the pasta is ⅛ inch thick (and the strips are shorter than 15 inches), you should pass them through the next-narrower setting. Roll the dough as thin as you like, as long as it doesn't tear or fall apart. If it does tear, fold the strip in half or thirds (making it shorter and enclosing the tear) and reroll at wider settings.

Set the finished strips down, lightly floured and not overlapping, in the big trays. If necessary, cover a layer of strips with a floured kitchen towel, and rest more strips on top.

Rolling the Dough by Hand

Have your dough at room temperature for rolling. Cut 1 pound of dough into three pieces (5 to 6 ounces each). Work with one piece and keep the others covered. Have flour close at hand for sprinkling when needed.

Lightly flour the work surface—preferably wood—and rub a little on your rolling pin. Press the first piece of dough flat, then dimple it all over with your fingertips. Begin rolling it into a rectangle, about twice as long as it is wide. Working from the center of the dough, roll up and down, left and right. Occasionally, flip the dough over and dust the surface with flour if the dough is sticking; periodically, turn the dough 90 degrees.

When the dough gets thin and floppy, you can also stretch it gently with your hands: grasp the edges and tug the dough on all sides to widen and lengthen it, evenly. Roll and stretch the dough until it is 20 to 24 inches on the long sides and about 10 inches on the short sides.

Hand-cut this sheet of dough into your chosen shape, as detailed below, before rolling out the next piece.

Cutting Pasta Shapes by Hand and by Machine

As soon as you have rolled all your dough pieces through the pasta machine or hand-rolled one piece, you can start cutting the shapes you want. Long flat shapes like tagliatelle (the same as fettuccine), tagliolini, or pappardelle are the quickest to cut (and cook). A machine attachment will cut tagliatelle or tagliolini precisely, but I like hand-cutting and the slightly irregular noodles I get. Details on both meth-

Rolling up and down, working from the center of the dough

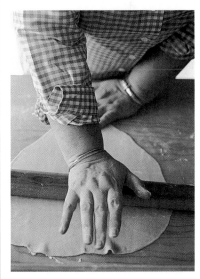

Continuing to roll and stretch the dough

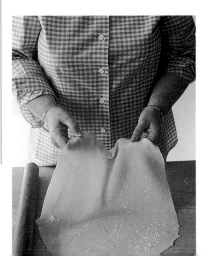

Stretching further with your hands

ods follow. Lacce (shoelaces) are hand-cut thicker strips (shorter than the others) that are also quick to produce and a good shape for doughs that don't roll very thin.

If you are not in a rush, however, try the other shapes shown here: Maltagliati—which means "badly cut"—are small diamond-shaped pieces (or rhomboids, in geometry). Garganelli are little quill-shaped tubes rolled from maltagliati. I especially love the last shape, boccoli, a spiral that resembles a little girl's ringlets (*boccolo* is Italian for a curl). All three are made from long ribbons of dough, so you can easily make some of each from the same batch. Get someone to share the fun!

Keeping Cut Pasta

You can cook all these shapes as soon as they are cut, or let them sit and dry at room temperature until you are ready, but use them within a day. Lay them out on trays as shown in the photos, lightly floured and separated so they don't stick together—arrange long shapes in separate small nests, and other shapes in a single layer. Pasta that has air-dried will take a bit longer to cook.

Folding in the short ends of the dough so they meet in the middle

Folding the strip in half

For papardelle, cutting the strips 1½ inches wide

For tagliatelle, cutting strips ½ inch wide

For tagliolini, cutting strips ⅛ inch wide　Tossing the cut pasta in flour

For lacce, cutting tagliatelle-shaped strips into 3- or 4-inch pieces

To freeze cut pasta for long storage, set the nests or individual pieces in single layers, floured and separated, on trays that fit into your freezer. After they're solidly frozen, pack them in small airtight plastic bags or containers. Don't defrost before cooking; simply drop the frozen pieces into the boiling water.

Three Hand-Cut Long Pastas: Pappardelle, Tagliatelle, and Tagliolini

Have a tray or two, kitchen towels, and flour handy. If you're cutting by hand, you'll need a sharp long-bladed chef's knife. When folding dough for these shapes, make sure any surfaces that will touch are sprinkled with flour so they don't stick together.

Lay out one pasta strip (rolled out by machine) on a cutting board, and dust it lightly with flour.

Fold in the short ends so they meet in the middle, sprinkle with flour if needed, then fold the strip in the middle, like closing a book.

You'll have a small rectangle with four layers of pasta. Slice this rectangle *crosswise* into strips, which will unfold as 15-inch-long noodles.

- For *pappardelle*, cut strips that are 1½ inches wide.

For maltagliati, cutting pasta ribbons into 2-inch-long rhomboids

- For *tagliatelle*, cut strips that are ½ inch wide.
- For *tagliolini*, cut strips that are ⅛ inch wide.

Now unfurl the layered strips by shaking them open (unfold them carefully if they're stuck). Sprinkle, then toss the strips lightly with flour, so they don't stick to each other, and pile them gently in a little nest on the floured tray.

Fold, slice, and unfurl the rest of the dough strips in the same way.

If you rolled dough by hand, fold in the short (10-inch) sides of your pasta sheet to meet in the middle, then fold again like a book. Now you'll have a narrow 10-inch-long rectangle to cut *crosswise* into pappardelle, tagliatelle, or tagliolini.

To cut long shapes with a machine: Most machines have ½-inch-wide rotary cutters for tagliatelle and much narrower cutters for tagliolini. Feed one of your wide strips, lightly floured, into the cutters you want. Support the strip with one hand, and crank with the other. As the pasta is drawn through the cutter, switch hands so you can catch and lift the cut noodles as they emerge.

Shoestring Pasta: Hand-cut Lacce

Lacce should resemble 3-to-4-inch shoelaces. Therefore, they should be cut like tagliatelle, only shorter, and the dough should be twice the thickness of tagliatelle.

Three Short, Unusual Shapes: Maltagliati, Garganelli, and Boccoli

Lay out two or three of your machine-rolled strips on a cutting surface; slice them *lengthwise* into three long ribbons, each about 1¾ inches wide, using a ruler or straight edge to guide your knife blade if you want. (If you've hand-rolled a 10-by-20-inch sheet of dough, slice it in six ribbons of equal width.)

- *Maltagliati:* Cut the long ribbons with diagonal slices into 2-inch rhomboids. Dust them with flour, pick them up with a dough scraper or spatula, and spread them on a lightly floured tray or towel.

- *Garganelli:* First make a bunch of maltagliati. Lightly flour a chopstick or similar-size thin rod. Following the illustration, roll one small piece around the stick, starting at one corner, as you see here.

Seal the roll at the opposite corner, as shown:

For garganelli, rolling maltagliati squares around a chopstick

Pushing the garganelli off

For boccoli, cutting 1-inch slices into a 4-inch ribbon of pasta

Winding the piece around a stick

Pulling it off the stick

Slide the little tube off the stick, and make another. Spread the garganelli on trays as you complete them.

• *Boccoli:* Cut the long ribbons into 4-inch strips. Following the illustrations, with a sharp-pointed small knife, slice two 1-inch slits inside each strip, as shown above.

Make sure you don't slice the edges of the strips. Using the handle of a wooden spoon, starting at one corner of the dough, roll it out diagonally, then slip it off gently. Do the rolling at the corner of your working surface, so that the spoon end of the wooden spoon hangs over the edge, allowing the dough to roll onto the handle. The slits open up when boccoli are cooked, accentuating the shape and allowing sauce to permeate the cylinder.

Get a rod, a stick, or the handle of a wooden spoon that's about ½ inch thick and rub it with flour. Wind one strip around the stick, in a spiral fashion, as above.

Don't overlap the dough as you wrap it, but seal at one end by pressing.

Slide the curl off the stick. Arrange the boccoli on lightly floured trays as you complete them.

The finished boccoli

Basics for Cooking Fresh Pasta

• For 1 pound of pasta, bring 6 quarts of water to a full boil and stir in 1 tablespoon kosher or sea salt. The dough has no salt, so it is particularly important that the cooking water be well salted.

• Before adding the pasta to the water, shake off excess flour, using a strainer or colander or just shaking it in your hands.

• Drop the pasta into the boiling water in several batches, stirring with each addition to separate the pieces.

• Keep the heat high but don't cover the pot. Let the water return to the boil, stirring occasionally. Start timing when the boil resumes.

• Cook at the boil at least until the pasta rises to the top; at that point, many pastas are done (but some are not). Remove and taste a bit of pasta when it surfaces. Cooking times will vary with the composition of the dough, the shape and thinness of the pasta, and the degree to which it dried before cooking.

• Here are some general guides to cooking times:

  • Fresh pastas are not cooked *al dente* like dried pastas. Cook them until they are tender all the way through *and you have tested them*.

  • Tender white-flour pastas will cook the quickest. Rich Man's Golden Pasta (page 158) will be done in as little as 2 minutes. Poor Man's Two-Egg Pasta (page 159) will take a bit longer.

  • Some mixed-flour pastas, like flaxseed and potato pasta, cook quite fast. Heavier, whole-grain pastas, like whole wheat, take considerably longer—about double the time.

  • Flat long pasta cuts will cook more quickly than rolled shapes like garganelli or boccoli.

• Remove pasta from the cooking pot with a spider, tongs, or other tool, let excess water drain into the pot, and drop with clinging water into a skillet containing the sauce.

• Finish the pasta and sauce together following the procedures outlined on page 105.

Egg Pasta with Whole Grains, Ground Beans, Seeds, Nuts, and Spinach?

W hy not? Almost any milled grain—and finely ground seeds, nuts, and dried beans—can be mixed with all-purpose wheat flour to create pasta doughs. Some of these are traditional: whole-wheat, buckwheat, chestnut, and semolina flours, among others, have long been incorporated into pasta by Italian cooks.

The mixed-flour doughs here are just a sample of the diversity of flavors, textures, and (not least important) nutritional qualities we can enjoy in pasta. These days there's an amazing variety of flours available, meeting a growing demand for healthful and flavorful whole foods. Next on my playing-around list are pastas with oat flour, corn flour, fava-bean flour, brown-rice flour, almond meal, pecan meal, and . . . Let me know if you discover any other good ones!

Suggested Shapes and Sauces

Cut into pappardelle and dress with Anytime Tomato Primavera (page 125). Also delicious with Long-Cooking Savoy Cabbage, Bacon, and Mushroom Sauce (page 138), or just Butter and Cheese (page 119).

Rustic sauces with game or sausages are also a good pairing here.

Whole Wheat Pasta

FOR I POUND OF PASTA

Some of the first pastas in Italy, made by the Etruscans and later the Romans, were made out of barley and chickpea flour. When wheat came on the scene, it was milled as whole wheat and used for pasta. We find 100-percent whole wheat a bit dense and hard to digest these days, so I use equal proportions of white and whole wheat here to make a light, fast-cooking pasta with a distinctive taste.

Food-processor mixing recommended, following the directions on page 160.

DRY

I cup all-purpose flour

I cup whole-wheat flour

WET

2 whole large eggs

¼ cup extra-virgin olive oil

3 tablespoons water

FRESH PASTA WITH NUTS: MIXING, KNEADING, AND CUTTING

Ground nuts can be incorporated into pasta doughs with great success. Try the ones I give here—walnuts in buckwheat dough, and hazelnuts in ceci dough—and experiment with other combinations, using almonds and pecans too. Follow these guidelines whenever you are adding nuts:

For a 1-pound batch of dough, start with a generous ⅓ cup of whole nuts (or halves) to get ¼ to ⅓ cup of ground nuts. First toast whole nuts lightly in a dry pan to bring out flavor. After they have cooled, pulse them in a food processor into tiny bits, smaller than ⅛ inch. This will take only 1 or 2 seconds—don't grind them into a powder. Pick out any remaining larger nut pieces; crush them smaller—or eat them.

Mix the dough by hand or food processor, as usual. When you turn it out for final kneading, spread the dough into a small rectangle and sprinkle the nut bits on top. Fold the dough over the nuts, and knead as you would normally, distributing the nuts well, until it is smooth and shiny; then let it rest.

To roll a dough with nuts using a pasta machine: Divide the dough in quarters and roll each piece slowly, at the widest setting, twelve times, folding and turning between rolls. Then roll through narrower machine settings. If you see any nut pieces that are making the dough tear, remove them. If a strip does tear, fold it over and reroll at a wider setting to repair it. Roll the dough as thin as possible (it will never be as thin as plain dough, however).

Cut any dough with nuts by hand, crosswise, into lacce, or shoe-strings (page 168). Or fold the strips and cut lengthwise to form pappardelle, as shown in the photos on page 166.

Buckwheat Pasta

FOR 1 POUND OF PASTA

I love buckwheat for the earthy, gritty character it brings to many dishes. Flour made from the buckwheat seed (it's not a relative of wheat) is used in Japanese soba noodles and is traditional in Italian pasta too. In the Valtellina they make a dish called pizzoccheri, *buckwheat pappardelle dressed with cabbage and bacon and Fontina.*

Food-processor mixing recommended, following the directions on page 160.

DRY

1 cup all-purpose flour

1 cup buckwheat flour

WET

2 large whole eggs

¼ cup extra-virgin olive oil

3 tablespoons water

Suggested Shapes and Sauces

Pappardelle with Long-Cooking Savoy Cabbage, Bacon, and Mushroom Sauce (page 138)—a wonderful winter pasta.

A tomato-based sauce, such as Mushroom Ragù (page 141) or Slow-Cooked Summer Tomato and Eggplant Sauce (page 259).

Do not smother the pasta with too much sauce.

Buckwheat Pasta with Walnuts

A few spoonfuls of chopped walnuts lend marvelous texture and flavor to buckwheat pasta. Use about ⅓ cup of finely chopped walnuts for 1 pound of pasta; see box, facing page, for details on incorporating nuts into dough.

Suggested Shapes and Sauces

Hand-cut lacce

Dress with Butter, Fresh Sage, and Walnut Sauce (page 120). For convenience, chop up the walnuts for the sauce when you're processing the nuts for the dough, but leave them larger, in ⅛-to-¼-inch nuggets.

Semolina Pasta

DRY

I cup all-purpose flour

I cup semolina flour

WET

2 large whole eggs

¼ cup extra-virgin olive oil

3 tablespoons water

Semolina is the grind of durum wheat—the wheat that makes the best dry pasta. Here, mixed one-to-one with all-purpose flour, it makes a fresh pasta that is nutty and resilient to the bite.

Food-processor mixing recommended, following the directions on page 160.

Suggested Shapes and Sauces

Any shape.
Good with vegetable and nut sauces.

Flaxseed Pasta

FOR I POUND OF PASTA

DRY

I ½ cups all-purpose flour

½ cup ground flaxseed meal

WET

2 large whole eggs

¼ cup extra-virgin olive oil

3 tablespoons water

If you are at all interested in eating healthfully from "whole foods," you have probably learned about flaxseed, hailed as a great source of fiber, beneficial fatty acids, and other good stuff. But did you know that it makes a really tasty fresh pasta too? Note that you need ground flaxseed meal— available in whole-food markets—for this dough.

Food-processor mixing recommended, following the directions on page 160.

Suggested Shapes and Sauces

Cut in any shape you like (easy to work).
Delicious with nothing more than olive oil and cheese (page 107).
Aglio e Olio (page 104).
A vegetable sauce such as Anchovies, Capers, and Fresh Tomatoes (page 91).

Cornmeal or Polenta Pasta

For this pasta use instant polenta flour. The cornmeal gives the pasta great texture, flavor, and color.

Food-processor mixing recommended, following the directions on page 160.

Suggested Shapes and Sauces

Cut in wide strips of polenta pasta.
Dress with a simple tomato sauce and fresh mozzarella.
Also good with *Brodetto* with Lobster and Corn (page 299).

DRY

1 cup all-purpose flour, plus a little for kneading
1 cup instant polenta flour

WET

2 large whole eggs
¼ cup extra-virgin olive oil
2 tablespoons water

Barley Pasta

This is one of the oldest pastas in Italy. The Romans would call it lasagnum—wide strips of pasta dressed with honey, cheese, and herbs. I love this pasta. When cooked, it is light and has a silky texture.

Food-processor mixing recommended, following the directions on page 160.

Suggested Shapes and Sauces

Cut in lacce (shoestrings) or boccoli (curls).
Dress with complex sauces, such as Bolognese *Antica* (page 143) or Asparagus, Green Pea, and Scallion Sauce (page 135).

DRY

1 ⅓ cups all-purpose flour
⅔ cup barley flour

WET

2 large whole eggs
¼ cup extra-virgin olive oil
3 tablespoons water

Ceci (Garbanzo Bean) Flour Pasta

DRY

1 ⅓ cups all-purpose flour

⅔ cup garbanzo-bean flour

WET

2 large whole eggs

¼ cup extra-virgin olive oil

3 tablespoons water

Flour from dried ceci—the Italian name for garbanzo beans or chickpeas—is one of a number of bean flours with which one can make pasta. Like the others, this yields a good pasta with a different nuance of flavor—complex, buttery, with a tinge of sweetness from the bean. It's a great carrier for vegetable, game, or nut sauces.

Food-processor mixing recommended, following the directions on page 160.

Suggested Shapes and Sauces

Cut the dough into garganelli, tagliatelle, maltagliati, or boccoli.
Dress with Sauce of *Broccoli di Rape* with *Ceci* and Bacon (page 114).

Ceci Pasta with Hazelnuts

Another good pairing of pasta and nuts. Incorporate ⅓ cup of finely chopped hazelnuts into the ceci dough (see box on page 172 for details on incorporating nuts into dough).

Suggested Shapes and Sauces

Cut by hand into lacce, and dress with Butter and Fresh Basil Sauce (page 118).

Chestnut Pasta

Italians enjoy many traditional foods made with farina di castagne—chestnut flour—especially cakes and sweets. Pasta with part chestnut flour is delicious too, as I hope you will discover. Imported farina di castagne is widely available in specialty markets (and from Web sites).

Food-processor mixing recommended, following the directions on page 160.

Suggested Shapes and Sauces

Be sure to try chestnut pappardelle with Butter, Dried Chestnut, and Rosemary Sauce (page 121). Rosemary and chestnuts have an established affinity; fresh rosemary often adorns *castagnaccio*, the famed rustic chestnut bread of Tuscany.

DRY

1 cup all-purpose flour

1 cup chestnut flour

WET

2 large whole eggs

¼ cup extra-virgin olive oil

3 tablespoons water

Potato Flour Pasta

Potato flour (not potato starch) makes pasta with a delicious and distinctly potato-ey flavor. The dough will feel stiff when just mixed, but after resting it gets soft and easy to roll and cut.

Food-processor mixing recommended, following the directions on page 160.

Suggested Shapes and Sauces

Cut into tagliatelle or tagliolini.
  Dress simply with Butter and Fresh Sage Sauce (page 118).
  Also delicious dressed with Bolognese or other meat sauce.

DRY

1⅓ cups all-purpose flour

⅔ cup potato flour

WET

2 large whole eggs, plus spoonfuls
    of beaten egg if needed

¼ cup extra-virgin olive oil

3 tablespoons water, plus spoonfuls
    if needed

Spinach Pasta Dough

*S*pinach pasta is essential to Pasticciata Bolognese (page 200), but you can
enjoy it in all the cuts and shapes of fresh pasta.

It is best to start prepping the spinach well ahead of time, as detailed in the recipe, for
the best texture. You can always freeze the dough until you need it. Spinach pasta is usually more moist than other fresh pastas and so will cook more quickly.

ABOUT 20 OUNCES SPINACH DOUGH, ENOUGH FOR ONE
PASTICCIATA BOLOGNESE OR CUT PASTA TO SERVE 8

One 10-ounce box frozen chopped
spinach, or 10 ounces fresh small-
leaf spinach

2 cups all-purpose flour, plus more for
kneading and rolling

2 large whole eggs

2 egg yolks

1 tablespoon extra-virgin olive oil

Preparing the Spinach in Advance

If you're using frozen spinach, start thawing it a day before making
the pasta. Take the frozen block out of the box, put it in a colander
over a bowl, and let it thaw completely and drain for a day in the refrigerator, or overnight at room temperature. Squeeze the thawed
spinach by handfuls to press out as much liquid as possible.

If you're using fresh spinach, try to start a day ahead. Wash it thoroughly in several changes of cold water, remove the stems, and cook
it for 5 minutes or more in a large volume of boiling water. Remove
the spinach from the pot, and let it drain and cool in a colander;
then squeeze out as much water as possible. If possible, let it drain
and dry in the colander overnight. Squeeze the spinach again the
next day.

With either kind of spinach, when you think you've squeezed it
enough, squeeze it again, by handfuls, using all your might. The drier
the spinach, the better the pasta.

Puréeing the Spinach and Making the Dough in a Food Processor

Crumble the spinach into the food-processor bowl and purée it thoroughly, scraping it off the sides. With the spinach and the blade in
place, add the flour and pulse to blend with the spinach, scraping as
necessary.

Whisk together the whole eggs, yolks, and oil in a bowl or measuring cup with a spout. With the food processor running, pour in the liquid ingredients on top of the green flour. Process for about 30 seconds, scrape down the workbowl, and scrape in all the egg residue too. Process another 20 to 30 seconds, until the dough has started to come together in a ball on the blade.

Turn the dough onto a lightly floured surface and knead briefly, until it's smooth. Wrap well in plastic wrap, and let rest at room temperature for 30 minutes before rolling. Store for 2 days in the refrigerator, or for 3 months in the freezer.

Homemade Ravioli, Big and Easy

The ravioli in the coming pages are different from the ones in my earlier books. These *raviolo grande* are more than 4 inches, with a plump pillow of stuffing in the middle.

I'm particularly fond of these ravioli because the pasta component is as important—and delicious—as the filling. Whereas the dough in small ravioli is too often compressed and thick, here the pasta retains its perfect texture—and there's more of it to enjoy. In the master method below, I'll show you how to roll out the dough and fill it so the ravioli stay thin and airy, with distinct top and bottom layers. This method, in fact, is simpler than the one used for small ravioli. Because you're working with larger dimensions, it is easier to seal and shape the ravioli correctly. And it all goes faster: there's less dough and filling to make, and less fuss in cutting and cooking.

You follow the same method with any of the fillings. All use uniform amounts: 2 cups of savory filling to stuff into 1 pound of Poor Man's Pasta dough (page 159) to yield twenty big ravioli. Since two or three ravioli make a nice *primo*, or first course, and four or five make a hearty main course, no one will go hungry, I am sure.

I've also chosen the fillings that can be done in a reasonable amount of time, most of them right on the spot—that is, you just put raw ingredients together and then stuff the dough. These simple fillings cook right in the pasta and have a delightful freshness about them. Then I show you how to take a small portion of one of my long-cooked meat sauces (from the recipes starting on page 134)—or from a large meat dish in chapter 5—and transform it almost instantly into a rich ravioli filling with a matching sauce. If you've got some sauce or roast leftovers in the refrigerator—or have saved some in the freezer—you can easily come up with your own creations.

Simple Ricotta Ravioli

*T*his is a simple, pure version of cheese ravioli, without the eggs that are usually added to firm up the filling. Use fresh whole-milk ricotta with large curds and drain it thoroughly to get the best consistency. With creamy fillings such as this one, I feel that a slightly thicker dough provides more texture and is preferable to a very thin dough. If you roll your dough strips to get eighteen or twenty ravioli—following the guidelines below—that's better than trying to stretch them to get twenty-four.

All you need is enough sauce to coat the ravioli lightly. So those small portions of sauces you have saved in the freezer might be just enough to dress a batch.

FOR FILLING ABOUT 20 RAVIOLI

12 ounces (about 1½ cups) fresh whole-milk ricotta, well drained (see page 181)

2 tablespoons or so extra-virgin olive oil

3 ounces fresh mozzarella, cut in ¼-inch cubes (about ⅓ cup)

½ teaspoon or more coarse-grained sea salt (see page 350)

½ teaspoon or so coarsely ground fresh white pepper

Filling the Ravioli

Following the master method, page 189, roll dough strips for filling.

For each *raviolo*, scoop a scant tablespoon of ricotta, shape it round, and drop in place. Press a shallow well in the soft top of the round and fill with drops of olive oil—barely ¼ teaspoon on each portion.

Press two or three cubes of mozzarella into the ricotta round, covering the oil. Sprinkle a good pinch of sea salt on and around the ricotta; do the same with a pinch of white pepper. Cover and cut ravioli as detailed in the master method below.

Finishing the Ravioli

Cook and sauce ravioli as on page 192. Remove pan from heat, sprinkle over them the freshly grated cheese, and serve.

FOR FINISHING

½ cup freshly grated Parmigiano-Reggiano or Grana Padano

Good Sauces for This . . .

Tomato sauces, the fresher the better: Slow-Cooked Summer Tomato Sauce (page 256), Marinara Sauce with Fresh Basil (page 130), or the Two-Minute Fresh Tomato and Basil Sauce (page 183), even frozen Simple Tomato Sauce (page 132), with shredded fresh basil.

Fresh Shrimp and Tomato Ravioli

*S*mall shrimp cook right inside these very fresh-tasting ravioli. You don't need fancy big shrimp for this: small and inexpensive "41/50s" (which means there are forty-one to fifty shrimp in a pound) are a good size, or even smaller rock shrimp. Make the simple flavored butter a bit ahead of time, and chill it in the freezer to facilitate handling.

MAKES 2 CUPS OF FILLING, FOR 20 TO 24 RAVIOLI

FOR THE FLAVORED BUTTER

3 tablespoons soft unsalted butter

1 ½ tablespoons chopped fresh Italian parsley

Freshly ground black pepper, a few grinds to taste

FOR THE SHRIMP

10 ounces small raw shrimp, 41/50 size or smaller

5 ounces whole fresh tomato, peeled, seeded, and juiced (½ cup) (see tips on fresh tomato peeling and seeding, page 261)

3 tablespoons shredded fresh basil leaves

¼ teaspoon salt

FOR FINISHING

2 tablespoons extra-virgin olive oil

Preparing the Filling

For the flavored butter, blend the soft butter, chopped parsley, and freshly ground black pepper well in a bowl. Scrape it onto a piece of plastic wrap, fold over the plastic, and shape the butter into a flat square about ⅓ inch thick, like a big butter pat. Chill in the freezer until very hard. Cut the square checkerboard-style into twenty-five little cubes, five rows of five; separate them and keep chilled.

To prepare the shrimp, remove the shells and devein them, rinse well, and dry. Cut the shrimp crosswise into pieces about ¾ inch long (halves or thirds, depending on their size—you may not have to cut tiny shrimp at all). Chop or dice the tomato flesh into small chunks, no larger than ¼ inch. Toss the shrimp, tomatoes, shredded basil, and salt together in bowl.

Filling the Ravioli

Following the master method, page 189, roll dough strips for filling. For each *raviolo*, drop in place a tablespoon of shrimp-tomato filling,

Good Sauces for This . . .

Two-Minute Fresh Tomato and Basil Sauce (page 183) (to make it easy, prep the tomatoes and basil for the sauce and the shrimp stuffing at the same time).

Aglio e Olio (page 104) and marinara sauce (page 130).

including in each portion two or three shrimp pieces and some tomato bits; then set a cube of flavored butter on top. Cover and cut ravioli as detailed in the master method.

Finishing the Ravioli

Cook the ravioli, transfer them to a skillet, and dress with sauce (see master method on page 192). Remove pan from heat, and drizzle with extra-virgin olive oil (1 tablespoon for a skillet with ten or twelve ravioli) and serve.

TWO-MINUTE FRESH TOMATO AND BASIL SAUCE

This is a fine fast sauce for Shrimp and Tomato Ravioli and Simple Ricotta Ravioli (preceding recipes) as well as for Potato, Leek, and Bacon Ravioli (page 186). Make the sauce *just* before the ravioli come out of the pot, for the freshest taste. You should definitely peel the tomatoes for this: see my method on page 261.

FOR 20 *RAVIOLI GRANDI* OR 1 POUND OF PASTA

¼ cup extra-virgin olive oil

4 tablespoons sliced garlic

Flesh from 1½ pounds ripe fresh tomatoes, peeled, seeded, and juiced, roughly chopped into ⅓-inch pieces (2 cups), juices reserved

¼ teaspoon salt

4 tablespoons shredded fresh basil leaves

In a 14-inch skillet, toast the garlic slices in the olive oil for 1 minute. Scatter in the chopped tomato, sprinkle on the salt, add the reserved juices and a few tablespoons of pasta water, then toss for a few more minutes, just barely cooking the tomatoes. Turn off the heat and stir in the basil. Toss with hot pasta right out of the cooking pot. Use half the sauce for dressing each batch of 10 *ravioli grandi*.

Here are easy variations of the fresh fillings on these pages:

Ricotta and Goat Cheese Ravioli
Use the formula and procedure for Simple Ricotta Ravioli, page 181, but replace half the ricotta (about 6 ounces) with an equal amount of fresh, creamy goat cheese.

I recommend the same tomato sauces or *cacio e pepe* sauce (see facing page).

Mozzarella, Tomato, and Basil Ravioli
Cut 12 ounces of fresh mozzarella into ⅓-inch cubes—about 1½ cups. Prepare ½ cup of fresh tomato, peeled and chopped—as you would for Shrimp and Tomato Ravioli above—and toss with 3 tablespoons shredded fresh basil leaves and a pinch of salt. Mound each *raviolo* with 1 tablespoon of mozzarella pieces and a teaspoon of tomato-basil.

I recommend saucing this with Raw Summer Tomato Sauce, page 265.

Fresh Pear and Pecorino Ravioli

T his delicate and quite simple ravioli is a lovely way to enjoy the affinity of pear and cheese. The filling is a lively blend of shredded ripe pear, shredded 3-to-6-months-aged Pecorino Romano (it should be semisoft), and mascarpone—just stirred together at the last moment.

MAKES 2 CUPS OF FILLING, FOR 20 TO 24 RAVIOLI

Preparing the Filling

Peel and core the pear, and shred it against the large holes of a box grater. Stir the shreds with the shredded cheese in a bowl, and blend in the mascarpone.

Filling the Ravioli

Following the master method, page 189, roll dough strips for filling. For each *raviolo*, scoop a scant tablespoon of the filling, shape it round and drop in place. Cover and cut ravioli by master method.

Saucing in the Skillet and Finishing

Cook the ravioli as in master method, page 192. Meanwhile, heat the butter until simmering in a large skillet and thin it with a cup of the boiling pasta water. Lay the cooked ravioli in the skillet, and coat with the hot butter. Remove the pan from the heat, and sprinkle over it the grated aged Pecorino, mixing gently so the cheese begins to melt into a sauce, then grind coarse black pepper all around.

A ½-pound firm ripe Bartlett pear (or 2 small pears); pears of most varieties will make a good filling, as long as they are ripe but firm

8 ounces 3-to-6-months-aged Pecorino Romano, freshly shredded

1½ tablespoons chilled mascarpone

FOR *CACIO E PEPE* SAUCE

6 ounces (1½ sticks) butter

4 ounces mild 12-months-aged Pecorino Romano, grated

Abundant coarsely ground black pepper, to taste

Good Sauces for This . . .

I serve these with a melted-butter sauce and sprinkles of black pepper and more Pecorino Romano—details are in the recipe. If you can, find a mild, one-year-old *aged* Pecorino for the finishing touch.

Potato, Leek, and Bacon Ravioli

*A*lmost every region of northern Italy has some version of potato-stuffed ravioli. The potato is a constant, whereas the flavoring may change, from onion to chard to raisins to pine nuts. You can come up with some of your favorites. But in my house everybody loves potato-and-bacon ravioli, even fussy kids. You can do all the cooking ahead of time if you want—just mash up the filling while it's still warm, then refrigerate.

MAKES 2 CUPS OF FILLING, FOR 20 TO 24 RAVIOLI

¾ pound Yukon Gold potatoes (3 small potatoes are best)

3 tablespoons extra-virgin olive oil

About 5 ounces bacon, cut crosswise in ¼-inch strips (¾ cup)

2 medium leeks, washed, drained, and finely chopped (1½ cups)

⅛ teaspoon salt, or more to taste

Freshly ground black pepper to taste

½ cup grated Parmigiano-Reggiano or Grana Padano for the filling

FOR FINISHING AND SERVING

1 cup grated Parmigiano-Reggiano or Grana Padano

Preparing the Filling

Cook the whole, unpeeled potatoes in a pot of *unsalted* water to cover at a steady boil for 20 minutes or longer, until just cooked through. Don't let them crack or get mushy on the outside. Let them cool briefly, then peel and slice them into rounds, ¼ inch thick.

Heat the oil and the bacon pieces in a skillet over medium heat, stirring occasionally, for 3 or 4 minutes, until the bacon is sizzling and has rendered much of its fat. Stir in the leeks and cook another 3 minutes or so, until they're wilted and sizzling. Spread the potato slices in the pan, season with salt and pepper, and toss with the bacon and leeks.

Cook for 8 minutes or more over medium-high heat, breaking up the potatoes into chunks. Spread and press the filling flat in the pan, and let caramelize for a couple of minutes. Turn the pieces, press, and fry; then repeat. When the filling is thoroughly cooked and has started to color, scrape it into a mixing bowl. Cool briefly, then crush the potatoes some more with a fork (I like to have little chunks left); add salt, pepper, and cheese to the filling to taste.

Good Sauces for This . . .

Butter and Fresh Sage Sauce (page 118) is the best, but Fresh Tomato Sauce (page 183) would go well too.

Filling the Ravioli

Roll dough strips following the master method, page 189. For each *raviolo*, scoop up a heaping tablespoon of potato filling, shape it round, and set in place. Cover and cut ravioli.

Finishing the Ravioli

Cook and sauce ravioli as on page 192. Remove pan from heat, sprinkle the freshly grated cheese over, and serve.

MAKING RAVIOLI WITH MEATY SAUCES

With a pint or so of a long-cooking meat sauce—or even a chunk of tender meat and a cup of pan sauce from one of the big meat recipes in chapter 5—you have both the filling and sauce for ravioli at hand.

Follow the procedures below to transform any of these into ravioli:

Pork or Duck *Guazzetto* (pages 151, 154)

Long-cooked *Sugo* and Meatballs, turkey or sausage, page 146

Salsa *Genovese* with Braised Pork Shoulder and pan sauce (page 348)

Roast Pork Shoulder and pan sauce (page 345)

Braised Beef Shoulder Roast with Venetian Spice and pan sauce (page 351)

Roast Breast of Veal with some of its stuffing and pan sauce (page 354)

Ragù alla Bolognese with some of its meat (page 143)

Separate the Sugo *from the Meat*

To fill and dress a whole batch of ravioli you'll need at least a cup of cooked meat and a cup of sauce. If you're using duck or pork *guazzetto*, take the meat off the bone and shred it or, even better, pass it through a meat grinder. Do the same with braised or roasted beef or pork. If you're using meatballs, crumble up two or three in a bowl to measure a cup of meat.

If you've already shredded and blended your meat with the cooking sauce (as I do with *guazzetti* and *salsa Genovese*), warm up a pint until the sauce liquefies, and pour it through a strainer. Press and scrape the meat in the sieve to separate the fibers and release more liquid—it should be fairly dry. (Use this sieving procedure to help shred and dry any moist meat you want to use as a filling.)

Prepare and Portion the Filling

Put the cup of shredded or ground meat in a bowl and blend in the following, to firm up the consistency and freshen the flavor:

- 2 tablespoons fine dry bread crumbs
- 2 tablespoons freshly grated Parmigiano-Reggiano or Grana Padano
- 1 tablespoon chopped fresh Italian parsley
- 1 teaspoon fine lemon zest

If pieces of meat passed through a meat grinder or chopped are too dry, add a few tablespoons of the sauce.

Adjust the amounts proportionally if you have more or less meat. The filling is now ready: scoop a tablespoon of filling—or a bit more or less—and mound in place on rolled strips of dough, in the usual way (see page 189). Cover and cut ravioli.

Cooking, Saucing, and Finishing

Cook meat-filled ravioli as usual (see page 192). Heat the cup of sauce in the large skillet and loosen it with a cup or so of boiling pasta water. Dress ravioli with this warm sauce, remove from the heat, and scatter ½ cup or more freshly grated Parmigiano-Reggiano or Grana Padano on top.

Master Method:
How to Roll, Fill,
and Form Big Ravioli

If you have made ravioli from my previous books, you will find this method is different. Instead of folding dough over the filling—which can be, literally, quite a stretch—you make separate strips of dough for the base and for the top of the ravioli. I think you will find this approach quite manageable—even if you are a novice at rolling pasta dough—and, because the finished pieces are larger, you'll have more room for adjusting your measurements (or making mistakes).

When making ravioli, though, it is always important to work quickly once you have rolled out the dough. If the dough surface dries out, it will be more difficult to work with and harder to seal the edges of the ravioli. Therefore, before you begin rolling, make sure you have all these items ready:

1-pound batch of Poor Man's Two-Egg Pasta dough (page 159), at room temperature

Finished filling or prepped filling ingredients, ready for portioning

Pasta machine and a large work surface

Flour for sprinkling

1 egg, well beaten, and a small pastry brush

A round tablespoon measure, or a very small ice-cream scoop, or other utensil to make small mounds of filling the size of a walnut

Rotary pastry cutter (pastry wheel) with a sharp wheel, fluted or straight, or a sharp knife for cutting the ravioli

A large tray or baking sheet, lined with a clean kitchen towel or parchment (that's the easiest to handle) or wax paper, lightly floured, and extra towels for covering the dough and the finished ravioli

ROLLING A NICE WIDE STRIP OF DOUGH

For these ravioli, your strips must be at least 5 inches wide. You can achieve this width when you first start rolling and folding the dough on the widest machine setting, as detailed in basic procedures for pasta dough (page 163). Repeat this step until your original piece is almost exactly 10 inches in length, fold it in half so it's 5 inches long, then feed that (doubled) edge into the rollers. Now you will be working with a 5-inch strip, and it will keep that width, or even get wider, as the dough stretches in length. But do not pull the dough through the rollers at any time—if you do, you'll lose your width.

If rolling by hand, roll first up and down until dough is about 10 inches long, then turn the dough 90 degrees and proceed to roll until it is about 20 to 24 inches long. Turn the dough 90 degrees back and forth to reach the right thickness and rectangular shape. To help stretch the dough, between rollings, press it lightly outward with the palm of your hands.

The dough for the ravioli rolled thin and wide

Brushing a border of beaten egg around each mound

Rolling the Dough

Cut the dough into four pieces. Work with one piece at a time, and keep the others moist in a closed plastic bag. Roll the first piece of dough using the machine method detailed on page 163—make sure your strips are 5 inches wide on the first setting (see box, page 189). When you have stretched the dough to approximately 20 inches—having narrowed the setting twice—cut it crosswise into two 10-inch strips. Roll each of these to 20 inches—long enough for five ravioli. Measurements need not be exact; if your dough stretches to 24 inches, make six ravioli; if your strips are a bit shorter, that's all right too.

Filling and Forming the Ravioli

Lay the two strips out on a very lightly floured surface. The strips should be the same length and width; stretch them gently by hand to widen or lengthen as needed. If one strip is clearly wider than the other, use that as a top strip to drape over the filling. Keep the strips covered with a moist cloth to prevent drying.

With a scoop or a spoon (or your fingers), place a measured amount of filling in a mound on the left or right end of your designated bottom strip. The center of the mound should be 2 inches in from the edge. Place the next portion of filling 4 inches from the first, measuring center to center of the mounds. You should have room for five or six mounds on the strip, as shown in the photo. Press the top of the mounds lightly to flatten and spread them just a bit.

Brush a thin stripe of beaten egg along the top, bottom, and side edges of the dough strip and right in between each mound of filling, as shown in the photo.

Pick up the top strip and drape it over the filling mounds, lining up the edges with the bottom dough strip on all sides, and stretching it gently so it covers the bottom completely.

Now press the dough layers together lightly, *but only along the stripes of egg "glue."* Do not press the dough together in the clear area around the filling mounds—in fact, you want to leave a bit of air space in each of the ravioli. If you see a *big* bubble of air around the

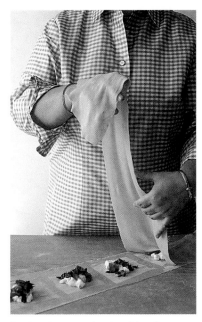

Laying the second strip of dough on top

Trimming the edges with a ravioli cutter

Cutting out the individual large squares

filling, though, push it out gently before you've pressed the edges together. Press the filling, flattening it lightly.

With your pastry-cutting wheel, cut along the top, bottom, and side edges of the ravioli strip in straight lines, trimming away as little of the dough as possible, as shown in photo; then cut in between the mounds, separating the ravioli, as shown in photo. (You can save and cook the dough trimmings, if you want, but don't try to reroll them.)

Arrange the finished ravioli on the lightly floured towel-lined or parchment-lined tray—check each one, and pinch closed any edges that may not be well sealed. Cover with a cloth, and make more ravioli from the next piece of dough.

A plate of *ravioli grande*

Master Method:
How to Cook, Sauce,
and Serve Big Ravioli

Ravioli, like most of the pasta dishes in this chapter, are boiled in a large pot and dressed with sauce in a large skillet. The important difference with ravioli—in particular these wide, thin big ravioli—is that you don't want them piled on top of each other while cooking or in the skillet, lest they stick together or break open. Use the *widest* pot you have for cooking (8-quart capacity or larger) and, if possible, two large skillets for the saucing, since even a 14-inch pan can only hold ten or twelve big ravioli at a time.

If you are serving twenty or more ravioli, you will probably need to cook them in batches, following the basic steps below. When the first batch of ravioli is cooked, lay them in the skillet with part of the sauce already well heated; coat with sauce and let them sit while you cook the rest of the ravioli. Dress with the remainder of the sauce in another skillet. If you only have one large skillet, transfer the first batch to a large warm serving platter when the second batch is almost ready to come out of the pot. Use the empty skillet for saucing once again.

Of course, if you'd rather not rush and worry, just cook, sauce, and enjoy your ravioli one batch after another. They'll all be perfectly hot and fresh, and your family or friends will not mind waiting, I am sure.

Here's an overview of cooking ravioli with any filling or sauce. (Refer to earlier sections for details on cooking pasta, page 98, and saucing in a skillet, page 105)

- Bring 6 quarts of salted water to a boil in a wide pot.

- Heat the amount of sauce you'll need in a large skillet, and keep it warm.

- Give the ravioli a final pinch around the edges to seal, then drop them quickly but gently into the boiling water—taking care not to splash your hands with hot water. Cook only ten ravioli at once, unless you know your pot can accommodate more.

- Stir gently with a wooden spoon to make sure the ravioli are not sticking together.

- Bring the water back to a full boil over high heat and start timing. Lower the heat slightly if the ravioli are being tossed around and might break.

- After a few moments, the ravioli will rise to the surface of the water. Using a slotted spatula or a wire spider, gently move them around so none are trapped underneath. Occasionally dunk, separate, and flip them over so they cook evenly on all surfaces and don't stick. (Caution! Use a *smooth* utensil: spiders sometimes have bits of wire that can puncture the ravioli.)

- Cook the ravioli for 3 to 3½ minutes. A good indication of doneness is when the top dough shrinks and tightly encloses the mound of filling (resembling a Chinese dumpling!). If you're not sure whether the pasta has been cooked through, taste a portion from the sealed edge, where the dough is thickest.

- Have a folded kitchen towel in one hand. With the other hand, lift out one *raviolo* (or two, side by side) on your slotted, smooth utensil and rest it momentarily on the towel—this will drain off and absorb excess water. Slide each *raviolo* into the skillet; continue to remove and drain the others.

- Keep the ravioli in one layer and coat them all over with hot sauce, spooning it on top of the ravioli and shaking the pan so they don't stick to the bottom. Keep the heat low while saucing; turn it off if the ravioli will rest in the pan.

- When ready to serve, remove the pan from the heat and sprinkle cheese or oil if suggested in the preceding recipes.

- Arrange individual portions of ravioli on warm plates and pour or spoon over any sauce left in the pan.

STORING RAVIOLI UNTIL YOU ARE READY TO COOK

You can make ravioli ahead of time. Just arrange them on a tray as directed and keep them covered with a towel or plastic wrap. If you will be cooking them within an hour (or two), leave them at room temperature; otherwise, refrigerate. Ravioli can keep this way for 2 to 3 hours.

I prefer not to freeze uncooked ravioli, since the brief cooking time that the pasta needs is not enough to cook the frozen filling, particularly with these ravioli, which will be overcooked by the time the filling has thawed and cooked through.

If you have cooked ravioli left, keep them refrigerated covered with plastic wrap, making sure they don't overlap. To reheat, put some sauce in a sauté pan, lay ravioli alongside each other, top with additional sauce— making sure there is enough sauce to reheat them, since the pasta will absorb sauce while reheating. Reheat, covered, over medium heat, for 8 to 10 minutes. Top with cheese, spoon on any remaining sauce, and serve.

Baked Pastas

Baked dishes always reveal another dimension of pasta flavor and texture. You'll find this true, I hope, in both the everyday casseroles made with dry pasta and, especially, in the baked fresh pasta dishes. For the first time in any of my books, I've included recipes for a lasagna and a *pasticciata* with many layers of fresh homemade pasta. If you love making and cooking fresh pasta, as I do, these will certainly open a new territory for you to explore.

Baked Shells with Cherry Tomatoes

Y ou can make this colorful and fresh-tasting dish anytime with a batch of Twenty-Minute Marinara Sauce and cherry or grape tomatoes, which are in the market almost year-round and often are sweeter than large tomatoes.

This is one baked dish in which I use fresh mozzarella in the filling. I love its texture and fresh taste in uncooked or quick-cooked pastas, and these can be lost in long cooking. Buy small whole mozzarella balls, an inch in diameter, if you can. Sometimes they are called bocconcini, *little mouthfuls*, but in my neighborhood the supermarket calls them ciliegine, *little cherries*. Toss them whole with the hot pasta so they keep their integrity in the baking dish—you don't want them to melt away like shredded mozzarella on top.

SERVES 6

Preheat the oven to 400°. Butter the bottom and sides of the baking dish, and spread half the marinara sauce in the bottom.

Cook the shells until slightly underdone, a minute or two less than package directions. While the pasta is cooking, heat the remainder of the sauce in the skillet.

Drain the cooked pasta in a colander, shake off excess water, and dump it into the pan. Toss pasta with sauce until coated, over medium-low heat, then toss with the sliced tomatoes for a minute or so to heat and soften them, but don't break them up.

Off the heat, toss the shells with half the grated hard cheese and half the shredded mozzarella, and turn everything into the baking dish. Scatter the fresh mozzarella balls or pieces and the shredded basil all over, and fold them into the pasta.

Spread the pasta level in the dish, sprinkle the remaining shredded cheese all over, and then the remaining grated cheese.

Bake, uncovered, for 30 minutes, or until the top is crusty and nicely colored.

2 tablespoons butter for the baking dish

3 cups Marinara Sauce (page 130)

1 pound dried pasta shells—preferably large (not giant), about 1½ inches

10 ounces (1 box) cherry or grape tomatoes, cut in half

¾ cup freshly grated Parmigiano-Reggiano or Grana Padano

1½ cups shredded low-moisture mozzarella (see box, page 197)

10 ounces fresh mozzarella, small whole *bocconcini* or *ciliegine,* or cut into 1-inch pieces if larger

¼ cup shredded fresh basil leaves

RECOMMENDED EQUIPMENT

A 14-inch skillet for tossing the pasta and fillings

A 3-quart baking dish for a heaping dish, or a 4-quart dish for a shallower dish with a larger, crispy top

Cavatappi with Sugo and Meatballs

If you happen to have some meatballs and sugo left over from the recipe on page 146, here's a simple baked dish that will put them to good use. Just toss them with cooked cavatappi—spiral pastas that do look like corkscrews—and cheeses, then bake.

You can also bake this in a mold and turn it out, as a lovely golden torta. Press the filling to fit into a 10-cup Bundt pan or soufflé dish, generously buttered and coated with bread crumbs. Sprinkle bread crumbs and grated cheese on the top (which will become the bottom), and bake at 400° until the edges are golden.

SERVES 6

1 pound cavatappi

2 cups *Sugo* (page 146)

4 tablespoons butter

6 to 8 turkey or sausage meatballs (page 149), sliced in ¼-inch rounds

1 cup freshly grated Parmigiano-Reggiano or Grana Padano

2 cups shredded low-moisture mozzarella or Muenster

RECOMMENDED EQUIPMENT

A 14-inch skillet for tossing the pasta and fillings

A 3-quart baking dish for a heaping dish, or a 4-quart dish for a thinner dish with a larger, crispy top

Preheat the oven to 400°.

Cook cavatappi in a large pot of boiling, salted water until slightly underdone, 8 to 9 minutes (always a bit less than package directions). While the pasta is cooking, pour the *sugo* in the skillet and heat it slowly. Butter the bottom and sides of the baking dish with 2 tablespoons of the butter.

Drain the cooked cavatappi in a colander, shake off excess water, and dump it into the pan. Toss pasta and sauce briefly until coated, then fold in the meatball slices for a minute or so to heat them.

Turn off the heat, sprinkle on ⅔ cup of the grated cheese and 1 cup of the shredded cheese, and fold in. Drop the remaining butter in bits on the pasta, fold in quickly, and turn everything into the baking dish.

Spread the pasta level in the dish; sprinkle the remaining shredded cheese all over and then the remaining grated cheese.

Bake, uncovered, for 30 minutes, or until the top is crusty and nicely colored.

CHEESES FOR BAKED PASTAS

In all my baked pastas, I use cheeses in abundance and variety, both for flavor and texture. In the recipes here, there's always a hard grating cheese and one or more of the semihard melting cheeses such as Muenster or mozzarella. Sometimes, you'll notice, these are only in the filling, sometimes on top as well—it all depends on the texture and look I want the dish to have when it comes out of the oven.

Here are a few tips and comments on the cheeses I use the most. But there are many others that are suitable for baked pastas. Try different cheeses, observe their flavor and melting qualities, and incorporate the ones you like into your cooking.

Freshly grated hard cheeses—either Parmigiano-Reggiano or Grana Padano— are essential to both fillings and toppings. I use them with besciamella (white sauce) or another sauce, as a thin filling between layers of pasta in lasagna. If I'm using a semihard cheese for a topping, I always put some Parmigiano-Reggiano over it to keep the other cheese from becoming leathery.

Semihard cheeses, the melting varieties:

- *Fontina—authentic Italian Fontina d'Aosta is one of the great melting cheeses and just a great cheese. I use it in stuffings and sandwiches, and I love it with a nice ripe peach.*

- *Low-moisture mozzarella—the compact kind that is perhaps the most widely melted cheese in this country. Much of it isn't good, and it becomes rubbery when melted as a topping. There are some good varieties available—including some small American artisanal cheesemakers—and I use it both in fillings and as a topping cheese. If I were shopping in the supermarket, I would check the fat content, making sure to buy whole-milk mozarella.*

- *Muenster—though it is not as flavorful and complex as European varieties, I prefer American Muenster to run-of-the-mill mozzarella. It's creamy, has a pleas- ant mild flavor, and melts nicely, though I never use it as a topping by itself.*

  Don't cut off the red (paprika) coating on Muenster, as you lose good cheese: just scrub it off under running water. Instead of shredding, I often shave it in thin slices with a vegetable peeler and lay them flat to make a layer in a pasticciata.

- *Ricotta—I use it in fillings for flavor and creaminess. If you can get real fresh ricotta, use it but don't drain it—you want the moisture in these dishes. Other- wise, packaged ricotta is fine in baked dishes.*

Ricotta Manicotti with Spinach or Asparagus Filling

M*anicotti are delicious and provide an easy way to enjoy the textures of stuffed fresh pasta baked in sauce.*

MAKES 12 MANICOTTI, SERVING 6

Asparagus Filling or Spinach Filling
(see below)

FOR THE MANICOTTI,
WITH EITHER FILLING

½ pound (½ recipe) Poor Man's
Two-Egg Pasta dough
(page 159)

Salt for pasta water

2 tablespoons butter, for the
baking pan

2 cups Simple Tomato Sauce
(page 132)

1 cup shredded Muenster

⅔ cup freshly grated Parmigiano-
Reggiano or Grana Padano

RECOMMENDED EQUIPMENT

A 9-by-13 inch baking dish

Prepare either the spinach or the asparagus filling, as instructed below, before rolling and cooking the manicotti squares.

Rolling and Cooking the Manicotti

Cut the dough into two pieces. Following the basic procedures on page 189, roll each piece until you have two strips, each about 30 inches long and 5 inches wide. Cut the strips into a dozen roughly 5-inch squares; lay them flat (not touching) on lightly floured towels.

Cook the squares, six at a time, in a pot of boiling salted water for 1½ minutes. Lift them out and lay them flat on damp towels. They may have stretched in cooking; if so, trim them to no more than 6 inches on a side before filling them.

Filling and Baking the Manicotti

Butter the bottom and sides of the baking dish. Heat the oven to 375°.

Spread ⅓ cup of the tomato sauce in the bottom of the baking dish.

Place ⅓ cup of the filling on one edge of a pasta square (the side that most needs to be hidden). Shape the filling into an even mound along the edge and roll up the square, snugly enclosing the filling.

Place the roll in the pan, seam side down. Fill and roll all the manicotti and arrange them so they don't touch each other in the pan. Spoon the remainder of the tomato sauce over, sprinkle on the shredded Muenster and then the grated cheese.

Cover the dish with foil and bake for 35 to 40 minutes, until the juices are bubbling and the pasta has started to crisp under the melted cheese. Remove the foil and bake another 4 or 5 minutes, to give the top a deep-golden color.

Asparagus Filling

Pour the oil into a medium skillet, stir in the sliced asparagus and scallions, sprinkle with ¼ teaspoon of the salt, and cook about 3 minutes over medium heat, until the asparagus is soft but not browned and the scallions are wilted. Let cool briefly.

Stir together the ricotta, egg, and grated cheese until smooth. Stir in the wilted vegetables, scraping the pan to include the oil, and fold together with the pepper and remaining ¼ teaspoon salt until evenly blended.

3 tablespoons extra-virgin olive oil

½ pound asparagus, trimmed and cut crosswise into ¼-inch pieces

2 bunches scallions trimmed and sliced crosswise into ¼-inch pieces (about 1 cup)

½ teaspoon salt

1 pound (2 cups) ricotta, fresh or packaged

1 egg

1 cup freshly grated Parmigiano-Reggiano or Grana Padano

¼ teaspoon freshly ground white pepper

Spinach Filling

Stir together the ricotta, egg, and grated cheese until smooth. Fold in the chopped cooked spinach, melted butter, and seasonings until evenly blended.

1 pound (2 cups) ricotta, fresh or packaged

1 egg

1 cup freshly grated Parmigiano-Reggiano or Grana Padano

20 ounces fresh spinach, cooked, drained, squeezed dry, and roughly chopped

2 tablespoons melted butter

½ teaspoon sea salt

¼ teaspoon freshly ground white pepper

A TREAT FOR TOMORROW

Double the amount of one of the fillings and you'll have enough for twelve manicotti using the full recipe—1 pound—of pasta. Wrap the extras individually in plastic wrap and freeze up to 2 months. To use these treasures, just bring the number you want to room temperature and bake as in the recipe.

Pasticciata Bolognese—
Lasagna with Spinach Noodles and Bolognese Sauce

I admit that I find the pasticciata Bolognese *one of the greatest pasta dishes ever. It is a messy dish, as the name* pasticciata *suggests, but it delivers great flavor. It sounds like quite a production, but if you break it up into its major components—making the pasta, preparing the two sauces—and do them ahead (some can even be done well ahead and frozen), then you need only a few hours for putting it all together and baking. You can put the assembled* pasticciata *in the fridge overnight if you like, and bake it the next day. You want to be relaxed and ready to enjoy this very special dish with your family and friends.*

The seductive texture of this baked dish depends on the lightness and delicacy of the pasta sheets. So it is extremely important to roll the dough out very thin, and for that reason I have given special instructions on how to do just that following the recipe.

SERVES 8 TO 10 OR MORE

1 recipe fresh Spinach Pasta Dough (page 178)

2 recipes (4 cups) *besciamella* (recipe follows)

4 cups *Ragù alla Bolognese,* either variety (page 143)*

2 to 3 tablespoons butter, for the baking pan

8 ounces freshly grated Parmigiano-Reggiano or Grana Padano (1½ cups)

12 ounces Muenster cheese or low-moisture mozzarella, shredded or very thinly sliced (3 cups) (see box on page 197)

Prepping
Roll the pasta dough into thin wide sheets, and briefly cook them, following the instructions in the box on page 205.

In separate saucepans, warm the *besciamella* and the Bolognese slightly, so they are loose and spreadable but not hot.

If you are going to bake the *pasticciata* right away, arrange a rack in the middle of the oven and preheat it to 375°.

Butter the insides of the baking dish.

Assembling the *Pasticciata*
As you follow the layering steps shown in the photos and outlined below, it is helpful to understand that the first two layers of pasta sheets together form a strong base—without this, the *pasticciata* would fall apart when it's served. Only a thin layer of sauces and a light sprinkling of grated Parmigiano-Reggiano separates these sheets, so they'll both cook thoroughly and won't stick together in a thick gummy mass.

Once you've created the base, you'll make three filling layers with generous amounts of sauces and cheeses. The last layers of pasta are, again, thinly dressed, to ensure they all have good texture. The final spreading of cheese and sauces should also be light—like makeup—as their purpose is just to make the *pasticciata* look beautiful.

Making the Base Layers

Coat the bottom *and* sides of the dish thinly with ⅓ cup *besciamella*.

Spread ⅓ cup Bolognese on the bottom, over the *besciamella*.

Following the illustrations, drape pasta sheets the length of the pan so that they cover the bottom of the dish completely and extend over the short sides of the pan by 6 inches or so.

Spread ⅓ cup *besciamella* over the pasta.

Spread ⅓ cup Bolognese over the *besciamella*.

Drape pasta sheets perpendicular to the first, across the width of the pan, with the ends of the sheets extending over the sides of the pan by 6 inches or so. Pasta sheets should now completely hide the sides of the pan.

RECOMMENDED EQUIPMENT

A pasta machine for rolling the *lasagne*

A 9-by-13-inch baking dish, 2 inches deep at least, or a similar 3-quart casserole, as in the photo; use a larger pan for a thinner, crisper *pasticciata*

Wide heavy-duty aluminum foil
A baking sheet

Sauce Note: If you are making the pasticciata with Bolognese Ricetta Antica, which has been cooked with milk already, I recommend using 5 cups of ragù Bolognese and decreasing the besciamella to 3 cups. Adjust the amount of each sauce proportionally in every layer.

Plunging the strips into ice water

Spreading them on a towel-lined tray

Lining the bottom of the dish with pasta sheets extended 6 inches over the long side of the dish

Arranging another layer of pasta sheets on top of the sauce

Making the Filling Layers

Spread ⅔ cup *besciamella* over the pasta. Sprinkle ¼ cup grated cheese all over. Spread 1 cup Bolognese in a thick layer. Cover with a third of the Muenster or mozzarella, shredded or in slices.

Fit another layer of pasta on top, covering only the inside of the pan now, cutting sheets if necessary to fit. Create another thick filling layer with ⅔ cup *besciamella*, ¼ cup grated cheese, 1 cup Bolognese, and another third of shredded cheese.

Make another layer of pasta sheets, cut to fit, and top with a final filling layer (⅔ cup *besciamella*, ¼ cup grated cheese, 1 cup Bolognese, and the last third of the shredded cheese).

Arrange another layer of pasta over the filling, cut to fit.

Making the Topping Layers

Spread ⅓ cup *besciamella* over the pasta, and sprinkle 2 tablespoons grated cheese all over.

Repeat with a final layer of pasta, then *besciamella*, and then grated cheese.

Fitting another layer of pasta on top, covering only the inside of the dish

Folding the overhanging flaps of pasta onto the top of the *pasticciata*

Sprinkling grated cheese over the filled dish

Fold all the overhanging flaps of pasta onto the top of the *pasticciata*. If they don't meet and cover the top, cut a piece of pasta to fit, or use all the remaining pasta here.

Spread the rest of the *besciamella* and Bolognese on, and sprinkle 2 tablespoons grated cheese all over.

Tenting the Dish and Baking

If you want, you can bake the *pasticciata* later, or the next day, covering it with plastic wrap and refrigerating it in the meantime.

Before putting it in the oven, tear a long sheet of foil to form a tent over the pan. This will give the insides time to cook before the top browns. Arch the foil so it doesn't touch the *pasticciata* anywhere, and crimp it against the rim and outsides of the pan so it stays in place and has formed a good seal. With the tip of a sharp knife, poke five or six small holes in the foil to vent steam.

Set the pan on a baking sheet, put it in the oven, and bake for about 45 minutes, or until bubbling juices indicate that it's cooking all the way through—peek under the foil to check. Take the pan (on the baking sheet) out of the oven to remove the foil tent. Loosen foil at the sides and lift it up carefully, so it doesn't touch the sticky top of the *pasticciata*. Return the pan to the oven, and bake for another 20 minutes or so, until the top is deeply colored and crisp.

Let the *pasticciata* sit uncovered for 20 minutes to settle before cutting it in squares and serving.

Besciamella—Béchamel, or Cream, Sauce

MAKES 2 CUPS

2 cups milk

Pinch of salt

Pinch of freshly ground white pepper

Pinch of freshly grated nutmeg

1 bay leaf

1 ½ tablespoons butter

2 tablespoons all-purpose flour

2 generous tablespoons freshly grated Parmigiano-Reggiano or Grana Padano

Pour the milk into a saucepan; add the seasonings and bay leaf. Bring almost to the boil and keep hot.

Melt the butter in a heavy-bottomed saucepan over medium heat. When the butter starts foaming, dump in the flour, and whisk to form a smooth paste or *roux.* Keep whisking and cooking 3 to 4 minutes, until the *roux* darkens slightly.

Pour in the hot milk in a stream, stirring to incorporate the *roux* into it. Cook, stirring constantly, until the sauce starts to boil. Adjust the heat to keep a steady perking until the sauce thickens, about 3 minutes.

Pour the sauce through a fine sieve, and whisk in the grated cheese.

Cover with plastic wrap, pressed right on the surface of the sauce, and let it cool. *Besciamella* can remain at room temperature for a few hours. Otherwise, refrigerate and use it within 3 or 4 days. I don't recommend freezing *besciamella,* as it becomes grainy.

HOW TO ROLL AND COOK PASTA SHEETS FOR BAKED PASTICCIATA AND LASAGNA

You'll use about 20 ounces fresh pasta dough for the recipes here.

Cut the dough into five equal pieces.

Working with one piece at a time, roll and fold it on the first setting of your pasta machine, to get a strip that is as wide as possible (see tips for making wide ravioli, box, page 189). Form the other pieces this way.

Stretch the strips as usual (see page 165), rolling all the strips through the machine before changing the setting—always maintaining the width. When the strips are 20 inches or longer, cut crosswise in two. Now you'll be rolling ten wide strips until they're as thin as possible. If they are too long you can cut them again for easier handling. Pieces of any length can be used in assembling the pasticciata or lasagna.

When each strip is as thin as you can get it, lay it flat on a lightly floured kitchen towel on a baking sheet. Arrange as many as you can on the cloth, making sure they don't touch, then cover them with another floured towel, on which you'll lay the next strips.

Cook and assemble the dish at this point, then store until you want to bake it.

To cook the strips, fill the widest pot you have with at least 6 quarts of water, more if possible, and 1 tablespoon kosher salt for every 6 quarts, then bring to a boil. Fill a big roasting pan (at least 3 inches deep) or a big bowl with cold water and ice. When the water is at a full rolling boil, slide in a pasta strip, letting the water catch and take it in as you lower it. Slide in another if there's room, but don't cook more than two at a time. If the lasagne puff and rise out of the water, push them under to cook on both sides.

For spinach pasta, take each strip out 50 seconds to 1 minute after it's gone in (usually before the water even returns to the boil).

For poor man's egg pasta, take it out 1½ minutes after it's gone in. The water should be back at the boil, and the strip should be just a little underdone.

Lift out one strip at a time. Let the hot water drain for a moment, then drop it into the ice water. After it has chilled for a few seconds, spread the strip out with your fingers, unfolding it if stuck or twisted. Let it cool for another ½ minute or less, then pick it up with your fingers by one end, let the cold water drain off, and lay it flat on a towel. Put the second strip (not touching) on the towel if there's room—the strips will be even wider now.

Cook, chill, and spread out all the strips this way, replenishing the cooking water and ice water as needed.

Lasagna with Meatballs and *Sugo*

I hope you've saved some meatballs and sugo *(page 146) for this wonderful fresh-pasta lasagna. But if you haven't, you can follow the basic procedure using sliced, cooked Italian sausage meat instead of the meatballs and another tomato sauce. Note that you'll need a bit more than a single batch of egg pasta dough—4 extra ounces to be specific—so just make two batches and freeze the extra.*

SERVES 8 OR MORE

1¼ batches (20 ounces) Poor Man's Pasta dough (page 159)

12 turkey or sausage meatballs, fully cooked, from *Sugo* and Meatballs, page 146 (defrosted if frozen)

About 4 cups of any of the following: *sugo* from *Sugo* and Meatballs; *sugo* with Simple Tomato Sauce, or just Simple Tomato Sauce (page 132)

2 to 3 tablespoons butter, for the baking pan

1 pound (2 cups) ricotta, fresh or packaged, not drained

1 cup freshly grated Parmigiano-Reggiano or Grana Padano

10 ounces Muenster or low-moisture mozzarella, shredded (2½ cups)

Getting Ready

Roll the 20 ounces of pasta dough into thin wide sheets and briefly cook them, following the procedures on page 205.

Slice the meatballs into rounds about ⅓ inch thick.

Warm the *sugo* or tomato sauce if necessary, to spreadable consistency.

Arrange a rack in the middle of the oven and preheat it to 375°.

Lightly butter the baking dish.

Assembling the Lasagna

Coat the bottom of the baking dish with ⅓ cup sauce.

Drape pasta sheets the length of the pan so that they cover the bottom of the dish completely and extend over the short sides of the pan by 6 inches or so. Spread ⅓ cup sauce over the pasta in the bottom of the pan.

Drape pasta sheets perpendicular to the first, across the width of the pan, with the ends of the sheets extending over the long sides of the pan by 6 inches or so. Over this pasta, spread ⅓ cup sauce and half the ricotta (1 cup), and sprinkle over it ⅓ cup of grated cheese and 1 cup of shredded cheese.

Lay down pasta to cover just the inside of the pan, cutting sheets to fit. Spread ⅔ cup of sauce over, and arrange the meatball slices side by side on top. Sprinkle on ⅓ cup grated cheese, and spread ⅓ cup sauce over that.

Lay down another layer of pasta to cover the fillings, cutting sheets to fit. Spread ⅔ cup of sauce over the pasta and the rest of the ricotta over the sauce.

Lay down another layer of pasta to cover the fillings, spread ⅓ cup sauce over the pasta, and scatter ¾ cup of shredded cheese on top.

Lay down another layer of pasta to cover, and spread ⅓ cup sauce over it.

Fold the overhanging flaps of pasta onto the top of the lasagna. If they don't meet and cover the surface, cut a piece of pasta to fit, or use all the remaining pasta here.

Spread the remaining ⅓ cup sauce, and sprinkle on the remaining ¾ cup of shredded cheese and the last ⅓ cup of grated cheese.

Tenting the Dish and Baking

Use a long sheet of foil to form a tent over the pan, as described in the *Pasticciata Bolognese* recipe (page 200). Make sure the foil doesn't touch the lasagna, and poke five or six small holes in the foil to vent steam.

Set the pan on a baking sheet, put it in the oven, and bake for about 40 minutes, or until bubbling juices indicates that it's cooking all the way through. Remove the foil without touching the top of the lasagna. Bake uncovered for another 20 minutes or so, until the top is deeply colored and crisp.

Let the lasagna sit uncovered for 20 minutes to settle before cutting it in squares and serving.

Laying one end of the pasta strip in the baking dish and covering it with sauce

Continuing to fold the strip back and forth to make layers before covering them with sauce

Finishing with a final layer of pasta

TOMORROW'S TREAT: RIBBON LASAGNA

Often when you're layering a lasagna or pasticciata you'll find yourself not using up a final strip or two of pasta. Don't throw it away. Freeze it, and pull it out one day when you have a few leftovers in your refrigerator, such as a small amount of meaty sauce, stewed or braised meat with a little gravy, maybe a couple of meatballs, or perhaps some seafood, as well as a little tomato sauce (which I trust by now you'll always have on hand). All you need is a small baking dish (3½ to 4 inches in diameter), which you'll fill with your ribbon of lasagna and sauce in your own special way.

So pop that strip of pasta into a pot of boiling water, fish it out after a minute, shock it in ice water, and drain. Following the illustrations, lay one end flat in the small, shallow, buttered baking dish. Spread a couple of tablespoons of whatever saucy, meaty leftover you're using, then fold and pull back the strip of dough over it to make a second layer; top that with a couple of tablespoons of tomato sauce and a few thin slices of a melty cheese to cover, fold again and make another layer of meaty sauce, then finish with a generous sprinkling of grated Parmigiano-Reggiano or Grana Padano. What you have made is an accordion-pleated mound of pasta ribbon, each layer generously cushioned with meaty filling and sauce and cheese. Now just bake it at 375° for 25 minutes, and when it comes out bubbly and melded together, you'll have yourself a rare treat.

Of course, you can multiply these ingredients and make as many individual ribbon lasagnas as you have hungry mouths to feed.

Gnocchi and Gnudi

I have given you instructions for making gnocchi before, but here I am working with smaller, easy-to-handle amounts. I am also opening up a whole new horizon by including different grains, herbs, and flavors in making gnocchi and exploring different condiments. And I am introducing you to a variation on the theme—gnudi, the "naked dumpling."

Potato Gnocchi

1 ½ pounds baking potatoes

¾ teaspoon salt

1 large egg, beaten well

1 ½ to 2 cups all-purpose flour

RECOMMENDED EQUIPMENT

A potato ricer or vegetable mill

Making and Shaping the Gnocchi

Boil the potatoes in water to cover until tender when poked with a fork. Don't let them overcook to the point that their skins split. Drain.

As soon as the potatoes are cool enough to handle, peel them and put them through the ricer or vegetable mill, using the medium disk and letting the shreds fall onto a large baking tray or board. Spread them out, sprinkle on the salt, and let them dry out and cool for at least 20 minutes.

Pour the beaten egg over the potatoes, and then 1 cup of the flour. Gather the mass together and knead, adding a little more flour as necessary to make the dough hold together. But keep it light; the more you work the dough, the more flour you'll need, and you don't want to incorporate too much or the gnocchi will be heavy and dry. A good criterion: slice the mass in half and examine the texture. It should look like cookie dough peppered with small holes.

Cut the dough into three equal pieces. Roll out each portion into a broomstick about 18 inches long, then cut crosswise into ⅔-inch pieces and toss them lightly in flour. You should have about seventy-two gnocchi.

Take one piece of gnocchi and place it, cut side down, on the tines of a fork, then with your lightly floured thumb press into it, at the same time pushing it off the end of the fork and onto a floured board. The gnocchi should have an indentation where your thumb was, and ridges from the fork tines on the other side. Repeat with all the remaining pieces, and cover with a clean towel. At this point they should be cooked immediately or quickly frozen.

Cooking the Gnocchi

Bring a large pot of salted water to a boil.

Drop the gnocchi, five or six at a time, into the boiling water—the larger the pot, the less time they will take to return to the boil.

Once they have, cook for 2 to 3 minutes, until they plump up and float to the surface; when done, they will have a softer feel and will no longer thump against the side of the pan as you fish them out with a strainer or slotted spoon. Drop them gently from your strainer into the waiting sauce.

VARIATIONS

Whole Wheat Gnocchi
Use half whole-wheat flour. It is better to sift the two flours together—¾ cup whole-wheat and ¾ cup all-purpose flour. Then follow the above directions. The dough will be firmer and needs to cook a bit longer—approximately 5 minutes. Finish with Pesto Asparagus or Green Bean Sauce (page 212), plus 1 tablespoon extra-virgin olive oil, some ground pepper, and grated Parmigiano-Reggiano. These whole-wheat gnocchi are also good with Mushroom Ragù (page 141).

Poppy Seed Gnocchi
Work 2 tablespoons toasted poppy seeds into the dough as you are kneading it. Then follow the above directions. The dough will need to cook about 3 minutes. Finish the gnocchi in a skillet with Butter and Fresh Sage Sauce (page 118). Or make a dressing of ⅓ cup bread crumbs toasted in a pan with a scant tablespoon of butter and 1 tablespoon or more poppy seeds.

Sweet Gnocchi
Finish the gnocchi with butter and a little sugar. You can also dress them with cinnamon and toasted bread crumbs. And a splash of maple syrup is delicious. The kids will love it. I know some who even like their gnocchi dressed with peanut butter and jelly!

Basil Gnocchi
Add 4 tablespoons basil paste (page 213) to the dough and work it in by hand, kneading until it is thoroughly distributed. Cook as

FREEZING GNOCCHI

Spread the gnocchi out, not touching, on a floured baking pan or whatever will fit in your freezer, and freeze them. When they are solid—in about 2 hours—gather them together, shake off excess flour, and store them in sealed plastic bags for future use. They will keep for up to 6 weeks.

To cook frozen gnocchi, do half a batch at a time and double the amount of cooking water. Because they are frozen, the cooking-water temperature drops, and if there are too many in the pot they will disintegrate before the water returns to the boil.

directed above, and finish with Pesto Asparagus or Green Bean Sauce (recipe follows).

Spinach Gnocchi
Work ¾ cup well-drained puréed spinach (for details, see page 178) into the dough, and cook as directed. Finish with the same Pesto Asparagus or Green Bean Sauce.

PESTO ASPARAGUS OR GREEN BEAN SAUCE

Trim and cut at an angle into 1-inch pieces about ¾ pound asparagus (you should have about 4 cups). Or trim an equal amount of tender green beans and cut into 1-inch pieces. When the pot of gnocchi water comes to a boil, toss in the asparagus or beans, cook 3 minutes, then add the gnocchi and cook 3 minutes more. Melt 4 tablespoons butter in a skillet, scoop up the gnocchi and asparagus or beans, and drop them into the pan, then add 1 cup Basil Paste (see below) and enough of the boiling water to make a sauce. To serve, top with ½ cup grated Parmigiano or Grana Padano.

SIMPLE BASIL PASTE

makes about 1 cup

3 cups firmly packed fresh basil leaves

4 tablespoons extra-virgin olive oil

¼ teaspoon salt

Process all the ingredients with the steel blade of a food processor to a very fine paste. Scrape the bowl occasionally so that all the leaves are puréed.

Gnudi

Gnudi *means "naked dumpling," because it's truly a stuffing without a pasta shell. So if you love those stuffings in ravioli, skip the pasta—this dish is for you.*

25 TO 30 GNUDI, SERVING 6 AS A FIRST COURSE OR 4 AS A MAIN DISH

Start heating a large pot of salted water.

Blend the ricotta and the egg together in a large bowl. Mix in the spinach, cheese, bread crumbs, flour, salt and pepper, and knead lightly.

Test the consistency of the dough by scooping up a heaping tablespoon, forming it into a ball, and flouring it. Drop it into the boiling water; if it does not hold its shape and rise to the surface of the water within a minute, add more bread crumbs to your dough.

When you have the right consistency, shape all of the dough into balls the size of golf balls, roll them lightly in flour, and lay them out on baking sheets covered in parchment paper.

Drop the gnudi gently one by one into the boiling water and cook for about 2 or 3 minutes, until they rise to the top, and come to a rolling boil. To test for doneness, scoop out a ball and press it with your fingers: the dumpling dough when cooked should bounce back, leaving no indentation.

Transfer to a sauté pan with Butter and Fresh Sage Sauce. Top with freshly grated cheese before serving.

I pound fresh ricotta, drained

I egg

I cup dry spinach purée, prepared from 20 ounces frozen or fresh spinach (see page 178)

¼ cup freshly grated Parmigiano-Reggiano or Grana Padano

6 tablespoons fine bread crumbs

¼ cup flour, plus flour for rolling

½ teaspoon salt

Freshly ground black pepper, a generous amount

I recipe Butter and Fresh Sage Sauce (page 118)

½ cup freshly grated Parmigiano-Reggiano or Grana Padano

RECOMMENDED EQUIPMENT

Baking sheet covered in parchment paper

Polenta

Corn, polenta, came to Italy from the New World, and yet, along with pasta and rice, it is one of the beloved starch dishes of Italy. Polenta was for the northeastern regions of Italy what potatoes were for Ireland. Corn grew in abundance there and fed many people and still does, so much so that the people of the Friuli-Venezia Giulia region are known as *polentoni*, polenta eaters. I come from the region, and I grew up eating polenta and still do eat it often. As a child I had just-cooked or leftover polenta for breakfast with milk and sugar or with caffe latte, or pan-fried with some sugar and cinnamon sprinkled on top, as well as in endless ways accompanying vegetables, meats, fish, and cheeses.

It is rather simple to cook—all you need is cornmeal, water, salt, olive oil, and a few bay leaves. When done, you can enjoy the polenta piping hot or let it cool and take shape, then cut and fry it, or grill and bake it, topped with anything you choose. In this chapter you'll find it with leeks, with bacon lardoons, with Montasio cheese, or with just an egg yolk nestled in a piping-hot mound of polenta.

Beyond the flavor of polenta, I look for the mouth feel, and that depends on the grind. Instant polenta will give you a smooth puddinglike texture, the medium grind a bit more texture, and the coarse will have almost a raspy feel in your mouth. There is also white polenta, milled from white corn, which is used much in the Veneto. And the *polenta taragna,* which has buckwheat milled along with the yellow corn, has much texture and flavor.

The one important caution in cooking polenta is to get it smooth. Start it in cold water and whisk well while it cooks; it may take a bit longer but ensures lump-free polenta.

Even though polenta might look done, make sure you cook it the recommended time; its digestibility and flavor increase with longer cooking time.

Basic Polenta

Put 10 cups cold water in the pot with the oil, salt, and bay leaves. Whisking vigorously with one hand, pour the polenta into the water in a thin steady stream (a spouted measuring cup is helpful here). Keep whisking until all the cornmeal is incorporated and the mixture is smooth. Turn on medium-low heat and gradually bring the polenta to a boil. This will take 10 minutes at least—don't rush it. You can leave the pot for a couple of minutes, but stir frequently and thoroughly, especially the bottom, sides, and corners. As soon as you feel thickening, use a sturdy wooden spoon in place of the whisk, so you can scrape the polenta from the corners and mix it in.

The polenta will become very thick as it gets close to the boil; then big bubbles will rise and burst in (and out of) the pot. At this point, lower the heat to get a continuous but slow perking—just a couple of bubbles at a time. Set a cover ajar on top, so polenta doesn't pop all over the stove. Because of its density, spatters can easily burn you, so be careful.

Cook the polenta at this rate for another 25 to 35 minutes, stirring frequently, and adjusting heat as necessary. Stir more continuously near the end, scraping up the thickest polenta from the bottom and corners.

When the polenta is glossy and just pulling away from the sides, it is done and you may turn off the heat. Or cook it longer, slowly, for more flavor; mix in more water if you want it softer, or turn up the heat, stirring vigorously, to thicken it. Polenta retains heat for up to 30 minutes, so you can cover the pot and leave it for 15 minutes or so before serving. As it cools, it will form a crust on top. To prevent, place a piece of plastic wrap directly on the polenta.

Finishing the Polenta

Stir 1 to 2 cups of freshly grated Parmigiano-Reggiano or Grana Padano into the pot after you have turned off the heat. If you want

FOR BASIC POLENTA

¼ cup extra-virgin olive oil

1 tablespoon salt

4 bay leaves

2 cups yellow polenta, medium-grind

FOR FINISHING POLENTA

1 to 2 cups or more freshly grated Parmigiano-Reggiano or Grana Padano

¼ pound (1 stick) butter (optional)

½ cup mascarpone cheese (optional)

RECOMMENDED EQUIPMENT

A heavy whisk

A heavy-bottomed saucepan, Dutch oven, or stovetop casserole, 10-inch diameter, at least 6-quart capacity; enameled cast-iron pots, like Le Creuset, are particularly good

more flavor at this point, you can mix in a stick of butter or ½ cup of mascarpone cheese also.

Ladle 1 to 2 cups of hot polenta into each warm bowl and top with more Parmigiano-Reggiano or Grana Padano, either grated or in shavings.

SIMPLE VARIATIONS FOR BASIC POLENTA

Basic Polenta with Leeks

Cut up into approximately 1-inch pieces enough leeks to fill 3 cups. After the polenta has perked for about 10 minutes, stir in the leeks and let them cook right in the pot. Alternatively, sauté the leeks separately, and fold them in for the last 5 minutes of cooking. Top each serving with Parmigiano-Reggiano or Grana Padano, grated or in shavings.

Basic Polenta with Bacon

You'll need 1 pound thick-sliced bacon. Stack the slices and cut them crosswise into lardoons, or matchstick strips about ¼ inch thick. Fry them over medium-high heat in a skillet, stirring and separating, until dark and crispy; then lift them out with a slotted spatula and let the fat drain off. Fold the bacon into the polenta, off heat, along with a cup of grated Parmigiano-Reggiano or Grana Padano. Top each serving with more cheese, either grated or in shavings. If you like, save some bacon for decoration on top.

Basic Polenta with Cheese

Cut a semihard cheese like Montasio or cheddar into ½-inch cubes. Stir into the cooked polenta, off the heat, with 1 cup Parmigiano-Reggiano or Grana Padano. Top each serving with more cheese, either grated or in shavings.

To flavor with gorgonzola, stir in the cup of grated Parmigiano-Reggiano or Grana Padano. Then crumble gorgonzola over each serving.

A BREAKFAST TREAT: A GOLDEN BOWL— POLENTA AND AN EGG YOLK

The enormous residual heat of polenta is sufficient, as the saying goes, "to cook an egg." Do just that to make this treat for breakfast or brunch.

Prepare Basic Polenta finished with freshly grated cheese, or in one of the simple variations. For every golden bowl, separate an egg and keep the yolk whole in a dish. Ladle a portion of steaming polenta into a warm bowl; press with a spoon to make a small nest. Slide the yolk into the nest. It will cook as you garnish it with freshly ground black pepper and surround it with Parmigiano-Reggiano, either grated or in shavings. To eat, stir the yolk into the polenta and really enjoy this dish.

The crowning glory of this dish is a shaving of fresh truffles on top of it all.

Polenta *Pasticciata*: Baked Polenta Layered with Long-Cooked Sauces

Polenta pasticciata *is a layered baked dish, just like lasagna, but made with warm, fresh polenta instead of pasta. And, like lasagna, it is marvelously versatile: you can put all manner of good things in between the layers of polenta—cheeses, vegetables, meats, or sauces, or a combination.*

I've narrowed down the possibilities for this pasticciata, *which is filled with one of the savory long-cooked sauces on pages 134 to 155. Most of them make great fillings, with intense flavor and chunky texture that complement the mild sweetness and softness of the polenta. So I am leaving the final choice of sauce to you: whether you decide to use one of the guazzetti or meat Bolognese or the mushroom ragù or Savoy-cabbage-and-bacon sauce, the procedure is exactly the same.*

Perhaps you have one of these in your freezer right now! If you've got 4 cups, that's enough to fill a pasticciata *that will serve eight as a main course, or even more as a side dish, perfect for a buffet or large dinner party. But don't give up if you only have 3 cups of mushroom ragù or guazzetto. If you also have Simple Tomato Sauce (page 132) on hand, blend in a couple of cups to extend your base sauce; or simmer up a quick marinara to use as an extender.*

You have lots of flexibility with polenta pasticciata: *use the cheeses you like in amounts you are comfortable with. To make a deep* pasticciata *with thick layers, which makes a great presentation unmolded, assemble it in a 3-quart baking dish or a 12-inch cast-iron skillet, filled to the brim. For a crispier texture and for more golden* gratinato *on top, spread the layers thin in a wide shallow casserole. Use* besciamella *to add moistness and richness, or do without it. With good basic polenta and a deeply flavored long-cooked sauce, your* pasticciata *will be delicious however you make it.*

SERVES 8 AS A MAIN COURSE, MORE AS A SIDE DISH

I recipe (about 10 cups) Basic Polenta (page 215), freshly made and hot*

4 to 6 cups of any of the following sauces:

    Mushroom Ragù (page 141)

    Savoy Cabbage, Bacon, and Mushroom Sauce (page 138)

Preheat the oven to 400° and set a rack in the center.

Put plastic wrap on fresh polenta to keep it hot and to prevent a skin from forming on top. Be sure to assemble the *pasticciata* within ½ hour, while the polenta is still warm and soft with no lumps.

If necessary, heat the filling sauce to quite warm. If it is too dense for spreading, thin it with some water. If you're extending the filling sauce with simple tomato or marinara sauce, warm them up together.

Butter the bottom and sides of the baking dish or skillet thoroughly. Use more butter on the bottom in particular, if you want to unmold the *pasticciata*.

Put ¼ cup *besciamella* in the dish or skillet and spread it around the bottom; it doesn't have to cover every bit.

Pour in half the polenta (approximately 5 cups) and spread it evenly in the bottom of the pan. Scatter ⅓ cup or more shredded Muenster or other soft cheese all over the top, then sprinkle on 2 to 4 tablespoons of grated Parmigiano-Reggiano or Grana Padano. Pour or ladle 2 cups of the warm sauce over the polenta and cheese, and spread it all over—use 3 cups sauce if you want a thicker layer.

Pour on a bit more than half of the remaining polenta (about 3 cups) and spread it. Spread another ¼ cup of *besciamella* on top, top with shredded soft cheese and grated hard cheese in the amounts you like. Pour in the remaining sauce and spread it evenly, reserving a cup, if you have enough and plan to unmold the *pasticciata*.

For the top layer, spread all the rest of the polenta and another ¼ cup *besciamella* on top of that. Sprinkle on more shredded soft cheese and grated Parmigiano-Reggiano or Grana Padano. If you're making a thin *pasticciata* in a big pan, or want it to have a beautiful deep gold *gratinato*, use enough *besciamella* and cheese to really cover the top. Do not compress the cheeses, though. See do-ahead note below.

Set the pan on a cookie sheet and bake for 45 minutes to an hour or more, until the top is deeply colored and crusted, even browned a bit on the edges. Let the *pasticciata* cool for a few minutes before serving. If you are serving portions from the baking pan, cut in squares like lasagna, or wedges if you've used a round skillet or pan, and lift them out with a spatula.

To unmold the *pasticiatta*, let it cool for at least 10 minutes. Run a knife around the sides of the pan, cutting through crust sticking to the rim or sides. Lay a cutting board, big enough to cover it, on top of the baking pan or skillet, hold the two together (with the protection of cloths and the help of other hands if necessary), and flip them over. Rap on the upturned pan bottom—or bang on it all over—to loosen the bottom. Lift the board, and give the pan a good shake. The *pasticciata* will drop out soon, with sufficient encouragement. Serve it on the board, or reflip it onto a serving platter and serve with a cup or more of warm sauce heaped on the top or served on the side.

Ragù alla Bolognese, *Ricetta Antica* or *Tradizionale* (page 143)

Duck Leg *Guazzetto* (page 154) or Pork Rib *Guazzetto* (page 151)

Tomato Primavera Sauce (page 125)

Sugo and Meatballs (page 146)

marinara sauce (page 130)

2 tablespoons or more soft butter, for the baking dish

1 cup *besciamella* (page 204) (optional; it will render the *pasticciata* richer and more complex)

1 to 2 cups shredded Muenster or other cheeses for shredding[†] (see box, page 197)

½ to 1 cup grated Parmigiano-Reggiano or Grana Padano

RECOMMENDED EQUIPMENT

A 9-by-13-inch 3-quart baking dish or 12-inch cast-iron skillet 3 inches deep, for a 3-inch-high *pasticciata* that you can unmold; for a crisper *pasticciata*, use an 11-by-15-inch pan

*Note: You can serve this with or without freshly grated Parmigiano-Reggiano; it will be richer with, but just as good without.

[†]Note: Good alternatives are dry-packed mozzarella, Italian Fontina, cheddar, or other cheeses of your liking.

Do-ahead note: If you want to prepare the *pasticciata* and bake later the same or next day, spread the last layer of polenta and coat it well with *besciamella* but don't sprinkle on the final layer of cheeses. Cover it lightly and leave it at room temperature, or wrap well and refrigerate overnight. Before baking, sprinkle on the cheeses and make a tent of foil (see page 203) over the baking dish, without touching the cheese. Poke a few small holes in the foil to vent steam. Set the pan on a sheet and bake for ½ hour at 400°, remove the foil, and continue to bake until deeply colored and crusted.

POLENTA JUST SAUCED

All of the sauces that I recommend for layering in a *pasticciata* are delicious just ladled on top of hot polenta. You'll need ⅓ to ½ cup of hot sauce for each serving of Basic Polenta (finished with freshly grated cheese) or any of the Simple Variations that follow (page 216). Put the polenta in warm serving bowls, sprinkle over more Parmigiano-Reggiano or Grana Padano—it melts best under the sauce—then spoon the sauce on top.

Hearty sauces like mushroom ragù or savoy cabbage and bacon are particularly delicious with *polenta taragna*, a coarse grind of whole-grain cornmeal and buckwheat. Prepare *taragna* exactly as you do yellow polenta, but give it an extra 10 to 15 minutes of cooking and more water as needed.

POLENTA LAYER CAKE WITH BUTTER
GORGONZOLA FILLING

This appetizer *torta* is made with chilled polenta, not soft polenta like a *pasticciata*. It's as rich as any dessert cake but much simpler and faster. Make it in any size you want, but even this small cake will be enough to serve six uninhibited eaters. You'll need:

- 3 cups pourable polenta from a fresh batch of Basic Polenta (page 215)

- 4 to 8 tablespoons or more butter

- ¼ to 1 cup or more crumbled or sliced gorgonzola

- 3 tablespoons to ½ cup or more freshly grated Parmigiano-Reggiano

- A round mold such as a 6-inch cake pan (at least 2½ inches deep) or a 1-quart soufflé dish, or an 8-inch square pan

When the polenta is fresh and hot, slosh the mold with cold water so it's damp. Pour in the polenta and level it to form a smooth disk at least 1½ inches thick. Chill until solidified, then invert the mold to get out the disk (wrap and refrigerate it for up to 2 days if you want).

Heat the oven to 400° when you are ready to make the cake.

Slice the disk into three equal round layers (as you would split a cake layer). Place one round on a well-buttered or parchment-lined baking sheet. Dot the surface, lightly or heavily, with bits of butter, using a third of the total, then with half the gorgonzola and a third of the grated Parmigiano-Reggiano.

Place a second polenta layer on the fillings and load it up the same way, using up the gorgonzola. Top with the third polenta round and decorate it with butter and Parmigiano-Reggiano.

Put the sheet in the oven and bake for 30 minutes—or 45 if the polenta is just out of the fridge—until the top of the cake is sizzling and deep golden and the filling oozes from between the layers. Lift with a wide spatula onto a cake plate. Serve very hot. You might want to bake some halved, cored pears alongside the polenta cake to serve with it.

Risotto: Cooking with All Your Senses

I love making risotto for family meals. It's not something I have time for every day—it takes a good 30 minutes, mostly at the stove—but it is one of those special dishes that focus my attention and engage all my senses in the amazing processes of cooking. I smell, see, and taste what's in the risotto pan, of course, but I am listening too: for the clicking sound that tells me the rice grains are sufficiently toasted and it's time to splash them with wine; for the distinctive bubbling as each addition of cooking liquid disappears in the pot, which tells me the rice is ready for more.

If I've stepped away from the stove—I do take a break from stirring risotto now and then, and you can too—that sound brings me back. I add more liquid and stir (and stir and stir), and feel, through the wooden spoon in my fingers, the corner of the pan where the rice is almost sticking, the resistance that tells me yet another cup of broth is needed before I wander away again.

The Basic Risotto recipe that follows is one that will give you this marvelous engagement of the senses. It's a simple formula that will let you focus on the critical steps in cooking—in the end, creating a great risotto is 100 percent technique—not on a long list of ingredients. You can make this right out of the cupboard, building flavor and superb texture with just olive oil, onions, rice, wine, water, salt, and cheese. Nothing else, not even butter, is necessary. I give you choices, though: use butter or leeks or broth if you want, or more or less of the ingredients listed in ranges. I want you in the driver's seat, following your senses and tastes, to achieve the texture and flavor you like best (see more on these choices in the box on page 228).

With risotto, you see, it is more important that you understand what you are doing than that you add things in prescribed amounts. When you are in control of what's happening in the pot, you will feel how powerful a few ingredients and a few techniques can be in creating an outstanding dish.

To sharpen your focus, you'll find each step of the recipe instructions accompanied by a brief explanation of its purpose and the chemistry of risotto—these are short, and, believe me, you will have plenty of time to read them while you are stirring! And if you have further questions about risotto, write me at www.lidiasitaly.com. I love teaching about this precious treasure of Italian cooking.

Basic Risotto

5 to 7 cups water, Turkey Broth (page 80), or Simple Vegetable Broth (page 288), or an additional 1 to 2 cups of flavorful sauce

¼ cup extra-virgin olive oil

10 ounces or more onions with (optional) leeks, shallots, and/or scallions, chopped medium-fine (2 cups or more)

1 teaspoon salt

2 cups short-grained Italian rice, either Arborio or Carnaroli

1 cup white wine

FOR FINISHING

2 tablespoons extra-virgin olive oil or butter

½ to 1½ cups freshly grated Parmigiano-Reggiano or Grana Padano

Freshly ground black pepper, to taste

RECOMMENDED EQUIPMENT

A 3-to-4-quart heavy saucepan at least 10 inches wide to allow for steady evaporation; enameled cast-iron or heavy-gauge stainless-steel pans with a heat-dispersing bottom layer are particularly well suited for risotto

Pour 7 cups of water or other cooking liquid into a large pot and bring it almost to a boil. Cover, and keep it hot over very low heat, on a burner close to the risotto pan.

Cooking the Onions

What You Are Doing: In this stage of cooking, you are softening and caramelizing the onions to form a flavor base for the risotto. You are keeping them from getting brown or crisp, and softening them by cooking in water, so that they will ultimately melt into the risotto. You then cook off the water completely, to prepare for the next step, toasting the rice.

Put the ¼ cup oil, onions, and ½ teaspoon of the salt in the big risotto pan, and set over medium heat. Cook the onions slowly, stirring frequently with a wooden spoon, as they sweat, soften, and gradually take on a golden color, 8 to 10 minutes. Adjust the heat if the onions are about to get brown.

Ladle ½ cup of water into the onions, stir well, and continue to cook the onions without letting them brown, still over low to medium heat, for another 5 to 10 minutes. The onions should be golden and glistening with oil, but all the water must be cooked away.

Toasting the Rice

What You Are Doing: In this critical step, every grain of rice becomes coated and cooked in hot fat (the oil). This forms a capsule on the outer layer of each grain that will prevent it from absorbing too much liquid too fast and possibly disintegrating. "Toasting" means that the rice must be cooked on the outside—not brown. Toasted rice will still look white, but you can hear a clicking sound when you stir it.

When the onions are completely devoid of water, add the rice all at once, raise the heat to medium, and stir constantly with the oily onions. Cook for about 3 minutes, until the rice grains have been toasted, but do not allow them to scorch or color. Have the wine ready to add.

Cooking with Wine

What You Are Doing: *In this quick step, you are balancing the starchy character of the rice with the acidity and taste components of dry white wine. These are quickly absorbed by the rice kernel, but the alcohol cooks off. Rice that is not tempered has less flavor and yields a starchy risotto.*

Pour in the wine all at once, and cook with the rice for 2 to 3 minutes, over medium heat. Stir constantly all around the pan, until the moisture has evaporated. Have the hot water close by, and be ready to add it with a ladle or measuring cup.

Creating the Creamy Risotto

What You Are Doing: *For the next 15 to 20 minutes, the gradual addition of hot liquid (it must be hot!) has two effects on the rice: it draws out the starches stored in the kernels, just a bit at a time, while the kernels are slowly absorbing liquid and cooking. Short-grain Italian rice has an abundance of a particular starch that, when released by the kernel into the warm liquid and fat in the pot, forms a creamy suspension. You must maintain a steady gentle simmering to maintain this process of "amalgamation." While some of the liquid is absorbed by the rice, it is also evaporating, and the risotto will thicken and heat up rapidly. You stir continuously to prevent the starches from scorching. And you must add more liquid in small amounts to continue the process as described, until you have reached optimal softening of the kernels and development of the suspension. It is OK to stop stirring and leave the rice shortly after each addition of liquid, when it is wet and the danger of scorching is minimal— but don't go far.*

For the first addition, ladle in 1½ to 2 cups of the very hot liquid, enough to barely cover the rice; stir it in continuously, all around the pan. Add the remaining ½ teaspoon of salt, and stir well. Lower the heat, if necessary, to maintain a very gentle perking.

Stir frequently at first, and then constantly as the risotto thickens.

Make sure the spoon is reaching in all the corners of the pan, on the pan bottom, and around the sides. When all the water has been absorbed, the risotto is harder to stir—the bubbling *sounds* thicker too—and the pan bottom is visible in the track of the spoon, ladle in another cup of water. (If you are flavoring your risotto with a sauce—see box, facing page—stir it in at this point, before the second addition of water.)

Cook, stirring always, and add another 2 cups of water when the risotto is ready for it, as just described—anywhere from 3 to 6 minutes between additions. Keep track of how much liquid you have added.

Finishing the Rice

What You Are Doing: *In this final step, you stop the cooking when the risotto reaches the consistency you want. You finish with olive oil, as a flavoring and amalgamating agent, and incorporate grated cheese and fresh pepper as flavor elements, to taste.*

After the addition of at least 5 cups of water, you can taste and gauge the degree of doneness of the rice kernels and the fluidity of the creamy suspension. At any time that you find the rice grains pleasantly *al dente* and the risotto creamy, you can choose to stop cooking. Or you may incorporate more water, up to about 7 cups total, if you want a softer, looser risotto.

When you are satisfied, turn off the heat and stir in the 2 tablespoons olive oil. Stir in grated cheese and freshly ground black pepper to taste. Serve the risotto immediately in heated bowls, with more cheese and pepper at the table.

RISOTTOS WITH FLAVORFUL
LONG-COOKING SAUCES

One of the joys of mastering risotto is the freedom to improvise and use it as a foundation for new dishes, without depending on recipes. My inspiration for a spur-of-the-moment risotto often comes from the refrigerator and freezer, where (thanks to my thrifty mother) are carefully stored small containers of flavorful pasta sauces. Often there's just a cup or two, not enough for a lasagna or a big pot of pasta, but a perfect amount to imbue a pot of risotto with its intense flavors and special personality.

Below I have listed several of the long-cooking sauces in this chapter which can make wonderful risotto variations. Follow these general guidelines and procedures with any sauce:

- Use at least 1 cup of sauce, and a maximum of 2, for a full batch of risotto. The more you use, the richer and more distinctive the risotto will be. With thin sauces, such as marinara or simple tomato, you should use 2 cups always.

- All sauces should be pourable: use water or broth to thin dense sauces like mushroom ragù, cabbage sauce, or meat sauces. Shred or cut meat in *guazzetti* (off the bone, of course) into small pieces that will distribute throughout the risotto.

- Heat the sauce to a simmer before adding to the risotto. Pour in all the sauce after the risotto has already absorbed 2 cups of hot liquid and the release of starch has commenced (as I have noted for you in the recipe).

- Stir in the sauce and let it cook briefly—the risotto should be bubbling gently—then add more of the basic hot liquid and continue with the cooking as usual.

- Sauce will not necessarily replace water or broth—you should have a full pot (5 to 7 cups) of hot water or broth to bring the risotto to the consistency you like.

THE BASICS OF RISOTTO

The Basic Risotto recipe above presents you with many choices. Here are some thoughts on these quandaries:

The Nature of the Liquid

Some people are surprised to learn that you can make risotto with plain water. Of course you can, since the chemical processes are the same whatever liquid you use. If you have broth of any kind, and you want its particular flavor in your dish, use it. If you are adding a long-cooking sauce for flavor (especially if you use 2 cups), water is a good choice, and better than a broth that might interfere with the sauce.

The Aromatics

Onions, cooked properly, provide a fine sweet base of flavor for simple risotto, but greater and more complex flavors will come if you add chopped leeks, shallots, or scallions. Shallots are have a strong flavor (don't use more than ½ cup), but they mellow during cooking and they completely disappear in the risotto. Leek pieces will not disappear but add lovely flavor, as do scallions. You can add up to 2 cups of leeks, scallion, and shallots to the pan, after the onions have started to sweat and wilt. But all moisture must be cooked out of them before you toast the rice. With each 1-cup increase of onion mixture, add 1 tablespoon of olive oil.

The Amount of Liquid

There's no set amount—here's an instance where you are really in control. A general guideline for liquid is three and a half times the amount of rice, and you should have this amount on hand, and hot. But you may need far less. For one thing, it will evaporate at different rates in different pans and with different heat intensities, and the amount of liquid it takes to produce a given consistency will therefore vary. Most important, you should add liquid until you have produced risotto with the texture you like.

The Finish—Olive Oil or Butter

This is a fascinating question with no single answer. It is important to understand that both olive oil and butter have an amalgamating property—bringing everything together texturally—that is always used to "finish" risotto (referred to as mantecare in Italian). Many people mistakenly think that butter—and lots of it—is required as the finish, to make risotto creamy. (And some chefs whip in butter to give risotto creaminess when it wasn't developed through proper cooking.) But our basic recipe shows that you develop the creaminess by the slow release of starch and proper cooking. And olive oil at the end adds a nice complexity that does not alter the essential flavor of the risotto: it is, in my opinion, a cleaner, more pristine finish. I like using olive oil as a finish with fish risotto and some vegetable risotti, because it leaves the pristine flavors of the fish and vegetables clean and vibrant.

Butter, on the other hand, is a marvelous liaison (or amalgamator): it makes the risotto even creamier and, no doubt, buttery. I use it with all meat, mushroom, and some vegetable risotti. The butter makes the dish rich and creamy, magnifies and to some extent alters the flavor. This can be desirable, and there are many risotti where I love to use it. For instance, butter has the effect in tomato sauces of balancing the acidity—but it changes the taste in a way that olive oil does not.

Sauces Good with Risotto . . .

Spicy Tomato Sauce (page 128)—not a long-keeping sauce, so make a half-recipe just for risotto.

Marinara Sauce with Fresh Basil (page 130)—use 2 cups sauce. *For a special finish:* off heat, just before serving, stir in 1 to 1½ cups small cubes of fresh mozzarella, 2 tablespoons shredded basil leaves, and just ½ cup freshly grated Parmigiano-Reggiano.

Simple Tomato Sauce (page 132)—use 2 cups sauce; finish with mozzarella and basil as above.

Summer Tomato and Eggplant Sauce (page 259)—use 2 cups sauce; finish with mozzarella and basil as above.

Savoy Cabbage, Bacon, and Mushroom Sauce (page 138)—use only ½ cup freshly grated Parmigiano-Reggiano.

Asparagus, Green Pea, and Scallion Sauce (page 135)—I suggest finishing with 2 tablespoons butter rather than olive oil.

Mushroom Ragù (page 141)—finish with butter.

Ragù alla Bolognese (page 143); can also be used for *Riso Sartu,* (page 230).

Duck Leg *Guazzetto* (page 154).

Pork Rib *Guazzetto* (page 151).

BUTTER OR OLIVE OIL, YOUR CALL

Here's a delicious experiment that will show you these differences better than I can describe. Make a basic risotto, incorporating two cups of Simple Tomato Sauce (page 132), as described above. Cook it to the consistency you like, and then pour half into a separate bowl—finish one half with 1 tablespoon butter and the other with an equal amount of olive oil. See what I mean? They are distinct, but it's hard to describe—and only you can say which you prefer.

Riso Sartù

With its developed flavor and moist, saucy consistency, risotto is still special the day after—it's not just cold rice. Riso Sartù is a dish I always enjoy when visiting my cousin Clara Pacelli in Naples. It is one of the most wonderful ways I know to transform cooked risotto into something new. The risotto is blended with meat sauce, green peas, and lots of grated cheese and packed into small molds with morsels of egg, prosciutto, and mozzarella hidden inside. Baked and then unmolded, the cakes are crisp and crunchy outside—as you can see in the photo below—and creamy and chock-full of treats inside.

This recipe makes six cakes with 2½ cups of risotto and a cup of Ragù alla Bolognese (page 143) as the meat sauce. It is easy to multiply the formula if you have more risotto and sauce, and ovenproof cups to serve as molds.

This dish might be made today with leftovers, but traditionally it was the specialty of the Neapolitan aristocracy, and risotto was made expressly for it.

---

6 SMALL MOLDED RICE CAKES OR *TIMBALES,*
SERVING 6 AS A FIRST COURSE

FOR COATING THE MOLDS

2 to 3 tablespoons soft butter

2 tablespoons or more grated cheese or fine dry bread crumbs

FOR THE SAUCE AND
RISOTTO MIXTURE

1½ cups Ragù alla Bolognese (page 143)

¾ cup frozen peas

2½ cups cooked risotto (page 224)

⅔ cup grated cheese*

Getting Ready

Set a rack in the middle of the oven and preheat to 450°. Butter the insides and top rims of all six cups or molds generously, using a teaspoon or more of soft butter for each. Sprinkle a teaspoon or more of grated cheese (or bread crumbs, if you prefer) inside each cup, and rotate and tilt it so the buttered surfaces are completely coated. Invert the mold and shake out loose cheese or crumbs (if cheese, be sure to collect and use it in the next steps).

To refresh your sauce, stir 2 or 3 tablespoons water into the Ragù alla Bolognese (or more water if the ragù is very thick) and heat to a simmer in a small saucepan. Stir in the frozen peas, simmer them in the sauce for a few minutes, until tender, then take the pan off the heat. You should have 2 cups of sauce, or a bit more.

Measure the risotto into a skillet, set it over low heat, and—assuming it is chilled and congealed from refrigeration—break up the lumps of rice with a spoon. Warm it up gently, and keep pressing and stirring until the rice loosens (don't cook or fry it), then stir in 1 cup of the warm Bolognese-and-green-pea sauce until thoroughly distributed. Take the skillet off the heat, and stir in ⅔ cup of grated cheese. The rice mixture should be warm, not hot: let it cool if necessary.

Filling the Cups

Fill each cup, one at a time, as follows: Measure a scant ½ cup of the rice and plop it into the cup. Press the rice level with a teaspoon or your fingers, then press in the center to form a hollow and move some of the rice up the unfilled sides to the rim, like walls around a crater.

To fill the crater, take two pieces of hard-boiled egg, a teaspoon of mozzarella cubes, and a teaspoon of prosciutto strips. Drop the pieces into the hollow, mixing them up a bit, press down gently, then top

FOR HIDING INSIDE THE RISOTTO

- I hard-boiled egg, peeled and sliced lengthwise in quarters, then crosswise in thirds, so you have 12 small chunks

- ⅓ cup packaged (pressed) mozzarella cut into tiny cubes, ¼ inch or smaller

- 2 ounces paper-thin prosciutto cut into small strips (each about the size of a paper clip!)

FOR THE FINISHING TOUCH

3 tablespoons grated cheese

RECOMMENDED EQUIPMENT

The best molds to form the dome-shape risotto cake pictured here are ceramic custard cups with a 5-ounce capacity and rounded bottom. Tapered metal *timbale* molds of the same size are also suitable. Miniature soufflé-type ramekins, 4- or 5-ounce capacity, can be used but may be harder to unmold, because of the broad bottom.

Note: Altogether you will need 1 well-packed cup of freshly grated Parmigiano-Reggiano or Grana Padano, used in the amounts given above.

off the hollow with a teaspoon or so of the reserved Bolognese; level it with a spoon.

The cup should be just about filled to the top. Cap it with 1½ tablespoons of risotto mixture: press it down firmly and spread it smoothly and evenly within the rim of the cup. Finally, sprinkle 1½ teaspoons of grated cheese lightly over the top—don't press down the cheese.

Fill each cup in this way. (You can refrigerate them at this point if you want; allow extra baking time for chilled cups.)

Baking, Unmolding, and Serving

For easy handling, set the cups on a baking sheet or in a shallow baking pan—spaced well apart for fast, even heating—and place it in the oven. Bake for 30 minutes, then rotate the sheet back to front. The top of each cup should be nicely colored but moist; juices from the insides should be hot enough to drip over the sides. Bake 20 minutes more, until the tops are dark gold and well crusted.

Remove the sheet from the oven and let the cups sit and cool for at least 5 minutes, and up to 10, before unmolding. Meanwhile, gently heat the remaining Ragù alla Bolognese; you should have almost a cup left in the saucepan—thin it with a bit of water if it's thickened up while sitting. Warm up six small (dessert-size) plates, which you will need for unmolding and serving.

Protecting your hands with pot holders or dry kitchen towels, set one hot cup on a clear counter. Insert a thin sharp knife blade into the cup, flat against the side, and run it all around, cutting through the crust on the rim and loosening the rice inside too. Lay one of the warm plates on top of the cup, and grip them firmly together—make sure your pot holders or towels won't slip when you move your hands. Quickly invert the cup and plate and, before setting the plate on the counter, give the pair a sharp shake to loosen the rice cake.

Center the upside-down cup in the plate and lift it up. What you hope is that it will come off the rice cake easily and completely. If some of the rice is stuck in the cup, just scrape it free and patch it in place. If the cup doesn't lift off the rice, give it a few good raps on the side and top with a heavy knife handle. You might have to invert the cup again and make sure you've cut through the crust completely. But you will succeed in unmolding each cup!

When they are all unmolded, spoon about 2 tablespoons of hot Ragù alla Bolognese on top of each rice cake and let it drip down the sides. Serve right away.

For a larger dinner party, this is a great way to serve facsimile risotto. Make the risotto and assemble the day before, then set in the oven to bake while your guests are arriving. Make sure to allow 20 minutes more of baking time if it is cold from the refrigerator.

USING LEFTOVER RISOTTO

Riso al salto, *rice with a jump,* is the traditional way of reusing risotto in Italy, and a delicious one. The secret with leftovers is always to create a new dish, not a reheated one.

To make rice with a jump you will need 2 cups of leftover risotto and ½ cup grated Parmigiano-Reggiano or Grana Padano, one beaten egg seasoned, and 2 tablespoons of chopped parsley or chives. Loosen the risotto with a fork, add the other ingredients, mix all well, and form hamburgerlike patties. Press them down slightly, and cook them in a hot non-stick skillet with butter till crispy on each side. Press them down with a spatula occasionally—but gently, because they are fragile—until they form a crust, which is the best part. They are great for breakfast in the morning with eggs, or as a side for braised meats; or eat them just as they are.

Leftover risotto makes also a good fried-rice facsimile. Sauté in some olive oil some leftover vegetables or meat cut in small pieces, seasoned with salt and pepper. In the meantime, break the risotto up with a fork, and add it to the skillet. Cook for a few minutes, stirring, then add chopped scallions, chives, or parsley, and drizzle on some balsamic vinegar—for 3 cups of fried rice, you'll need 3 teaspoons of aceto balsamico. Let the rice cook for 2 or 3 minutes, tossing, then serve.

For the Love of Vegetables

Recently, at a food conference where I was speaking, I was asked the question "What is missing on Italian menus in America?" I did not have to think for a moment—it's vegetables. Everyone is into pasta, risottos, and polenta, and vegetables are relegated to a secondary role, if they have any role at all. Well, vegetables are as important as pasta and rice and at times even more important than meat in an Italian home.

Italians love their vegetables. Appetizers are largely made up of pickled, grilled, marinated, and steamed vegetables; the diversity and beauty of Italian soups lies in the legumes and vegetables enriching them; the repertoire of pasta and risotto dishes would diminish by half if there were no vegetables; and Italy would need to double the amount of meat or fish for their main courses if vegetables were not served alongside.

I love cooking with vegetables, and it is ever more encouraging that Italian varieties of vegetables are increasingly available, such as *broccoli di rape*, fennel, radicchio, *cavolo nero* (black kale), cardoons, and *cocuzza* (goose-necked squash) and its tendrils. Simply braised with virgin olive oil and garlic, these vegetables will turn into a delectable dish or serve as a dressing for pasta. As if that were not enough, try stuffing these vegetables between two slices of crusty bread and a deliciously juicy sandwich will emerge without the need of mayo or mustard, the juiciness of the vegetables dressing the bread, with the olive oil as condiment. When I was young, on many days the lunch I took to school would be a sandwich of egg-battered and fried zucchini.

Italians love fresh leafy salads, from sweet spring baby greens to intense and bitter chicory, tossed with red wine vinegar and virgin olive oil. But when those leaves are not available, Italian cooks will turn most vegetables, simply steamed or boiled, into a great salad using the same condiments. There is nothing better on a hot summer day than poached zucchini sprinkled with some sea salt and drizzled with extra-virgin olive oil. It is a pure clean taste, sweet and delicate.

For a more complex flavor try *verdure gratinate*, lasagnas made of vegetables and day-old bread. It may seem like a novelty, but most regions of Italy will have their own version of vegetables baked with yesterday's bread and some cheese. Here I share with you some of my favorites. I'm sure you'll find that the use of vegetables as a main course with a little protein as an accompaniment is a delicious, nutritional, and delightful way to cook.

The Abundance of Summer

Poached Whole Zucchini with Lemon and Olive Oil

*P*oaching is not a common preparation here in the U.S., but in season all over Italy you will be served zucchini cooked this way, simply seasoned with salt and olive oil.

It is a perfect method when excellent zucchini are abundant—convenient to do the cooking ahead. Let the zucchini cool and you can serve them many delicious ways—as an appetizer, a side dish, or the centerpiece of a summer salad. (See page 238 for some good ideas.)

You can expand this recipe as much as you want for large parties.

SERVES 6 TO 8

Rinse the zucchini but do not trim them. Bring a large saucepan or stockpot of water to a steady boil. Add the zucchini, but don't cram them together or boil them too vigorously, because you want them to remain whole.

Cook for about 20 minutes, partially covered. Near the end of the cooking time, check for doneness by lifting one squash from the water with a large slotted spoon or spatula. A perfectly cooked zucchini will be just soft enough to droop a bit on the spoon but won't break apart. Carefully remove the zucchini, one at a time, to a colander or wire rack and lay them flat. Sprinkle about ½ teaspoon of the salt over the squash, rolling them to distribute the salt evenly. Let cool for a few minutes.

When you can handle them comfortably, trim the ends from each zucchini and cut them in half crosswise, into 3-inch pieces. Slice all of these lengthwise in half, and again into quarters, to form wedges. Arrange the wedges neatly on a serving platter, cut side up, in one or two layers, so you can dress them easily.

2 pounds (5 or 6) small tender zucchini (see box, page 239)

I teaspoon coarse *fleur de sel* or kosher salt, plus more to taste

3 tablespoons best-quality extra-virgin olive oil

I teaspoon finely shredded lemon zest

I teaspoon freshly squeezed lemon juice, or more to taste

Poached Whole Zucchini with Lemon and Olive Oil (cont.)

Good So Many Ways

Once you've cooked and cooled whole zucchini—and cut them into wedges, rounds, or cubes—dress them with any good salad dressing or with any of these cold sauces:

- *Salsa Verde* (page 362)
- Smooth Sweet Red Pepper Sauce (page 364)
- Cucumber, Yogurt, and Mint Sauce (page 363)

Another way is to slice the poached zucchini into thin lengthwise strips and layer them into a *gratinate* with country bread, following the recipe on page 240.

Sprinkle another ½ teaspoon of salt evenly over all the slices (you may need a bit more if using very coarse grains of *fleur de sel*). Then drizzle the 3 tablespoons of oil all over and scatter the lemon zest. Let the zucchini absorb the flavors for a while before the final seasoning. Just before serving, sprinkle the lemon juice over the wedges. Taste a piece, and add more salt or lemon juice if you like.

 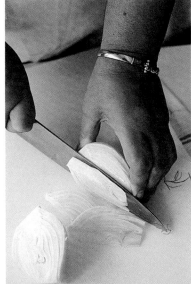

Zucchini Salad with Potatoes, Boiled Eggs, and Red Onion

Poached zucchini, cut into rounds or cubes, is a terrific salad ingredient. This salad is a lovely combination of tastes and colors, but you can follow the same basic approach without the potatoes, without the eggs, or even without the onions.

If you are preparing zucchini and potatoes for salad, it's easy to cook them in one pot of water. Start boiling them together and remove the zucchini when they are "droopy," as described in the main recipe. Usually the potatoes will need to cook a bit longer, until they are easily pierced with a fork or sharp knife. Let everything cool, then toss your salad and dress it just before serving.

THE IDEAL ZUCCHINI

Zucchini are most flavorful and appealing when they are young and firm. For all the dishes in this chapter, choose unblemished squash, about 6 inches long and no fatter than 2 inches in diameter. Three zucchini of this ideal size weigh about 1 pound.

SERVES 6

Put the whole, unpeeled potatoes in a pot of boiling *unsalted* water to cover. Bring to a boil, cooking steadily—but not violently—for 20–25 minutes. Test for doneness—the potatoes should be easily pierced with a fork. Don't let them crack or get mushy on the outside. When they are just cooked through, remove them, sprinkle the ¼ teaspoon salt over them, and let cool.

If you are using uncooked zucchini, cook them along with the potatoes, removing them after 20 minutes.

Trim the ends of the zucchini and cut them crosswise into rounds, about ½ inch thick. (If the squash are "fat," first slice them lengthwise to form half-round or quarter-round pieces.) Peel the potatoes and cut roughly into 1-inch chunks, about the size of the zucchini pieces. Peel the eggs and cut into wedges.

To finish the salad, toss the squash and potato pieces together in a bowl, scatter the egg wedges and onion slices on top, and toss lightly. Drizzle over all the olive oil and the vinegar, sprinkle on the salt and grinds of pepper, and toss thoroughly to distribute the seasonings.

Serve right away.

½ pound Yukon Gold potatoes (2 small potatoes are best)

1 pound small Poached Whole Zucchini (see main recipe), or 5 or 6 small tender uncooked zucchini

¼ teaspoon coarse sea salt or kosher salt

2 hard-boiled eggs

1 small-medium red onion, cut in thin half-moons (about ⅔ cup)

3 tablespoons extra-virgin olive oil

2 tablespoons red wine vinegar

¼ teaspoon salt, plus more to taste

Freshly ground black pepper to taste

Zucchini and Country Bread Lasagna

Another wonderful way to use bread—something that we always have in abundance in our house, fresh, day-old, and dried—is as an element of many savory dishes. It is used in appetizer gratinate, soups, and salads, and day-old bread is great in desserts.

Here bread slices are the base and substance of a summertime vegetable lasagna, in place of pasta. I give you two versions, one with raw zucchini, one with briefly sautéed eggplant slices. Assembly and baking are the same for both. You could multiply the recipe and make this as a big party or picnic dish. It's wonderful warm or at room temperature as a hearty side dish.

To vary: use egg-battered zucchini strips (page 21) for a scrumptious lasagna; or roast the eggplant instead of frying it; or combine zucchini and eggplant (sauté zucchini slices first, though).

The good flavor comes from Summer Tomato Sauce. The recipe on page 256 will give you enough for a big casserole and for several pasta dishes too. But you could use other sauces, such as a marinara or a plain tomato sauce.

SERVES 8 TO 12 AS A SIDE DISH

FOR THE ZUCCHINI

2 pounds firm, unblemished zucchini (6 small or 4 medium)

½ teaspoon salt

2 tablespoons extra-virgin olive oil

FOR ASSEMBLING THE LASAGNA

12 or so day-old slices of country bread (from a 1½-pound loaf)

2 tablespoons soft butter, for the baking pan

Rinse and dry the zucchini, slice off the stems, and trim the blossom ends. With a sharp long-bladed knife (or a mandoline if you have one) cut very thin lengthwise slices, about ⅛ inch thick. Put them in a large bowl, sprinkle over them the ½ teaspoon of salt and the 2 tablespoons of oil, and toss to coat the slices with the seasonings.

Assembling the Lasagna

Arrange a rack in the center of the oven and preheat to 400°. Cut the crusts off the bread slices. If they are soft and fresh, you can dry the slices briefly in the oven, but don't let them get crisp or brown.

Butter the bottom and sides of the baking pan generously. Spread a cup of the tomato sauce in a thin layer in the bottom of the pan. Cover the bottom with a single layer of bread slices. Trim the slices and cut them in pieces so they fit close together and lie flat (but you don't have to fill every small crack or hole). Spoon about 2 cups of sauce onto the bread and spread it evenly.

Make a layer of zucchini (or sautéed eggplant), using half the slices. You can lay them crosswise or lengthwise in the pan, whichever way fits best. Overlap the slices as necessary to make an even layer that completely covers the sauce. Press down gently to condense the lasagna and make more room in the pan, then sprinkle 1 cup of grated cheese evenly over the top.

Now repeat the layering: Arrange another layer of bread slices and trimmed pieces. Cover the bread with 2 more cups of sauce, spread evenly. Lay out the rest of the zucchini (or eggplant) slices in an overlapping layer. Spread the remaining tomato sauce, about a cup, in a thin layer. Sprinkle another cup of cheese (or more!) in a generous layer over the top of the lasagna.

Baking the Lasagna

Cut a sheet of aluminum foil about 2 feet long—preferably from a wide roll of heavy-duty foil. Press the foil so it hugs the sides of the pan and bend it to make a "tent" over the lasagna that doesn't touch the surface anywhere.

Bake the lasagna covered for about 45 minutes, giving the zucchini plenty of time to cook. Remove the pan from the oven; carefully unfold the foil from the sides of the pan and lift it off completely. Don't get burned by the pan or the steam that is released—keep your face and hands out of the way. And don't let the foil mess up the cheesy topping! (In a glass casserole, you should be able to see the sauce bubbling up around the sides of the pan.)

Return the lasagna to the oven and bake for another 15 to 20 minutes, or until the top is deep golden-brown. Let the casserole settle for a few minutes before serving (it will stay hot for some time). Cut in squares or rectangles of whatever size you like, and lift out individual pieces with an angled spatula.

6 cups Summer Tomato Sauce (page 256) or Anytime Tomato Primavera Sauce (page 125) or marinara sauce (page 130)

2 cups grated Parmigiano-Reggiano or Grana Padano, or more to taste

RECOMMENDED EQUIPMENT

A 9-by-13-inch Pyrex baking pan or a similar shallow casserole with 3-quart capacity

Wide, heavy-duty aluminum foil

THE BEST BREAD FOR COUNTRY BREAD LASAGNA

A hearty European-style chewy wheat bread, made with all-white or white and whole-grain flour, is best for these savory lasagne. Cut the slices yourself and let them dry a bit. Day-old (or briefly oven-dried) ½-inch slices will soak up lots of vegetable juices and give the lasagna a marvelous texture. Don't get a skinny or low loaf with lots of crust, though— like a baguette or ciabatta— since the crust is trimmed away. Instead get a lofty bread— a large round or oval loaf— for big slices with lots of "insides."

Eggplant and Country Bread Lasagna

3½ pounds medium eggplants

About 2 cups flour, for dredging

½ cup canola oil, for frying,
    or more if necessary

½ teaspoon salt, or more if necessary

FOR ASSEMBLING THE
LASAGNA

Same ingredients as for main recipe

RECOMMENDED EQUIPMENT

A 12-inch or larger skillet, non-stick
    preferred

Trim the stem and bottom ends of the eggplants. Peel off all the skin if it is tough, or, with tender eggplant, remove ribbons of peel in a striped pattern (see box, page 254).

With a sharp chef's knife, cut all the eggplant lengthwise into slices, about ⅓ inch thick. Toss a few slices at a time in the flour (in a large bowl or on a tray) to coat completely on both sides; shake off the excess and pile in another bowl or tray.

Pour 2 or 3 tablespoons of the canola oil into the skillet and tilt it so the entire bottom is coated with a thin film of oil. Set the pan over medium-high heat for a couple of minutes.

Lay a batch of eggplant slices in the pan with plenty of space between them. You want to brown the pieces quickly, with minimal oil, so keep the heat up but don't let the oil smoke or the vegetables burn. Fry the slices for about 2 minutes, until lightly colored on the underside, then flip them over and fry 2 minutes on the second side. Drain the slices on sheets of paper towel and sprinkle with a couple pinches of salt while hot.

Brown the remaining floured eggplant in batches, adding oil to the pan as needed. Remove to paper towels and salt them right away, using about ½ teaspoon for all the slices.

Assemble and bake the lasagna as in the main recipe.

TO SALT OR NOT TO SALT THE WATER

I always used to boil vegetables in salted water. But recently I started salting certain vegetables after they were cooked, tossing them immediately after draining with medium-coarse salt, while they were still steaming hot, and I found I liked it. Does it make that much difference? Indeed it does. Instead of making a saline solution out of the boiling water that permeates the vegetable throughout, salting later allows the vegetable to retain its pure vegetable flavor, and then the sprinkled salt adds another dimension of flavor by seeping in gently while it is still hot. The vegetables that best respond to this method are string beans, broccoli, and zucchini. But I find it also true of cabbage, beets, chard, and other greens.

Broccoli and Cauliflower *Gratinate*

These crispy, cheesy, caramelized florets of broccoli and cauliflower are a wonderful mealtime vegetable. But they're so tempting, easy to pick up and pop in your mouth, that they would make a hard-to-resist impromptu hors d'oeuvre before dinner begins.

You can prepare either broccoli or cauliflower alone with this recipe, though a combination is especially colorful. The florets are partly cooked by my covered-skillet method, then tossed with grated cheese and bread crumbs and baked until golden. The cauliflower and broccoli cook at different rates in the skillet, as detailed in the recipe. If you're preparing just one kind of florets, simply adjust your timing.

SERVES 6

Prepping and Skillet Cooking

Place a rack in the center of the oven and preheat it to 375°.

Snap or slice off the big clusters of broccoli and cauliflower florets from the stems. Trim the stalks of the broccoli pieces but don't separate the tiny florets. Slice the cauliflower clusters in half or quarters so that they're roughly equal in size to the broccoli pieces. You'll need only the floret pieces for this dish, so save all the good stalk and stem pieces for soup or another dish.

Set the skillet over medium-high heat, pour in the oil, and scatter the garlic slices. Let them cook, tossing them in the pan once or twice, until they just begin to color, 3 to 4 minutes.

Drop in the cauliflower pieces and sprinkle on ¼ teaspoon of the salt and the *peperoncino*. Cover the skillet, give it good shake to roll the florets around, and cook for about 5 minutes, over medium heat, shaking the pan again once or twice.

Uncover and add the broccoli florets, sprinkle another ¼ teaspoon salt on top, and pour in ¼ cup water.

Cover and cook another 4 to 5 minutes, shaking the pan now and again, until the broccoli has started sizzling and softening too. Remove the pan from the heat and scrape all the florets into a large mixing bowl, with all of the oil and garlic.

1 pound broccoli

1 pound cauliflower

3 tablespoons extra-virgin olive oil

3 tablespoons sliced garlic

½ teaspoon salt

¼ teaspoon dried *peperoncino* (hot red pepper flakes)

FOR THE *GRATINATE*

2 tablespoons soft butter, for the baking sheet

⅔ cup plus a few tablespoons grated Parmigiano-Reggiano or Grana Padano

¼ cup fine dry bread crumbs

Lemon slices, for serving

A 14-inch skillet or sauté pan, with a
  cover

A 12-by-18-inch baking sheet

FEEL THE VEGETABLES

*Always touch your vegetables
when you are buying them and
when you are cooking them.
Touching any ingredient is very
telling. I am always told that I
am very sensual with my ingredients when I cook, and maybe I
am. But I know that I understand them much, much better
once I have handled them. I can
tell whether a certain meat is
grainy and tough, I can tell how
fresh a fish is by how firm it is.
And I can tell that vegetables are
fresh when an artichoke squeaks
under my fingers, the string bean
snaps when I bend it, the pepper
squirts when I break it open, and
an eggplant is shiny and firm to
the touch.*

Broccoli and Cauliflower Gratinate (cont.)

Assembling and Baking the *Gratinate*

Let the florets cool for a few minutes while you coat the baking sheet
with the butter. Mix the ⅔ cup of grated cheese and the bread
crumbs together.

Pour about half the crumbs on top of the florets and toss all together. Pour over the rest of the crumbs and toss again, until the florets are well coated and the crumbs are moistened.

Lay the florets on the baking sheet, in one layer with space between them, so all surfaces will crisp and caramelize in the oven.
Scrape up any crumbs in the bowl and sprinkle them on the vegetables. Finally, sprinkle extra cheese lightly all over the florets, using
another 2 or 3 tablespoons, if you love cheese as much as I do.

Put the baking sheet in the oven and bake for about 10 minutes,
rotate the pan back to front for even browning, and cook 10 minutes
more. The florets should be crispy and nicely colored but may need a
few more minutes for deep color. If they're still not dark enough after
5 minutes, raise the oven heat or move the sheet to a higher rack and
bake a bit longer.

Let the vegetables cool on the sheet briefly, then arrange them on
a serving platter. Scrape up the crispy bits of crumbs and cheese and
crumble them over the florets.

Serve warm or at room temperature, with sliced lemon. Eat
them by squeezing a few drops of
juice onto a floret and popping it
in your mouth!

Chopping basil leaves

Green Bean *Gratinate* with Cherry Tomatoes, Mozzarella, and Basil

*O*ne day, when I was wondering what to make with a nice batch of fresh green beans, my daughter Tanya remembered a salad she'd had on a recent trip to Italy—perfectly cooked green beans, cherry tomatoes, basil, and cubes of fresh mozzarella.

Because I love to take things a step further, I decided to combine the very same ingredients in a casserole and bake them with a crosta (crust) of bread crumbs and grated cheese. It was wonderful. And it is a fine example of how one simple procedure—baking ingredients coated with cheesy bread crumbs—can work so well with so many foods. The Broccoli and Cauliflower Gratinate (page 243) and the Crispy Baked Turkey Cutlets (page 310) use the same method.

Of course, there's another kitchen principle evident here: good ingredient combinations lend themselves to different preparations. If you want to try Tanya's original salad with green beans, tomatoes, basil, and mozzarella, I give a formula following the main recipe.

SERVES 6 OR MORE

Arrange a rack in the top half of the oven and preheat to 375°. Fill a large pot with water (at least 5 quarts) and bring it to the boil.

Trim both ends of the beans and remove strings (if they're an old-fashioned variety and have strings). Dump them all into the boiling water, cover the pot until the water boils again, then cook uncovered, for 10 minutes or so, until they are just cooked through—tender but still firm enough to snap (see box, page 247).

Drain the beans briefly in a colander, then put them in a big kitchen bowl. Sprinkle ¼ teaspoon of salt on the hot beans and toss them so they're all seasoned. Let the salt melt and the beans cool for a couple of minutes.

Meanwhile, rinse and dry the tomatoes; if they're larger than an inch, slice them in halves; otherwise, leave them whole. Cut the mozzarella into ½-inch cubes. Slice the basil leaves into thin shreds or a *chiffonade*.

Toss the grated cheese and bread crumbs together in a small bowl. Lightly grease the insides of the baking dish with a teaspoon or more

1 ½ pounds fresh green beans

½ teaspoon kosher salt

¾ pound cherry tomatoes (about 3 cups), preferably small grape tomatoes

½ pound fresh mozzarella

4 to 6 fresh basil leaves

1 cup grated Parmigiano-Reggiano or Grana Padano

½ cup dry bread crumbs

3 tablespoons butter

3 tablespoons extra-virgin olive oil

RECOMMENDED EQUIPMENT

A shallow baking dish, 2- or 3-quart capacity

of the butter. Sprinkle ¼ cup of the cheese-and-bread-crumb mix all over the bottom of the dish.

When the beans are no longer steaming, drop the tomatoes, cubes of mozzarella, and basil shreds on top. Drizzle the olive oil over all, sprinkle on the remaining ¼ teaspoon salt, and toss together a few times. Sprinkle ¾ cup of the cheesy bread crumbs on top and toss well, so everything is coated.

Turn the vegetables, scraping up all the crumbs, into the baking dish, and spread them in an even layer. Sprinkle over the remaining ¼ cup of crumbs; cut the rest of the butter in small pieces, and scatter them all over the top. Place the dish in the oven.

Bake the *gratinate* for 10 minutes, then rotate it back to front and bake another 10 minutes. Check to see that it is browning and bake a few minutes more, until the *gratinate* is dark golden and crusted. (If the crumbs still look pale after 20 minutes in your oven, raise the temperature to 400° or 425° and bake until done.)

Serve the hot *gratinate* in the baking dish.

Green Bean, Cherry Tomato, and Mozzarella Salad

Prep and cook green beans (1 or 2 pounds) as for the *gratinate*, but have ready a bowl of ice water to refresh them and set the color. As soon as they are cooked to a soft snap (see box, facing page), lift the beans and drop them in the ice water. Chill thoroughly, then drain and dry them well.

Toss the blanched beans with cherry tomatoes, mozzarella cubes, and basil *chiffonade* (in the same proportions as for main recipe). To dress the salad, sprinkle over it 2 tablespoons wine vinegar, ¼ cup extra-virgin olive oil, and salt and freshly ground pepper to taste.

Toss well and serve.

Giovanni Bencina peeling garlic

Skillet Green Beans with Gorgonzola

Green beans are delicious, but they can get boring. But letting a little gorgonzola melt into the beans gives them a marvelous complexity. This is great as an appetizer or a side dish with grilled meats.

SERVES 6 TO 8

Rinse and dry the beans and trim off both ends.

Set a large skillet over medium heat, pour in the oil, and toss in the smashed garlic cloves. Cook 4 to 5 minutes, until the garlic has just lightly colored.

Put the beans in the pan, shake it a few times to spread them out, pour in ¼ cup water, and cover the pan. Lower the heat and cook, covered, for about 15 minutes, shaking the pan and checking the green beans occasionally, until they are tender to the bite and lightly caramelized.

When they're done as you like, salt lightly (bearing in mind that the gorgonzola will be salty), uncover the pan, raise the heat, and drop bits of crumbled gorgonzola into the beans, all around the skillet.

Cook—no cover now—tossing and stirring the beans with a spatula or tongs, while the cheese melts, about a minute and a half. When the cheese has melted and coated the beans—but before it coats the bottom of the pan in a thick layer—spoon and scrape the green beans into a deep bowl and serve immediately.

2 pounds green beans

¼ cup extra-virgin olive oil

6 garlic cloves, peeled and smashed

Salt to taste

½ pound gorgonzola, crumbled

RECOMMENDED EQUIPMENT

A 14-inch skillet

GREEN BEANS: COOK TO A SOFT SNAP

For both recipes here—and anytime I cook green beans in water—I check the doneness of the beans carefully. I don't like undercooked beans, which are still crunchy and have a raw taste, and I don't like overcooked beans, which are mushy and a drab olive color. I want them to be cooked all the way through, which brings out their full flavor, be tender to the bite, but still give you something to chew. And I want green beans to be bright green.

There are various tests to check the beans (which I do after about 10 minutes of cooking): poke one with a fork, take a bite, slit one open to see the interior, or hold one up to see if it droops. But my favorite test is to fold a bean in the middle: it shouldn't break sharply, and it shouldn't just fall apart. It should snap, but softly.

Grilled Corn and Figs with Balsamic Reduction

*Y*ou probably have enjoyed grilled corn; you may or may not have tasted a grilled fresh fig. I'm almost sure, however, that you never had them together in one dish. But when late summer brings them to market at the same time, I hope you will try this recipe. It's a simple one to do ahead: you grill the corn on the cob and then grill the figs (they take barely a minute). You slice off the corn kernels, toss them with the figs, and serve the dish at room temperature.

The golden vegetable and dark fruit are a great-tasting and pretty combination just as they are, but if you happen to have some *Drizzling Sauce of Balsamic Vinegar* already made (or a bottle of balsamic vinegar to reduce), it's definitely worth applying the final swirl of sauce. The acidic tang sets off the sweetness of all the sugars in the corn and figs, already intensified by the heat of the grill. You can use either a gas or a charcoal grill for this, but keep the fire moderate (and pay attention, especially with the figs) so the sugars are caramelized, not burned.

SERVES 6

6 large ears sweet corn

2 tablespoons extra-virgin olive oil

¾ teaspoon salt, plus more to taste

1 pound (about 1 pint) ripe fresh figs, preferably a dark variety

FOR SERVING

1 or 2 tablespoons Drizzling Sauce of Reduced Balsamic Vinegar (page 39)

Clean the grill rack very well. Heat it with medium heat, if you're using a gas grill. If a charcoal grill, ignite and spread a bed of coals in a low layer that will cook all the ears of corn over moderate—not searing—heat. (If you can, adjust the height of the rack, too, to avoid burning the corn.)

Shuck the corn and remove all the silks. Put the ears in a big bowl or on a tray; pour the olive oil and sprinkle ½ teaspoon of salt all over them. Roll them around and rub them with your hands so they're well coated.

To prepare the figs, trim their stems and slice them all in half (through the stem end to the pointy blossom end).

Lay the ears of corn on the grill, and cook them for 7 minutes or more, turning them frequently, until the ears are nicely grill-marked and the kernels are tender. Don't burn them, and do shift them around the grill so they cook evenly. Let them cool while you grill the figs.

Wipe off the rack, if necessary, and have it hot so the figs don't stick. Set the fig halves on the rack, cut side down, and cook them only for a minute or so, to caramelize the cut side and soften the flesh. Don't let them burn or get mushy.

With a sharp knife, slice the grilled kernels off the cobs and gather them in a mixing bowl (see box, page 276, for my method of cutting off kernels). Put in the fig pieces and toss together with the corn, adding the remaining ¼ teaspoon of salt or more to taste.

Serve warm or at room temperature in a wide bowl or platter. If you're drizzling with the balsamic reduction, it's best (and prettiest) to spread the corn and figs out in a shallow layer on a platter and swirl the vinegar with a teaspoon or fork in thin streaks over the top. This will give every spoonful of corn a delicate accent of sauce.

SMELL THE HERBS

The use of fresh herbs has exploded in the American kitchen today and that is wonderful, but I recall, as a young apprentice at my great-aunt's apron strings, for every pot that went on the stove there was an herb somewhere in the garden to match. Some herbs were better to cook; others were better added to the finished dish. Rosemary, bay leaves, and thyme were mostly used for long cooking, where their oils would be extracted slowly out of their leaves, but sage, oregano, and marjoram needed very little cooking time, and basil, parsley, and mint were tossed raw, which is enough to release their aroma.

When I cook I love to crush herbs in my hands and then inhale their perfumes; it invigorates me, it refreshes me, and I get a good sense of what I am adding to the pot.

I gently begin crushing herbs for my grandchildren in their early months of life, so they can begin to collect the smells of the wonderful world of herbs and foods.

Zucchini and Scallions with Vinegar and Mint

*H*ere is another unusual preparation of zucchini that will heighten your appreciation for a wonderful vegetable that is often abundant and underused. It's my simplified version of a traditional method—in escabesce—in which sautéed zucchini is marinated in vinegar with fresh mint. Here, zucchini and scallion slices caramelize slowly in a skillet, are quickly coated with sizzling vinegar, and are tossed with fresh mint. The resulting layers of flavor are distinct but harmonious.

This is a versatile addition to your repertoire of fresh-from-the-garden recipes. Made ahead and served at room temperature, it's a lively side dish all summer long, especially good with anything off the grill.

SERVES 4 TO 6 AS A SIDE DISH OR CONDIMENT

2 pounds small tender zucchini (5 or 6; see box, page 239)

½ teaspoon salt, approximately

½ pound scallions

¼ cup extra-virgin olive oil

1 tablespoon red or white wine vinegar, or 3 tablespoons Reduced Wine Vinegar for Vegetables, or more to taste (facing page)

8 to 10 small fresh mint leaves, shredded or torn

RECOMMENDED EQUIPMENT

A 12- or 14-inch skillet

Wash the zucchini well and pat them dry. Trim the ends of the zucchini and slice them crosswise into ⅓-inch-thick rounds. Gather all the pieces in a bowl and toss them with ¼ teaspoon of salt.

Trim the root ends of the scallions, remove all the wilted green and loose white layers, and cut into 1-inch lengths.

Pour the oil into the skillet and set over medium-high heat. After a couple of minutes, turn the zucchini slices into the hot oil and spread them out evenly to fill the pan. Push down on the top zucchini with a spoon or spatula, pressing the bottom slices against the pan. Scatter the scallion chunks on top of the zucchini and sprinkle them with a pinch or two of salt.

Let the zucchini cook and caramelize on the bottom without disturbing them for 8 minutes or so. Lift some of the bottom slices with a spatula to check: when they're nicely browned and a bit shriveled, turn the vegetables over so the top pieces can caramelize. Cook for a couple of minutes, turn again, cook a bit more, and turn, until all the pieces are golden, sizzling, and shrinking.

Drain off the oil. Set a colander or a strainer in a small bowl, tilt the skillet over the strainer, and let the vegetables slide in. Quickly scrape the oil out of the pan, shake the colander to drain the zucchini, then turn the vegetables back into the skillet, set on medium-high heat. Cook briefly, shaking the pan and tossing the vegetables.

When they're sizzling again, push them to one side of the pan, clearing a hot spot. Pour the tablespoon of wine vinegar (or 3 tablespoons of reduced wine vinegar) into the hot spot, let it heat and start to bubble, then toss and stir the zucchini in with the vinegar to coat them.

Cook for a minute or so, remove the pan from the heat, and taste a piece of zucchini. If you like, salt the vegetables lightly. And if you want a more assertive vinegar taste, return the pan to the heat, heat another spoonful of vinegar, and incorporate it into the vegetables.

When it tastes right, turn off the heat, scatter the mint on top, and toss with the vegetables. Let the zucchini cool in the pan and absorb the flavors for a few minutes. Arrange the slices in a serving dish, scrape in any juices, and cool to room temperature before serving.

REDUCED WINE VINEGAR FOR VEGETABLES

For these slowly sautéed zucchini, and other vegetables (both cooked and raw), I prefer to use concentrated wine vinegar, which has a mellower but more intense flavor than vinegar straight from the bottle. To make the reduction, boil any amount of red or white wine vinegar in a saucepan until reduced by half. If you start with a pint, for instance, boil it down to a cup. Stored in a tightly sealed small jar, reduced vinegar will keep indefinitely.

Poached Eggplant with Vinegar, Garlic, and Mint

*M*any people love eggplant but dread the frying of it and don't like all the oil the eggplant absorbs. I am a lifelong eggplant lover, but I do like to eat—and cook for my family—in a healthy way. So I like this preparation, which gives you all the good flavor of eggplant without the frying: you poach small eggplant wedges in water and red wine vinegar, then season and marinate them in fresh mint, garlic, and drizzles of olive oil. After an hour, the layers of bright flavor in each slice are developed and you have a delicious and versatile dish. The wedges are a treat by themselves and a fine complement to many other dishes; see page 253.

SERVES 6 OR MORE AS A SIDE DISH;

12 OR MORE AS AN ANTIPASTO

FOR POACHING

2¼ pounds small, firm eggplants (preferably 6 to 8 ounces each; see box, page 254)

2 cups red wine vinegar, white wine vinegar, or cider vinegar

FOR MARINATING

¼ teaspoon salt

15 to 20 small fresh mint leaves, shredded

3 garlic cloves, thinly sliced

3 tablespoons extra-virgin olive oil

RECOMMENDED EQUIPMENT

An 8-quart pot or saucepan for poaching

A flat baking sheet or platter for cooling the eggplant

Prepping and Poaching the Eggplant

Trim the stem and bottom (blossom) ends of the eggplants. Slice the eggplant in half lengthwise, then slice each half into wedges, about 1½ inches wide on the outside (peel side). You should have thirty or more wedges.

Pour the vinegar and 10 cups water into the pot, cover, and heat quickly until boiling. Drop in all the eggplant slices, cover, and return the liquid to the boil rapidly, then set the cover ajar and adjust the heat so it's at a moderate boil.

Push the eggplant under the surface frequently, shifting the pieces around a bit so they all poach evenly. After about 10 minutes, reduce the heat so the liquid is perking gently and won't break up the softening wedges. Cook for a total of 15 to 20 minutes, until the flesh of the eggplant appears completely translucent—any opaque streaks means it is not cooked through. Don't cook any longer than necessary; as soon as they are done, turn off the heat and carefully lift the wedges out of the liquid with a wide, perforated spatula or strainer—let the liquid drain off briefly—and lay them on the baking sheet. Spread the slices apart from each other in one layer and let them cool for a few minutes.

Marinating the Eggplant

Using a paring knife, cut out the stuck-together mass of seeds on each slice and discard, taking care not to tear the flesh; don't worry if a few seeds are left.

As you seed them, lay a third of the wedges in the small gratin dish in one layer, and top them with the seasonings: sprinkle on a third of the salt and a third of the mint-leaf shreds, scatter a third of the garlic slices, and drizzle a third of the oil all over. Arrange and season two more layers of eggplant in the same way.

Marinate the eggplant for about an hour at room temperature before serving or using in a dish (though they'll be tasty in 30 minutes if you need them sooner). See my serving suggestions below.

If you're making this ahead for serving the next day, seal the dish with plastic wrap and refrigerate; remove at least an hour before using so it comes to room temperature. To keep after the second day, remove the garlic slices from the dish, wrap, and refrigerate; use within a week.

POACHED FISH FILLETS WITH POACHED EGGPLANT WEDGES

Marinated eggplant wedges are a great accompaniment to grilled and poached fish of all kinds, including sea bass, swordfish, cod, snapper, and grouper. And here's a basic method to follow with all fish.

After you have poached the eggplant strain the vinegar water (removing eggplant seeds) into a wide sauté pan. Marinate the eggplant as in the main recipe for ½ hour or so, then reheat the vinegar water to a simmer, slide in up to four serving-size pieces of fish fillet, and poach for about 4 minutes.

Lift the fillets carefully out of the poaching liquid and lay them in a baking dish. Drizzle some of the juices from the marinated eggplant over the fish, then lay eggplant wedges on top. Serve immediately, or let the flavors marry for 30 minutes at room temperature or longer in the refrigerator. Lift portions of fish and eggplant together onto serving plates and drizzle with marinating liquid.

Poached shrimp are also delicious with eggplant—better than traditional shrimp cocktail. Proceed as above, except poach the shrimp in the vinegar water for 2 minutes. Cool before serving.

A narrow oval or rectangular gratin or baking dish—about 6 by 10 inches— for marinating the eggplant in layers

Other Ways to Enjoy Poached Eggplant

As an antipasto: as a *crostini* topping—chopped into small bits; with thin slices of prosciutto; with Tuna *in Olio* (page 10); with Marinated Mackerel (page 3); in Raw Tomato Sauce for Pasta (page 265)

In pasta: added to Raw Tomato Sauce (page 265)

As a marinade: on top of Poached Fish Fillets (above)

As an accompaniment: for grilled fish steaks (page 302); for grilled lamb chops

As a chutney: chopped up with fresh black figs; for anything grilled

WHAT TO LOOK FOR IN AN EGGPLANT

I love eggplants but I am fussy about them. Here's what I look for:

For almost all dishes, I prefer small eggplants, weighing 6 to 8 ounces each. These generally have fewer and smaller seeds, and since seeds are the source of bitterness, there is usually no need to slice, salt, and drain—the time-consuming procedure used to extract bitterness from big eggplants. In recipes where the seeds must be removed, like the preceding vinegar-poached wedges, fewer seeds also means less work and waste, and more delicious flesh.

In the summer it is easy to find small eggplants, especially at farmers' markets and stands, or to grow them. When you can't find any 8 ounces or under, choose the smallest ones available, preferably of a uniform width. I find that "big-bellied" eggplants are more likely to have lots of mature seeds.

My ideal eggplant must be fresh. It should have firm flesh with no bruises; glossy skin, with no blemishes; and a tight skin that covers the flesh so well that it "squeaks" when you rub it. A long green stem is also an indicator that the fruit has been recently picked and is still drawing nourishment from the stem. Indeed, a fresh vital stem, rather than a withered brown one, is a reassuring sign of freshness for most vegetables, as is the presence of fresh leaves on root vegetables like carrots, beets, and turnips.

Naturally, I prefer Italian eggplant varieties, but slender Asian eggplants are very good, I find, with few seeds. And there are beautiful multicolored heirloom varieties of eggplant at farmers' markets too. Some of these are quite good.

About eggplant skin and peeling: I always leave skin on small eggplants with thin skins—it adds texture and color to a dish, and often I think it is the most delicious part. When the skin of an eggplant is tough and thick, as happens in some varieties and mature fruit, it can prevent even cooking of the flesh. In such a case, I might peel the skin completely, but if I want the skin's taste and effect, I'll peel off strips in a zebra-striped pattern all around the eggplant.

Sweet Summer Tomato Sauces

The ripening of the first tomatoes from Grandma's plants (usually late July in New York City) starts a special season of cooking and eating at our house. Though I can cook with decent tomatoes anytime, nothing matches the flavor of our own garden-grown, sun-sweetened tomatoes. I welcome them as a treasured seasonal vegetable—which is why I've put my summer tomato sauces here, rather than with the "year-round" tomato sauces in chapter 3.

These represent very different kinds of sauces: the first, "slow-cooking," sauces require hours to make and will last for months; my "raw" sauce takes a couple of minutes to make and most likely will disappear in one meal. But they all capture the essence of tomatoes—tomatoes I hope you've grown yourself—at the peak of flavor.

Slow-Cooked Summer Tomato Sauce

*A*bout half the tomato plants I put in our garden beds each summer are plum tomatoes, mainly Italian varieties but also some of the old-fashioned American "heirlooms" that are being revived. Of course, New York is not Naples, and our San Marzano and Roma tomatoes don't absorb the intense sunlight that they would in Italy, but with my mother's careful tending (and the kids' attention too), the plants are prolific and the tomatoes big and sweet.

When they ripen—by the bushel, it seems—we make these sauces, one with just tomatoes and the other with tomatoes and eggplant. They are simple sauces, mostly the primary vegetables and big "bouquets" of fresh-cut basil branches (and olive oil, onion, garlic, and peperoncino, naturally). Yet they have a freshness and intensity that are distinct from any sauce made with canned tomatoes, even the finest San Marzano tomatoes.

We make both of these in large quantities, in part because the plants are so productive (and Grandma won't let anything go to waste), but mostly because they are so delicious and versatile. I put them on pasta, eggs, meats, and other vegetables. They are key components in some of my favorite summer creations, including the vegetable lasagna and skillet gratinate that you will find elsewhere in this chapter. And I freeze as much of both sauces as I can—they keep for months and retain their fresh, summery flavor. It's a joy to cook with them in December or January!

MAKES ABOUT 3 QUARTS OF SAUCE

8 pounds ripe plum tomatoes

¾ cup extra-virgin olive oil

About 1 ¼ pounds onions, finely chopped (5 cups)

2 teaspoons salt, plus more to taste

5 large garlic cloves, finely chopped (about ⅓ cup)

½ to 1 teaspoon *peperoncino* (hot red pepper flakes), to your taste

Prepare the tomatoes for sauce, following one of the methods detailed on page 261, and mix all the pulp and strained juices together.

Initial Sautéing

Put the oil in the saucepan, add the onions and 1 teaspoon of the salt, set over medium heat, and stir well. Cook and soften the onions for 7 minutes or so, stirring frequently and adjusting the heat to make sure they don't brown.

When the onions are wilted, golden, and translucent, push them aside to clear a space in the bottom of the pan. Drop the garlic in the "hot spot," spread the bits and let them caramelize slightly, for a minute or more, then stir them together with the onions. Pour 2 tablespoons of water into the pan, stir everything well, and let the vegetables cook and soften for another minute.

Adding the Tomatoes and Seasonings

Pour the prepared tomatoes into the saucepan (slosh out your tomato bowl with a cup or two of water, and pour in those juices too). Sprinkle in the *peperoncino* and another teaspoon of salt, and stir well to blend the seasonings and sautéed onion and garlic into the tomatoes. Finally, push the "bouquet" of basil branches into the pot, pressing them down with a spoon until they're completely submerged.

Cover the pan, raise the heat to high, and bring the sauce to a boil, stirring occasionally, then turn the heat down so the surface is just bubbling gently, and cook covered. Stir occasionally, and adjust the heat to maintain the slow perking.

When the tomatoes have cooked thoroughly and broken down, after 30 minutes or so, remove the cover. Raise the heat slightly, so the perking picks up a bit and the sauce begins to reduce in volume. Stir now and then, more frequently as the sauce thickens, to prevent scorching. Don't rush—it will take an hour or more of steady slow cooking to concentrate the tomatoes.

When the sauce is no longer watery and has the consistency you like, remove the pan from the heat. Taste it, and stir in salt if needed. Let it cool, and before using or storing, pull out the basil branches, shaking them over the pot to get every last bit of sauce.

The sauce can be stored in the refrigerator for about a week, or in the freezer, in a properly filled and sealed container, through the winter.

8 large branches fresh basil with lots of leaves (or smaller stems, tied together)

RECOMMENDED EQUIPMENT

A heavy-duty saucepan or Dutch oven, 8-quart capacity or larger, with cover

A DELICIOUS DISCOVERY!
SWEET CORN POACHED IN SUMMER
TOMATO SAUCE

After many summers of preparing fresh tomato sauce—and boiling thousands of ears of sweet corn in water—it was only when I was working on the recipes for this book that I had a brainstorm: perhaps I could use the enormous potful of crushed plum tomatoes perking away on the stove to cook up the fresh sweet corn we were having for lunch. . . .

Why not?

I shucked the corn and removed all the "silk," rinsed the ears, and dropped four of them in the pot. I covered the saucepan so it quickly returned to a gentle boil, and cooked the ears for about 8 minutes, until the kernels were tender.

Dripping with sauce, the corn looked beautiful and tasted great—and no one needed butter. In addition, the sauce in the pot gained extra sweetness.

Try this whenever you make this summer tomato sauce. It's easy to cook a half-dozen ears of corn when the large batch of tomatoes is cooking for the first time. Or you can reheat a quart or more of finished sauce and poach a couple of ears in it at a time.

Slow-Cooked Summer Tomato and Eggplant Sauce

H ere you prepare the tomatoes and sauté the base of onions and garlic in the
exact same way as in the previous recipe, but the final sauce is unique. First
you soften the eggplant chunks in the pan before adding the tomatoes. Then you cook
the vegetables covered for a long time, so the chunks break down even more. The aim is
to soften the eggplant so much that it almost melts into the tomatoes—which explains
the traditional name for this sauce, melanzana affogata: literally, "suffocated eggplant."

    The eggplant does not disappear, though, either in flavor or texture, I assure you. If
you love eggplant as much as I do, you will want to make this sauce—and plenty of it.

MAKES ABOUT 3 QUARTS OF SAUCE

Prepare the tomatoes for sauce, following one of the methods on
page 261.

Trim and peel the eggplants (or, if the skin is tender, peel in
stripes; see box, page 254). Cut them lengthwise in ¾-inch-wide
slices, stack the slices, and cut them into ¾-inch-wide strips, then
chop into ¾-inch chunks.

Following the procedures for "Initial Sautéing" in the main
recipe, stir together the oil, the onions, and ½ teaspoon salt in the
saucepan. Cook for 5 or 6 minutes, add the garlic and let it
caramelize in a "hot spot," then stir in a couple tablespoons of water
and cook the onions and garlic together for a minute or two.

Now pour the eggplant pieces into the pan, sprinkle on 1 teaspoon salt, and turn to coat the pieces with the oil and sautéed onion
and garlic. Cook over medium-low heat, uncovered, stirring and
turning the eggplant frequently. If the pan gets dry and the pieces
start to brown, stir in several spoons of water; lower the heat if
needed.

Cook for 12 to 15 minutes, or until the eggplant chunks are very
soft, almost mushy, but still retain their shape. Pour in the prepared
tomatoes and juices, rinsing the tomato bowl with 2 or 3 cups water
and pouring it into the pan (the eggplant needs the additional liquid). Sprinkle on the remaining ½ teaspoon salt and the *peperoncino*,

5 pounds ripe plum tomatoes

3 ½ pounds firm eggplants

½ cup extra-virgin olive oil

About 1 ¼ pounds onions,
    finely chopped (3 cups)

2 teaspoons salt, plus more to taste

4 garlic cloves, finely chopped (about
    ¼ cup)

½ teaspoon dried *peperoncino*
    (hot red pepper flakes), or to taste

3 or 4 large branches fresh basil
    with leaves

RECOMMENDED EQUIPMENT

A heavy-duty saucepan or Dutch oven,
    8-quart capacity or larger,
    with cover

Slow-Cooked Summer Tomato and Eggplant Sauce (cont.)

and stir to blend everything together. Submerge the basil branches in the sauce, cover the pan, and raise the heat to medium.

When the sauce reaches the boil, lower the heat to keep an active simmer and cook, covered, for 40 minutes or so. The eggplant should now be broken down and melting into the tomatoes.

Uncover the pan and let the sauce bubble gently and gradually reduce. Stir carefully as it thickens, to make sure the eggplant doesn't stick to the pan bottom; lower the heat if necessary. Cook, uncovered, for a total of 45 minutes to an hour, until the sauce has the consistency you like, then turn off the heat. Pull out the basil before using, and store sauce as in the main recipe.

A MEMORY FROM CHILDHOOD: SUFFOCATED EGGPLANT WITH SCRAMBLED EGGS

A simple dish that I loved as a child (and still adore) is beaten eggs cooked in a small pan of bubbling *melanzana affogata* (or Slow-Cooked Summer Tomato and Eggplant Sauce, page 259). Here's how to make enough for 4 servings:

Heat 3 cups of sauce in a skillet until simmering. Crack 4 fresh eggs in a bowl and beat them with a couple pinches of salt. Pour the eggs on top of the hot sauce, raise the heat to high, and scramble up the eggs and sauce together with a fork for 1 minute. Serve hot for a great breakfast, lunch, or brunch—or supper.

Instead of scrambling the eggs, try poaching them: make an indentation in the simmering sauce, crack an egg into it; do the same for each serving. Cover the skillet, and cook slowly (about 4 minutes) until the egg is done to your liking. With a spatula, lift out a portion of sauce with an egg nestled on top, and serve.

PREPARING FRESH TOMATOES
FOR SUMMER SAUCES
(AND WINTER SUPPERS)

Making a big batch of sauce from fresh tomatoes is a summer tradition in my family, and we do it the old way. We blanch the tomatoes and peel them, remove the cores and seeds, crush the pulp, and press out every bit of good juice—all before the cooking starts.

It does take time and effort, especially when you are preparing many pounds of tomatoes, but in my opinion this method yields the largest volume of sauce, with the best flavor and texture.

Here I've detailed how I set up my kitchen to process tomatoes efficiently, with minimal mess. To me, it's an enjoyable task.

I also suggest a shortcut method that eliminates peeling the tomatoes and employs a food processor. It will make a tasty sauce and certainly save you time.

First test your tomatoes: some garden varieties can be peeled without blanching, especially if they are very ripe. Slit the skin around the core and lift it with your knife or fingernail. See if you can peel off a strip all the way down the fruit, as you would a banana, without tearing the flesh of the tomato. If you can—lucky you!—you can skip the work at the stove, or blanch only those tomatoes with tight skins.

Here's the arrangement I find most efficient and easy:

At the stove:

- start heating a big stockpot of water, for blanching

- nearby, have a large bowl or pot filled with water and lots of ice, to shock the tomatoes and stop the cooking

- have a spider or long-handled strainer for moving the tomatoes

- put a colander in another bowl to drain the chilled tomatoes (or put this colander right in the sink)

At the worktable:

- a bowl for the tomato peels and cores

- a sturdy wire sieve (medium-mesh) set inside another bowl, for the seeds

- a large bowl, for the crushed tomato flesh (or pulp)
- large rubber scrapers or spoons for pressing out the tomato juices

Loosening the Tomato Skins

While the water is heating (or kept near boiling), make two slits in the skin at the "bottom" end of each tomato, in an X shape. Each slit should be an inch long; don't cut the flesh.

When all the tomatoes are slit, bring the blanching water to a rolling boil and drop in about a dozen tomatoes. Cover the pot to bring the water back to a boil quickly, and cook the tomatoes for no more than a minute. As soon as the skin peels back at the slits, lift out all the tomatoes and plunge them into the ice water. Drain in the colander when chilled.

Blanch, shock, and drain all the tomatoes this way. Add more ice as needed to keep the water shockingly cold.

Peeling, Seeding, Crushing

This part *is* fun—and faster with helpers.

Bring the drained tomatoes to the table. Working over the first bowl, with a sharp paring knife, cut out the core of one tomato (usually smaller in plum tomatoes than in regular tomatoes); drop the core in the bowl. Then peel off the loosened skin and let the strips fall in the bowl.

Still holding the tomato, slice it in half crosswise . Grasp one half, hold it, cut side down, over the sieve, and gently squeeze out the seeds and juice. Clear out any sticky seeds with your finger, if necessary, then really squeeze your fist closed, letting more juice fall into the sieve. But don't open your hand yet—drop the crushed tomato flesh in the third, large bowl.

Peel, cut, squeeze, and crush all the tomatoes this way. When you've got the rhythm, use a two-fisted technique to squeeze out the seeds and crush both halves of each tomato simultaneously. Now press and rub the pile of seeds against the sieve to extract all the remaining juice. Dump out the seeds and rinse the sieve; pour the collected juice into the bowl of crushed pulp. Set the empty sieve back in the empty bowl.

Next pour cool water into the bowl of skins and cores, just enough to cover them. Soak and stir the peelings for a few moments, then empty the bowl into the sieve, draining off the juicy rinse water. Mash the skins against the sieve until they're dry, to release more juice.

Finally, discard the skins and cores and pour the collected juice into the bowl of pulp. Stir to blend; if you see any big pulp pieces, crush them up. Rinse out all the bowls with a little slosh water and add that too.

You're ready to start cooking the sauce.

Preparing Plum Tomatoes: A No-Peel Shortcut Method

You won't work at the stove with this technique. Do, however, set up your worktable and equipment for efficient processing. Here's what you'll need:

- a bowl with a sieve set in it to catch the seeds and cores
- a food processor with a steel blade to chop up the tomatoes
- a large bowl for the chopped tomato pieces
- large rubber scrapers or spoons

Removing the Seeds and Processing

Rinse the tomatoes and drain them in a colander.

Working over the bowl with the sieve, remove the core of each tomato and drop it in the sieve. Then cut the tomato in half and squeeze the seeds and juice into the sieve. (Refer to the instructions above for details.)

You can't crush the tomatoes with their peels on, so drop the halves into the workbowl of the food processor. When the bowl is about half full, pulse the motor a few times, just to chop the tomatoes roughly. Empty the pieces into a large bowl.

Process all the tomatoes in this manner. Next scrape and press the seeds and cores in the sieve, collecting all the juices in the bowl beneath it. Discard the seeds and cores and mix the juices in with the chopped tomatoes. Rinse the bowl with slosh water, add that, and you're ready to start cooking the sauce.

THE BEST TOMATOES FOR SUMMER TOMATO SAUCE

Plum tomatoes, preferably Italian varieties, are the tomatoes you want for these sauces. They have thin skins, small cores, and few seeds—all the parts you will discard—and a large amount of sweet, flavorful flesh or pulp, which provides the substance of your sauce. You can use other types of tomatoes (if you have a garden surplus, for example) but you will get less usable flesh and juices from the initial preparation (see page 261) and ultimately less sauce, since so much of the water in the vegetable has to be evaporated.

You don't have to grow your own plum tomatoes for sauce (though it does give a special flavor). In late summer, you can usually find plum tomatoes at farmers' markets, farm stands, and even many supermarkets, often at low prices compared with slicing tomatoes. As with other vegetables, buy firm, unblemished tomatoes without bruises or mushy spots; avoid any that are overripe and starting to break down.

Indeed, unless you are in a rush to make sauce that very day, don't insist on perfectly ripe tomatoes; slightly hard ones will do. Plum tomatoes will continue to ripen after picking—ours often sit on the windowsill for days or even weeks until I get a chance to cook them—so you can always give them a few days to soften and sweeten up.

Raw Summer Tomato Sauce for Pasta

*T*his is the pasta "sauce" I make in August, when just-picked tomatoes in all shapes and colors are piled on our kitchen windowsills—and it is too hot to hang around the stove. It's a fast no-cooking preparation, but it requires ripe and juicy tomatoes, preferably homegrown or heirloom tomatoes from the farmers' market. Be sure to have them at room temperature.

The sauce actually develops in the hour or two when it marinates: salt draws the juices from the tomatoes, and they become infused with the flavors of basil and garlic. Then all you do is toss piping-hot pasta with the tomatoes and enjoy one of the rare treats of the whole year.

MAKES 3 TO 4 CUPS, ENOUGH TO SAUCE
I POUND OF DRY PASTA

Rinse the tomatoes, drain, and wipe dry. Cut out the core and any other hard parts. Working over a big mixing bowl to catch all the juices, cut the tomatoes—cherry tomatoes in half; regular tomatoes into 1-inch chunks—and drop them in the bowl.

Smash the garlic cloves with a chef's knife and chop into a fine paste. This is easier if you add some of the salt as you chop; mash the garlic bits and salt with the flat side of the knife too. Scatter the garlic paste and the rest of the salt (½ teaspoon in all) over the tomatoes and stir gently.

Pile up the basil leaves and slice into thin strips (called a *chiffonade*). Strew these over the tomatoes, then the *peperoncino* flakes. Pour in the oil, stir, and fold, to coat the tomatoes and distribute the seasonings.

Cover the bowl with plastic wrap and let it marinate at room temperature for 1 to 2 hours. Toss the marinated sauce with freshly cooked and drained pasta. Serve as is, or toss in 1 cup freshly grated Parmigiano-Reggiano. For additional complexity, you could add 1 cup or more cubed fresh mozzarella.

2 pounds ripe summer tomatoes, preferably heirloom varieties in a mix of colors and shapes

3 or 4 plump garlic cloves, peeled

½ teaspoon salt

6 large basil leaves (about 3 tablespoons shredded)

¼ teaspoon dried *peperoncino* (hot red pepper flakes), or more or less to taste

½ cup extra-virgin olive oil

I cup or more grated Parmigiano-Reggiano or cubed fresh mozzarella (optional)

Skillet-Cooked Vegetables

Cooking vegetables in a large skillet is very much a part of Italian cooking tradition, particularly in the south, where vegetables prepared this way are called *strascinate*, or "dragged," in reference to the way the vegetables in the pan are pulled around with a fork.

Tradition, though, isn't the main reason I skillet-cook so many of my favorite vegetables—it's because a wide pan lets me cook almost any vegetable to perfect tenderness with still some texture to the bite. At the same time, I can surround and infuse it with my favorite flavoring agents—olive oil, garlic, and *peperoncino*—and I can, if I want to, give it a delicious layer of caramelization. All this is done with little or no added liquid, maximizing each vegetable's distinctive flavor and minimizing loss of nutrients. It's a relatively fast method, too—and there's only one pot to clean!

All you need is a heavy-bottomed skillet, either a slope-sided fry pan or a straight-sided sauté pan. For most recipes, a 12-inch pan is adequate, though for larger batches (2 pounds of vegetables or more), a 14-inch pan is better. What you want is a pan large enough to hold all your vegetables in a single layer with room to move, so every piece can cook and caramelize on all sides.

And you need a good cover. Covering the skillet allows the vegetable to soften in its own moisture as the liquid evaporates gradually and caramelization develops. When you make lovely gold-tinged cauliflower or green beans in a pan that has been covered, you'll understand that you don't need blazing heat, lots of fat, or rapid sautéing to produce those hues and textures.

Employ all your senses to know what's going on in the pan: even when covered, the smell and sounds can tell you how fast something is cooking and if caramelizing may in fact be burning. You get to know the foods you cook, sensing when a vegetable needs more moisture, more heat, or longer cooking.

Skillet Asparagus

In springtime, when farmers' markets sell really fresh, locally grown asparagus—or if you're lucky enough to pick spears in your own asparagus bed—cook them by the skillet method. You'll find it concentrates the natural sweetness and subtle asparagus flavors that are at their peak for only a day or two. Butter and cheese are natural complements to asparagus, and here they both get a final delicious toasting.

For details on how I trim asparagus—and a fine cooking method for the year-round spears that have been shipped to supermarkets—see the Scallion and Asparagus Salad recipe (page 35).

SERVES 4 TO 6

Melt the butter in the skillet over medium heat. When it is just starting to bubble, lay in the spears in a single layer, sprinkle with salt, and shake to roll the asparagus and coat them.

Cover the pan and let the spears cook and steam for 4 to 5 minutes (or more, if they are very thick), shaking them around now and then.

Uncover, raise the heat slightly, and continue to cook another 4 minutes or so, shaking frequently, until lightly caramelized. Lift the asparagus onto a warm platter. The butter left in the pan should be starting to color; if not, cook a bit more, and when browning starts, swirl the pan to spread the color.

Remove from the heat, and scatter the cheese around in the hot pan, swirling again to blend it into the browned butter. Pour the sauce over the asparagus and serve immediately.

¼ pound (1 stick) butter

1½ pounds fresh asparagus, trimmed and peeled

½ teaspoon salt

⅓ cup freshly grated Parmigiano-Reggiano or Grana Padano

RECOMMENDED EQUIPMENT

A 14-inch heavy-bottomed skillet with a cover

ABOUT SAVORY SAUCES

For each vegetable on pages 268 to 280, I give you a recipe for a small, intensely flavored sauce. You'll need only ½ cup or so for a big batch of vegetables, yet it can transform the dish.

The intensity of the sauce won't mask or interfere with the flavor of the vegetable. On the contrary, it will be brighter and more distinctive—I like to think of such sauces as making the vegetables happy.

The five sauces here are also good with many other vegetables. You can make them in larger batches if you like—all of them will keep for several days or up to a week in the refrigerator.

Skillet Cauliflower

I cook cauliflower many ways and my family loves them all (certainly I do). But if some in your family don't like the distinctive, "sulfur" quality in cooked cauliflower, try this skillet method. It eliminates the sulfur taste and produces a cauliflower floret that's entirely different from a boiled one—crispy on the edges, and almost coated with a sweet caramelization. It's delicious by itself but even better with the lively contrast of Garden Tomato Elixir.

SERVES 6 TO 8 AS A SIDE DISH

1 large cauliflower (1½ to 2 pounds untrimmed, with leaves and stem)

¼ cup extra-virgin olive oil

4 plump garlic cloves, peeled and sliced

¼ teaspoon dried *peperoncino* (hot red pepper flakes)

½ teaspoon salt

FOR SERVING

1 cup or more Garden Tomato Elixir (recipe follows): infused with basil and garlic, at room temperature (optional)

RECOMMENDED EQUIPMENT

A large skillet or sauté pan with a tight-fitting cover

Tear or cut off all the outer leaves attached to the base of the cauliflower, then cut out the bottom core.

Separate the head into big florets, snapping them apart or slicing them from the inner stem. Now cut the big florets into 1-inch chunks or thick slices (don't break up the clusters of tiny florets) so you have 6 cups or more of roughly equal-sized cauliflower pieces.

Pull off the outer leaves

After cutting the core, separate the florets

Put the olive oil in a large skillet or sauté pan (one that has a cover) and set over medium-low heat. Scatter the garlic slices and *peperoncino* in the oil, and pile in all the cauliflower. Sprinkle the salt all over the florets, give the pan a few good shakes, and cover.

Let the cauliflower "sweat," giving the pan an occasional shake, for about 4 minutes. Then remove the cover and toss everything together well, by jerking the pan (like chefs do) or just turning the vegetables with a spoon. Cover, cook another 3 minutes, then toss well again. By this time, the edges of some of the cauliflower pieces should have started to brown. If not, turn the heat up just a bit.

Cover the pan again, and let the cauliflower continue to caramelize slowly, tossing the pieces every few minutes, until they are tender, fragrant, and beautifully browned—12 to 15 minutes in the pan in all.

To serve, spread a cup or more of tomato "elixir" to cover the bottom of a serving platter. Pile the warm cauliflower in the middle of the red pool—make sure all the colors are showing—and spoon out serving portions, scooping up sauce and vegetables together.

Well-browned and ready to serve

Garden Tomato Elixir

In ancient times, an elixir was thought to cure anything, make one immortal, or turn metal into gold. And this elixir, a seasoned purée of really ripe raw homegrown tomato, certainly can turn ordinary vegetables into something delectable. I've paired it here with caramelized cauliflower, but it will make even a boiled potato an exciting dish.

This is a great way to use very ripe homegrown or farm-stand tomatoes that are almost too juicy to cut up—and are often a bargain at the farm stand. If you have a lot of tomatoes, you can easily multiply this formula for larger quantities.

Store elixir in the refrigerator for a week and enjoy it as a beverage as well as a vegetable sauce. I've been told it makes a great Bloody Mary. But my favorite is a small glass of chilled tomato elixir in the morning. Try it—it will change your day!

MAKES ABOUT I PINT

1 ½ pounds very ripe and juicy summer
   tomatoes

¼ to ½ teaspoon salt

3 tablespoons extra-virgin olive oil—
   the best you have!

4 plump whole garlic cloves,
   peeled

6 large fresh basil leaves

A pinch of dried *peperoncino*
   (hot red pepper flakes) (optional)

A squeeze of fresh lemon juice
   (optional)

Good With . . .

Braised endive

Pan-sautéed peppers and/or
   eggplant

Sautéed or boiled zucchini

Have a couple of mixing bowls handy, and place a sturdy wire sieve (with small but not tiny holes) in one of them. Rinse the tomatoes if necessary; cut out the cores and any other hard parts.

Following the instructions for preparing tomatoes on page 261, peel the tomatoes, slice them in half, and squeeze out the seeds. You should collect all the skins and seeds in the sieve, all the juices in the bowl underneath it, and all the crushed tomato pulp in the second bowl.

After you have pressed the seeds and skins to extract their juice, dump out the residue and rinse the sieve. Now put the crushed pulp in the sieve and push and scrape it all vigorously, forming a purée that drops into the juice.

(Here's a quicker procedure, if you prefer: Core and trim the tomatoes but don't peel them. Cut them into quarters, or smaller pieces, and drop into the sieve. Press and rub the tomatoes—skins, seeds, and all—until the scrapings are as dry as you can get them. It's faster, but you won't get quite as much purée this way.)

With a wire whisk, blend the puréed pulp and juice, adding the ¼ teaspoon salt. Now drizzle in your best olive oil, a tablespoon at a time, whisking steadily, as the oil emulsifies. Taste and add more salt if you like.

Smash the peeled garlic cloves under the big blade of a chef's knife; drop them into the emulsion. Crumple up each basil leaf in your fingers to release the oils and drop them in as well. If you like a bit of heat, add a pinch of *peperoncino*.

Cover the bowl, give the garlic and basil 2 to 3 hours to infuse the tomato, at room temperature, then scoop out the cloves and leaves and discard. Whisk up the "elixir," add salt or drops of lemon juice to taste, and enjoy.

Serve at room temperature as a vegetable sauce, then keep it in the refrigerator.

Skillet Brussels Sprouts

*B*russels sprouts are a love/hate vegetable. Let this recipe surprise you—even the dubious will fall in love with sprouts. But it's the experience of tasting the vegetable in an unexpected form—all the leaves separated, tossed in the skillet until tender and sweet—that really makes the difference. They are wonderful as is, but the Lemon Sauce that follows provides a tangy counterpoint to the delicately caramelized green-gold leaves.

SERVES 4 TO 6

1 ½ pounds fresh, firm Brussels sprouts

3 tablespoons extra-virgin olive oil

4 plump garlic cloves, peeled and sliced (about 3 tablespoons)

¼ teaspoon dried *peperoncino* (hot red pepper flakes)

¼ teaspoon salt

FOR SERVING (OPTIONAL)

½ cup Lemon Sauce (recipe follows)

RECOMMENDED EQUIPMENT

A 12-inch skillet or sauté pan with a tight-fitting cover

Undoing the Brussels Sprouts

Rinse and drain the sprouts.

Working over a big bowl with a sharp paring knife, cut off (and discard) ¼ inch or so of the base of each sprout, freeing the outer leaves. Now stick the point of the knife into what's left of the base and slice out the tiny core, in one cone-shaped piece—just as you would cut out the bigger core of a cabbage or cauliflower. This loosens the inner leaves. Discard the small core.

Begin peeling off the outermost leaves, discarding only wilted or blemished leaves; drop all the fresh dark-green leaves, even thick ones, into the bowl. Keep peeling off the leaves until you reach the tiny ones that can't be pulled apart. Cut this bundle in slivers and drop them into the bowl. When all are done you will have a large fluffy pile of leaves.

Skillet-Cook the Brussels Sprouts

Put the oil and the garlic in the skillet and set over medium heat. Let the garlic cook and caramelize lightly for 4 minutes or so, shaking the pan now and then.

Dump in the sprout leaves, shake the pan to spread them out, then sprinkle the *peperoncino* and salt all over.

Cover the skillet and let the leaves cook and wilt for 4 to 5 minutes, giving the pan an occasional shake, then uncover and turn them well with a big spoon or tongs. The leaves should be sizzling but not browning—lower the heat if necessary. Cover again.

Cut out the cores of each sprout

Peel off all the leaves

Skillet Brussels Sprouts (cont.)

Cook another 4 to 5 minutes, until the leaves are soft, greatly reduced in volume, but still green and glistening. Serve the Brussels sprouts hot right from the skillet or turn them onto a warm platter.

To serve with lemon or another sauce, spread ½ cup of warm sauce in the bottom of a platter and pile the Brussels sprouts on top. Scoop up sauce with each serving-spoonful of leaves.

Lemon Sauce

Lemon is such an everyday flavoring that we forget how unique it can make a dish.

2 lemons

4 or 5 fat garlic cloves, peeled

2 medium onions, peeled and cut in wedges or big chunks (about 3 cups)

½ teaspoon salt, or more to taste

¼ teaspoon dried *peperoncino* (hot red pepper flakes)

2 tablespoons extra-virgin olive oil

1½ cups water

Rinse and dry the lemons. With a sharp vegetable peeler or paring knife, shave off the outer yellow zest in strips, taking none of the bitter white pith, until you have about ¼ cup of strips, packed together. Juice some or all of the lemons, straining to remove seeds and pulp, to get about ⅓ cup of lemon juice.

Put the juice, strips of peel, garlic, onion, and salt in a 2-quart saucepan; pour in the water and 1 tablespoon of the oil. Bring to a boil, cover, and cook for about 20 minutes at a gentle boil. Remove the cover and cook rapidly for 20 or 30 minutes, or until the overall volume has reduced by half and the onion pieces are barely covered in liquid.

Purée the warm sauce in a blender or food processor. With the machine running, pour the remaining tablespoon of olive oil in a thin stream to incorporate it into the sauce.

Taste the sauce and blend in salt if needed; reheat if necessary before serving. Store in the refrigerator.

Good With . . .

Asparagus

Broccoli

Zucchini

Green beans

Poached carrots

Just about anything goes well

MORE ELIXIRS FROM THE GARDEN

The intensity of other raw vegetables at the peak of flavor can be captured in a small sauce, similar to my method for tomato elixir.

Try sweet red and yellow peppers: purée them in the food processor and pass through a strainer. Then whisk in salt and your best olive oil to create an "emulsion" sauce with body and texture.

Cucumbers are another good base: seed, skin, purée the flesh of small cukes, then emulsify with oil. Serve chilled with hot vegetables, for an unusual treat.

Skillet-Cooked Sweet Corn and Lima Beans

*S*weet corn and fresh lima beans are natural garden partners and one of my favorite vegetable combinations. I like traditional American succotash (originally a Native American dish, in fact), in which the vegetables are cooked together in water, milk, or cream. But limas and corn are especially delicious when prepared by my covered-skillet method, with olive oil and garlic (and a bit of peperoncino).

You must use fresh-cut corn kernels and lima beans right out of the shell for this dish—frozen corn and limas will get mushy and just don't have the flavor.

Cutting corn kernels off the cob is easy. For a fast method, see box on page 276. And shucking lima beans is a pleasant task that I enjoy. Though I admit that Gianni, my mother's boyfriend, is always happy to help me when I've got pounds of beans to shell.

SERVES 8 OR MORE AS A SIDE DISH

4 to 6 ears sweet corn

3 1/2 to 4 pounds fresh lima beans in the shell

3 tablespoons extra-virgin olive oil

3 or 4 plump garlic cloves, sliced

1/2 teaspoon salt

1/4 teaspoon *peperoncino*

FOR SERVING

1 cup Basil Onion Sauce (recipe follows)

RECOMMENDED EQUIPMENT

A 14-inch skillet or sauté pan with a cover

Cut the kernels from the ears of corn until you have 4 or 5 cups (see page 276).

Shell all the lima beans. You should get at least a quart of shelled beans from 4 pounds of beans in the shell. Rinse the shelled limas, getting rid of any bits of the pods, and drain them well.

Put the olive oil in the skillet, toss in the garlic slices, and cook them over medium-high heat for just a minute. Dump all the limas from the bowl into the pan—keep your face away, as there will be a lot of sizzling when the damp beans hit the oil. Immediately cover the pan, give it a good shake, and turn down the heat to medium-low.

Cook the limas, covered, and shake the pan frequently. Uncover it every 3 minutes or so and quickly check that the beans are sizzling and softening but not burning. After 10 minutes, sprinkle over beans the salt and *peperoncino*; cover and cook for another minute. Then add the corn kernels and stir them into the beans. Cook, covered, another 5 minutes, then add 1/2 cup of water to the pan and cover again.

Cook another 8 to 10 minutes, until the beans and the kernels are tender to the bite but not mushy, and have caramelized lightly on the edges.

Serve the corn and limas right away, straight from the pan or piled on a platter covered with a thin layer of Basil Onion Sauce. Scoop up some of the sauce with each serving spoonful.

Basil Onion Sauce

You have certainly played around with fresh basil, particularly with pesto. Here the flavor is more subtle in its cooked form.

MAKES ABOUT 1 CUP

Reserve 5 or 6 bright-green basil leaves (about 2 tablespoons) and 2 tablespoons of the olive oil. Put the remainder of the basil in a small saucepan with all the other ingredients (including the remaining tablespoon of olive oil). Bring the water to a boil, cover the pot, and boil gently for 15 to 20 minutes.

Remove the cover and boil steadily another 20 minutes or longer, reducing the contents of the pot to 1 cup—about a quarter of the original volume. Lower the heat if necessary, as liquid evaporates, to avoid burning the sauce ingredients.

When it is sufficiently concentrated, scrape everything from the pot into the bowl of a food processor and purée. Roughly chop the reserved basil leaves with a knife, then add the pieces to the food processor and purée until they're incorporated. Finally, with the machine running, drizzle in the reserved 2 tablespoons of excellent olive oil, to form a light emulsion.

Serve the sauce warm with cooked vegetables; reheat on the stove if it has cooled off. Store in the refrigerator.

2/3 cup fresh, unblemished basil leaves, packed

3 tablespoons best-quality extra-virgin olive oil

1/2 pound onions, cut in 1-inch pieces (about 1 1/2 cups chunks)

1 cup leek chunks (1-inch pieces)

2 cups water

1/2 teaspoon salt

Good With . . .

Brussels sprouts

Boiled eggs

Poached leeks

Fresh tomatoes with mozzarella

Poached zucchini

CUTTING FRESH CORN KERNELS

Sweet corn on the cob is special, but for many dishes I want the fresh kernels only. Here's how I cut them from the cob—quickly:

With a big chef's knife, chop off an inch or two at the top and the bottom of the ear. This removes much of the silk and the stem and makes peeling the husk easy. Strip off the husks and remove any cling-ing silks. Now stand the ear on the cut flat bottom end, on a tray or inside a wide bowl, so the kernels don't fall all over the place. Slice down with the blade of the knife, close to the cob, going the full length of the cob and shaving off a band of kernels. Rotate the cob and slice off more kernels, turning and slicing until it's clean shaven.

You may get anywhere from ½ cup to nearly 2 cups of kernels from each ear, depending on the size of the corn and the maturity of the kernels.

Corn cobs can add a lot of flavor to stocks, a soup base, or Simple Vegetable Broth (page 288). Save a few cobs when you make these summer corn dishes: wrap them airtight, freeze them, and drop them into the pot the next time you are making stock or soup.

Skillet-Cooked Broccoli

T his way of cooking broccoli opens a whole new world of flavors for one of the most available vegetables. Make a medley in the skillet by cooking cauliflower, zucchini, or other cut-up vegetables at the same time. And even reluctant vegetable eaters (we have a few in my family) find broccoli irresistible with my Creamy Garlic Sauce.

SERVES 6

Rinse and drain the broccoli heads and cut apart all the main branches where they join or are attached to a central stem. Separate the clusters into medium-size florets, 2 to 3 inches wide at the top. If they are wider, slice them lengthwise. Cut their long stems so the florets are about 4 inches long.

Peel the tough skin from the stem pieces and slice them lengthwise in half, or in quarters if they are thick. You can also peel or slice off the tough fibrous layer of the large branches and central stems and slice up the fresh core into 4-inch sticks. Discard all dry and hard pieces.

Set the skillet over moderate heat, pour in the oil, and strew in the garlic. Cook the garlic slices for about 5 minutes, with an occasional shake. When they're lightly caramelized, dump the broccoli pieces into the skillet, sprinkle the salt and *peperoncino* all around, and pour in ½ cup water.

Cover the pan, raise the heat slightly, and cook for 5 minutes, shaking the pan a couple of times. Lift the cover and toss everything very well, then cover again.

Let the broccoli cook another 3 to 5 minutes, and poke or taste a piece to check the tenderness. Cook longer, covered, if you want it softer. Remove from the heat and uncover the pan as soon as the broccoli is cooked through and still brightly colored.

Serve right away, in a pool of Creamy Garlic Sauce.

1 ½ to 2 pounds fresh broccoli on the stem

¼ cup extra-virgin olive oil

6 plump cloves garlic, sliced

¼ teaspoon salt, plus more to taste

¼ teaspoon dried *peperoncino* (hot red pepper flakes)

FOR SERVING

½ cup or more Creamy Garlic Sauce (recipe follows)

RECOMMENDED EQUIPMENT

A 12- or 14-inch skillet or sauté pan with a cover

Creamy Garlic Sauce

It may scare some of you, but garlic lovers will be excited about transforming 1 whole cup of raw garlic cloves into 1 cup of creamy garlic sauce. But don't be intimidated: this simple reduction of garlic in a pan of milk creates a sauce that is surprisingly mild—though unmistakably garlicky. And if the whole-cup idea seems too extreme for you, despite my assurance, by all means make this with just ½ cup of cloves.

At full or half strength, this is delicious with all sorts of vegetables—use it warm with hot vegetables and cold with crudités.

MAKES 1 CUP

2 cups milk

2 heads garlic cloves, peeled

4 bay leaves, preferably fresh

¼ teaspoon salt, plus more to taste

1 tablespoon excellent extra-virgin olive oil

Put the milk, garlic, bay leaves, and ¼ teaspoon salt into a 2-quart saucepan. Bring to a boil and cook at a steady boil for 30 to 40 minutes or even more, gradually reducing the contents of the pot to 1 cup.

Pour and scrape everything into a wire sieve set over a bowl. Remove the bay leaves, and press and scrape the soft garlic through the sieve, making sure you get every bit of the delicious purée into the bowl.

Whisk the sauce until smooth, then whisk in the tablespoon of olive oil and pinches of salt to taste.

Reheat the sauce on the stove until warm. Thin it if you wish with milk or cream. Store in the refrigerator.

Good With . . .

Asparagus

Tomatoes

Zucchini

Leeks

Spinach

Just about everything goes with this

Roasted Winter Squash

S quash is one of those vegetables that, when in season, are celebrated in Italy. It is used in pasta, stuffings, risottos, and soups. By being roasted, as it is here, the squash, like Cinderella, is transformed. It becomes the centerpiece rather than a side dish.

SERVES 6

Preheat the oven to 400°.

Cut the squash in half through the stem and blossom ends. Scoop out all the seeds and fibers so the flesh is clean. Place each half cut side down, and, with a sharp chef's knife, cut straight across to trim the ends of the squash. Then cut the squash into even slices (cutting crosswise) or wedges (cutting lengthwise)—all about 2 inches thick at the widest part.

Remove the peel from the squash slices with a sharp vegetable peeler or paring knife. (With acorn squash, strip off the peel just from the top of the ridges; this will help the pieces cook faster and creates a decorative striped look.)

Pile the squash in a mixing bowl, drizzle the oil and sprinkle the salt over the pile, and toss to coat the slices with the seasonings.

Spread the butter on a large baking sheet (or line it with a non-stick silicon sheet). Lay the slices flat on the sheet with plenty of space between them for even caramelization.

Bake about 20 minutes, then flip the pieces over; bake for another 20 to 25 minutes, until they are tender all the way through (poke with a fork to check) and nicely caramelized on the edges.

Serve hot, piling up the squash pieces on top of a pool of Orange Sauce; drizzle balsamic reduction in thin streaks all over the top.

The squash is also delicious with just one of the sauces, or with only a final drizzle of good olive oil and another sprinkle of salt before serving by itself!

TO PREPARE AND BAKE THE SQUASH

3 pounds winter squash, such as butternut, buttercup, or acorn squash

3 tablespoons extra-virgin olive oil

½ teaspoon salt

2 to 3 tablespoons butter, for the baking sheet

TO SERVE (OPTIONAL)

½ cup or so Orange Sauce (recipe follows)

1 to 2 tablespoons Drizzling Sauce of Reduced Balsamic Vinegar (page 39)

Orange Sauce

Using orange brightens and brings sunshine to fall and winter vegetables.

3 or 4 medium-size oranges

1 ½ cups leek chunks (1-inch pieces)

1 cinnamon stick

1 cup water

3 tablespoons soft butter, for thickening the sauce

MAKES ABOUT 1 CUP

Rinse and dry the oranges. With a sharp vegetable peeler or paring knife, remove the outer peel of three of the oranges, in strips. Don't take off any of the bitter white pith—if you do, trim it away from the strip. Put the strips of peel in a small saucepan, 2-quart or so.

Cut the oranges in half and squeeze to get out all the juice: you should have a bit more than a cup. (Juice another orange if you have a cup or less.) Add the juice to the saucepan along with the leek pieces, cinnamon stick, and water. Place the pan over high heat and bring to a boil. Reduce the heat to maintain a perking boil, and let the sauce cook for about 30 minutes, reducing to about a third of the original volume.

Pour the sauce into a sieve set over a bowl. Remove the cinnamon stick and the pieces of peel (wiping them off and saving any juices), then press and scrape the leek pieces with a spoon or spatula to retrieve as much liquid as you can.

You should have about ¾ cup of orange "soup." To thicken this into a sauce, whisk the butter into it bit by bit.

Serve the sauce hot. Reheat on the stovetop if necessary, and whisk until smooth.

Good With . . .

Cauliflower

Parsnips

Turnips

Leeks

Celery root

Skillet Gratinati

You may be surprised to find recipes with chicken, veal, and pork cutlets in my vegetable chapter. But the inspiration for this distinctive group of dishes is the vegetables that cover and surround the small portions of meat. When zucchini, eggplant, and (especially) tomatoes are at their best in the summer—and when I've an abundance of fresh tomato sauce in the refrigerator and freezer—I cook these beautiful one-pot dinners.

I call these "skillet *gratinati*" because a large skillet or sauté pan is an essential part of the cooking.

First you sauté your vegetables (in some instances) in the skillet; then you gently brown the meat cutlets in the skillet; then you layer lovely individual servings in the skillet; and then you develop your sauce in the skillet.

Finally, you place the whole skillet in a hot oven, where the meat and vegetables cook until tender, the sauce thickens, and the crowning layer of grated cheese turns into a golden, crisp *gratinato*. (The whole cooking process takes little more than half an hour.)

The first stage, on top of the stove, is the most fun, when you create your main dish and sauce in one pan in minutes. Having all your components ready and staying close to the pan will ensure success with this simple dish.

The *gratinati* here are similar in technique but offer different ideas for ingredients. The most detailed instruction is in the main recipe that follows, with briefer descriptions in the equally delicious variations.

Once you understand the process, do experiment, using different meats, vegetables, herbs, and sauces—make the skillet-*gratinate* technique your own.

Skillet *Gratinate* of Zucchini and Chicken

2 pounds skinless, boneless chicken breasts or chicken "tenders"*

3 small or 2 medium zucchini (1 pound, or slightly more)

3 tablespoons extra-virgin olive oil, or more if needed

1 cup or more flour, for dredging

½ teaspoon salt, or more to taste

FOR THE SAUCE

3 tablespoons soft butter

1 cup Summer Tomato Sauce (page 256)

¼ teaspoon dried *peperoncino* (hot red pepper flakes)

1 cup white wine

12 small fresh mint leaves, or 1 tablespoon large mint leaves, shredded

¾ cup grated Grana Padano or Parmigiano-Reggiano

1 cup hot Simple Vegetable Broth (page 288) or stock, if needed

Note: I recommend 3 small whole chicken breasts, or 6 breast halves, weighing 2 pounds. If you have only larger breast halves (some are 8 to 10 ounces), you can slice each in 2, on the bias, to make 2 portions.

Preparing the Chicken and Zucchini

Place a rack in the center or upper third of the oven and preheat to 425°.

If the chicken breasts are whole, cut them in half. Trim off any bits of fat, skin, or tendon. Flatten each breast half with a mallet (or the flat bottom of a heavy pan) to an even thickness, about ¾ inch.

Trim the stem and blossom ends of the zucchini and wash well. Slice across the squash on a sharp angle, creating long ovals, ¼ inch thick. You should have about twenty pieces at least 3 inches long, and a few shorter pieces from the ends.

Put 3 tablespoons of the olive oil in the skillet, tilt to coat the bottom, and set it over medium heat.

Toss about half the zucchini pieces in flour to coat well (set flour aside to use for chicken), pat off any excess, and lay them in the pan. Keep the heat moderate, and let the pieces caramelize slowly for about 4 minutes. Turn when the edges are nicely browned on the underside; fry for about 2 minutes on the second side. With a slotted spatula, lift the pieces to a plate or tray (no paper towels are needed here) and salt lightly. Fry the remaining zucchini ovals in the same way and salt them. While frying, monitor the heat, keeping it high enough to brown the zucchini but not let them burn.

When the zucchini are done, turn off the heat but leave all the oil in the skillet.

Starting on the Stovetop

Have all of your *gratinate* and sauce ingredients handy to the stove.

You should have at least 2 tablespoons of olive oil in the skillet (add a bit if needed). Add 1 tablespoon of the butter and set the pan over medium-low heat.

Salt the chicken pieces lightly, flop them in the dredging flour to coat on both sides, and pat off excess. When the butter is just beginning to sizzle, arrange all six cutlets in the pan. Cook them gently for 1½ minutes, then turn them over; they should be very lightly colored, with no browning.

Maintain the gentle cooking while you assemble the *gratinate*.

- Sprinkle the chicken again with salt (using ½ teaspoon total for the dish).

- Spread a heaping tablespoon of tomato sauce on top of each cutlet.

- Arrange the zucchini slices on top of the sauced chicken, overlapping the ovals so each portion is neatly covered. Use all the zucchini.

Now raise the heat a bit and begin to develop the sauce:

- Sprinkle the *peperoncino* onto an open "hot spot" where it will sizzle and toast briefly.

- Drop the remaining butter, in small pieces, in between the layered cutlets.

- After a few seconds, pour in ⅔ cup of the wine around the cutlets and let it heat briefly, 10 to 20 seconds.

- Spoon the rest of the cup of tomato sauce into the pan (not on the chicken).

- Bring to a simmer, then drop the mint into the sauce all around the pan.

- Give the pan a gentle shake or two, to mix and emulsify the sauce ingredients.

- Finally, sprinkle 2 tablespoons of grated cheese evenly over each zucchini-topped mound.

At this point, the sauce should be about ⅓ inch deep in your pan or even higher, coming well up the sides of the chicken cutlets. If not, pour in the rest of the wine and as much hot vegetable broth or stock as necessary. Raise the heat again to bring the pan sauce to an active simmer.

RECOMMENDED EQUIPMENT

A 14-inch heavy-bottomed, ovenproof skillet or sauté pan for 6 portions; or a 12-inch pan for 4 portions

Finishing in the Oven

When the sauce is simmering, place the skillet in the oven. (Put the handle in front and the food in the back.)

Bake for about 10 minutes—and have thick pot holders or dry towels in hand before you touch the handle or the skillet!—then open the oven and check the pan.

Right on the rack, give the skillet another gentle shake. There should still be plenty of sauce, and the cheese should be lightly colored. If the sauce appears syrupy, or close to evaporating, add more vegetable broth, stock, tomato sauce, or wine to raise the level.

Bake for another 8 to 10 minutes, until the chicken is fully cooked and tender and the *gratinate* top is deeply and evenly browned. If the cheese layer still appears too light, raise the heat in the oven as high as possible (turn on the broiler if it is top-mounted) and bake briefly until it is as dark and crispy as you like.

Carefully remove the skillet from the oven, handling it with plenty of thick cloths. I carry it right to the dining table, where it makes a beautiful presentation (see the photo on page 286). While it is on the table, leave the cloths covering the hot handle. With a large, angled spatula, lift one portion of chicken-and-zucchini *gratinate* onto a dinner plate, then spoon over it some of the sauce.

Skillet Gratinate of Eggplant and Veal

SERVES 6

Place a rack in the center or upper third of the oven and preheat to 425°.

If you have a single chunk of veal, slice it across the grain into six equal pieces. Pound each piece with a mallet (or the flat bottom of a heavy pan) to flatten to a ½-inch thickness. Trim the stem and bottom ends of the eggplants. If they're 6 inches long or less, cut them lengthwise into ¼-inch-thick slices. If they are longer, slice them on the diagonal at a sharp angle, creating large ovals. You should have two or three pieces to cover each veal cutlet.

Put ⅓ cup of canola oil in the skillet and set over medium heat.

Dredge the eggplant slices in flour, and when the oil is hot, put about half the pieces in the pan. Fry gently 2 to 3 minutes, and flip when lightly caramelized; fry for another 2 minutes on the second side. Remove to paper towels; salt lightly. Add remaining canola oil to the pan (if it seems dry) and brown the rest of the eggplant; drain on paper towels and salt lightly. Remove the skillet from the heat and pour out any remaining canola oil.

Starting on the Stovetop
Put the 3 tablespoons of olive oil and 1 tablespoon of the butter in the skillet and set over medium-low heat.

Salt the veal slices, dredge in flour, and when the butter is just sizzling, arrange all six in the pan. Cook them gently for a minute or so, then turn and let them brown slowly while you make the *gratinate* and the sauce.

- Season the veal with pinches of salt and grinds of fresh pepper.
- Lay one or two basil leaves flat on each cutlet.
- Spoon a heaping tablespoon of tomato sauce on top of each.
- Cover the sauced cutlets with overlapping slices of eggplant.
- Raise the heat; drop the remaining butter, in pieces, around the pan.

2 pounds boneless veal, preferably in one piece*

1½ pounds small eggplants (2 or 3)

½ cup canola or other vegetable oil

1 cup or more flour, for dredging

½ teaspoon salt

FOR THE SAUCE

3 tablespoons extra-virgin olive oil

3 tablespoons soft butter

Freshly ground black pepper

2 dozen fresh basil leaves

1½ cups Summer Tomato Sauce (page 256)

½ cup white wine, plus more if needed

¾ cup grated Grana Padano or Parmigiano-Reggiano

1 cup hot Simple Vegetable Broth (page 288) or stock, if needed

Note: Try to get a 2-pound chunk of veal (from the leg or shoulder), which you will slice into 6 individual cutlets, about 5 ounces each. If your market has only pre-cut small scaloppine, pound them, then cook 2 or 3 of them together for each gratinate portion.

FOR THE LOVE OF VEGETABLES * 285

- Pour the ½ cup of wine into the pan and let it heat briefly.

- Spoon the remaining tomato sauce in between the veal portions.

- Shred the rest of the basil leaves and drop into the sauce.

- Shake the skillet to mix up the sauce, and add more wine or water if the level is too low.

- Finally, sprinkle 2 tablespoons or so of grated cheese on each cutlet.

Finishing in the Oven

Follow the instructions in the main recipe for zucchini and chicken.

Skillet Gratinate of Summer Tomato and Pork

SERVES 6

Place a rack in the center or upper third of the oven and preheat to 425°.

Slice the pork loin crosswise into six equal pieces. Trim fat if there's a lot, but leave a thin layer, for moisture and flavor. Nick the fat and skin around each cutlet so it won't twist and tighten the meat during cooking. Pound each piece with a mallet (or the flat bottom of a heavy pan) to tenderize and flatten to ½-inch thickness.

Rinse and dry the tomato (or tomatoes). Cut out the core neatly and slice off this "top" ½ inch of each tomato, where the core was, and about ½ inch of the curving "bottom." Cut these pieces into ½-inch chunks for the pan sauce.

Now slice the center of the tomato into ½-inch-thick rounds. Repeat with the second tomato if necessary so you have one beautiful round to top each cutlet.

Starting on the Stovetop

Put the olive oil and 1 tablespoon of the butter in the skillet, and set over medium-low heat. Strew the sage leaves around the pan and cook them slowly for a minute or two as the butter melts and starts to sizzle.

Salt the pork pieces, dredge them in the flour, then arrange all six in the pan. Cook for about 2 minutes, then turn them over and let them brown slowly while you make the *gratinate* and the sauce as follows:

- Pick out the cooked sage leaves and lay two on each cutlet.

- Season each with pinches of salt and grinds of fresh pepper.

- Place a thick tomato round on each cutlet and sprinkle with salt.

- Raise the heat, and drop in the remaining butter, in pieces.

- Spread the small chunks of tomatoes (and juices) in "hot spots" and let them start to cook for a minute.

2 pounds boneless pork loin, in one piece*

1 or 2 large, firm beefsteak-style tomatoes (about 1½ pounds total)

½ teaspoon salt

½ cup or more flour, for dredging

Freshly ground black pepper

FOR THE SAUCE

¼ cup extra-virgin olive oil

3 tablespoons soft butter

12 fresh sage leaves

½ cup white wine, plus more if needed

½ cup hot Simple Vegetable Broth (page 288) or stock, plus more if needed

¾ cup grated Grana Padano or Parmigiano-Reggiano

*Note: Ask for a 2-pound (boneless) piece from the rib (or shoulder) end of the loin with a thin layer of fat left on the meat. These cuts are all slightly fatty; if you want lean, you can use filets of pork loin.

Skillet Gratinate of Summer Tomato and Pork (cont.)

- Pour in the ½ cup of wine and ½ cup of vegetable broth; shake the pan and raise the heat. Add more wine or water if the sauce level is too low.

- Finally, sprinkle 2 tablespoons or so of grated cheese on each cutlet.

Finishing in the Oven

Follow the instructions in the main recipe for zucchini and chicken.

A SIMPLE VEGETABLE BROTH
INSTEAD OF STOCK

One of the mistakes I see many cooks making is automatically reaching for a can of chicken broth whenever a recipe calls for a bit of stock or a sauce needs an additional ⅓ cup of liquid. But the strong flavors of a broth—and the saltiness of canned broth in particular—can often change the flavor direction from where you want to go. And it's an unnecessarily expensive and sometimes wasteful habit, if you only use a bit of the can and discard the rest.

Instead, I encourage you to adopt one of my favorite thrifty kitchen practices: making your own simple vegetable broth when you are cooking, using it as a multi-purpose "moistening agent" for a host of dishes.

All you need for this clean-flavored and cost-free liquid are a saucepan, a few cups of water, a cup or two of fresh vegetable pieces, and a few sprigs of herbs. Just rinse off all the flavorful trimmings from vegetables you are prepping, and throw them in the pot with water to cover by an inch or two, with a bit of salt and maybe a dash of olive oil. Cook ½ hour or more, until the liquid is reduced by a third and the flavor is extracted, then strain and use in sauces, roasts, a *gratinate*, or to steam vegetables. Put the remainder in the refrigerator or freezer so it's there when you want it—and you won't need that can of stock.

Any combination of the following will give you a good broth:

Chunks of onion, with peel

Trimmed leaves of leek or scallion, cut up

Chunks or peelings of carrot

Chunks or peelings of celery

2 or 3 cloves of garlic with peel, smashed

Several sprigs and stems of parsley

Stalks and leaves of basil, oregano, marjoram, sage, or other herbs

Optional flavor enhancers:

Pinch of *peperoncino*

Strips of lemon peel

The *Piatto Forte*— Seafood, Poultry, and Meat

This book is all about "Lidia's Family Table," and at our table there are definite family favorites. My favorites tend to reflect my own philosophy of life and of cooking. I love, for instance, preparing and eating secondary cuts of meat—the shoulders, tongue, butts, bony breasts, all those underused parts of the animals we butcher. We talk a lot these days about the need to be more conscious of our environment. So shouldn't we use every part of the animal for nourishment and make that food chain really efficient? But, leaving social awareness aside, secondary cuts just taste good. In most instances these cuts come with bones, muscles, and cartilage, and when cooked they have great flavor and succulence.

The same applies to fish; skate, monkfish, mussels, cod steaks all follow the road less traveled. They are underused and they are particularly delicious. So let's try to keep a balance in our oceans and bring great flavors to our tables.

You may want to turn the page when you come to recipes for rabbit, duck legs, or chicken livers. But don't. You'll be depriving yourself and your family of some unique flavors you may never have tried.

Red *Brodetto* of Skate

Brodo *means "soup" in Italian, and* brodetti *are savory, soupy preparations that usually refer to fish. A* brodetto *is uncomplicated, quick, and very delicious—a preparation that you can use for many kinds of seafood. For this recipe I've chosen skate, an ocean fish that some of you may not be familiar with. It is immensely popular in Europe and one of my lifelong favorites. Fortunately, it is now widely available here, reasonably priced, and, when fresh, as sweet and luscious as lobster. It is particularly well suited for a* brodetto, *having naturally gelatinous flesh and bones, which enhance the richness and viscosity of the sauce. If you can, buy skate with the center cartilage, which is how I like it; see box on skate, page 294.*

SERVES 6

2 pounds skinless skate wing with
    cartilage, or 1 ½ pounds skate fillet

¾ teaspoon salt, or more to taste

1 to 2 cups flour, for dredging the fish

1 cup canola oil, or more if necessary

6 tablespoons extra-virgin olive oil

1 large or 2 medium onions, chopped

2 tablespoons tomato paste

2 tablespoons red wine vinegar

2 cups water or Simple Vegetable Broth
    (page 288)

¼ teaspoon *peperoncino*
    (hot red pepper flakes)

2 tablespoons chopped fresh Italian
    parsley

RECOMMENDED EQUIPMENT

A 14-inch sauté pan or skillet, with
    3-inch sides or deeper

Cutting and Frying the Skate

Slice the skate wing into 1½-inch-wide strips, cutting along the rib lines that extend from the body side to the edge—a whack with a chef's knife will cut through the tough band of cartilage. If using thin skate fillet, cut the strips a bit wider, about 2 inches, so each piece has some substance. If any strips are longer than 6 inches—from a large wide skate wing—cut them in half crosswise.

Sprinkle all the pieces with salt on both sides, using about ⅛ teaspoon of salt in all. Roll them in the flour to coat on all surfaces; shake off any excess and set them down on a plate or a piece of wax paper.

Meanwhile, pour enough canola oil into the pan to cover the bottom with a ⅛-inch layer. Heat over high heat for a couple of minutes or more, until the oil sizzles instantly if you dip a piece of fish into it. Lay a batch of fish strips in the pan, with an inch or two of space in between the pieces. Fry for 2 minutes or more, until the first pieces you put into the pan are crisped and golden brown, then turn them over in the same order that you put them in the pan. (If they are coloring much quicker or much slower, adjust the heat down or up.) Cook on the second side for another 2 minutes or more, until it is nicely colored too: thin fillet pieces will need less time; skate pieces with cartilage will need more. When caramelized on both sides, lift the pieces with tongs and lay them in a bowl lined with paper towels to drain. Sprinkle lightly with salt.

Fry all the pieces the same way, adding oil to the pan as necessary; drain on paper towels and salt lightly (use only three or four pinches in all). Pour the hot canola oil out of the skillet—I use a ½-gallon cardboard container, from milk or orange juice, to collect the cooled used oil.

Making the Brodetto

Put the skillet back on the stove, pour in ¼ cup of the olive oil and dump in the onions, sprinkling ¼ teaspoon salt over them. Cook over medium-high heat, stirring, for 3 to 4 minutes, as they sizzle and wilt, then pour in a couple tablespoons of water to steam and soften them. Continue to cook for another 3 minutes, stirring frequently. Clear a space in the pan, and drop in the tomato paste. Stir and toast it for a minute in the hot spot, then stir in with the onions.

If you're cooking skate pieces with cartilage, return them to the skillet now. Turn and toss them (with tongs) to mix with the onions, and start cooking again. As they heat, stir the red wine vinegar into the 2 cups of hot water or vegetable broth in a measuring cup. When the fish is sizzling, pour the vinegar water into the pan and turn the heat to high. As it heats up, stir to amalgamate the onions, tomato paste, and fried bits, then shake the pan and move the skate pieces around gently, so they're bathed with liquid but don't break apart.

Add more water or broth to bring the sauce level just over the top of the skate; drop in the *peperoncino*, and drizzle the remaining 2 tablespoons of olive oil all over; shake the pan to stir things up a bit. When the sauce comes to a boil, adjust the heat to keep it actively simmering all over the surface. Cook for about 5 minutes, then taste, and add more salt if needed.

If you're cooking skate fillet pieces, return them to the skillet now. Lay them in the pan and cover with the simmering sauce, without breaking the pieces apart.

Cook for another 5 minutes or so—10 minutes of simmering in all—until the sauce has thickened and reduced slightly. Sprinkle the chopped parsley all over the *brodetto* and take the skillet off the heat. Serve right away.

Serving Suggestions . . .

Skate *brodetto* is delicious served over hot polenta, or grilled polenta.

It's also a great condiment for pasta or risotto when removed from the bones.

Follow the basic procedure in the recipe, using 2 pounds of trimmed monkfish pieces—trimmed and cut as they are for the brodetto on page 296—in place of the skate. Cook monkfish in the brodetto the whole time, like sturdy skate pieces with cartilage.

Other good seafood to prepare in red brodetto are black bass, eel, and grouper.

ABOUT SKATE

Skate is a flat, ocean-bottom creature with wings on either side that move it through the water, like a ray. The fan-shaped wings—weighing 1 to 2 pounds each—are the parts of the skate that get to market. The thick, inedible skin on the top and bottom of the wing is removed to expose a wide, thin slab of sectioned flesh. Actually, there are two layers of flesh, with a middle layer of thin cartilage that extends out to the edge of the wing. What you are most likely to find in the supermarket are pieces of skate fillet—wing meat already sliced from the cartilage. You can see the narrow ridges and grooves where the branches of cartilage were attached.

When they are fresh, skate fillets are fine for this recipe. But if you have a fish market where they get the whole wings, I recommend that you have the fishmonger remove only the skin and leave the skate still on the cartilage. There are several advantages: skate pieces with cartilage taste better than fillets, just like meat cooked on the bone; the pieces are sturdier and can cook longer with other seasonings in the pan, the cartilage lending flavor and body to your brodetto. Finally, if you are an omnivore, as I am, you will find that most of the wing cartilage (except for one tough edge) is a delicious treat to chew on. And it's good for you, too!

Freshness is more critical with skate than with other fish, because the flesh begins to deteriorate and gives off an ammonia smell within a day or two after the wing has been skinned, faster when it has been filleted. This is another reason it's best to find a market where they get the whole wing and you can see it with the skin on, before you buy it. Fresh skate will smell like the clean sea.

EVERYBODY LOVES FRIED SKATE!

Simple fried skate was a supper treat when I was growing up, and it is still one of my family's favorites of all fried seafoods. . . . Salt the strips of wing, flour them, fry until golden on all sides, remove to paper towels to drain, and salt lightly again.

I suggest you slice the wing pieces narrower than for *brodetto*—I cut them into fish fingers, which the kids love. Since there is no further cooking in sauce, fry the pieces slightly longer than in the *brodetto* recipe, to make sure they are cooked through, especially if the cartilage is still inside. And one more thing: if you are just frying skate and not making a *brodetto*, you will need lots more fish, because it disappears fast.

RED *BRODETTO* WITH CANNELLINI BEANS

Fish cooked with beans is traditional fare in Tuscany, and this basic skate *brodetto* can easily become a hearty one-dish meal with the simple addition of cannellini.

You'll need 3 cups of cooked beans, either home-prepared or canned. When you start frying the onions for the *brodetto*, heat the beans in a saucepan with a cup of their cooking liquid, vegetable broth, or water. After the tomato paste and vinegar water have cooked for 3 or 4 minutes, pour the hot beans and liquid into the pan, and gently stir to incorporate into the *brodetto*; if you have big fish pieces in the pan already, don't break them up. Add more water or broth if the sauce is thick. Cook for another 8 to 10 minutes; as in the basic recipe, add 2 tablespoons olive oil, salt to taste, and the skate fillets (if you are using them) for the last 5 minutes of cooking. Serve fish and beans together in warm soup bowls.

Monkfish *Brodetto*

This brodetto *follows essentially the same steps as the preceding skate recipe, flouring and frying to seal and caramelize the fillets, then returning them to the skillet as you create the sauce. But here the sauce is built on a light purée of poached garlic, lemon juice, and white wine, rather than onions, tomato paste, and red wine vinegar.*

You can take other fish and seafood in this direction. Skate is as delicious in white brodetto as it is in red. Shrimp and scallops—even chicken breast—are excellent done this way as well. An important point to remember, though, with seafood variations: shrimp, scallops, and fillet of skate will be overcooked if they're in the sauce too long. After the initial browning of these delicate fish, get all the sauce liquids cooking first, then add them to the brodetto for just the last couple of minutes before serving.

SERVES 6

8 plump garlic cloves, peeled

3 pounds monkfish fillet

1½ teaspoons salt

1 to 2 cups flour, for dredging the fish

1½ to 2 cups canola oil

4 tablespoons butter, in chunks

1 tablespoon freshly squeezed
   lemon juice

½ cup white wine

¾ cup Simple Vegetable Broth
   (page 288) or water

¼ cup dry toasted pine nuts

¼ cup shredded fresh basil
   (about 12 big leaves)

RECOMMENDED EQUIPMENT

A 14-inch skillet or sauté pan

Making the Garlic Purée

Put the garlic cloves in a small saucepan with about 1½ cups of water. Bring the water to a steady, bubbling boil and cook, uncovered, for 15 minutes. Drain, then add a fresh 1½ cups of water and boil again, for about 30 minutes, until the cloves are completely soft but still whole and hardly any water is left in the pot. Reduce the heat as the water evaporates so nothing burns. Purée the cloves and any drops of cooking liquid in a food processor, mini-chopper, or blender; you should have about ⅓ cup of purée.

Preparing and Frying the Fish

If the monkfish fillets are covered with a translucent membrane (the fishmonger may have trimmed it), use a sharp paring knife to lift and strip it off. Cut the monkfish into chunks, about 2 inches wide, and sprinkle ½ teaspoon salt over all the surfaces.

Roll the chunks in the flour to coat well; shake off excess. Pour enough oil into the pan to reach a depth of ⅓ to ½ inch, and heat rapidly for several minutes, until the oil bubbles instantly if you dip a piece of fish into it.

Lay a batch of fish chunks in the pan, with plenty of space in between the pieces. Fry for a couple of minutes on each side, until crusted and golden brown all over, about 6 minutes in all, then remove them to a bowl lined with paper towels to drain. Sprinkle lightly with salt. Fry all the pieces the same way, adding oil to the pan as necessary; drain on paper towels, and salt lightly with an additional ¼ teaspoon of the salt. Pour the hot vegetable oil out of the skillet.

Making the *Brodetto*

Set the skillet back on the stove; put in the chunks of butter, and start melting them over medium heat. Return all the monkfish to the pan and heat, turning the pieces on all sides, until everything is sizzling again, about 3 minutes.

Clear a large hot spot in the skillet, and scrape in every bit of the garlic purée. Raise the heat a little, and shake the pan to spread the garlic, rolling the fish pieces in it at the same time. After a minute, when the purée is sizzling, sprinkle the lemon juice and the remaining ¾ teaspoon salt all over, and turn the pieces.

Pour in the wine and the broth; bring the sauce to a bubbling boil, and cook 3 minutes or more, turning the fish chunks, as the sauce thickens and coats them. Scatter the pine nuts in the pan, and toss them with the fish.

When the sauce has the density you like, turn off the heat, sprinkle the basil shreds over the fish, turn the chunks in the sauce one more time, and serve right away.

Serving Suggestions . . .

White *brodetto* is usually eaten with some grilled or hearty country bread, but white polenta or some boiled rice is very good with it too.

I also like adding some cooked fava beans or peas in the last 5 minutes of cooking.

Mussel *Brodetto*

This is one of those almost miracle dishes: it is ready in 10 minutes, it is quite inexpensive, it is full of flavor and texture and very gratifying, and all of my grandchildren love it. The brininess of the sea will come forth with the underlying garlic, lemon, and olive oil, the flavors all tied together by bread crumbs, then captured in the opening shells of this sweet mollusk.

But one thing is required of you in order for this miracle to happen. The mussels you buy must be absolutely the freshest; otherwise, turn the page and go to another recipe.

To enjoy this dish best, you must serve it piping hot in hot bowls, because the shells cool quickly. Grilled country bread and spoons will help scoop up every last drop.

If you have some left over, remove mussel meat from the shells and return it to the sauce to make a great condiment for a plate of pasta the next day.

SERVES 6

½ cup plus 2 tablespoons extra-virgin olive oil, for cooking and finishing

4 fat garlic cloves, peeled and smashed

½ large lemon, cut into very thin half-moon slices (¾ cup)

2 medium onions, peeled and cut into thin half-moon slices (about 2 cups)

½ teaspoon salt

3 pounds mussels, rinsed and scrubbed

1 cup white wine

Freshly ground black pepper to taste

3 tablespoons fine dry bread crumbs

6 tablespoons chopped fresh parsley

RECOMMENDED EQUIPMENT

An 8-quart or larger wide saucepan or Dutch oven, preferably 14 inches or more in diameter, with a cover

Pour the ½ cup of olive oil into the big pan, toss in the garlic, and set over medium-high heat. After 2 to 3 minutes, when the garlic is sizzling nicely, drop in the lemon slices, raise the heat to high, and cook, stirring, for a minute or so, until the lemon is sizzling and melting into the oil and the garlic is just starting to turn golden.

Toss in the onion slices, sprinkle on ¼ teaspoon of salt, and cook, stirring and shaking the pan, for 2 to 3 minutes or so, until wilted.

Dump in all the mussels, and immediately begin tossing them in the hot oil, lemon, and onion, for ½ minute or so.

Cover the pot, and cook for a minute, shaking it often; uncover, pour in the wine, and toss the mussels; add the remaining ¼ teaspoon salt and grinds of pepper, toss the mussels well, and cover.

Cook 2 minutes or so, until most of the mussels are opening and are still plump. Sprinkle the bread crumbs over all and toss well, mixing the crumbs with the sauce; then toss the mussels with the parsley.

Finally, turn off the heat, drizzle the 2 tablespoons of olive oil all over, and toss, coating the mussels with the hot sauce.

Serve right away, in hot bowls, ladling some of the *brodetto* over each portion of mussels.

Brodetto with Lobster and Corn

T his beautiful brodetto is brimful of colors, tastes, and textures, and extends the flavor of lobster to bowls of polenta or pasta. Lobster and corn cooked together in a brodetto is not traditionally found in Italy. I discovered this combination of flavors when I was traveling through Maine and other parts of the Northeastern coast of the United States, and I liked it so much that I took the liberty to Italianize the duo.

The preparation follows the basic steps of all red brodetti: First the floured lobster pieces are fried to seal the flesh and caramelize it. Then they're put back in the skillet with aromatics, tomato, and seasonings to create the brodetto, and the addition of corn adds sweetness and texture.

Most people eat only the tails and the claws of lobsters, but don't you disregard the heads and tiny legs—they are the sweetest parts. After having enjoyed the polenta and the sought-after parts of the lobster, set yourself up with a wet towel and a clean plate, and begin to nibble and suck on those little legs, biting into them now and then to squeeze out the meat. Then pull the head piece up close and pull the inside part from the shell, lick the shell, and set it down. Slowly begin to pry open the chest chambers, and with an oyster fork pry out morsels of some of the sweetest lobster meat.

At our house it is the heads of the lobsters that are rationed, not the tails.

SERVES 6

Cutting Up the Lobsters

About 30 minutes before cutting them up, put the lobsters in the freezer, in whatever bag or paper wrappings they are in. They will become inactive as their temperature drops.

Before cutting up the lobsters, put towels under your cutting board, extending out, to catch the juices that are released.

You will split the lobster lengthwise in two strokes of the chef's knife. Hold the lobster flat on a cutting board with your left hand on the tail, put the point of the knife just behind the head, and with a sharp stroke cut through the top of the shell, bringing the knife blade down between the eyes and antennae of the lobster. This splits the head part in two. Turn the lobster so you are now holding with

2 live lobsters, each about 1 ½ pounds

½ cup flour, or more if needed

½ cup canola oil, or more if needed

½ cup extra-virgin olive oil

1 medium onion, chopped into ¼-inch pieces

2 tablespoons finely minced shallots

¾ teaspoon salt, or to taste

2 cups chopped leeks in ½-inch pieces

2 tablespoons tomato paste

One 28-ounce can plum tomatoes and
their juice, passed through a food
mill, or 2 cups Summer Tomato
Sauce (page 256) or Simple Tomato
Sauce (page 132)

4 cups or more Simple Vegetable Broth
(page 288) or water

¼ teaspoon *peperoncino*
(hot red pepper flakes)

3 cups fresh corn kernels (and juices)
scraped from the cob
(see page 276) or frozen corn
kernels

1 cup chopped scallions

RECOMMENDED EQUIPMENT

A heavy chef's knife and sturdy kitchen
shears, for cutting up the lobsters

A 14-inch sauté pan or skillet, 3-inch
sides or higher

Brodetto *with Lobster and Corn (cont.)*

your left hand the split front, and split the entire tail in one stroke.
Let the split halves lie with their cut sides open, so flesh and innards
and juices stay in the shell.

Next, cut the claws off where they attach to the head; then cut
the meaty pincer part of each claw from the jointed knuckle. Crack
the heavy shell of the pincers on both sides, using the back of the
knife blade. Cut lengthwise slits in the knuckle joints with the knife
point—this will make it easier to remove the cooked meat.

Now look in the split halves for a pale vein (the digestive tract)
that runs from the tail forward, along the top side only; pick it out
and discard. Next, pick out and discard the stomach sacs, located behind and underneath the eyes, in both head sections.

Using the shears (or the knife if you prefer), cut off the eyes and
antennae and the bit of shell that holds them. Snip off the small legs
where they attach to the front shell.

Cut the tail section from the head section, leaving as much of the
meat in the tail as you can, and all of the tomalley and roe in the
head.

Split and cut up the second lobster in the same way. You should
now have four split head sections, four split tail sections, four
cracked pincer claws, four slit knuckle joints, and sixteen small legs.

Frying the Lobsters

Flour the eight split head and tail sections by sprinkling flour over
the cut sides and patting the flour to cover the meat, tomalley, roe,
and the rest of the insides completely. You can't press or roll the lobster in flour, because the innards will come out—and you don't need
to put flour on the outside shells.

Pour the canola oil into the skillet, using enough to coat the bottom completely. Set over medium-high heat; when the oil is hot,
quickly lay the split pieces, floured side down, in the pan. Don't
move them for 2½ to 3 minutes, until caramelized and crusted
evenly—give the wider head pieces a bit more time in the pan than
the tail pieces. Remove each piece with tongs and set it on a board or
a tray, cut side up. Put the claw pieces in the pan—no flouring
needed—and fry them for 20 seconds or so on each side, then remove them too.

Making the *Brodetto*

Pour out the canola oil and pour in ¼ cup of the olive oil. Set over medium-high heat and stir in the onion and shallots. Sprinkle on ½ teaspoon of salt, and stir as the onion heats for a minute or so; then lay the four head pieces in the pan, fried side up. Strew the sixteen small lobster legs in the skillet, and stir them around with the onion.

Cook for another minute, and then scatter the chopped leeks into the pan; stir them and heat for a minute. Clear a space, and drop in the tomato paste; toast it in the hot spot for a minute, then pour in the milled tomatoes or tomato sauce and 2 cups of broth or water—or more, if necessary, so the lobster shells are just covered. Raise the heat to high, sprinkle the remaining ¼ teaspoon salt and the *peperoncino* all over, and stir and shake the pan as the sauce comes to a boil.

When it is boiling, cover the pan and adjust the heat so the sauce is perking nicely all over the surface. Cook for 10 minutes or so, shaking the pan now and then; uncover and add broth or water, if necessary, to keep the pieces barely covered. Cover the pan and cook another 5 minutes or so.

Now uncover the pan, and push the claw and tail pieces into the sauce all around the skillet. Bring the sauce to a good simmer again, and cook uncovered. After 4 minutes or so, lift up one of the head pieces with tongs, holding the shell so the meat is free to drop out. Shake the shell sharply; I usually bang the tongs vigorously on the side of the pan to dislodge the meat into the sauce. Empty all the head pieces this way, while the sauce keeps simmering. (If you can't fit the tail and claw pieces into the pan, empty out a couple of head pieces earlier.) When the heads are gone, stir the sauce, taste, and add salt if needed.

Stir the corn kernels into the skillet, and drizzle over pan the remaining ¼ cup of olive oil. Simmer about 4 minutes covered—or cook uncovered over high heat if the sauce needs thickening—then stir in the scallions and cook for another minute, or until the corn is tender and the *brodetto* is flowing yet dense and rich.

Serve in warm bowls over loose hot polenta or grilled polenta slices, or use to dress spaghetti or other pasta. Have grilled country bread to dunk in the sauce. If you are serving more than four and everyone wants lobster tail, cut the tail pieces crosswise in half; claws must be distributed whole and shared peacefully.

Seafood on the Grill

Simple Grilled Cod Steaks

Fresh cod fillets are flaky and sweet and a favorite in my family for baking or broiling. In summer, I love thick cod steaks, cooked on the grill. Unlike fish more commonly cut for steaks—tuna, swordfish, shark, and others with firm texture—the softer flesh of cod can be a challenge to the griller, sometimes sticking to the rack or flaking apart. These problems are lessened by tying the steaks with twine, marinating in garlic oil, and searing on a hot clean grill. But even if you lose the perfect appearance or a flake of fish tears off, cod steaks are so sweet and delicious when grilled, it's worth it.

I serve cod with any (or all) of the cold sauces listed below; grilled lemon slices (see box, page 304) are a nice garnish too. Follow this basic procedure for any fish steak—tuna and the other firm-fleshed ones, or salmon, halibut, or bass.

SERVES 2 OR MORE

2 or more cod steaks, 1½ inches thick

¼ teaspoon salt, or to taste

½ cup garlic-infused oil
  (box, facing page)

Stems of fresh thyme or other fresh
  herbs

FOR SERVING

Salsa Verde (page 362), Salmoriglio
  (page 366), Smooth Sweet Red
  Pepper Sauce (page 364), cold
  cucumber sauce (page 363),
  or Fresh Tomato-Lemon Salsa
  (page 308)

To keep the steaks from falling apart, fold the long, thin end pieces—the belly flaps—inward to form a compact round of flesh. Tie a length of kitchen twine in a loop around the outside band of skin of the fish, securing the flaps within; pull to tighten, and knot it securely.

Sprinkle both sides of the steaks with salt, coat with garlic oil, and place in a dish with a few garlic slices and the herb stems strewn over them. Marinate for an hour or two at room temperature, or longer if refrigerated.

Preheat the clean rack of a grill over high heat until very hot. Just before putting on the fish, rub the grill with an oiled towel or a piece of pork fat. Wipe excess garlic oil off the steaks, and set them on the grill.

Sear the steaks without moving them for 4 to 5 minutes. Brush the tops with garlic oil. If the fish isn't sticking, check the cooked undersides and flip the steaks over as soon as the grill marks are golden brown. If the flesh sticks, grill another minute to sear, then turn the steaks over, using a sharp-edged broad metal spatula if necessary, to separate the flesh from the grill.

Grill to mark the second side, 3 to 4 minutes; brush the top side with a small amount of garlic oil, and lower heat to medium. If the flesh is not sticking, you can make crosshatch grill marks if you wish: lift the steak after 3 minutes, rotate it 90 degrees or so in relation to the grill rack, then lower it on the same side.

When the second side has grilled for 4 minutes or more, check for doneness by feel and sight: when the exterior flakes and the center of the steak is opaque but moist (push aside the flesh with a knife blade to see inside), remove steaks to a platter.

Sprinkle with salt and drizzle with garlic oil. Serve right away with sauce on the side, or top with spoonfuls of *salsa verde*, or drizzle *salmoriglio*, or dress with just a plain slice of lemon and some extra-virgin olive oil.

Serving Suggestions . . .

Cooked Carrot Salad with Pine Nuts and Golden Raisins (page 45), Scallion and Asparagus Salad (page 35), or Eggplant *all'Uccelletto* (Poached Eggplant with Vinegar, Garlic, and Mint; page 252) would be an ideal accompaniment for grilled cod.

FIRST MAKE GARLIC OIL—
AND OTHER TIPS FOR GRILLED SEAFOOD

Just a few steps from my kitchen is the door to a shady *terrazzo* where we relax and eat many of our summer meals. On one wall is a beautiful old-fashioned brick fireplace for cooking meats over wood coals. But often, I have to confess, I do my everyday grilling on a convenient gas grill with adjustable burners. And usually I grill fish or shellfish—it's always quick, and my family loves it.

Here are my basic preparations for all fish or shellfish before grilling. They're useful for either gas or charcoal grills, although every grill differs in heat output and cooking times:

- First, make plenty of garlic-infused oil, ahead of time, to flavor all fish and shellfish, including clams, mussels, and oysters in the shell.

For one cup of oil, drop ¼ cup of sliced garlic in 1 cup extra-virgin olive oil with ¼ teaspoon salt. Let the oil infuse for ½ hour to 1 hour before using; then remove the garlic slices. The oil can be refrigerated for a week or more.

- Marinate the seafood in garlic oil: pour just enough oil over to coat; toss and turn to oil all surfaces. Toss in some of the garlic slices if the garlic oil is freshly made, or a few newly cut slices, as well as fresh herb stems or branches—such as thyme, bay leaves, or rosemary. Marinate all fish for an hour or two if possible before grilling, or even overnight (refrigerated, of course).

- Clean and scrape the grill rack well, and get it intensely hot over high heat or hot piled coals before putting on the fish.

- Grease the hot grill rack lightly before putting on food, with an oiled paper towel, or a piece of cured pork skin from prosciutto end (page 129).

- Sear fish without turning until deeply marked by the grill, anywhere from 2 to 5 minutes. Thorough searing minimizes sticking.

- For large fish or steaks, initially cook over high heat, then, halfway through, lower heat to medium; for smaller pieces, lower the heat (or spread the coals) and cook only over medium heat.

- Keep garlic oil handy, and drizzle or brush on seafood sparingly while grilling—usually on turning the pieces. Avoid spilling any oil onto the lava rocks or coals and starting smoky, bad-tasting flare-ups.

- Grill simple garnishes and accompaniments for seafood at the same time. I grill rounds of lemon on the rack alongside my fish or shellfish, until nicely caramelized, 5 minutes or more, turning them occasionally. Another favorite: brush slices of country bread with garlic oil, and mark well on both sides (over a cool section of the grill), to serve with the fish.

Grilled Tuna *Rollatini* under Tomato-Lemon Marinade

When traveling through Sicily, you will often encounter tuna or swordfish rollatini—or involtini, as the Sicilians call them. It is a traditional dish. What makes the dish particularly delicious and interesting is that they roll the rollatini in seasoned bread crumbs before grilling.

The way I prepare the rollatini, they get a marvelous range of flavors by marinating before grilling in garlic, olive oil, and fresh thyme; then I smother them with a fresh tomato-and-lemon salsa after they've cooked (and try not to eat them for a couple of hours). The longer they sit—before and after grilling—the more flavorful they become.

This is also a versatile preparation. Make as many rollatini as you want from a big piece of tuna, as I explain in the box, and schedule their marinating periods and quick grilling to your convenience. Serve them hot off the grill or later, at room temperature, when they taste even better. One rollatino makes a beautiful first course; two make a satisfying main course; a few rollatini slices make a terrific tuna sandwich for a picnic. And if you want to enjoy these any time of year—or if you don't have a grill—just pop them in your oven (see page 309).

---

8 ROLLATINI, SERVING 4 OR MORE

Preparing the Garlic Oil and Crumbs

Stir the garlic slices and salt into olive oil. Allow to infuse for at least ½ hour, preferably an hour or more.

Mix all the seasonings with the bread crumbs, then stir in the 2 tablespoons of garlic oil. Rub the crumbs with your fingers so they're evenly moistened.

Preparing the *Rollatini*

As shown in the photos on the next page, slice the tuna into 3-ounce scallops; flatten and spread them (if necessary) to ¼-inch thickness with a meat mallet.

Sprinkle each scallop with a couple of pinches of salt, then cover with a thin layer, about 1½ teaspoons, of the seasoned bread crumbs.

Roll up and secure the *rollatini* with toothpicks, and place them all in a baking dish, close together in one layer. Drizzle over them

FOR THE GARLIC-INFUSED OIL

2 fat garlic cloves, sliced

⅛ teaspoon salt

½ cup extra-virgin olive oil

FOR THE FLAVORED BREAD CRUMBS

½ cup fine dry bread crumbs

½ teaspoon finely chopped fresh thyme

Grated zest of ½ lemon

1 tablespoon finely chopped fresh Italian parsley

¼ teaspoon salt

¼ teaspoon *peperoncino* (hot red pepper flakes), chopped into little bits

2 tablespoons finely chopped toasted pine nuts

2 tablespoons finely chopped golden raisins

2 tablespoons garlic-infused oil (ingredients above)

FOR GRILLING AND
MARINATING THE *ROLLATINI*

1½ pounds fresh tuna loin in one piece (see box)

½ teaspoon salt

About 6 fresh thyme branches

About 2 cups Fresh Tomato-Lemon *Salsa* (a full batch; recipe follows)

Grilled Tuna Rollatini *under Tomato-Lemon Marinade (cont.)*

2 tablespoons of the garlic oil, scatter in a spoonful of the oily garlic slices, drop in the thyme branches, and turn the *rollatini* to coat with oil on all sides. Let them marinate for at least an hour, preferably a couple of hours or overnight (refrigerated).

Grilling and Marinating with Tomato *Salsa*

Heat the clean grill rack over medium heat, using gas or charcoal. Take the *rollatini* out of the marinating dish and roll them in the bread crumbs. Press a bit, so a light coating of crumbs adheres to the rolls on all sides.

When the grill is ready, lay the *rollatini* at right angles to the grill bars and let them sear without moving for 2 to 2½ minutes, until they've been branded with nice gold marks on the bottom. The crumbs should be toasted but not burned. If the fish and crumbs are darkening much faster, lower the heat, raise the rack, or spread the coals out.

Using tongs, rotate the *rollatini* 180 degrees, so the first marks are on top; grill and mark the opposite side for about 2 minutes. Turn

Cutting thin slices from a tuna loin

Flattening the slices with a meat mallet

Covering a slice of tuna with seasoned bread crumbs

Rolling up the *rollatini*

Securing the filled roll with a toothpick

90 degrees and grill about 1½ minutes on a third side. Finally, rotate them all top to bottom again, so the remaining unmarked side of each roll is on the grill. They should need only a minute or so to mark. Drizzle garlic oil in tiny amounts on the *rollatini*, if you wish, after each turn.

After being grilled on all sides, about 6 to 7 minutes total, the *rollatini* should be cooked through but moist in the middle (you can cut one open if you are concerned about doneness). Immediately remove them to a clean baking dish (I usually just wash and dry the one in which they marinated in garlic oil). Pull out the toothpicks.

Serve the hot grilled *rollatini*, if you want, with any of the cold sauces beginning on page 362. For the most flavor, spread the Tomato-Lemon *Salsa* (recipe follows) over the top of the *rollatini* and marinate for 2 to 3 hours, until the rolls have cooled and been infused with the sauce. Serve at room temperature, one or two per person, with sauce on top. For longer marinating, refrigerate the sauced *rollatini* after 3 hours at room temperature and serve the next day—leftovers will keep and taste fine for about 4 days, properly sealed.

Spooning garlic oil over the *rollatini*

Fresh Tomato-Lemon *Salsa*

2 medium summer tomatoes, seeded,
   chopped in ⅓-inch pieces
   (about 2 cups)

½ cup finely diced red onion

¼ teaspoon coarse sea salt

1 wedge (lengthwise quarter)
   of a large lemon

1 tablespoon balsamic vinegar

2½ tablespoons extra-virgin olive oil

1½ tablespoons finely chopped fresh
   chives or Italian parsley

Toss the chopped tomatoes in a bowl with the red onion and the salt. Trim the ends of the lemon wedge and pick out any seeds. Lay it on one of its flat sides and slice the wedge lengthwise thinly, then crosswise. Let the slivers of lemon fall apart, and slice or chop any long pieces into short bits. Scrape all the lemon into the bowl, and toss with the tomatoes. Then toss with the vinegar, oil, and chopped herbs.

Spread the marinade over grilled tuna *rollatini*, or serve as a condiment for other grilled or steamed seafood.

BUYING TUNA FOR ROLLATINI

To make the rollatini, I start with a compact, evenly shaped chunk of tuna loin, which is easy to cut into thin slices, or scallops, about 3 ounces each. It is also simple to figure out how much tuna to buy: just multiply 3 ounces by the number of rollatini you need and ask the fishmonger for a single piece of tuna that total weight. Then mark off equal pieces and slice the chunk crosswise. For example, the chunk in the photo on page 306 is 1½ pounds, or 24 ounces, and I cut it in eight equal scallops. To make twelve rollatini (to serve six or more), I'd start with a 36-ounce, or 2¼-pound, section of tuna loin.

If pre-cut tuna steaks are all you can find, make your 3-ounce scallops by laying each steak flat and slicing it in layers as you would a cake. You could also have the fishmonger slice the scallops. However, uncut tuna stays fresher longer, so I recommend that you buy one solid piece and cut it yourself.

For rollatini—as for marinated Tonno sott'Olio (page 10)— I prefer loin pieces with the belly flap, or ventresca, attached. The flesh has more fat and flavor and is easier to grill without drying it out. If it's a small tuna, you should be able to cut the loin and ventresca as one slice; if the tuna is big, then separate the ventresca and cut it separately. The ventresca is a bit flatter, so cut on a bias.

TUNA *ROLLATINI* IN THE OVEN

When grilling is not possible, baked *rollatini* can be almost as delicious. Follow the same preparation as for grilling. Arrange the rolls an inch or so apart in a shallow baking pan (lightly filmed with garlic oil) and bake in a preheated 400° oven for about 10 minutes, or until the crumbs are crusty and nicely colored and the fish is just cooked through but still moist. Serve any way you like: marinated under tomato-lemon *salsa* or hot from the oven.

The *rollatini* with Fresh Tomato-Lemon *Salsa*

Crispy Baked Turkey Cutlets

I make a platter of these crumb-coated baked morsels for the kids when they come over because I know they will enjoy them and be nourished. But I notice most of the adults take a piece too. The cutlets have the crunchy appeal of fast-food-style fried "nuggets" and "fingers," but they are better in every way. (You may notice that the coating is the same blend of grated Parmigiano-Reggiano and bread crumbs that is so good on broccoli-and-cauliflower and string-bean gratinati, in chapter 4, pages 243 and 245.)

Turkey has great flavor and texture, but chicken-breast pieces are also good prepared this way. I usually buy turkey-breast cutlets (organic or naturally raised) and slice them up; packaged turkey tenders (the meaty flap inside the breast) are even more convenient—cut them in half, or pound them flat and use the whole tender.

The crispy tenders are great served with a green salad. Instead of the usual ketchup condiment, try some Summer Tomato Sauce (page 256), or the Quince, Cranberry, and Apple Sauce on page 367. They are wonderful served as a main course with Skillet Brussels Sprouts (page 271) or Skillet String Beans with Gorgonzola (page 247).

SERVES 6, OR MORE IF SERVING SMALL EATERS UNDER 4 YEARS OF AGE

2 pounds turkey-breast cutlets or "tenders," or skinless, boneless chicken breast

¼ teaspoon salt

3 plump garlic cloves, sliced

3 tablespoons extra-virgin olive oil

1 to 2 tablespoons butter, for the baking sheet

FOR THE CHEESY CRUMBS

½ cup dry bread crumbs

¾ cup freshly grated Parmigiano-Reggiano or Grana Padano

Rinse and dry the breast pieces, and trim off all fat and tendons. Slice the meat (with the grain rather than across it) in strips roughly 2 inches wide and 4 inches long: you should get ten to fifteen pieces. Pound thick or uneven pieces, if necessary, with a meat mallet or other heavy flat object, so they're an even ½-to-⅔-inch thick.

Put the strips in a bowl and toss them with the salt, garlic slices, and olive oil. Let them marinate for at least 15 minutes, preferably ½ hour, at room temperature.

Meanwhile, set a rack in the upper third of the oven—nearer the top for browning—and heat it to 425°.

Toss and stir together the bread crumbs, grated cheese, parsley, 2 tablespoons of olive oil, and the salt until thoroughly blended. Lightly butter the baking sheet.

When the meat has marinated, lift out a few pieces and pick off the garlic slices. Drop the strips in the crumbs and roll them around, then pick them up one by one and press the crumbs so they stick to the meat on both sides. Try my one-hand technique: scoop up a turkey strip and crumbs in the palm of your hand, then close your fingers and squeeze tight.

Lay the coated strips flat on the baking sheet, spaced at least ¼ inch apart. If you see bare spots of meat, press on a few of the remaining crumbs. Drizzle a bit more olive oil on each strip, and put the pan in the oven.

Bake for 10 minutes, rotate the sheet back to front, and bake for another 10 minutes, or until the crumbs are golden brown on top and the meat is cooked through but still moist. Cut a piece open to check doneness: if the crumbs are browning quickly while the meat is still uncooked, set the tray lower in the oven and/or lay a sheet of foil on top of the cutlets. Don't let them overcook, and move them to a platter as soon as they come out of the oven, so they don't dry out on the hot baking sheet.

Serve hot or warm. They are still very good reheated, and they make great sandwiches.

2 tablespoons chopped fresh Italian parsley

2 tablespoons extra-virgin olive oil, plus more for drizzling on the cutlets

RECOMMENDED EQUIPMENT

A 12-by-18-inch rimmed baking sheet

A SECRET FLAVORING

From a cook's point of view, the turkey gains in flavor immensely from a short marinating period in olive oil with lots of sliced garlic. Marinating is a great way of imbuing flavor into meats and fish in a gentle fashion. When you feel they do not have enough intrinsic flavoring, marinate them even though the recipe might not call for it. You must give the ingredients enough time—at least 15 minutes to several hours or overnight—to have an exchange.

Marinating is also a successful way of introducing new flavors to your family, especially children. Strong flavors like garlic, rosemary, bay leaves, and ginger can be difficult for a finicky eater to take directly, but in marinades they come through in soft dosages. This is how I develop and train my grandchildren's palates. The palate communicates information, which is stored in the brain, like a reference library, and becomes a resource for enjoying, recognizing, and preparing food. It is important that we fill up our reference library so that we can recall information when needed. There is no stronger memory recall than that of our olfactory sense. I am sure that all of you at some time or other have been brought back by an overpowering sense of smell to something that seemed lost in memory. As I describe on page 249, I introduce my grandchildren in their early months to herbs by crushing them under their noses. I am training their palates and expanding their repertoire of tastes in much the same way I am introducing them here to the gentle infusion of flavors that marinades give.

Skillet Chicken Breasts *Aglio e Olio*

Starting with a base of garlic and olive oil, similar to many of my pasta sauces, you build layers of flavor, toasting the garlic, peperoncino, and capers on the pan bottom, then draw the components together with broth and reduce the liquid to perfect saucing consistency. It's all done in less than 15 minutes.

The added challenge here is that you must cook six plump chicken breasts to perfection, in the same pan, in the same short time. The chicken takes up most of the room, so the hot spots will be harder to find. More important, you need to control the heat and timing with care: the chicken has to caramelize lightly at first, then, as the sauce comes up around it, cook to doneness in a couple of minutes of high-heat braising. You'll be thickening the sauce with bread crumbs in the exciting finale too—so it's good to have all the ingredients ready to go.

Quick, tasty, requiring little effort, this is the kind of cooking I love to do for my family. I guarantee that after you've served this amazingly moist chicken and superb sauce to your family they'll be requesting it often.

SERVES 6

6 chicken-breast halves, skinless and boneless (about 2 pounds)

¾ teaspoon salt, plus more as needed

½ cup flour, for dredging the chicken

¼ cup extra-virgin olive oil

2 tablespoons butter

8 or more big garlic cloves, sliced

¼ teaspoon *peperoncino* (hot red pepper flakes)

3 tablespoons tiny capers in brine, drained

2 tablespoons red wine vinegar

I cup Turkey Broth (page 80) or Simple Vegetable Broth (page 288)

I tablespoon fine dry bread crumbs

Trim the chicken-breast halves of all bits of fat, skin, or connective tissue with a paring knife. Do *not* cut off the "tenders"—the small loose flap of muscle on the underside of each half—but flatten each firmly against the larger piece, to form a neat oval.

Sprinkle both sides of the breasts with salt, using about ½ teaspoon in all. Spread the flour on a piece of wax paper and press and toss each breast to coat lightly on all surfaces; shake off excess.

Heat 2 tablespoons of the oil and all the butter in the pan over medium heat. When the butter is almost completely melted, lay the breasts in the pan, with space between them. Let them cook in place, without moving them, until they're sizzling. After 2 minutes or so, lift the first breast you put in the pan and check the underside. You want it to be lightly tinged with brown (not merely pale, but not brown all over either). Cook longer if needed, then turn all the breasts over when they've just begun to color.

Quickly scatter all the garlic slices into the spaces between the chicken pieces, turn the heat up slightly, shake the pan, and stir the garlic slices around in the hot fat so they separate. After a minute or a bit more, when the garlic has begun to sizzle, sprinkle the *peperoncino* flakes in a hot spot; toast for a minute; then spill the capers in several hot spots around the pan. Give the skillet a few good shakes to distribute the seasonings, and run the hot juices all around the breasts.

Raise the heat another notch. When everything's sizzling hard, pour the red wine vinegar into the open spaces and shake the pan to spread it. Let the vinegar sizzle and reduce for ½ minute or so, then pour in the broth.

Cook at full blast now, quickly bringing the liquid to a boil. As it cooks, drizzle the remaining 2 tablespoons of oil all around the pan, and sprinkle on another ¼ teaspoon of salt. Let the sauce bubble and reduce for a couple of minutes, shaking the skillet frequently, then sprinkle the bread crumbs into the sauce (not on the chicken) and stir and shake to mix them in. Within a minute or two, the crumbs will thicken the sauce visibly; cook, shaking the skillet, until it has the consistency you like. Turn off the heat, scatter the parsley over everything—and shake the skillet again.

Serve right away. I usually bring the pan to the table and serve family-style. For a more formal presentation, spoon a pool of sauce onto a warm dinner plate, place a breast half on top, and moisten with a bit more sauce. Serve the chosen vegetable in the same plate.

Serve With . . .

Many vegetables will go well with this dish, depending on the season: Roasted Winter Squash (page 279), Warm *Broccoli di Rape* and Yukon Gold Potato Salad (page 46), or crispy baked Broccoli and Cauliflower *Gratinate* (page 243).

Polenta with Leeks (page 216) could also be served to mop up the zesty sauce.

3 tablespoons chopped fresh Italian parsley

RECOMMENDED EQUIPMENT

A 14-inch skillet or sauté pan*

*Note: If you only have a 12-inch pan, do no more than 4 or 5 small breast halves at a time.

MY WAY OF SALTING

I find that, when cooking, I like to salt progressively—that is, to season with salt as I add each major ingredient to the pot. So it's difficult in recipe instructions to stop and tell you: Now salt the onions, now the meat, now the sauce, and so on. And the chances are that you would end up oversalting.

I suggest, therefore, with each recipe that you are about to cook, measure out the total amount of salt called for, and use a little of it to salt at different stages, gauging it so that you have a little left to adjust to taste at the end.

Sautéed Chicken Livers and Onions

Most of the time when you buy a whole chicken, the packet of neck, gizzards, and chicken liver tucked in the cavity will leave you wondering what to do with them. Well, these are some of the best-tasting parts. So, packet by packet, collect and freeze the necks and gizzards for a good chicken soup, and the livers for this quick and delicious dish.

Quickly sautéed chicken livers and slowly caramelized onions are such natural complements in taste and texture that they're always a welcome supper dish in our house. The kids are a bit finicky about this dish, but I prepare it when Grandma, Giovanni, and I are at home. There's nothing fancy about my version—though I do embellish the onions with a sweet-and-sour finish of vinegar and golden raisins. Chicken livers need a bit of attention—thorough trimming and rinsing, and fast cooking in a small amount of oil—and they'll be crispy on the outside and tender on the inside.

SERVES 4

2 tablespoon golden raisins

1 pound onions, peeled

4 tablespoons extra-virgin olive oil

4 tablespoons butter

¾ teaspoon or more salt

2 or 3 fresh bay leaves

2 tablespoons red wine vinegar

1 pound chicken livers

Freshly ground black pepper, to taste

RECOMMENDED EQUIPMENT

2 large skillets, preferably 12 inches in
   diameter

Frying the Onions

Put the raisins in a bowl with warm water to cover, so they plump up for a few minutes.

Slice the onions in half and then crosswise into ¼-inch-thick half moons (see photo, page 28). Put 2 tablespoons of oil and 2 of butter in one of the skillets and set it over medium heat. As the butter melts, stir in the onions, sprinkle with ½ teaspoon salt, and drop in the bay leaves. Shake the pan and turn the onions as they heat and start to sizzle, then lower the heat slightly and cook the onions slowly as they gradually wilt and start to color, stirring and tossing them occasionally.

After 15 minutes or so, when the onions are deep gold all over, raise the heat a bit, pour in the vinegar, and cook for a minute, stirring the onions in the vinegar as it steams and evaporates. Drain the raisins, and gently squeeze out the excess liquid; scatter them in the skillet and toss together with the onions. Now lower the heat, and continue cooking the onions until they're as dark and caramelized as you want them be. Turn off the heat, and let the onions rest in the hot pan.

Cleaning and Frying the Chicken Livers

While the onions are cooking, clean the livers (I do this on paper towels): with a paring knife remove all the fat, veins, and membranes, and slice the livers into separate lobes. Rinse them well, then pat dry with fresh paper towels. Sprinkle ¼ teaspoon salt and grind pepper on all surfaces of the livers.

Heat the remaining 2 tablespoons of olive oil and 2 of butter in the second skillet, over medium-high heat, until the butter is melted and foaming. Before the butter begins to color, lay the livers in the pan, without crowding them. With the heat high, cook the livers for 2 minutes or a bit more, until they're browned and crisped on the underside, then turn them over (in the order in which you put them in the pan). Cook about 2 minutes on the second side, until they are nicely crisped all over, and lift them—a couple at a time—with a spider or slotted spoon; let the oil drain off, and place them in the first, warm skillet, next to the onions. Don't overcook the livers: they should still be slightly pink inside when you move them. Taste a piece and season with more salt and pepper if you want.

If you will be serving right away, heap the onions on top of the livers, then spoon onions and liver together onto warm serving plates. If serving is delayed, leave the onions and livers in separate parts of the pan so the livers don't get soggy. Smother the livers with onions when you serve.

Serve With . . .

Some piping-hot Basic Polenta (page 215), or grilled polenta (page 216)

Poached Whole Zucchini with Lemon and Olive Oil (page 237)

Skillet-Cooked Broccoli (page 277) or Skillet Cauliflower (page 268)

My Mother's Chicken and Potatoes (with My Special Touches)

In my family, favorite dishes are always being altered according to what is available and what is best—especially when I'm cooking.

Here's a perfect example: chicken and potatoes, fried together in a big skillet so they're crisp and moist at the same time, is my mother's specialty. Growing up, my brother and I demanded it every week; our kids, Tanya and Joe and Eric, Paul and Estelle, clamored for it too. And now the next generation of little ones are asking their great-grandmother to make chicken and potatoes for them.

When I am at the stove—and though I follow my mother's basic procedures—I can't resist playing around. Some days I add sausage to Grandma's recipe, or capers or olives; I might douse the chicken with a splash of vinegar; sometimes I cut up a whole chicken, other times I'll split little poussins or Cornish hens. If I'm in a hurry, I quickly cook small pieces of chicken breast with the potatoes. (You can see what experiments have worked well if you look through my previous books.)

This recipe gives you Erminia's classic formula—chicken, small potatoes, a bit of onion, and fresh rosemary—with two of my latest twists: pickled cherry peppers and bacon strips, in bite-sized rolls. Cherry peppers are plump golf-ball–sized antipasto peppers in vinegar that you'll find in jars on the pickle shelves of the supermarket. They come in sweet and hot varieties—and the latter are explosive, if you take just a bite. But when they're seeded, sliced, and added sparingly to the chicken, they imbue the dish with a mellow heat that I love. If you and your family are hot heads, cut up two or more peppers; otherwise slice only one, or use the sweet cherry peppers and see how you like that.

My latest spin on our chicken-and-potato tradition is one everybody loves, especially the kids: we roll bacon slices into little bundles, pin each one closed with a toothpick, and caramelize them along with the chicken. The bacon fat slowly renders and lends the meat a layer of flavor that's picked up by the potatoes and onions too. By the end of cooking, the rolls have turned into crisp morsels that are a treat to eat with the juicy chicken and tender potatoes. (But be sure to remove all the toothpicks!)

SERVES 4 OR MORE

FOR THE BASIC CHICKEN
AND POTATOES

2½ pounds chicken legs or assorted
pieces (bone-in)

Prepping and Browning the Chicken (and Bacon) and Potatoes
Rinse the chicken pieces and pat dry with paper towels. Trim off excess skin and all visible fat. Cut the drumsticks from the thighs. If using breast halves, cut into two small pieces.

Make the bacon roll-ups: Cut the bacon slices in half crosswise and roll each strip into a neat, tight cylinder. Stick a toothpick through the roll to secure it; cut or break the toothpick so only a tiny bit sticks out (allowing the bacon to roll around and cook evenly).

Pour the canola oil into the skillet and set over high heat. Sprinkle the chicken with ¼ teaspoon salt on all sides. When the oil is very hot, lay the pieces in it, skin side down, an inch or so apart—watch out for oil spatters. Don't crowd the chicken: if necessary, fry it in batches, with similar pieces (like drumsticks) together.

Drop the bacon rolls into the oil around the chicken, turning and shifting them often. Let the chicken pieces fry in place for several

½ cup canola oil

½ teaspoon salt, or more to taste

1 pound red bliss potatoes, preferably no bigger than 2 inches across

2 tablespoons extra-virgin olive oil or more

2 medium-small onions, peeled and quartered lengthwise

2 short branches fresh rosemary with plenty of needles

FOR MY SPECIAL TOUCHES — TRY EITHER OR BOTH

4 to 6 ounces sliced bacon (5 or 6 slices)

1 or 2 pickled cherry peppers, sweet or hot, or none—or more!—cut in half and seeded

RECOMMENDED EQUIPMENT

A 12-inch cast-iron or other heavy-bottomed skillet with 3-inch-high sides or deeper, with a cover

My Mother's Chicken and Potatoes in the pan

minutes to brown on the underside, then turn and continue frying until they're golden brown on all sides, 7 to 10 minutes or more. Fry breast pieces only for 5 minutes or so, taking them out of the oil as soon as they are golden. Let the bacon rolls cook and get lightly crisp, but not dark. Adjust the heat to maintain steady sizzling and coloring; remove the crisped chicken pieces with tongs to a bowl.

Meanwhile, rinse and dry the potatoes; slice each one through the middle on the axis that gives the largest cut surface, then toss them with the olive oil and ¼ teaspoon salt.

When all the chicken and bacon is cooked and out of the skillet,

Erminia serving my version of her chicken and potato dish

pour off the frying oil. Return the skillet to medium heat and put in all the potatoes, cut side down in a single layer, into the hot pan. With a spatula, scrape all the olive oil out of the mixing bowl into the skillet; drizzle over it a bit more oil if the pan seems dry. Fry and crisp the potatoes for about 4 minutes to form a crust, then move them around the pan, still cut side down, until they're all brown and crisp, 7 minutes or more. Turn them over, and fry another 2 minutes to cook and crisp on their rounded skin sides.

Cooking Everything Together

Still over medium heat, toss the onion wedges and rosemary branches around the pan, in with the potatoes. If using cherry peppers (either hot or sweet), cut the seeded halves into ½-inch-wide pieces and scatter them in the pan too.

Return the chicken pieces—except breast pieces—to the pan, along with the bacon rolls; pour in any chicken juices that have accumulated. Raise the heat slightly, and carefully turn and tumble the chicken, potatoes, and onion (and bacon and/or pepper pieces), so they're heating and getting coated with pan juices—but take care *not* to break the potato pieces. Spread everything out in the pan— potatoes on the bottom as much as possible, to keep crisping up— and cover.

Return the heat to medium, and cook for about 7 minutes, shaking the pan occasionally, then uncover, and tumble the pieces and potatoes (and bacon rolls) again. Cover, and cook another 7 minutes or so, adding the breast pieces at this point. Give everything another tumble. Now cook covered for 10 minutes more.

Remove the cover, turn the pieces again, and cook in the open skillet for about 10 minutes, to evaporate the moisture and caramelize everything. Taste a bit of potato (or chicken) for salt, and sprinkle on more as needed. Turn the pieces now and then; when they are all glistening and golden, and the potatoes are cooked through, remove the skillet from the stove and—as I do at home— bring it right to the table. Serve portions of chicken and potatoes, or let people help themselves.

Rabbit *Cacciatore*

Please try this recipe. Nothing would make me happier than to see more dedicated home cooks in this country cooking rabbit. And for those of you just starting to cook, you really should make use of this delicious and healthful meat. It's always been an important food on our family table. When I was a child, in our town of Busoler, every family had a pen of rabbits—including my namesake Aunt Lidia, my mother's sister—and even as I gathered grass to feed them and played with them, I understood how important it was to nourish them, so they would nourish us.

Today, though, while rabbit dishes are popular in my restaurants, especially as a pasta condiment, I notice that customers still regard rabbit as a fancy and different food, especially the saddle (the loin section) of rabbit. The truth is, rabbit is easy to cook and is as versatile and tasty as chicken.

Here, then, is a typical rabbit dish from my kitchen, which I still prepare often for family dinners. I always buy whole rabbits and cut them up myself, as I demonstrate in the photos alongside. Like poultry, rabbit is easy to divide. Let the joints show you where to cut off the meaty leg pieces. The back pieces are easy to chop with a sturdy chef's knife or a small cleaver. If you prefer, though, ask your butcher to cut up the rabbit into eight or ten pieces for you.

I am sure you'll love this cacciatore (hunter's-style) rabbit. During the first 40 minutes, the cooking is purposely slow and relaxed, as the meat gradually caramelizes with herbs, fresh peppers, and other vegetables and seasonings. Add these as you prepare them—you don't need to rush. Once you've developed many layers of flavor, you pour in some broth, cover the pan, and let the rabbit braise for another 20 minutes.

SERVES 4 WITH LEFTOVERS

1 rabbit, about 3 ½ pounds

1 ½ teaspoons coarse sea salt, plus more to taste

⅓ cup plus 2 tablespoons extra-virgin olive oil

5 or 6 plump garlic cloves, peeled and smashed

8 or 9 large fresh sage leaves

Cutting Up the Rabbit

Following the photographs, lay the rabbit on its side; lift up the thigh of the meaty hind leg, then twist it around and bend it back to expose the joint. Cut into the flesh there and through the joint to separate the leg-thigh piece. Turn the rabbit over and separate the other hind leg in the same way.

Lift the foreleg on one side, find and sever the shoulder joint, and pull off the leg from the backbone.

1. The rabbit lying on its side

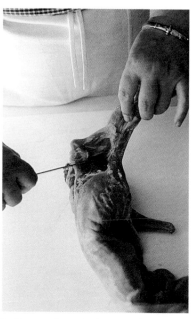

2. Cutting through the meat down to the joint of the hind leg

3. Cutting off the hind leg at the joint

4. Severing the foreleg at the joint

5. Separating the rib cage from the loin

6. The cut-up rabbit, top to bottom: two legs with one small piece of tail in the center; next, two pieces of loin; the rib cage cut in half; two forelegs with a small piece of neck at center

3 sprigs fresh rosemary

¼ cup oil-packed sun-dried tomatoes, halved, drained, and dried

4 large shallots, peeled and sliced in half (about 4 ounces)

1 ½ teaspoons tomato paste

2 or 3 pickled hot cherry peppers, drained, seeded, and quartered, or an equivalent amount of Tuscan preserved peppers plus ⅛ to ¼ teaspoon *peperoncini* (hot red pepper flakes)

1 ½ tablespoons red wine vinegar

¾ cup white wine

3 large bell peppers, red and yellow (1 ½ pounds), cored, seeded, and cut in 1-inch pieces

1 cup or more hot Turkey Broth (page 80) or Simple Vegetable Broth (page 288) or other light stock

RECOMMENDED EQUIPMENT

A cleaver or heavy chef's knife, for cutting up the rabbit

A 12- or 14-inch deep skillet or braising pan with a tight cover

Rabbit Cacciatore (cont.)

Clean all the fat from the cavity. Cut off the neck, slicing crosswise through the backbone just above the rib cage. Cut off the tail end of the backbone, slicing crosswise just below the meaty flaps of the saddle—chop the backbone here with a cleaver or a sturdy kitchen knife.

Cut crosswise through the meat flaps and backbone where the saddle meets the rib cage; make an initial cut with your knife, then chop with the cleaver to separate the rib piece from the saddle.

Cut and chop the saddle in half, crosswise. Spread open the two sides of the rib cage and split them apart down the middle.

You now have eight good serving pieces plus the two small pieces of neck and tail.

Cooking the Meat and Seasonings

Toss the rabbit pieces with 1½ teaspoons of salt to season them on all sides.

Pour the ⅓ cup olive oil into the braising pan, swirling it around, and set over medium heat. As the pan heats, lay in the meatiest rabbit pieces, close together in one layer, tucking the remaining pieces (like the rib pieces) on top.

Cook, without turning, to let the meat caramelize slowly, and scatter the garlic, sage leaves, and rosemary sprigs on top. After 6 or 7 minutes, or whenever the undersides of the rabbit pieces are opaque and just lightly browned, turn them over and move them around. Brown gently now for 10 minutes or so, turning again once to let the seasonings tumble in between.

Scatter the sun-dried tomato halves over the rabbit pieces, turning them again so the tomatoes fall to the bottom. Clear a space and drop in the shallots; cook them in the hot spot for a minute or two, then tumble them in with the rabbit pieces. Clear another spot, drop in the tomato paste, toast it for a minute, then turn and move the pieces around in the pan, distributing the tomato paste.

The rabbit should be browned all over by now; if not, turn any pale sides to the pan bottom. Drop in the cherry-pepper pieces in hot spots and toast them for a minute.

Turn the heat up a bit, and pour the vinegar into the pan in several clear places; let it steam and sizzle, then pour the white wine all around. Turn the rabbit pieces as the wine heats and starts to cook off.

Now scatter the bell-pepper pieces into the pan and continue to cook, turning occasionally and maintaining the heat so the juices in the pan are gently sizzling and evaporating and light browning continues.

After 12 minutes or so, when the pepper pieces have softened and the rabbit has caramelized more and the pan bottom is nearly dry, drizzle over another tablespoon or two of the olive oil and turn the pieces. Pour in the cup of hot broth and stir it with the seasonings, scraping the bottom to dissolve any glaze.

Covered Cooking and Serving

When the broth is simmering, cover and cook about 15 minutes, then sprinkle on another ¼ to ½ teaspoon of salt (taste to determine how much). Turn everything again, stirring to deglaze the bottom of the pan; the liquid should be reducing and thickening gradually; adjust the heat if necessary.

Cover and cook a final 10 to 15 minutes, or until broth and juices have concentrated into a small amount of thick sauce, enough to coat the rabbit, and the meat is tender. If there's not enough liquid, pour in broth, a few tablespoons at a time, heat, and stir to blend.

Remove the pan from the heat. Serve right away, or cover the pan to keep the rabbit warm. If it has cooled or the sauce thickens, reheat the rabbit gently with small amounts of broth to refresh and moisten it. Taste for seasoning before serving.

Serving Ideas . . .

- Rabbit *cacciatore* is delightful served as is with some piping polenta or a good crusty bread to mop up the silky sauce.

- You can also use the sauce to dress pasta and serve it with the rabbit, especially Whole Wheat Pasta (page 148) or Poor Man's Pasta shaped into *boccoli* (page 133), or garganelli (page 143).

- Potato Gnocchi (page 210) and Whole Wheat Gnocchi (page 211) are also good companions for this dish.

- If you have any leftovers, pick the meat off the bones and mix with what sauce you may have left. Add this to the Basic Risotto (page 224), halfway through the cooking.

Skillet Duck Legs with Olives and Anchovies

*D*uck has in most cases been something you eat in a restaurant. I love duck, and I love serving it at home to family and guests. I hope that this two-step method of cooking cut-up duck pieces in a big skillet or casserole will make you comfortable with cooking duck at home. First you fry the duck by itself for about an hour, slowly; the skillet takes all the fat out of the bird and melts it into a frying medium which leaves the skin golden and crispy and the meat moist, flavorful, and, amazingly, not at all greasy. In the second stage, you build a small sauce and infuse the duck with its savor.

I prefer cooking just the duck legs here, as I do for the guazzetto on page 154, as they require minimal trimming and the meat stays moist through the long cooking. If your supermarket doesn't have duck legs, ask if they can order them; call a few specialty butchers or even a local restaurant provisioner if necessary. Duck legs are worth looking for, because they're not only convenient and delicious but often less expensive than whole duck.

If a whole duck is all you can get, though, it will work fine in this recipe. See box (page 326) for a simple cutting-up procedure.

SERVES 4

4 large duck legs (about 3 pounds), or a whole duck (4 to 5 pounds)

¾ teaspoon salt, or more to taste

6 tablespoons or more extra-virgin olive oil

3 plump garlic cloves, sliced

I tablespoon finely chopped anchovies

I cup flavorful black and green olives, pitted

2 sprigs fresh rosemary (2-inch tender branches with lots of needles)

3 tablespoons red wine vinegar

I cup white wine

Cooking the Duck Legs in Their Own Fat

Trim the excess skin and all the visible fat from the duck legs; cut the skin and fat into 1-inch pieces. Sprinkle ½ teaspoon of the salt on all sides of the legs.

Pour 2 tablespoons of the oil into the pan, and set over medium heat. Arrange the legs in the pan, skin side down, and scatter all the skin and fat pieces in the spaces between them. As the fat starts to sizzle, lower the heat slightly and partially cover the skillet, leaving a gap of an inch or so for moisture to evaporate. Let the fat sizzle away, as you occasionally nudge and shift the leg pieces so they don't stick to the bottom.

After 15 to 20 minutes, turn the legs over—the skin should be gold and lightly crisped already. Cook the legs on the flesh side for about 15 minutes, shifting them a bit, then turn them skin side down again and continue cooking for another 20 minutes—cook an hour altogether—until they are thoroughly crisp and deeply colored. Lift the leg pieces from the pan, letting fat drip off, and put them in a bowl. Carefully pour out the fat into a heat-proof container, but leave the crusty bits on the bottom and sides of the skillet. See box on uses for duck fat, which follows.

Flavoring and Finishing the Duck

Return the skillet to the stove; pour in 3 more tablespoons of olive oil, and set over medium heat. Stir in the garlic slices, and cook for a minute or two, until they start to sizzle. Drop the chopped anchovies in a hot spot; cook, stirring, for a minute or more—the anchovies will melt away in the oil. Now drop in the olives and stir them around, scraping up some of the browned bits in the pan as you do, for a minute or more, until they're starting to cook.

½ cup or so Turkey Broth (page 80), Simple Vegetable Broth (page 288), or water, if needed

RECOMMENDED EQUIPMENT

A 12-inch heavy-bottomed sauté pan or casserole pan, with 4-inch sides or deeper

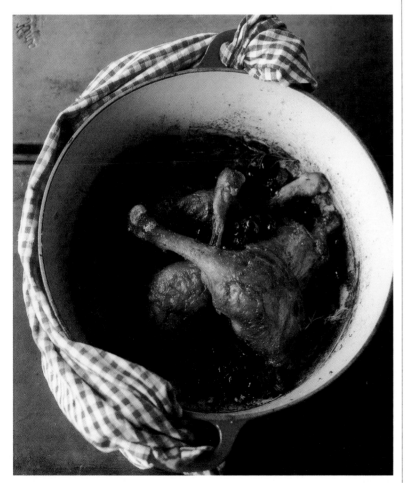

Skillet Duck with Olives and Anchovies

Put the duck legs back into the pan, toss in the branches of rosemary, and get the duck cooking again, turning the legs over in the oil and seasonings for a minute or two. When everything is hot, pour the red wine vinegar in several clear spaces around the pan; toss and stir everything as the vinegar steams and the acidity cooks off. After a minute, sprinkle on another ¼ teaspoon of salt and pour in the wine, also on hot spots, and stir for a minute, then cover the pan completely.

Cook covered for 4 or 5 minutes over low to medium heat, then uncover and turn everything well, coating the duck with the liquid and using it to deglaze the browned bits in the pan. Taste the sauce and add salt if necessary; drizzle over a tablespoon or two of olive oil if the sauce needs more viscosity.

Cover the pan, and cook another 4 to 5 minutes. Uncover, and give everything a final stir so the duck is well coated with thick sauce

IT'S EASY TO CUT UP A DUCK

To make this wonderful dish with a whole duck rather than duck legs, here's a simple way to cut it up. I suggest you have a heavy chef's knife, kitchen shears, and a small cleaver.

- *Rinse and dry the duck. Save the giblets and neck for soup (or cook the neck in the skillet, as I would). Trim and cut excess skin and fat, and cut them up for the skillet.*

- *Grasp a wing near the body and bend it back firmly, exposing the armpit—you'll feel the connecting joint. Cut through it to remove the wing; repeat on the other side. Slice off the outside thin wing piece for the soup pile; cook the meatier wing pieces in the skillet.*

- *Set the breast facing up, and slice a line right down the middle, exposing the cartilage where the breast halves meet. Now cut through the cartilage and bone with your shears or knife, following your line, splitting the duck open.*

- *Open the breast halves and spread them apart, like opening a book, with the spine down the middle. Now cut the duck apart along the spine, chopping with the base of your knife or cleaver at the tough parts. One cut is all you need; leave the backbone attached to one of the long duck halves.*

- *Cut each half crosswise, dividing the breast meat from the leg meat—there's a natural dip between them.*

- *Now you have four big pieces, two small wings, one neck, and lots of fat and skin to fry, following the recipe.*

and bits of olives. If there's loose, wet sauce in the pan, cook and stir until it is thickened. But if the duck is dry and there are stuck brown bits on the pan, pour in a bit of broth to loosen things up and get the duck moist and glistening with the sauce. Remove from the heat and serve. Let the duck rest in the pan, partially covered, if you want; re-fresh and reheat it with a bit of broth before serving.

DELICIOUS DUCK FAT AND CRACKLINGS

Don't discard delicious duck fat!

You'll get almost a pound of fat with skin attached when you're trimming duck legs for this recipe or for guazzetto (page 154). Both the fat and the skin are full of flavor and easy to render, giving you a snack of delicious cracklings and a small crock of pure duck fat. Here's how:

Cut the trimmings into rough ½-inch pieces and put them in a heavy-bottomed saucepan over medium-low heat. Within a few min-utes, the fat will have started rendering and the skin will be sizzling. Cook slowly for 20 minutes or more, until the skin cracklings are crisp and browned all over.

Lift out the cracklings with a spider or strainer, and toss them on a paper towel with a little salt. Pour the rendered duck fat into a heat-proof bowl or small crock. (If you're not sure whether it's heat-proof, put a spoon in the crock to temper the heat.) Store duck fat in a closed crock; it will solidify and keep for a month and more. To use, just spoon into a pan; it will melt immediately, like butter. Use it as a cooking fat when frying eggs, making sauces like Bolognese, and braising meats.

Enjoy the cracklings as a snack, or dress a soup with them. You can use them instead of bacon in a quick pasta dish, or add them to a recipe like Spaghetti with Asparagus Frittata (page 99). Also, duck cracklings are delicious tossed in a green salad, in Poached Whole Zucchini with Lemon and Olive Oil (page 327), in scrambled eggs, or kneaded into focaccia just before baking.

Serving Ideas . . .

This skillet duck is delicious served just with cooked or grilled polenta.

Skillet Brussels Sprouts (page 271) is a harmonious accompaniment with or without polenta.

To serve on individual plates, arrange a whole leg, thigh and drumstick, on each plate, and top it with the pieces of olives and drops of remaining sauce. Or you can cut the leg at the joint and serve two pieces.

If you are cooking the whole duck pieces, either serve as they are or cut in smaller pieces. Duck bones are more brittle and splin-ter easily, so cutting at the joints is the way to go.

Poached Chicken and Vegetables in Broth

I know that "boiled" anything is not a popular concept these days (one reason I call this "poached"), but don't disdain or neglect this elemental dish. It is still one of the easiest and most satisfying one-pot meals we can give our families. It's also faster to make than ever: the big birds I buy—plump, meaty, and best when organically raised—are thoroughly cooked, tender, and moist after barely 45 minutes in the broth. When you really want to make it festive, substitute a capon for the chicken. And with markets that offer an unprecedented array of produce and herbs in all seasons, we can surround the chicken with a greater variety of vegetables than our great-great-grandmothers ever had at one time.

In this recipe, I've loaded the pot with seven hearty and aromatic vegetables (almost 5 pounds' worth), but you can certainly choose others or vary the amounts. Just cut enough vegetables overall to give everyone a bountiful serving, drizzling the meat and vegetables with some extra-virgin olive oil and a few grains of sea salt to make it complete. But I also hope you'll top each portion, as I do, with a dollop of salsa verde, a traditional condiment for boiled foods. The bright, acidic flavor and fresh, uncooked texture of the finely chopped salsa are a perfect counterpoint to the poached meat and vegetables—it makes a meal of boiled chicken exciting as well as comforting.

SERVES 6 TO 8, WITH EXTRA BROTH

FOR THE BROTH

6 quarts cold fresh water

¼ cup coarse sea salt, or 3 tablespoons kosher salt

1 tablespoon whole black peppercorns

¼ cup (¼ ounce) dried porcini slices

2 bay leaves, preferably fresh

1 or 2 pieces hard rind of Parmigiano-Reggiano or Grana Padano, if available, rinsed and scraped (see page 66)

Starting the Broth and Vegetables

Pour the water into the pot, set it over low heat to get started, and add the seasonings—salt, peppercorns, porcini, bay leaves, and cheese rind. Cut up all vegetables as follows, and drop them into the pot:

- Cut the leeks crosswise into 4-inch lengths, but don't slice them open.

- Cut the carrots and parsnips crosswise into 3-inch lengths; slice thick sections lengthwise in half or quarters, so all pieces are about 1 inch thick (throw the skinny pointed ends of the parsnips into the broth too).

- With a vegetable peeler, shave off the outer layer of the celery stalks, then cut crosswise into 3-inch lengths.

- Slice the celery root into 2-inch, roughly square chunks.

- Trim off the tough root end of the fennel bulb, but leave the core intact so the leaves are held together; slice the bulb into six or eight wedges, through the core.

- Trim the onions but leave the root ends intact, so the layers are held together.

When all the vegetables are in the pot, put on the cover and turn the heat to high. Bring the water to a rolling boil, set the cover ajar (I prop it up on a big wooden spoon), and lower the heat to maintain a moderate bubbling. Cook the broth and vegetables for about 30 minutes, while you prepare the chicken.

Prepping the Chicken

Remove the giblets and neck from the chicken, rinse well, and drop them all (including the liver) into the broth. Rinse the chicken under cold running water. Set it on a cutting board; chop off the tail piece and add it to the pot. Pull off all clumps of fat and discard. Twist and fold the wingtips against the neck, so they stay in place under the breast.

Put the seasonings into the body cavity: the salt, the peppercorns, the smashed garlic cloves, and the bay leaves. Rinse the lemon, cut it in half crosswise, squeeze the juice from both pieces into the cavity, then push in the squashed lemon halves too. Press the bird's legs together, close to the body, so the cavity is covered and the chicken is compact and evenly shaped.

Spread out the cheesecloth square and place the chicken in the center. Lift two diagonally opposite corners, draw the cloth up and around the bird, and tie the corners in a simple overhand knot. Tighten the knot so it rests on the chicken breast and the cloth is snug against the bird. Now lift the other corners of the cheesecloth and bring them together, tie in another knot, and tighten it to wrap the chicken up completely. Tie the loose ends in square knots that won't unravel.

Finally, cut a length of twine about a yard long (I double it for strength) and tie one end of the twine under the bulging cheesecloth topknots, in a secure knot. You should now be able to lift the cloth-wrapped chicken with the string—test it now, over the worktable,

THE VEGETABLES

¾ pound leeks, 1 ½ inches thick, trimmed and rinsed

½ pound large carrots, trimmed and peeled

½ pound small parsnips, trimmed and peeled

½ pound large celery stalks, trimmed

¾ pound celery root, completely peeled and trimmed

1 fennel bulb, stalks trimmed and coarse outer leaves pulled off

8 small onions (each about 2 ounces), peeled

THE CHICKEN AND SEASONINGS

3½-to-4-pound roasting chicken with giblets

1 teaspoon coarse sea salt or kosher salt

2 teaspoons whole black peppercorns

3 large garlic cloves, peeled and smashed

2 fresh bay leaves

1 small or medium lemon

FOR SERVING

Salsa Verde (page 362) and/or Smooth Sweet Red Pepper Sauce (page 364)
Gnoccho Grande (page 336)

RECOMMENDED EQUIPMENT

A 10-to-12-quart stockpot

Cheesecloth to make a 30-inch square, triple thickness

Kitchen twine

because you'll need to lift the cooked chicken out of the boiling broth the same way.

Cooking the Chicken and Serving

When the broth and vegetables have been cooking for ½ hour, uncover, and lower the chicken into the broth with your strong string. Make sure the chicken is submerged, then loop the string around a handle of the stockpot, or any anchor point. Bring the broth back to a good boil, then adjust the heat to keep a steady but gentle bubbling on the surface.

Cook the chicken, uncovered, for 40 to 50 minutes (less for a smaller chicken, more for a larger one or if you are using a capon). Set a big bowl close to the chicken pot. Turn off the heat, grasp your twine, lift the chicken bundle straight up above the stock, and lower it into the bowl.

Let the chicken rest in the cheesecloth while you check the vegetables—they should be soft but not falling apart. Cook longer or lift them out of the broth with a spider or other big strainer, into a big bowl. Ladle a bit of hot broth onto the vegetables, and cover with foil or a pot lid to keep them warm.

To free the chicken, lift it from the bowl onto a tray, a board, or a big piece of foil, which will catch the juices. Cut the twine, untie the cheesecloth knots—try to keep the cloth whole—and unwrap the bird. Spoon out the lemon, bay leaves, and other seasonings from the cavity and discard. To keep the chicken warm, put it back in the bowl, doused with fresh hot broth and covered.

To strain the broth, drape the moist cheesecloth inside a colander or large strainer and set it over a big pot or bowl (you'll still have several quarts of stock). Pour the broth through the cheesecloth. Taste it for flavor; use (and store) as is, or bring it to a boil and reduce it if you want to concentrate it.

To make a two-course meal, cook some thin pasta such as capellini or stelline (little stars) or rice in the broth and serve with some grated Parmigiano-Reggiano for the first course. Then serve the chicken, whole or cut up, on a warm serving platter, surrounded with the vegetables. (If they have cooled off, warm them up in broth.) Pass around *salsa verde* and/or pepper sauce at the table.

A Simple Soup with Savory Chicken Broth

This recipe gives you the bonus of several quarts of tasty broth. Whether you serve the broth as a soup right away, or save most of it for future meals, garnish it with any of the choices suggested for Turkey Broth (page 80): passatelli, tagliolini, quickly cooked tender spinach leaves, Cheesy *Crostini* (page 60), or just a heap of freshly grated Parmigiano-Reggiano or Grana Padano.

For my family, I like to carve the whole hot chicken at the table and assemble plates, arranging a few pieces of every vegetable around the chicken and spooning 2 tablespoons or more of *salsa verde* all across the top of the chicken and vegetables, with more *salsa verde* on the side.

WARM CHICKEN SALAD

If you have leftover poached chicken, the moist meat makes a wonderful warm salad, with raisins and pine nuts and a lively, sweet dressing (similar to the Cooked Carrot Salad with Pine Nuts and Golden Raisins, page 45). Three cups of dressed chicken would serve 3 or 4.

For the dressing, put ½ cup water, 3 tablespoons white vinegar, and 1 teaspoon honey into a small saucepan and bring to a boil. Drop 3 tablespoons of golden raisins into the pan, and poach them gently for 4 minutes; then lift them out with a slotted spoon. Return the liquid to a boil, and cook rapidly until it is reduced to 3 tablespoons. Pour the dressing out of the pan to cool.

To assemble the salad:
Toast 3 tablespoons pine nuts in a dry pan until golden.

Shred chicken meat to make 3 cups or so. Put the chicken in a pan with a few spoonfuls of broth (or water), and toss the shreds over low heat just to warm up and refresh. Put the shreds in a mixing bowl, and toss with the warm vinegar-honey dressing, 2 tablespoons extra-virgin olive oil, and ½ teaspoon salt—or more to taste. Scatter the plumped raisins and toasted pine nuts over the chicken, and toss together.

Arrange the salad on a bed of greens, on a large platter or individual salad plates, and serve while the chicken is still slightly warm.

Roast Turkey and Pan Sauce

The turkey is a North American native that was taken to Europe, food historians tell us, by the early Spanish explorers. In Italy, it became a culinary favorite of the aristocracy quite quickly: I've been delighted to learn that sixty-six turkeys were served at a feast for Catherine de' Medici in 1549.

In my family, however, turkey was not a big deal until we came to North America, 400 years later. Like most of our neighbors in the 1950s, we mainly cooked and ate turkey as the centerpiece of Thanksgiving and other holiday feasts. But over the years, it has become a significant part of our everyday eating. As you've seen, turkey wings flavor our basic broth, and turkey breast cutlets are a family favorite.

A whole roast turkey is still something special on our table. And after years of Thanksgiving and Christmas feasts and birthday dinners, I have perfected the two-stage, wet-then-dry turkey-roasting procedure that I present here. It's unusual but it works. In fact, I roast all kinds of meats and poultry this way (as I explain in the box on page 338) to produce marvelously moist and flavorful meat with a crispy, caramelized exterior—and a rich pan sauce at the same time.

For the autumn and winter holidays, I serve the turkey with seasonal trimmings—Quince, Cranberry, and Apple Sauce (page 367), Cotognata—Quince Chutney (page 368), and Gnoccho Grande for a stuffing. And I glaze the bird with balsamic-vinegar reduction for a deep mahogany sheen. Roast turkey is so good, though, and so economical, I hope you'll cook it often, not just for Thanksgiving. For everyday dinners, follow the basic procedure for cooking a chicken or a small turkey (page 338). You don't have to give it the holiday touches every time: the bird will be beautiful without the glaze and delicious with just its natural pan sauce.

SERVES 12 OR MORE, WITH LEFTOVERS

1 fresh turkey, 12 to 14 pounds, including neck and giblets

1½ tablespoons kosher salt

¼ cup extra-virgin olive oil

Prepping the Turkey and Vegetables

Arrange a rack low in the oven, making sure that the fully prepared turkey will fit in easily and roast well below the oven ceiling. Remember that the foil tent will be an inch or two higher than the turkey itself. Preheat the oven to 375°.

Take out the giblets and neck from the turkey, and save. Remove and discard any lumps of fat from the cavities. Rinse the bird inside and out, in cool running water, clearing the cavity of any residue.

Rinse the giblets too. Pat everything dry with paper towels.

Set the wire roasting rack in the pan and the turkey on the rack, with the neck and giblets on the pan bottom. Sprinkle 2 teaspoons of the kosher salt inside the main turkey cavity and the rest of the salt (1½ tablespoons in all) over the outside of the bird. Pour the olive oil on the turkey, a bit at a time, and spread it with your hands to coat the entire skin, including the back. Twist the tip joint of each wing down, and forcefully fold it so it stays in place under the neck (think of placing both your hands behind your neck). Rest the oiled turkey on the rack, flat on its back, wings folded and breast up.

Toss together in a bowl the vegetables and seasonings, except the salt and broth, with the ¼ cup olive oil, mixing everything well. If you are using my turkey broth or other salted broth, don't add salt. If using an *unsalted* stock, mix 1 teaspoon kosher salt with the vegetables.

Put a handful or two of mixed vegetables (and one of the rosemary branches) loosely into the cavity of the turkey. Spread all the rest in one layer on the pan bottom, all around the turkey. Push the vegetable pieces under the rack if your pan is small, so they will cook in the stock.

Before pouring in the broth, move your pan near the oven, so you won't have far to carry it. Pour the broth into the roasting pan on the side, without wetting the turkey. Depending on pan size, you'll need 4 to 6 cups of stock to fill the bottom about ⅓ inch deep. Add more stock (or water) if necessary.

Putting Up the Tent and Roasting the Turkey

Tear two long sheets of aluminum foil. Cover one side of the pan with the first sheet, arching it well above the turkey. Crimp the foil against the rim of the pan so it stays in place without touching the bird. Cover the rest of the pan and turkey with the second sheet of foil (or more if needed), overlapping the sheets several inches. Press the bottom of the foil tightly against the sides of the pan, all around, sealing the tent completely.

Carefully place the covered pan on the oven rack—it will be heavy, so you may need some help. Push it well to the back of the oven for the maximum heat, and let the turkey roast undisturbed for 2 hours. Open the oven, pull the roasting pan to the front, and lift off the foil sheets. The pan juices should be bubbling away, and the

VEGETABLES AND
SEASONINGS

1 pound carrots, peeled and cut into
    2-inch chunks

2 large onions, peeled and chopped
    into 1-inch pieces

¾ pound celery stalks with leaves,
    rinsed and cut into 2-inch chunks

1 ounce dried porcini slices, crumbled
    into ½-inch pieces

1 tablespoon whole black
    peppercorns

6 short branches fresh rosemary,
    with plenty of needles

¼ cup extra-virgin olive oil

1 teaspoon kosher salt, if needed

4 to 6 cups Turkey Broth (page 80) or
    Simple Vegetable Broth
    (page 288)

FOR GLAZING THE TURKEY
(OPTIONAL)

¼ cup Reduced Balsamic Vinegar,
    glaze consistency
    (page 39)

SERVING SAUCES AND
ACCOMPANIMENTS
(OPTIONAL)

Turkey Gravy (page 335)

Quince, Cranberry, and Apple Sauce
    (page 367)

Cotognata (page 368)

Reduced Balsamic Vinegar
    (page 39)

A heavy-duty roasting pan,
    at least 12 inches by 18 inches,
    preferably larger
A flat wire roasting rack, big enough
    to hold the turkey but small enough
    to leave space for vegetables on the
    pan bottom
Wide heavy-duty aluminum foil
A saucepan, a medium-mesh sieve,
    and a potato masher, to make the
    sauce
A kitchen brush, for painting the
    turkey with glaze (optional)

Roast Turkey and Pan Sauce (cont.)

steaming turkey will be mostly pale. With a ladle or bulb baster, baste the turkey all over with the pan juices and return it to the oven. Save the foil.

Roast the turkey uncovered for 30 minutes to an hour, to brown the skin and cook the meat to a safe internal temperature. (Because every oven thermostat is different and turkeys will vary in size, cooking times will vary.) After 30 minutes, baste again and check the internal temperature of the turkey (see box, page 337), then continue roasting, if necessary, until the meat reaches the right temperature. If the breast is getting too dark, cover it loosely with a sheet of foil.

Starting the Sauce

Carefully remove the roasting pan and lift the turkey out of the pan and onto a baking sheet or platter. Cover the turkey loosely with the foil, and keep it in a warm place while you make the sauce. (The oven should remain on at 375° if you're going to glaze it.)

Remove the turkey neck but not the giblets (nor the liver) from the roasting pan and put into the saucepan. With a potato masher, crush the cooked vegetables and giblets in the roasting juices, breaking them up into little bits. Set the sieve on the saucepan, and pour everything out of the roaster into the sieve, scraping up all the juices, vegetables, the liver, and flavorful caramelized bits. Press the vegetables and other solids against the sieve with a big spoon to release their liquid, then discard what's left in the sieve.

You should have 1 to 2 quarts of pan juices (depending on how much stock you started with and the roasting time). Set the saucepan over high heat, bring the juices to a boil, and let them reduce, uncovered.

Optional Glazing of the Turkey and Final Steps

To make a glaze for turkey, if you like, mix ¼ cup of balsamic-vinegar reduction and 2 tablespoons of the pan sauce until spreadable; heat and thin it as needed. Put the turkey, still on the rack, back in the empty roasting pan. Brush the glaze all over the bird in a smooth, even coat. Return the turkey to the oven for 10 to 15 minutes, or until the glazed skin is crisp, shiny, and deeply colored. Let it rest in a warm place, tented with foil, if you wish.

To finish the sauce: Pour into the boiling sauce any turkey juices that accumulated on the baking sheet. When the sauce has reduced almost by half, taste it for salt and add a bit more if you like, and bring back to a simmer.

Strain it once again, this time through a fine-meshed sieve into a measuring cup or other narrow container. Let it rest for a minute, then spoon off the fat layer that's accumulated on top. Thicken the sauce with bread crumbs if it's too liquid (see box).

To serve: for formal occasions, you can present the whole turkey and carve it at the table. For most family dinners, I cut the bird up in the kitchen as follows. Cut the wings off, slice the breast meat, then remove the legs at the joint and slice the leg and thigh meat from the bones for dark-meat lovers; arrange all the pieces on a serving platter. Pour any juices left in the pan or on the cutting board over the meat, then nap all the pieces with a cup or more of the finished sauce. Bring the platter to the table, and let people serve themselves. Put the rest of the sauce in a bowl and pass it.

TURNING PAN SAUCE INTO TURKEY GRAVY

The reduced sauce from the roasting pan juices will be fully flavored but sometimes thinner than a typical turkey gravy. Here's how I thicken the juices and give them more texture (without using flour or starch). Put the strained and reduced sauce in a pan or skillet, set over medium heat, and whisk in fine dry bread crumbs—about 1 teaspoon for each cup of sauce. Keep whisking as the sauce starts to bubble; let it cook and thicken for a minute. You'll have a delicious and natural-tasting gravy in no time. Strain and serve.

An Unusual Turkey Stuffing:
Poached Gnoccho Grande

The way I roast turkey, I never stuff it. Instead, for holidays and special occasions when a turkey needs a special dressing, I make a gnoccho grande, a large loaf-shaped dumpling of bread crumbs, eggs, seasonings, and festive tidbits of dried fruits and nuts, wrapped in cheesecloth and poached in broth. Since I usually cook a big pot of turkey broth the day before I roast the turkey (to have plenty for the roasting pan), I'll poach the gnoccho grande while it's bubbling away.

The next time you make turkey broth, try this wonderful big dumpling. It's a great accompaniment to any poultry or meat dish, not just turkey, and a fine soup garnish, or cook it in the broth from Whole Poached Chicken (page 328).

A 2-POUND *GNOCCHO GRANDE* SERVING 10 OR MORE

8 large eggs

½ teaspoon salt

2 cups fine dry bread crumbs

2 cups freshly grated Parmigiano-Reggiano or Grana Padano

⅛ teaspoon freshly ground black pepper

½ teaspoon freshly grated nutmeg

Zest of 1 lemon, finely grated

Zest of 1 small orange, finely grated

¼ cup chopped fresh Italian parsley

⅓ cup golden raisins

⅓ cup dried apricots, chopped into ¼-inch pieces

¼ cup pine nuts, toasted

⅓ cup cooked chestnuts (page 71), chopped into bits (optional)

3 to 4 quarts Turkey Broth (page 80) or broth of Poached Chicken (page 328), heated to boiling in stockpot

To make the dough, whisk the eggs in a large mixing bowl, add the salt, and then whisk in the bread crumbs. Stirring with a wooden spoon, incorporate all the remaining ingredients except broth; when the dough gets too stiff to stir, work it with your hands. It's ready when it holds together, although it will still be slightly sticky. Shape the dough into a cylindrical loaf about 8 inches long and 4 inches thick.

Cut a 40-inch length of cheesecloth and fold it lengthwise so it's 18 inches wide. Set the loaf at one narrow end of the band, centered, with a margin of cloth on either side. Roll up the loaf in the cheesecloth, so it is wrapped in many layers. Twist the open sides of the cloth in opposite directions, tightening them against the loaf like a piece of candy in a twisted wrapper. Tie the twists on both sides with long pieces of kitchen twine so they can't unravel. Leave at least a foot or so of twine dangling from each knot.

Now lower the *gnoccho grande* into a stockpot of boiling turkey broth—you should have enough to cover the *gnoccho* by 1 inch. It can be cooked in a pot of salted water like pasta, but it will be a bit less flavorful, although still good. Tie the free ends of twine to the pot handles or to a big spoon lying on the pot rim, so the *gnoccho* is suspended in the broth and can't fall to the bottom. Bring the broth back to a gentle boil, and poach the loaf for 40 minutes or so, then lift it out of the broth and into a bowl (the broth may, of course, be used again). Untie the twine, and roll the loaf out of the cheese-cloth. Slice into the center to check that the dough is cooked all the way through—uncooked dough will be wet and mushy. If necessary, rewrap the *gnoccho* and cook it a bit longer.

You can slice and serve cooked *gnoccho grande* right away, or let it cool, wrap and refrigerate it, and reheat the slices in a pan of broth. As an accompaniment to roast turkey or other main courses, slice in ½-inch-thick rounds, then in half-rounds or wedges, and serve on a warm platter. *Gnoccho grande* also makes a lovely soup garnish: cut the rounds into small cubes and heat them in broth.

CHECKING TURKEY FOR DONENESS

When is the turkey roasted enough?

After 2½ hours total of roasting, insert an instant-read meat thermometer into the thickest part of the thigh (the part that cooks most slowly). A reading of 165° to 170° will indicate that the thighs are almost done, and you can remove the bird from the oven, make the sauce, and complete the glazing. If the temperature is lower (likely with a bigger turkey), continue roasting and check again in 15 minutes.

If you don't have a thermometer, check the juices that flow from the thigh when you pierce it near the joint. Any sign of pink in the juices indicates that more roasting is needed.

ROASTING IN TWO STAGES: FIRST WET, THEN DRY

When you read this recipe—or the ones for roast pork, lamb shoulder, or stuffed veal breast later in this chapter—you'll see that my way of roasting involves more than sticking a piece of meat in a hot oven. In all these recipes, the ingredients list calls for lots of cut-up vegetables, seasonings, and a quart or more of broth. All the vegetables and liquid go into the roasting pan, underneath the meat, and I seal everything in a tent of aluminum foil for the first hour or two in the oven. This wet cooking serves to break down and soften the fibers in the meat and vegetables. As the fibers loosen, they release their flavors. And as the liquid boils and steams within the closed environment, it permeates the meat with all the flavors it has picked up.

The second stage, dry cooking, begins when the tent is removed and the meat is exposed to the direct dry heat of the oven This uncovered cooking produces the crispy and caramelized exterior that is essential in a roast.

When you simply roast meat, as most recipes suggest, you get the caramelization but not the tenderizing of the meat fibers and the development and exchange of flavor. And, often, I find that dry heat alone toughens the fibers; lean meat, like the breast of poultry, will quickly dry out.

ROAST CHICKEN IN A TENT

I roast chicken exactly as I do turkey, with a few small differences: the oven temperature is higher; the vegetables, which are cut smaller, cook with the pan juices on the stove top so they soften up.

For a 3½-to-4-pound chicken: Heat the oven to 425°. Season the chicken with 1 teaspoon salt and 2 teaspoons oil. Use a third to a half of the vegetables and seasonings given for turkey; chop them all into ¼-inch pieces. Add a pint of broth to the pan, and enough water to fill the pan to about ⅓ inch deep.

Seal the chicken in a foil tent over the pan, and roast it covered for 1 hour. Remove the foil, and scrape all the vegetables and liquid into a saucepan *together*—don't strain the vegetables as you do with turkey—and cook over high heat.

To finish the chicken, return it to the oven and roast 20 to 30 minutes uncovered, checking it occasionally and basting with the juices in the saucepan, until the skin is crisp and golden. To finish the sauce, reduce the pan juices by half, strain out the soft vegetables, and purée them through a sieve into the sauce.

Meat Main Dishes

Thin-Cut Lamb Shoulder Chops in a Skillet with Sauce

Here's an uncommon preparation for one of the most common and popular cuts of meat in the market: thin-cut lamb shoulder chops. They're inexpensive, wide, and meaty. Barely ½ inch thick, they look like they'll cook in a minute, perfect for fast family suppers. But shoulder chops also have lots of cartilage and gristle, and usually two sets of bones, which call for slow cooking (and the meat is tougher than it looks).

Though it is a thin chop, it will take about 20 minutes to cook. Get out the big skillet to caramelize the meat and flavoring agents, and then bring everything together in a superb sauce. With surprising ingredients, this is a good recipe to add to your growing repertoire of aglio e olio base sauces. Also, as the sauce reduces, it actually braises the chops for a few minutes, which tenderizes the meat a bit, although it will still be chewy (which I love).

What is surprising about the sauce? In addition to my usual aglio, olio, e peperoncino, I drop a couple of chopped anchovy fillets into the pan, where they quickly disintegrate. As part of the sauce, their flavor has a subtle presence but a remarkable impact: taste a bit of lamb by itself, then a morsel with sauce, and you'll see. Here is delicious evidence that the anchovy is a potent source of umami—the amino acid that makes other foods taste better.

You can omit the anchovies entirely, but I hope you'll give this food synergy a try: if you're doubtful, use just one fillet of anchovy. We all need to be adventurous!

SERVES 4

Trim the fat from the outside edges of the chops. Salt them on both sides lightly, using ¼ teaspoon. Spread the flour on a plate or on a piece of foil; dredge the chops in it on both sides to coat lightly, then shake off the excess flour.	4 lamb shoulder chops, ½ inch thick or less (6 to 8 ounces each)
	¾ teaspoon kosher salt
	½ cup or so flour, to coat the chops
Put the oil and butter in the skillet, and set over medium-high heat. As the butter foams, lay the chops in the pan. Fry them on the first side for 2 minutes, then flip them over and fry for 2 more	3 tablespoons extra-virgin olive oil, plus more if needed
	2 tablespoons butter

4 fat garlic cloves, sliced

1 or 2 teaspoons finely chopped
   anchovies (1 or 2 small fillets)

¼ teaspoon *peperoncino* (hot red
   pepper flakes), or to taste

¼ cup red wine vinegar

2 tablespoons Dijon-style mustard

1 cup or more Simple Vegetable Broth
   (page 288), Turkey Broth
   page 80), or water

RECOMMENDED EQUIPMENT

A 14-inch skillet or sauté pan; you can
   cook 2 or 3 chops in a 12-inch pan

Serving Ideas . . .

This intensely flavored dish beck-
ons a mellow *contorno*, such as
mashed or baked potatoes, or the
Potato, Parsnip, and Scallion
Mash (page 361).

   Polenta (page 215) would also
be quite nice, or *riso al salto*
(page 233), would be delicious
to mop up the sauce.

Thin-Cut Lamb Shoulder Chops in a Skillet with Sauce (cont.)

minutes—the meat should only be light brown; if chops are darkening too fast, lower the heat.

Scatter the garlic in empty hot spots in the pan. Cook for a
minute, stirring the slices until they're sizzling, then drop the anchovy bits into the hot spots and stir as they heat and melt away.
Shake the skillet and sprinkle the *peperoncino* in the hot spots, and
give them a minute of sizzling.

Turn the meat over, so the first side is down again. Fry for 2 minutes—shaking the pan now and then—and flip over once more; by
now there should be some nice caramelization on the meat.

Spill the vinegar into the hot spots; shake the pan and tilt it to
distribute the juices all around; sprinkle another ¼ teaspoon salt all
over. After about 2 minutes, turn the meat pieces again.

Now plop the mustard into several different hot spots; shake and
stir and caramelize it for a minute.

Turn the meat one more time—it will be getting darker—and
pour the broth into the skillet. It should come well up the sides of
the meat, almost but not quite over the top. Get the juices boiling,
then lower the heat to keep a lively bubbling simmer in the pan.

Relax! Let the meat cook, the sauce thicken, and the flavors come
together for 4 or 5 minutes. Taste the sauce—sprinkle in more salt if
you like. Drizzle another tablespoon of olive oil all over to give the
sauce more shine, if you want.

When the sauce has become syrupy and looks the way you like it,
sprinkle the parsley all over. Turn the meat once more, shake the
skillet one last time, and take it off the heat.

To serve, put a chop on a warm plate and spoon over some of the
sauce.

Roast Thick Lamb Chops with Roast Carrots and Parsnips

*Y*ou'll need lamb shoulder chops again for this great dinner dish, but, unlike the thin chops for skillet cooking, the right ones for roasting won't be in the meat case. Don't just pick up a package of thick-looking chops: ask the butcher to cut lamb shoulder chops expressly for you, each one 2½ inches thick (or as close to that as possible). If he or she looks surprised, it's because she's never cut them that thick before. The chop size is unusual, but the meat is exactly the same as everyday thin chops—so make sure she gives you the same price!

Thick chops are treated here like roasts, following my covered/uncovered roasting procedure. To shorten the roasting time, I divide each chop into two pieces. Still, the meat needs 90 minutes or more in the oven, typical of the long cooking all shoulder cuts need, to melt the connective tissue and fat, to extract the flavor of bones, and to soften the meat fibers. Bigger pork and beef shoulders will take twice as long as these lamb chops.

SERVES 4 OR MORE

Setting Up the Roasting Pan

Place a rack in the bottom third of the oven and, if possible, another rack in the top third, with enough space on both for the filled roasting pan. Preheat the oven to 425°.

Trim most of the fat from the chops, leaving only a very thin layer on the outside surfaces. To divide each chop into two pieces, lay it on a flat, cut side so you can see the divisions of the muscles. On one side are muscles attached to rib and backbones; on the opposite are the muscles around the thin shoulder-blade bone. It is easy to see where to separate them, because thick ribs tend to break apart naturally between these muscles—cooperatively, in the middle. Pull with your fingers to separate the pieces; slice apart the small section of meat that may hold them together. Sprinkle the meat pieces on all sides with salt, and pat it on, using ½ teaspoon in all.

Put all the cut vegetables, the herbs, porcini, and peppercorns in the pan. Drizzle about ¼ cup of the olive oil and the remaining teaspoon of salt over and toss and tumble everything together with your

2 lamb shoulder chops, cut 2¼ to
  2½ inches thick (3 pounds total)

1½ teaspoons or more coarse sea salt
  or kosher salt

¾ pound carrots, peeled, trimmed, and
  sliced into even 3-inch chunks

¾ pound parsnips, peeled, trimmed,
  and sliced into even 3-inch chunks

1 celery stalk, peeled, slit lengthwise,
  and cut into 3-inch lengths

4 plump garlic cloves, peeled

1 medium leek, about 8 ounces,
  trimmed for roasting (see box)

2 medium onions, peeled and quartered
  in wedges, attached at root end

2 fresh bay leaves

2 tablespoons fresh rosemary needles

2 tablespoons (packed) fresh mint
leaves, roughly chopped

2 tablespoons dried porcini, chopped
or broken into small bits

I teaspoon whole black peppercorns

⅓ cup extra-virgin olive oil, plus more
if needed

I cup white wine

1½ cups Turkey Broth (page 80),
Simple Vegetable Broth (page 288),
or water

RECOMMENDED EQUIPMENT

A large, heavy-duty roasting pan,
12 by 18 inches preferred

Aluminum foil

hands, distributing the seasonings and oiling all the pieces. Put the lamb pieces in with the vegetables, turn them in the pan, and rub them to coat with more olive oil. Arrange them several inches apart from each other, with vegetables all around, so they will cook and caramelize evenly. Pour the wine and a cup of broth (or water) into the pan; if necessary, add more broth or water to bring the liquid to ½-inch depth.

Cover the pan with one or more long sheets of aluminum foil, arching the foil if necessary to keep it from touching the meat and vegetables. Crimp the foil around the rim of the pan, and press it tightly against the sides all around, sealing the lamb and vegetables in a tent.

Roasting, Covered and Uncovered

Roast for 45 minutes, undisturbed, on the lower rack. Remove the pan, and carefully take off the foil; the pan juices should be bubbling away around the meat and vegetables. With tongs, turn over each piece of lamb as well as the vegetables.

Place the pan on the upper oven rack, and roast for about 10 minutes, then turn the lamb pieces over. Roast 10 more minutes and turn again (tumbling the vegetables over too). Roast another 10 minutes, until the lamb is crusty brown all over and has shrunk back from the bones.

Caramelizing the Vegetables and Making the Sauce

Remove from the oven, and transfer the lamb pieces to a bowl or platter—letting the juices drip back into the pan for a moment. Keep in a warm place, loosely covered with the foil sheet.

Set a sieve over a saucepan, and carefully pour the juices out of the roasting pan, leaving the vegetables intact in the pan. It's fine if the small seasonings go into the sieve, but you don't want the vegetables to break. Pick out the bay leaves and discard. Spread the vegetables out in the pan—they will still be moist—and put them in the oven, on the high rack, to caramelize.

Meanwhile, start the sauce: press the juices from any seasonings or solids in the sieve. Skim the fat off the surface of the juices, and set the saucepan over high heat. Bring the juices to a boil, and reduce them by about half, to a slightly syrupy consistency: you should have about ¾ cup.

After 5 minutes or so, check the roasting vegetables: turn them in the pan, and rotate the pan on the rack. Roast until the chunks have crisped on the sides and caramelized on the edges, checking and turning them frequently. If they haven't colored nicely in 10 minutes, raise the oven temperature; if they appear dry, drizzle a bit of the sauce or olive oil over them.

Finishing and Serving

While the vegetables are roasting, warm a serving platter (or plates). If you want, cut out the blade bone, which protrudes from the meat—just lift the cooked meat off it and remove the bone. Cut the meat off the rib pieces too, or leave them intact (for those who like gnawing bones).

To serve family-style, heap the hot vegetables and meat on the serving platter and drizzle some of the sauce over. Or arrange a portion of vegetables in the center of a warm dinner plate, lay one of the lamb pieces on top, and moisten with sauce. Pass the remaining sauce at the table.

Serving Ideas . . .

The vegetables roasted alongside the meat are ideal and delicious as an accompaniment. Some hot polenta (page 215) would be a good addition too.

SAVE THE VEGETABLES!
A ROASTED CONTORNO TO EAT WITH YOUR MEAT

The way I roast, aromatic vegetables fill the pan to lend flavor to the meat during their hours together in the oven. Later, the vegetables are usually mashed and sieved to extract their juices, flavor, and rich pulp for the sauce. I sometimes hate to lose these sweet vegetables—if you've tasted a carrot or onion wedge that's roasted with turkey or pork shoulder, you know what I mean. So I suggest you split the goods and use some to make sauce and save the rest as contorno, as I do in this recipe.

You can do the same in any of the roasting recipes in this chapter. Follow these guidelines (and see the preceding lamb recipe for details):

- Increase the amount of sturdy root vegetables (or add them), such as carrots, parsnips, whole shallots, and rutabagas, as well as celery. Cut 3- or 4-inch-long wedges, evenly thick, at least ½ inch, or thicker if they must roast a long time. Short wedges cook through, look good, won't break, and will caramelize on the edges too.

- Cut onions in wedges, but trim them so the layers remain attached at the root end and they don't fall apart.

- Cook leeks whole. Use medium-thick leeks (1 ½ inches); trim off tough leaves; wash thoroughly; trim the hairlike roots, but leave the root base that holds the leaves together. Do not cut the leek crosswise; split the leaves—but not the root end—lengthwise. When serving, slice off the root and cut into short lengths.

- Use thick, big celery stalks; peel to remove tough skin. Cut celery sticks about 1 inch wide, so they don't fall apart.

- Caramelize the vegetables in the roasting pan after pouring out the pan juices for sauce. Roast them with the meat or by themselves. As detailed in the preceding lamb recipe, vegetables usually need more dry roasting than the meat, because they have been covered in liquid. Speed caramelization by raising the heat or the level of the roasting pan in the oven.

Roast Pork Shoulder with Roast Vegetable Sauce

Pork shoulders (also called butts or Boston butts) are terrific roasts, in my opinion, more delicious than pork loin and definitely less expensive. With a nice layer of fat on top, a good proportion of fat through the muscle, and lots of connective tissue, the roasted meat has wonderful flavor and soft, moist texture. It's easy to roast—you don't need to erect a foil tent for it—and the shoulder-blade bone, which adds flavor and speeds roasting, is simple to remove when you're serving the meat. (It is also easy to braise, as you will find in the following recipe for Salsa Genovese).

Shoulder roasts range from 4 to 8 pounds, bone-in, or larger. This procedure will work for any-size roast, though the vegetable and seasoning amounts are for a 5-to-7-pound shoulder, the size you'll usually find in the butcher's case. To feed a big crowd, ask the butcher to cut a larger shoulder for you, or cook two smaller roasts in one very big roasting pan. Be sure to increase the vegetables, seasonings, and cooking liquids proportionally with your meat.

Some of the other choices you have with this easy roast: should you mash all the roasting-pan vegetables into the sauce—the simplest method—or cut and caramelize them to serve as a side dish? Or a bit of each? (See page 344 for more information.) It's up to you. Do you want to glaze the roast? I've got a good maple syrup glaze to share—see recipe that follows.

SERVES 6 OR MORE

Prepping the Roast and Vegetables

Arrange a rack in the middle of the oven, and preheat to 400°.

Rinse and dry the roast; leave the entire layer of fat on the top. Place it in the roasting pan, and sprinkle salt on all sides, patting the crystals so they stick to the meat and are evenly distributed. Pour on the olive oil, and rub it all over the roast. Set the roast, fat side up, in the center of the pan.

Scatter all the chopped vegetables and seasonings—except the remaining 1 teaspoon of salt—around, and toss everything together with the 3 tablespoons of olive oil. If you are using water as cooking liquid, toss the 1 teaspoon salt with the vegetables; if using broth, less or no salt is needed, depending on the saltiness of the broth

5-to-7-pound pork shoulder (butt) roast, bone-in

1 ½ teaspoons coarse sea salt or crystal kosher salt

2 tablespoons extra-virgin olive oil

FOR THE PAN AND SAUCE: VEGETABLES,* SEASONINGS, AND BROTH

4 medium onions, peeled and chopped into ½-inch pieces

2 medium carrots, peeled and cut into ½-inch chunks

2 medium leeks (including green trimmings), rinsed, split, and chopped into ½-inch pieces

3 celery stalks with leaves, rinsed and cut into ½-inch pieces

About ½ ounce dried porcini slices, crumbled or chopped into small bits (¼ cup)

1 teaspoon whole black peppercorns

6 whole cloves

1 packed tablespoon fresh rosemary needles, stripped from the branch

2 large bay leaves

3 tablespoons extra-virgin olive oil

1 teaspoon kosher salt, or less to taste

3 cups or more Turkey Broth (page 80), Simple Vegetable Broth (page 288), or water

1½ cups dry white wine

RECOMMENDED EQUIPMENT

A heavy-duty roasting pan, about 12 by 17 inches, big enough for the roast with the vegetables around it

A medium saucepan (2-quart capacity or more), a sturdy sieve, and a potato masher to make the sauce

Note: Cut into small pieces, as listed, if you are mashing them for sauce; larger pieces, cut as described on page 344, to serve as an accompaniment

Roast Pork Shoulder with Roast Vegetable Sauce (cont.)

(taste to determine). Pour the white wine and 2 cups or more broth (or water) into the side of the pan so the cooking liquid is 1 inch deep, coming well up around all the vegetables.

Slow Roasting the Pork and Vegetables

Set the pan in the oven and roast for an hour, then open the oven and bring the roasting pan up front, turn the vegetables over, and rotate the pan back to front, for even cooking.

Roast for another hour or hour and a quarter (depending on the size of the roast); the internal temperature should be 170 degrees or a little higher. The meat should be browned all over with dark edges; the top (especially the fat) should be crisp and caramelized. There will still be a considerable amount of juices in the pan, and the vegetables should be cooked through and lightly browned. The dish is ready to serve now, unless you want to glaze the roast or get it darker and more crisp, in which case raise the oven temperature to 425° and proceed as directed later.

Making the Sauce and Finishing the Roast

Lift the pork out of the roasting pan with a large spatula, or by holding it with towels, and rest it on a platter while you start the sauce. If it's not going back in the oven, set the roast on a warm corner of the stove, covered loosely with foil.

With a potato masher, crush the cooked vegetables in the juices, breaking them up into little bits. Set the sieve in the saucepan, and pour everything from the pan into the sieve, including any flavorful caramelized bits that can be scraped up. Press the vegetables and other solids against the sieve with a big spoon to release their liquid, then discard them. Let the liquid settle, and when the fat rises, skim it off. Set the saucepan over high heat, bring the juices (you should have 3 to 4 cups) to a boil, and let them reduce, uncovered.

For further browning, return the roast to the roasting pan, including its juices. When the oven is at 425°, set the pan on a higher rack and roast until browned and crusty. This could take just a few minutes or 15 or more; check the meat frequently, and turn pan if browning unevenly.

When the roast is out of the oven, let it sit for 10 minutes or so before serving. I like to remove the blade bone, which is visible on the side of the roast. Insert a long knife blade into the meat so it rests on the flat bone; draw the blade along the bone, following its contours, and the meat will lift off. Arrange the boneless pork on a warm serving platter.

To finish the sauce, cook until the strained roasting juices have reduced by half, or to a consistency you like. Thicken it, if you wish, with bread crumbs (see box, page 335). Moisten the roast with some of the sauce and pass the rest.

A VERMONT FINISH FOR ROAST PORK: MAPLE SYRUP GLAZE

When I was testing this roast pork recipe at the Vermont home of my editor, Judith Jones, her cousin dropped by with jugs of the maple syrup he produces on his nearby farm. With the pan sauce on the stove and the pork ready for its last blast of heat, a taste of the syrup inspired this glaze. Though the roast will be wonderful without it, a coating of maple syrup (mixed with mustard to balance the sweetness) gives it a dark-golden veneer and a tantalizing layer of flavor too. (Crusty pieces will be in high demand when people taste the meat.)

For a regular-size roast, whisk together 2 tablespoons maple syrup—preferably the strong, dark cooking grade of syrup—with 2 tablespoons Dijon or other sharp mustard. After you've started the sauce and the pork is back in the empty roasting pan, brush it all over with the glaze—a thin coat is fine. (If you have a big roast and run out of glaze, just mix up more.) Roast, as instructed, for 5 to 10 minutes more, or until the roast is dark and caramelized.

Serving Ideas . . .

This pork roast is delicious with the usual mashed potatoes, but it is equally good with the Potato, Parsnip, and Scallion Mash (page 361), as well as with any of the skillet vegetables beginning on page 266.

Or, as I like it, serve simply with its own roasted vegetables.

Roast Pork Shoulder with Pan Vegetables

Salsa Genovese—Braised Pork Shoulder with Onions

*P*ork shoulder is delicious braised as well as roasted. Salsa Genovese provides a *wonderful sauce as well as a large amount of meat—indeed, this traditional Neapolitan Sunday dish gives you two options, for two different meals.*

In the custom of "Sunday sauces," the freshly cooked pork and its braising sauce are served separately the first time: the sauce with the meat extracted is tossed with pasta for a first course, and the meat is sliced and served as a main course. (In Italian and Italian-American homes, these might be different courses or on the table at the same time.)

Whatever sauce and meat are left from the first feast are then combined into a meaty sauce to dress pasta another day. A 5-pound pork shoulder cooked, in my recipe, with 5 pounds of chopped onions will give you plenty of meat and sauce to enjoy all these ways. Braise a bigger shoulder butt for even more leftovers—just be sure to buy plenty of onions: a 7-pound pork roast gets 7 pounds of onions!

SERVES 6 OR MORE

FOR THE *PESTATA*

4 ounces bacon, cut in 1-inch pieces

½ cup whole peeled garlic cloves

1 small carrot, peeled and finely shredded or chopped

1 stalk celery, finely shredded or chopped

5 to 7 pounds onions, peeled and chopped into ¼-inch pieces

5-to-7-pound pork shoulder (butt) roast, bone-in

1 tablespoon coarse sea salt or kosher crystal salt

½ cup extra-virgin olive oil

¼ teaspoon *peperoncino* (hot red pepper flakes), or more to taste, or none

Making the *Pestata* and Starting the Braise

Using the food processor with the metal blade, mince the bacon and garlic cloves together into a fine *pestata* (paste).

Since you have the machine out, use it to chop the carrot, celery, and onions if you want (you don't need to wash the bowl). Process each vegetable separately. Cut the carrot and the celery stalk into chunks before chopping; pulse each to small bits. Chunk up the onions into 1-inch pieces, put them into the food-processor bowl in batches, and pulse them to ¼-inch bits, not too fine. Put the onions in a big bowl—you will have 4 to 5 quarts of chopped onion when you are done.

(Of course, you may shred and chop the vegetables by hand, or even mince the bacon-garlic paste with a heavy cleaver, as I did growing up. It takes longer but is quite satisfying.)

Rinse and dry the pork, then sprinkle about ½ teaspoon salt lightly on all surfaces, patting it on. Pour the oil into the braising pan, and set it over medium heat. Before it gets hot, lay the pork in and brown it—lightly—turning it after a minute or so on each side.

While the meat is browning, scrape the *pestata* into the pan bottom; spread it out and let the bacon begin to render. Drop in *peperoncino* now, if you want some heat in the *salsa*; toast it on the pan bottom.

After 3 minutes or so of browning the pork, drop the tomato paste into the fat; stir and caramelize a minute. Dump the shredded carrot and celery into the pan bottom; stir for a minute, just to get them cooking. (Keep turning the meat so it browns evenly and slowly.)

Now scrape the chopped onions into the pan, all around the meat. Sprinkle the remaining coarse salt over the onions; raise the heat a bit, stirring the onions up from the bottom and mixing them with the oil, *pestata*, and tomato paste. Cook over medium-high heat, stirring, for about 5 minutes, until the onions are all hot and starting to sweat. Cover, and turn the heat to medium-low.

Braising the Pork

The pork is now going to cook for about 3 hours. Leave it alone for the first 45 minutes, then uncover, turn the meat, and stir the onions. They should be wilting and releasing liquid; if there is any sign of burning, lower the heat. Cover, and cook for another 45 minutes, turn the meat, and stir the onions. They should be quite reduced in volume, in a thick, simmering sauce. Stir in 2 cups of hot broth, bringing the liquid higher around the pork.

Cook, covered, for another 45 minutes, then stir. If the sauce level has dropped a lot and is beginning to stick, stir in another cup or two of broth. Taste, and add more salt if necessary.

Cover, and cook another ½ hour to 45 minutes. Check the consistency of the onions—they should be melting into the sauce, and the meat should be soft when pierced with a fork. If satisfactory, remove from the heat; otherwise, cook longer, adding more broth, or, if the sauce seems thin, uncover and cook to reduce it.

2 tablespoons tomato paste

4 cups, or more or less, hot Turkey Broth (page 80), Simple Vegetable Broth (page 288), or water

RECOMMENDED EQUIPMENT

A food processor

A heavy-bottomed braising or saucepan, or Dutch-oven casserole, 8-quart capacity or larger, 10-inch diameter or larger, with a good cover

SERVING *SALSA GENOVESE*, THREE WAYS

- As a *primo*, first course, for six: Remove 2 cups of the fresh onion sauce from the pot and put it in a large skillet. Cook 1 pound of rigatoni or other pasta, and toss it in the skillet with the simmering sauce. Finish with extra-virgin olive oil and freshly grated Parmigiano-Reggiano or Grana Padano.

- As a *secondo*, main meat course, for six or more: Remove the pork from the braising pot and cut out the blade bone (just lift the cooked meat off it and remove the bone). Slice the pork against the grain in ⅓-inch-thick slices, and moisten with hot sauce from the pot.

- As a meaty sauce for pasta: Traditionally, the leftover meat and sauce from Sunday dinner were combined and served another day as a dressing for pasta, but you can dedicate any amount of *Salsa Genovese* to this marvelous mixture.

If you want to make this with freshly braised meat and sauce, let cool briefly, then pull the meat apart with forks (or fingers) into shreds, about ½ inch wide or more, and toss with the sauce. Refrigerate or freeze for another day.

To dress 1 pound of pasta with meaty sauce: Heat 2 cups of sauce in a large skillet; refresh and extend it with a bit of extra-virgin olive oil and broth, and bring to a simmer. I like to serve this with rigatoni or ziti. Fresh garganelli or cavatappi would also be a fine pasta choice. Finish with more oil and freshly grated cheese.

Braised Beef Shoulder Roast with Venetian Spice

*B*eef shoulder, usually called the chuck, is the source of many flavorful cuts of meat. One of my favorites for braising is the compact boneless chuck roast, taken from underneath the shoulder blade. There's so much connective tissue and fat in the meat that long, moist cooking will produce soft, delicious meat, whatever you put in the pot.

This braise, however, is a special one, inspired by my connection to and love for Venice and its special place in culinary history—La Serenissima, as the state of Venice was called, was a center for the spice trade and the silk route through the Middle East to the Orient for over 600 years. The use of exotic, imported spices in cooking signaled a well-to-do household with a rich kitchen. I get excited just assembling the spices and flavorings (including coffee and cocoa) for this. And when the exotic perfume arises from the bubbling wine that fills the pot, I hate to leave the kitchen, even though there's almost no work to do once the beef begins its 3 hours of braising.

SERVES 6 TO 8

Preparing the Venetian Sachet

Cut a piece of cheesecloth to form a double layer, about 1 foot square. Pile the spices, bay leaves, and coffee beans in the center, then fold the cheesecloth to enclose them in a neat bundle. Tie the bundle securely closed with kitchen twine.

Preparing and Cooking the Meat

Sprinkle the teaspoon of coarse salt all over the roast and pat it into the flesh. Spread out the flour and plop the meat into it, turning it and patting the flour to coat all sides of the roast. Shake off excess flour.

Pour the olive oil into the pot and set it over medium-high heat for a minute or two, until the oil is hot. Lay in the roast on one of its large, flat sides and let it sizzle in place for 2 to 3 minutes, until lightly browned. Turn it over and brown the other flat side, another 2 minutes or so, then briefly brown the narrow sides of meat. With

FOR THE VENETIAN SPICE SACHET

2 cinnamon sticks, 2 inches in length

8 whole cloves

2 teaspoons whole black peppercorns

½ nutmeg clove, freshly grated

3 bay leaves, preferably fresh

2 tablespoons whole coffee beans

FOR THE BRAISING POT

A 5-pound boneless beef chuck roast (also called "chuck pot roast" or "underblade chuck")

1 teaspoon coarse sea salt or crystal kosher salt, for seasoning the meat

1 cup flour, for dredging

½ cup extra-virgin olive oil

1 pound or so onions, peeled, chopped in ¼-inch pieces (about 5 cups)

2 tablespoons tomato paste

1 ½ teaspoons Dutch-process cocoa powder

⅓ whole nutmeg, grated

1 ½ pounds carrots, peeled, cut in chunks 4 inches long and ½ inch wide

10 cups or more (three 750ml bottles) red wine

Simple Vegetable Broth (page 288) or water, as needed

2 teaspoons coarse sea salt or kosher salt

RECOMMENDED EQUIPMENT

Cheesecloth and kitchen twine

A heavy-bottomed braising or saucepan, or Dutch-oven casserole, 8-quart capacity, with a good cover*

*Note: For this dish, use the narrowest pan you have in which your chuck roast will fit lying flat on the bottom, with only a bit of space between the meat and the sides of the pot. The less empty space in the pot, the less wine you'll need to cover the meat.

Braised Beef Shoulder Roast with Venetian Spice (cont.)

tongs or a large spatula, lift the meat from the pot and set it on a large plate.

Scatter the chopped onions into the pot, lower the heat a bit, and cook them, stirring frequently, as they sweat, wilt, and soften; scrape up the browned meat bits in the pan too. After 6 to 8 minutes, when the onions have started to color lightly (don't let them get dark), clear a hot spot in the pan bottom and drop in the tomato paste. Spread and toast the paste for a minute or so, then stir it in with the onions.

Sprinkle the cocoa powder and grated nutmeg over the onions, stir to blend, then drop in the carrot chunks and toss them well with the hot onions.

Replace the roast in the pot, laying it flat on top of the vegetables; pour in any juices that accumulated in the plate. Tuck the sachet of spices next to the meat. Now pour in as much wine as needed to come up and over the top of the meat. You may need less than three bottles (2,250ml) of wine, or more; if you run out of wine, add vegetable broth or plain water to just submerge the beef in cooking liquid.

Sprinkle the 2 teaspoons of salt into the pot, put on the cover, and bring the wine to a boil, over high heat. Lower the heat to maintain a gentle, steady bubbling over the surface of the liquid, and let the meat cook, tightly covered, for 2 hours. Check the level of the liquid occasionally, and add wine, broth, or water if it has fallen much below the top of the meat. If the liquid is reducing rapidly, lower the heat. If the level hasn't fallen at all after an hour or so, raise the heat slightly and set the cover ajar.

After 2 hours, remove the cover and adjust the heat to maintain the steady perking of the braising liquid. Check the tenderness of the meat by poking a large fork into it in several places to gauge doneness. Any resistance indicates that more cooking is needed. Keep cooking—it should take a total of about 3 hours—until the meat is tender. The braising wine should be reducing slowly during this last hour too.

Finishing the Sauce and Serving

When the meat is thoroughly cooked, turn off the heat and, using wide spatulas, carefully lift the roast out of the pot and into a baking dish. Extricate the carrot pieces too, and put them in the dish. Place it in a warm spot, covering the roast loosely with foil.

To finish the sauce, set a sturdy mesh sieve over a large saucepan. Pour the braising liquid through the sieve, pressing on the vegetables and the spice sachet to extract their juices, then discard. Let the liquid settle briefly, then skim off the fat on top. Bring the sauce to a boil over high heat, and cook rapidly to thicken it to a consistency you like. Taste, and adjust the seasoning.

When you're ready to serve, move the roast to a cutting board and slice it crosswise in generous thick slices, using a very sharp serrated knife and holding it together with your hands. Don't try to slice it too thin while it's warm or it will fall apart.

I serve this family-style, in the baking dish or on a platter, fanning out the meat slices, and surrounding them with carrots. Ladle some of the sauce over the meat in the dish, and pass more sauce at the table. Hot polenta (page 215) is the perfect *contorno* for this dish, so serve a bowlful with the meat.

WINE FOR BRAISING

For braising the beef (and the great sauce you get at the end), you'll need three bottles or about 10 cups of red wine, or even more, depending on the size of your pan. This does not need to cost a fortune, though. I recommend that you buy a good but average wine. It should be fruity with lots of body, like a Merlot, Cabernet, Zinfandel, or Syrah. Of course, the better the wine the better the sauce, but don't go overboard.

Two Veal Delicacies

Roast Stuffed Breast of Veal

This recipe will seem long to you, but read it through once or twice and it will become very clear that all we are doing is stuffing a piece of meat, roasting it, and making gravy to serve it with. That's something I'm sure you have done any number of times—only in this case it is a breast of veal, which will yield delicious results.

Breast of veal—bone-in breast specifically—is another wonderful meat cut that I hope you come to love as much as I do. Like the preceding shoulder cuts, it has a good deal of connective tissue, bones, and cartilage, which contribute to the flavor and texture of the meat, especially during long cooking. Because it comes from young animals, the ribs in the breast are just developing: there's lots of soft cartilage, and you can just pull out the ribs after cooking, so serving and slicing are convenient.

Stuffing the breast is the fun part. The muscle layers easily separate and hold a generous amount of savory filling; then, when it's cooked and sliced, the cross sections of meat and stuffing make a beautiful presentation. It looks like an eye, with the meat as the lids.

If you've tried any of the other roasts in this chapter, the procedure here will be familiar: covered roasting for tenderness and flavor, dry roasting for deep color and crisp textures—and developing a great sauce at the same time.

The only difficulty you may find with this recipe is getting a nice big piece of veal breast, preferably the tip cut. It's not always easy for me either, as you'll understand when you read the box and study the technique photos here and on page 357. But if we all keep asking our butchers for veal-breast tip cuts, they'll get the message—we want those excellent, traditional cuts of meat, and we want to stuff them ourselves!

SERVES 6 OR MORE
(DEPENDING ON SIZE OF VEAL BREAST)

FOR THE STUFFING

3 cups country bread, day old or
   slightly dried, crusts removed,
   cut in 1-inch cubes

Making the Stuffing

Put the bread cubes in a small bowl and pour the milk over them; toss together, and let the bread soak up the milk, tossing the cubes every few minutes so they moisten evenly.

Meanwhile, put the mortadella, onion, carrot, and celery pieces in the food processor, fitted with the steel blade, and chop them together into fine bits, processing continuously for about ½ minute; scrape down the sides of the bowl, and process briefly until everything is a pastelike mix.

Pour the olive oil into a 10- or 12-inch skillet, and set over medium-high heat; scrape in the chopped stuffing and spread it in the pan. As it starts to sizzle, lower the heat considerably, stir, and sauté gently for 3 or 4 minutes to bring out the flavors—don't let the stuffing get crusty or colored.

Mixing the eggs with the bread crumbs

Squeeze the bread cubes firmly by handfuls to get out excess milk, and scatter them over the stuffing. Still cooking over low heat, break up the bread clumps with a spoon or spatula, and stir to incorporate completely. Mix in the chopped prunes, and cook them with the stuffing for a minute or so. Take the pan off the heat and scrape the stuffing into a bowl.

Let the stuffing cool, then stir in the pine nuts, grated cheese, parsley, salt, pepper, and the beaten egg, mixing thoroughly.

At this time, set a rack in the middle of the oven and preheat it to 400°.

Trimming and Stuffing the Veal Breast

As I explain in the box (page 359), and as you can see in the photos, your stuffing method will vary with the size and cut of veal breast (and your own preferences). Follow these general steps to prepare the breast: Rinse and dry it thoroughly. Check the breast for pockets of fat and remove. There is often a clump of fat on the bony side, where you will see a flap of meat partially covering the ribs. Lift this

¾ cup milk

½ pound mortadella (or ham), cut into 1-inch chunks (about 1 cup)

1 medium onion, peeled and cut into 1-inch chunks

1 medium-large carrot, peeled and cut into 1-inch pieces

2 stalks celery, cut into 1-inch pieces

2 tablespoons extra-virgin olive oil

4 big prunes, pitted, chopped into ⅓-inch pieces

¼ cup toasted pine nuts

3 tablespoons freshly grated Parmigiano-Reggiano or Grana Padano

2 tablespoons chopped fresh Italian parsley

¼ teaspoon salt

⅛ teaspoon freshly ground black pepper

1 egg, beaten with a pinch of salt

FOR THE VEAL

3½-to-5-pound veal breast, bone-in (see box)

1 teaspoon coarse sea salt or crystal kosher salt

1 tablespoon extra-virgin olive oil

FOR THE ROASTING PAN: VEGETABLES,* SEASONINGS, AND LIQUIDS

5 medium onions, peeled and cut into 1-inch chunks

3 medium to large carrots, peeled and cut into 1-inch chunks

4 celery stalks, cut into 1-inch pieces

4 plump garlic cloves, peeled

8 large pitted prunes, whole

1 packed tablespoon fresh rosemary
needles

6 whole cloves

1/4 cup dried porcini slices, crumbled
or chopped into small pieces

1 teaspoon whole black peppercorns

3 tablespoons extra-virgin olive oil

1/2 to 1 teaspoon coarse sea salt or
crystal kosher salt, or more to taste,
or none

1 cup white wine

2 cups or more Turkey Broth
(page 80), Simple Vegetable Broth
(page 288), or water

RECOMMENDED EQUIPMENT

A food processor

Kitchen twine, for tying the stuffed
breast

A heavy-duty roasting pan, preferably
17 by 20 inches, or as large as
possible

Wide heavy-duty aluminum foil

A medium saucepan, a sturdy sieve,
and a potato masher, to make the
sauce

*Note: Cut them in small pieces, as listed,
for sauce. To serve roast vegetables, cut
them as described on page 344.*

Roast Stuffed Breast of Veal (cont.)

flap, and cut away the fat hidden inside. Do not remove the skin on the bottom—either from the ribs or the meat flap—as it helps hold the breast together.

This flap of meat, under the ribs, is the one I use to wrap around the stuffed breast in the photos. Cut it off, shave off the silver skin from both sides, then pound it with a meat hammer or tenderizer until it is paper-thin, like *carpaccio*. And there's your wrapper!

To stuff: Follow the method shown in the photos, first cutting a pocket in the meaty layers on top of the ribs, then filling it with your stuffing. Enclose the breast and exposed stuffing with the pounded veal flap (or use bacon strips or prosciutto slices), and tie securely with kitchen twine.

If you have a whole veal-breast tip cut, you need only slice open the pocket on the wide side down to the tip and push the stuffing in toward the closed tip. Then tie the roast closed.

Note: This stuffing is excellent for turkey and chicken.

Filling the Pan and Roasting the Veal

Put the tied breast in the roasting pan and sprinkle the salt all over, patting the crystals into the meat. Pour on the olive oil and rub it all over. Set the breast, rib side down, in the center of the pan.

Put all the chopped vegetables, the prunes, and the seasonings (except the salt) in a big bowl, and toss with the 3 tablespoons of olive oil. If your broth is unsalted, add 1 teaspoon salt to the vegetables—use less salt or no salt if your broth is salted already. Scatter the vegetables and seasonings around the veal in the pan. Pour in the white wine and 2 cups or more broth or water, so the cooking liquid is about 1/2 inch deep in the pan.

Cover the pan with one or more long sheets of aluminum foil, arching the foil if necessary to keep it from touching the meat and vegetables. Crimp the foil around the rim of the pan, and press it tightly against the sides all around, sealing the veal and vegetables in a tent.

Set the pan in the oven and roast for an hour, then bring the roasting pan up front and carefully remove the foil. The veal should be lightly browned and the juices bubbling. Baste with the juices, turn the vegetables over, and push the pan back into the oven.

1. Trimming the fat

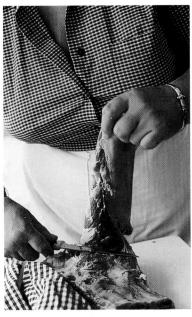

2. Cutting off the flap

3. Cutting a pocket

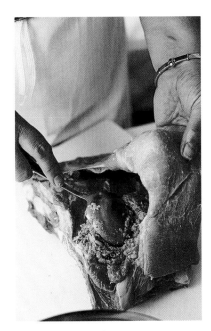

4. Filling with stuffing

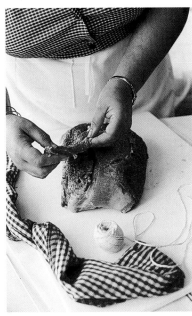

5. Enclosing the breast with the pounded veal flap

6. Tying securely with twine

Roast for another hour or so, uncovered, basting every 20 minutes and rotating the pan back to front for even cooking. The top of the veal breast should be brown and crusty, the vegetables lightly browned as well, and the liquid considerably reduced. Remove from the oven.

Making the Sauce and Finishing the Roast

Lift out the veal breast with a large spatula, or by holding it with towels, and rest it on a platter while you start the sauce.

With a potato masher, crush the cooked vegetables in the juices, breaking them up into little bits. Set the sieve over the saucepan, and pour everything from the pan through it, pressing the solids against the sieve with a big spoon to release their liquid, then discard the remains. Let the juices rest, and when the fat rises to the top, skim it off. (Putting the pan in a bowl of ice water will help the fat to congeal, if you are in a hurry.) Set the saucepan over high heat, bring the juices to a boil, and reduce them, uncovered, until they've thickened to a syrupy sauce.

Meanwhile, return the veal to the roasting pan and pour any accumulated juices into the saucepan. Baste the veal one more time with hot juices, and put it back in the oven to roast for 30 minutes more, until it is dark and crusty on top and the sides are browned as well.

To make sure the stuffing is cooked too, insert an instant-read thermometer into the stuffing layer. At 160°, it is ready.

Deboning the Veal and Serving

Remove the veal from the oven, and let it rest for 10 minutes.

Cut away the kitchen twine. Remove the ribs, loosening them with a knife, and pulling them out one at a time while holding the roast steady.

Slice crosswise into thick slices with a sharp, serrated knife. Lay the slices on a warm platter, showing off the stuffing layer, and moisten with the sauce. Pass more sauce at the table.

The roasted stuffed breast of veal

THE PERFECT VEAL BREAST—OR MAKING DO

The meat business has changed in my lifetime. Most retail butchers don't get meat in large quarters and "primal" cuts that they skillfully divide any way we ask. Supermarket meat departments, I've found, only get pre-cut sections of the most popular meats, which require minimal cutting before they go out in the case.

Unfortunately, the ideal veal breast for this recipe is not an item much in demand. It may take dedicated searching to find a butcher in your area who can fabricate the perfect piece: a 5-pound bone-in breast cut, from the tip. That's the very end of the breast, farthest from the front leg, and it has two advantages: lots of cartilage, which adds flavor and richness, and a naturally closed pocket at the tip, which makes stuffing easy.

On the day we tested this recipe and took these photos, I couldn't get a breast tip anywhere. The piece shown here (which came from a Manhattan supermarket) is only 3½ pounds and cut from the middle, not the closed end of the breast. As you can see, the pocket that I cut for the stuffing is open on both ends.

I wondered, though, how would I keep the stuffing in? My first idea was to wrap bacon or prosciutto slices around the openings and tie them in place. But we didn't have any in the kitchen that day—and there was no time for shopping. So I did something quite acceptable in cooking—I improvised. I took a flap of veal meat that is hidden under the ribs, next to the cutting board in the photos. I trimmed and pounded it and made a sheet that covered the holes neatly. Tied in place, the patch worked fine. No stuffing was lost, and we enjoyed our roast and delicious sauce for lunch and supper too.

One of the important—and challenging—lessons in cooking is that we cooks learn to make do with what we have.

Poached Veal Tongue with Potato, Parsnip, and Scallion Mash

Poached veal tongue is one of the ingredients in the classical Italian dish bollito misto, boiled mixed meats. It is one of my favorite dishes, but even without the other four or five meats I enjoy the poached tongue. The brining somewhat cures the meat and makes it retain the lively pinkish color throughout.

SERVES 4

FOR BRINING

¼ cup kosher salt

2 quarts water

FOR POACHING

2 bay leaves

2½ quarts water

2 celery stalks

I carrot

I medium onion

½ teaspoon black peppercorns

½ teaspoon salt

I fresh veal tongue, about 1½ pounds

FOR SERVING

Grated fresh horseradish
    (about 2 teaspoons per serving)

Salmoriglio (page 366; optional)

Salsa Verde (page 362; optional)

To brine the tongue, mix the salt with the water in a large bowl and submerge the tongue in it. Refrigerate for 6 hours or overnight.

Bring the ingredients for the poaching liquid to a boil in a pot large enough to accommodate the tongue later, and let boil vigorously for 20 minutes.

Remove the tongue from the brine, and lower it into the boiling broth. Cook, partially covered, at a lively simmer for 1¼ hours, then turn off the heat and leave the tongue submerged in the hot liquid for at least ½ hour. While the tongue is resting, get the potatoes and parsnips going (recipe follows).

Fish the tongue out of the broth, and as soon as it is cool enough to handle, remove the peel (the warmer the tongue, the easier that will be). Following the photographs, start at the butt end to remove the peel; once you have gotten started, it should come off quite easily in big pieces. Trim away any gristle and fat at the butt end, and when ready to serve, cut into slices.

Serve the tongue warm with the potato, parsnip, and scallion mash and at least one of the recommended condiments. The grated horseradish should be sprinkled on while the tongue is still warm, to infuse the slices with its sharp flavor. Leftover tongue is delicious cold, with the suggested sauces or others in this chapter. It makes a great sandwich with some mustard.

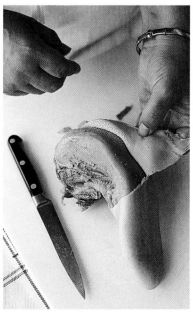

Making the initial cut at the butt end to loosen the skin

Pulling off the skin

Slicing the poached tongue

Potato, Parsnip, and Scallion Mash

SERVES 4 TO 6

Peel the baking potatoes, cut them in half, and submerge them in a pan of cold water to cover. Bring to a boil and cook 20 minutes, then add the parsnips and cook another 20 minutes, until both are tender. If the parsnips are getting too soft, fish them out of the pot with a wire sieve. When both the potatoes and parsnips are done, put them through a ricer, or strain and mash them in a bowl, with the butter and salt. Fold in the scallions. If the mash has to wait a little while before being served, put the bowl in a skillet with a small amount of boiling water, and simmer to keep warm.

2 medium russet baking potatoes (1½ pounds)

6 medium parsnips, peeled and trimmed (1½ pounds)

4 tablespoons butter

1 teaspoon salt

Two ¼-pound bunches scallions, finely chopped (1 cup)

RECOMMENDED EQUIPMENT

A potato masher or ricer

Savory Sauces

Salsa Verde

This is a classic cold sauce for boiled meats, poultry, and fish, but I find wonderful new uses for it all the time.

MAKES ABOUT 2½ CUPS

½ cup finely chopped red onion

2 tablespoons finely chopped shallots

½ cup very thinly sliced scallions

2 tablespoons finely chopped fresh chives

½ cup finely chopped roasted red peppers (jarred pimientos)

½ cup finely chopped baby gherkin pickles

2 hard-cooked eggs (page 36), yolks and whites separated, finely chopped

2 tablespoons drained and chopped tiny capers in brine

¼ teaspoon powdered mustard

I cup extra-virgin olive oil

½ cup red wine vinegar

¼ cup finely chopped fresh Italian parsley

Salt to taste

Put all the ingredients except the chopped parsley and salt in a mixing bowl, and stir to blend. Just before serving, stir in the chopped parsley and salt to taste.

Store refrigerated for 4 or 5 days. Refresh before using with additional red wine vinegar and extra-virgin olive oil, if the sauce seems dry, and fresh chopped parsley to liven up the color.

Serving Ideas . . .

Delicious with:

Homemade *Tonno sott'Olio* (page 10)

Marinated steamed mussels (page 16)

Poached Whole Zucchini (page 238)

Grilled Cod Steaks (page 302)

Poached Chicken (page 328)

Poached Veal Tongue (preceding recipe)

Any steamed or boiled vegetables. It also makes a great sandwich dressing.

Cucumber, Yogurt, and Mint Sauce

I remember having this condiment someplace in the Balkans, and it has been a summertime staple at my house ever since, especially when small crisp pickling cucumbers are abundant. A couple of hours before we eat, I salt the cuke slices and let them wilt. Just before we sit down, I toss the slices in yogurt with mint from the garden. A spoonful is enough to sauce a portion of fish, but I make it in big batches, because everyone heaps it on their plates as a dinner vegetable. Double the formula here to make a generous side dish serving six.

MAKES ABOUT 2½ CUPS

Rinse and dry the cucumbers, but don't peel them. Trim the ends and slice thinly crosswise, ⅛ inch or less. Put all the slices in a bowl, and toss them well with the salt; turn the slices into a colander, and set it over the bowl (or in the sink). Let the cukes wilt and release their juices for at least an hour, but 2 to 3 hours is better; then toss the slices gently once or twice so the liquid drains off.

Shortly before serving, pick up a handful of slices and press them between your palms. Don't crush or break them, but squeeze firmly, to get out as much liquid as you can. Put all the squeezed slices in a bowl, separating them if they're stuck together; plop the yogurt into the bowl, and fold it into the cukes. Fold and toss in the mint, lemon juice, and olive oil. Taste, and add more salt (or more yogurt, or any of the other seasonings) as needed. Heap into a small bowl for serving.

Refrigerate any leftovers—the yogurt may get watery, but the slices will still be tasty, and it will last for 2 or 3 days.

1¼ pounds of small pickling (Kirby) cucumbers, each preferably 4 ounces or smaller

1½ teaspoons kosher salt, or more to taste

1 cup plain whole-milk yogurt, cold

1 tablespoon chopped fresh mint leaves

1 tablespoon freshly squeezed lemon juice

1 tablespoon extra-virgin olive oil

Serving Ideas . . .

A refreshing complement for grilled and poached fish or chicken

Good with anything spicy, roasted, or grilled

A spoonful will make any sandwich better and juicier

Smooth Sweet Red Pepper Sauce

This is a great sauce for poached or grilled fish or poultry. It is customary in Italy to serve a poached or boiled meat with two or more sauces. Salsa Verde (*page 362*) and this sauce make a delightful pair.

And it's a snap to make right out of the pantry. It's got a brilliant color and surprisingly complex flavor for such a simple preparation: sweet, mildly acidic, and piquant—or as hot as you want, if you add more peperoncino or Tabasco. Fresh eggplant, poached with the onions, gives the sauce even more depth (see box that follows).

ABOUT 1 ½ CUPS

FOR THE POACHED
VEGETABLE BASE

2 cups water

⅓ cup red wine vinegar

2 bay leaves

3 plump garlic cloves, peeled

1 medium onion (about 4 ounces), peeled and quartered

2 large shallots, peeled and sliced in half

FOR FINISHING THE SAUCE

1 cup roasted red peppers (brine-packed), drained and cut in 1-inch pieces

1 ½ to 2 tablespoons roughly chopped drained sun-dried tomatoes (oil-packed)

¼ teaspoon *peperoncino* (hot red pepper flakes), or more or less to taste

¼ teaspoon salt, or more to taste

3 tablespoons extra-virgin olive oil

Poaching the Vegetable Base

Pour the water and vinegar into a small saucepan and drop in the bay leaves, garlic cloves, onion, and shallots. Bring to a boil, and cook, uncovered, at a gentle boil for 25 minutes or so, until the vegetables are cooked through, translucent, and easily pierced with a

Removing the ribs and seeds from a half pepper

Cutting the pepper into 1-inch pieces (or in slices—whatever a given recipe calls for)

fork. Turn off the heat, lift out the vegetables, and let them drain and cool briefly. Discard the bay leaves, and reserve ½ cup of the cooking liquid.

Processing the Sauce

Purée the poached vegetables along with the remaining sauce ingredients in a food processor fitted with the metal blade for about 1½ minutes, scraping down the bowl now and then, until absolutely smooth. Taste the sauce, and add more salt, *peperoncino,* or other seasonings if you like; mix in a little more poaching liquid for a thinner consistency.

Serve the sauce at room temperature. Store for a week in the refrigerator.

3 tablespoons poaching liquid, or more as needed

RECOMMENDED EQUIPMENT

A food processor

Serving Ideas . . .

A dipping sauce for the crisp turkey tenders on page 310

A second sauce for the Poached Veal Tongue on page 360 or the Poached Chicken on page 328

SMOOTH SWEET RED PEPPER SAUCE WITH EGGPLANT

I love the body and flavor that eggplant lends to this sauce.

Follow the main recipe exactly, but add to the poaching pot 1½ cups of firm eggplant peeled and cut in 2-inch chunks. (In summertime, I poach young tender-skinned eggplant without peeling.)

Cook and drain the eggplant along with the onions and garlic. Before adding the eggplant to the food processor, remove any seeds from the chunks.

And one more suggestion:

If you happen to have on hand some homemade marinated eggplant *all'Uccelletto* (Poached Eggplant with Vinegar, Garlic, and Mint; page 252), you can use that instead. Take a cup (or two) of the eggplant wedges, with some of the mint in which they are marinating, and purée with all the other red-pepper sauce ingredients. This version of the sauce is so good, you should make the marinated eggplants just to try it!

Salmoriglio

Salmoriglio, *a traditional sauce for seafood, is nothing more than a dressing of olive oil, garlic, lemon juice, salt, peperoncino, and fresh parsley. There's nothing to it—except remembering to make it ahead, so the garlic and pepper infuse the oil.*

MAKES A BIT MORE THAN A CUP, ENOUGH FOR SAUCING 8 OR MORE MAIN-COURSE SERVINGS

1 cup extra-virgin olive oil

3 plump garlic cloves, thinly sliced

4 tablespoons freshly squeezed lemon juice, or more to taste

¼ teaspoon salt, or more to taste

¼ teaspoon *peperoncino* (hot red pepper flakes)

2 tablespoons chopped fresh Italian parsley

Put all the ingredients except the parsley into a bowl, stir together briefly, and let it steep for ½ hour to an hour, to develop flavor. Stir, and taste the sauce; add more salt or lemon juice if you like. Just before serving, add parsley and stir.

Serve the *salmoriglio* at room temperature; stir the sauce well to blend, and remove the garlic slices only if you wish to. Spoon over fish and other foods.

Serving Ideas . . .

A favorite of mine for grilled fish, like the Grilled Cod Steaks on page 302, or any grilled fish, chicken, or lamb

Very good with Poached Veal Tongue (page 360)

A wonderful dressing for steamed vegetables or a green salad

Quince, Cranberry, and Apple Sauce

If you haven't cooked quince before, this is a good way to start. The sauce is tangy, not overly sweet, and because the fruit pieces tend to stay intact when cooked, you will enjoy the distinctive taste and texture. Though it is not as sweet as cotognata (the quince sauce that follows), you can enjoy it in many of the same ways, such as spooned onto buttered toast or stirred into a bowl of yogurt, for a tangy snack.

MAKES ABOUT 4 CUPS

6 whole cloves, and/or a small piece of cinnamon stick

Grated zest of a large orange

Fresh juice of a large orange

½ cup honey, plus more to taste

½ cup warm water, plus more as needed

2 or 3 ripe quince (about 12 ounces)

1 large or 2 small tart, firm apples

12 ounces (1 bag) whole cranberries, fresh or frozen

Put into saucepan the spices, orange zest, orange juice, and honey, sloshing out the cup with the warm water.

Rinse the quince, cut them in quarters, and peel off the skin. Pare out the core and the seeds, then slice each wedge crosswise in pieces about ⅓ inch thick. Drop the quince chunks into the saucepan, and set it over moderate heat. Stir as the honey dissolves and the liquid comes to a bubbling simmer. Cover the pan, lower the heat, and cook slowly for about 5 minutes, until the quince chunks have started to soften; don't let them get mushy. Remove from the heat.

While the quince are cooking, peel, quarter, and core the apples, and cut into pieces the same size as the quince. Rinse and drain the cranberries. Stir the apple pieces and the berries into the pan. The syrupy liquid should just reach the top of the fruit; add water (or more orange juice) if there's not enough.

Put a cover on the pan and set it over medium-high heat. Bring the syrup back to the boil, and cook about 4 minutes, until the cranberries are starting to pop (a bit longer if the berries were frozen).

Uncover, and simmer until the cranberries have broken up and turned to sauce, about 10 minutes. Stir frequently but gently, so the quince and apple chunks stay intact. Remove from the heat while the sauce is still pourable—it will thicken as it cools. Taste, and stir in honey if you want a sweeter sauce.

Cool briefly, then lay a piece of plastic wrap on top of the sauce to keep a skin from forming. Serve slightly warm or at room temperature. Store in the refrigerator, for up to 2 weeks. (You can freeze the sauce; the consistency will change, but the flavor will be fresh.)

Serving Ideas . . .

Good with roast turkey at the holidays, or any other roast poultry, meats, or winter vegetables

A great condiment for cold meats: try it on a turkey or roast-pork sandwich

Cotognata—Quince Chutney

This simple quince preserve is a specialty in many Italian regions. It seems to have its origins in the fourteenth century, when some of the most noted were from Reggio Emilia and Genova. The translucent, pastel fruit in a jellied syrup is a delightful accompaniment to all sorts of sweet and savory dishes.

If you have a large batch of fresh quince, just multiply this recipe and make a big pan of cotognata. It will keep for a month refrigerated. Pack it in little jelly jars and give as a gift: cotognata is a colorful and delicious way to introduce others to the pleasures of quince!

MAKES ABOUT 2 CUPS OF FRUIT IN THICK SYRUP

1 pound ripe, unblemished quince

1 cup sugar

1 cup white wine

1 cup water

A 3-inch section of vanilla bean

Serving Ideas . . .

With roast meats and poultry

With cheese (it's especially delightful with gorgonzola)

Put it on toast, or French toast or pancakes; stir it into yogurt; soften it with Grand Marnier and spoon it over vanilla ice cream for a gorgeous quince sundae.

Rinse the quince, and cut each into wedges through the stem and blossom ends. Peel the skin, or, if it is thin and unblemished, you may leave it on (which I do). Pare out the core and the seeds, then slice each wedge crosswise in pieces about ⅓ inch thick.

Put the quince, sugar, wine, and water in a heavy-bottomed 3- or 4-quart saucepan; stir together. Slit the vanilla bean lengthwise to split it open; scrape the tiny seeds into the pot, and toss in the pod too.

Bring the syrup to a boil, and cook, uncovered, at a steady simmer for an hour or longer, until the syrup has thickened visibly, with big bubbles popping all over the surface. Remove the pan from the heat and let it cool; pick out the vanilla pod.

Pack the *cotognata* into a pint jar or smaller jars; seal with plastic wrap and jar lids. Keep refrigerated. Stir in a small pan to warm it for serving; thin with liqueur or wine for a looser consistency.

HINTS ON QUINCE: A PERFUME FROM THE PAST

When I want to check a quince for ripeness, I hold it to my nose and inhale deeply. There's no mistaking a perfectly ripe one: the scent transports me back to the home of Nonna Rosa (my mother's mother) in Busoler, where I spent much of my childhood. The heady, floral scent of quince was everywhere in late fall and winter—in the kitchen, where the cut-up fruit slowly cooked into jam; in the dark pantry, where whole quince were set on wooden shelves, to dehydrate slowly over the winter months; and—perhaps most intensely of all—emanating from the drawers of folded linen, where Grandma tucked the quince to ripen and serve as a sachet.

Anyone who has grown up with quince, one of my favorite fruits, probably has happy memories of it, like me. It is cultivated and cooked all around the world, though it is much less popular in America now than in past generations, when it was commonly made into jams and preserves. If you are not familiar with it—yet—here are a few basics: it is an autumn tree fruit, like apples and pears, but has a starchy, tannic flesh difficult to appreciate raw. Cooked, however, quince brings a rich and complex flavor to both sweet and savory dishes. It keeps its shape yet has a lovely soft and melting texture, and the flesh takes on a lovely pinkish color too. In addition to sauces, I use quince in tarts, meat stuffings, and braised dishes.

Fortunately, the fruit is still readily available. I see it on occasion in the supermarket but more often find it at farmers' markets and orchards in autumn. Buy firm, unblemished fruit (don't worry if they're covered in fuzz: that's a sign of freshness); store them in a dark, well-ventilated place or brown paper bag, where they will mature and last for a month or two. Ripe quince will be lemony yellow all over, with a distinctive perfume you can't miss—even if it doesn't take you back to your grandmother's house.

Fruits and Crusts

When I reminisce about the sweet desserts of my childhood, inevitably I remember lots of fruits and some form of dough always at the base. I loved that then, and I love it even more today. I relish the flakiness of a good strudel, the crumbliness of a good tart shell, the softness of a sponge cake, the crunchiness of a sweet focaccia—all sensory memories that guide my dessert-making today.

In the pages that follow, juicy plums are cradled in a crumbly rustic tart shell, sweet ricotta is enveloped in a purse of strudel dough, summer figs are embedded in focaccia, and inebriated blueberries are suspended in a velvety sponge cake. My aesthetic of dessert-making in this book is very simple: give me some good seasonal fruits and I'll give you some good crusts to bake them in.

The recipes are easy to follow and also very flexible, open to all kinds of substitutions and embellishment. Being a good cook does not always equate with being a good baker or pastry chef, and if that is how you feel about your cooking skills, do not shy away from this chapter. I am certain that with any of these recipes you will succeed in making a good dessert.

Apple Crisp Parfait

Desserts with Fruit and Country Bread

Bread and Berry Pudding

In our house, where nothing goes to waste, you can bet that bread pudding is a highly esteemed dessert. This is a simple, delicious version (with a new twist that I just discovered). It is great in summer with any fresh berries—and frozen berries work fine the rest of the year. I like to use blueberries because they remain whole—especially small wild ones. I also like raspberries and other soft berries, precisely because they melt into the pudding and leave bursts of flavor where they baked. So you can experiment: firm strawberries would be nice, cut up, as would other semifirm fruits, like ripe pears. I would avoid very juicy fruits, though.

I like white breads for pudding, but, as with the Peach Lasagna (following recipe), it should be a hearty homemade or country white bread, not sourdough. I don't like sour breads in general, and certainly not for desserts. But when we were testing recipes in Vermont, we had only day-old bread that was a bit more sour than I liked, and that prompted me to develop a new twist on the recipe. There was a jug of maple syrup on the kitchen counter at my editor Judith's house, and I decided to balance the sourness by drizzling the bread with syrup and toasting it in the oven to sweeten and caramelize it lightly. As I am sure you will agree when you taste the pudding, it's worth using the maple syrup whether your bread is sour or not.

A 2-QUART BAKING DISH OF PUDDING, SERVING 8 OR MORE

FOR THE BREAD

5 to 6 cups 1½-inch cubes of hearty white bread—day-old but not stale, crusts removed

¼ cup maple syrup, preferably dark

Arrange one rack in the middle of the oven with space for the pudding dish, and one rack above it, to toast the bread on a baking sheet; preheat to 400°.

Put the bread cubes in a large bowl and drizzle over them the maple syrup, tossing so all the cubes absorb a little bit of syrup. Spread the cubes out on a baking sheet, place it on the upper rack in the oven, and toast for 15 minutes or so, until they're crisp and slightly caramelized all over. Remove the sheet, turn the oven down to 375°, and let the bread cubes cool while you make the custard.

To prepare the custard, beat the eggs, egg yolks, sugar, and salt well with a hand whisk, using the same bowl as for the bread if you wish, then whisk in the lemon zest, milk, cream, and vanilla.

Butter the inside of the baking dish generously. Pile the bread pieces in the dish, and scatter the berries all over (if you want to use more berries, go right ahead). Pour the custard over the bread and berries; turn the bread cubes over gently to moisten them on all sides and to distribute the berries.

Set the dish in the oven, and bake 50 minutes or so, until the top is golden brown and crusty and the custard is set throughout.* Test for doneness by inserting a thin knife blade into an eggy bit of pudding and the middle of a bread cube too: the knife blade should come out clean both times. During baking, rotate the pan on the rack for even cooking. After 50 minutes, if the top is browning slowly, move the dish onto a higher rack. If the top is dark but the custard needs more cooking (if you are using a deeper pan), lay a piece of foil loosely over the top.

Serve the pudding warm with a splash of cream, if you like, or a dollop of sour cream with additional berries on top and a little maple syrup drizzled over.

FOR THE CUSTARD

4 large eggs

4 egg yolks

½ cup *zucchero di canna* or white sugar

⅛ teaspoon salt

2 teaspoons freshly grated lemon zest

2⅔ cups whole milk

1⅓ cup heavy cream

1 teaspoon vanilla extract

2 tablespoons soft butter, for the pan

2 cups fresh or frozen berries (see headnote)

FOR SERVING (OPTIONAL)

Heavy cream or sour cream

Maple syrup

RECOMMENDED EQUIPMENT

A 2-quart baking dish, either shallow (7 by 11 inches) for more crustiness, or deeper (8 by 8 inches) for more creaminess

*Note: Custards are known to be creamier when baked in a water bath. If you choose to do so, make sure you have a baking pan that will hold your bread-pudding pan comfortably. Set the pudding pan in the larger pan, put them on the rack of the preheated oven, and with a measuring cup pour hot water into the bottom pan until it is ¾ inch from the top. Bake as above, but add 10 minutes to the baking time.

Peach Lasagna

Peaches are delightful prepared this way, but apricots, cherries, or a mixture of both will yield equally good results. Serve warm in a bowl with vanilla ice cream.

SERVES 8

FOR THE PEACH LAYERS

3 pounds ripe peaches

Grated rind and juice of I medium-small lemon

¾ cup sugar

FOR THE BREAD LAYERS

¾ stick (6 tablespoons) butter

8 slices (approximately 5 by 3 ½ inches) country bread, cut, not too thick, from a round country loaf

I ½ tablespoons sugar

FOR THE CRUMB TOPPING

⅓ cup flour

¼ cup sugar

I tablespoon dark-brown sugar

¼ teaspoon cinnamon

A pinch of salt

½ stick (4 tablespoons) butter

3 tablespoons finely chopped almonds

RECOMMENDED EQUIPMENT

A shallow baking dish, approximately 8 by 10 inches

Preheat the oven to 350°.

Peel the peaches and cut them into approximately ¼-inch wedges. Toss them in a bowl with the lemon rind and juice and ¾ cup sugar.

Melt 3 tablespoons of the butter in a large skillet and lay in half of the bread slices. Brown them lightly on one side, then turn them and brown the other side. Repeat with the remaining butter and bread slices, and when all are done, sprinkle the 1½ tablespoons sugar over them.

Line the bottom of the baking dish with half the bread slices; they should just cover the bottom. Spoon half of the peaches and half of their juices on top, then arrange a second layer of bread slices over the surface, and a final layer of peaches and juice.

Prepare the topping by tossing together in a bowl the flour, sugar, brown sugar, cinnamon, and salt. Cut the butter into small cubes and mix them with the dry ingredients, using your fingertips or a pastry cutter to incorporate the butter, but not too thoroughly—leave small, flaky pieces of butter throughout. Fold in the chopped almonds.

Sprinkle the topping evenly over the peach lasagna, and bake in the preheated oven for 1 hour. Test after 50 minutes; if the peaches were very ripe and juicy, it will be done. Otherwise, it will take the full hour or a little more; the peaches should be tender, the juices bubbling all around, and the top nicely browned. If the peaches seem done (and you don't want them to dry out) but the crumb topping is still pale, slip the dish under a hot broiler for a minute or two. Serve warm.

Fig Focaccia

When we arrived in Vermont to visit my editor for several intensive days of work on this book, she had made the focaccia from her children's bread book for our lunch. Several days later, when we were winding up, I noticed on the windowsill a pint basket of fresh figs we hadn't used up, and, remembering how much I loved the sweet fruit-studded focaccias I had had as a child, I suggested we improvise with those figs. So here is the recipe we put together, which celebrates a warm childhood memory reborn in the northern hills of Vermont. It fits right in with our dessert theme in this book of fresh fruits embedded in crusts, and is lovely for breakfast, for tea, or with after-dinner coffee.

MAKES I FLATTISH OVAL LOAF

Put the yeast in the large mixing bowl of the mixer and pour ¼ cup of the warm water over it. Because this is quite a wet dough, it is easier to knead in a standing mixer, but if you do not have one just use a big bowl and mix by hand. Let the yeast stand a few minutes to dissolve, then smear it around with your finger to make sure it is softened. Mix the salt with the rest of the water, and pour it into the bowl along with 2½ cups of the flour. Attach the dough hook, and let it knead the dough for about 2 minutes, adding just a little more flour if it seems very wet (or knead with a light touch by hand for 2 to 3 minutes).

Lightly flour your work surface, and scrape the dough out of the bowl onto it. Turn the dough over on itself several times, using a dough scraper and your floured hands; don't try to knead vigorously, because the dough is too wet and sticky.

Clean out the mixing bowl and oil it lightly. Dump the dough in, and turn it to grease all over. Cover the bowl tightly with plastic wrap, and leave the dough to rise until it has more than doubled in volume—about 1 hour, depending on the warmth of your kitchen.

Select eight plump figs of uniform size, and save them for the topping. Chop the rest roughly into about six pieces per fig, and mix them in with the risen dough, deflating it and distributing them evenly.

I package (I scant tablespoon) active dry yeast

1 ¼ cups warm water

I teaspoon salt

About 2¾ cups unbleached all-purpose flour

2 teaspoons olive oil

About ⅓ cup cornmeal

TOPPING

I pint fresh figs

2 tablespoons sugar, or more if you like

RECOMMENDED EQUIPMENT

A standing mixer with dough hook

A baking sheet

Fig Focaccia (cont.)

Generously sprinkle cornmeal over an 8-by-12-inch area of the baking sheet. Turn the dough out onto the cornmeal, and smear the remaining oil over the top, spreading it around with your fingers. Now pat and stretch the dough out into an oval shape approximately 8 inches wide and 11 to 12 inches long. Cut the reserved figs in half, stem to bottom, and arrange them at even intervals on top of the dough, cut side up, pressing them in slightly. Sprinkle the sugar all over the top.

Preheat the oven to 425°. Let the dough rest for 20 minutes while the oven heats, then bake it for 25 minutes. Remove the bread to a rack. It should settle and cool for at least 10 minutes; then serve it warm. It can, of course, be reheated.

DEALING WITH IDIOSYNCRATIC OVENS

When I bake at home, I don't hesitate to move things around the oven. It's a large professional oven with spots of quite variable heat, and, perhaps because of the massive griddle that sits on top, it retains heat long after the thermostat is lowered. Even if the dial is at 300°, my oven's top heat continues to brown foods like a broiler. These idiosyncrasies are a blessing in a way, because they demand that I pay attention to what is happening in the oven, and they've taught me how to move my dishes up and down on the racks and from the front to the back, to cover and uncover them as needed: to do whatever I need to do to get the dish that I want.

I have incorporated these practices into many of my recipes, because using your whole oven to control the rates of cooking and browning will help you deal with the peculiarities of your own oven. And, of course, oven thermostats vary so much, just setting the dial for the same temperature does not ensure the same heat.

The bread-pudding recipe on page 372 is a good example of how you can use the heat zones in your oven— and your racks—to your advantage. In the first step, you set both the heat and the pan of bread high up, so the top heat will quickly caramelize the bread without drying it out. But you set a rack in the middle—and lower the thermostat—to get more bottom heat on the baking dish, and slower cooking, to set the custard in the pudding. Stay flexible, though: you might want to move the pudding higher if the top is not browning as you want it—or you might need to cover it if it's darkening too fast even at a lower temperature setting. And when you are roasting or braising in the oven and there is too much liquid in the pan, just set the pan directly on the floor of the oven, where you get the most intense bottom heat.

So please don't just let your oven do whatever it wants—there are ways to control it.

Two Simple Butter Cakes with Fruit

These are my favorite kind of cakes to make: mix a batter in a bowl; put it in a pan with fruit; set the cake in the oven; remove when done—and that's it! They're ready to enjoy, with no fancy finishing or decorating needed. Such cakes are perfect for afternoon tea or as a simple dessert after a big dinner. But you know when I most love these cakes? In the morning—I just cut a small piece from the pan and sit down with a cup of excellent coffee, a copy of the *New York Times,* and my *torta.* It's a great way to start the day.

Simple as they are, both of these cakes have interesting, and lovely, touches: the *torta invertita* is (as you may have guessed) an upside-down cake. You put sugared rhubarb in the bottom of the pan, spread the batter on top, and bake. The fruit cooks and caramelizes and moistens the cake on top; then, when the *torta* is partly cooled, you invert the pan so the fruit turns into a glossy topping.

I love rhubarb, and in this recipe I've incorporated a great technique I learned from my editor, Judith, who grows rhubarb in Vermont. The cut-up fruit is tossed with sugar and sits overnight, to soften and release lots of its liquid. The drained pieces go right into the cake pan, and I cook down the juices to make rhubarb syrup (to drizzle on the cake). When rhubarb isn't available, other fruits make a great *torta invertita:* ripe stone fruits like apricots, nectarines, peaches, or plums; ripe pears, figs, and pineapple are good, too.

Crostata Invertita with Rhubarb

FOR SOFTENING THE
RHUBARB

2 pounds rhubarb, washed, trimmed,
and cut into 1-inch pieces

¾ cup *zucchero di canna* or white
sugar

FOR THE PAN

3 tablespoons soft butter

2 tablespoons *zucchero di canna* or
white sugar

FOR THE CAKE BATTER

1¾ cups all-purpose flour

2 teaspoons baking powder

⅛ teaspoon salt

8 tablespoons (1 stick) soft butter

1 cup sugar

2 eggs

½ teaspoon vanilla

1 cup milk

FOR SERVING (OPTIONAL)

Unsweetened whipped cream

Vanilla ice cream

Preparing the Rhubarb

The night before baking the cake (or at least 8 hours earlier), put all the rhubarb in a large bowl and toss with the sugar to coat all the pieces. Let the fruit steep as long as possible, then drain through a sieve or colander; save the exuded rhubarb juice. The pieces should be soft and reduced to 4 cups in volume. (If they haven't had time to wilt, put the fruit in a skillet with ½ cup or so of the juice; bring to a simmer, and cook for 5 minutes, or until the pieces are soft and have released more juice, but still have their shape. Drain and cool, again saving the juice.)

Preparing the Pan and Mixing the Batter

Arrange a rack in the lower third of the oven and preheat to 375°— you can bake this on a stone, if you have one.

Smear the butter to coat the insides of the pan with a thick layer of butter. Sprinkle the 2 tablespoons of sugar over the bottom (not the sides). Spread the drained rhubarb pieces in an even layer in the prepared pan; press gently just to flatten the layer.

Sift or stir together the flour, baking powder, and salt.

With the mixer on low speed, cream the butter and sugar together in a big bowl; when blended, beat on high speed for a couple of minutes, until smooth and light. Scrape down the sides of the bowl, and beat in the eggs, one at a time, mixing well at moderate speed, then mix in the vanilla. Beat on high speed for 2 minutes or so to lighten and smooth the batter.

Scrape down the sides and, at low speed, mix in the dry ingredients, alternating with the milk. Add a third of each at a time, and beat for a few seconds before the next addition. When everything's been incorporated, scrape the sides (and bottom) of the bowl, and beat on high speed for about a minute, until the batter is light and completely smooth. Pour it over the layer of rhubarb, and spread it evenly to fill the pan and to level the top.

Set the pan in the oven and bake for 25 to 30 minutes, until the top of the cake has set and is starting to brown. If using a glass pan, lift it carefully and check to see that the fruit is cooking and bubbling on the bottom. (If the fruit is not cooking actively but the top is browning, keep baking and lay a piece of foil loosely over the cake before it gets too dark. If the juices are bubbling so much that they're about to spill over the sides, place a sheet of foil *under* the dish.)

Bake for a total of 45 to 50 minutes, or until both the cake and fruit are done. The cake should be set so that a tester or toothpick inserted into the middle comes out clean; the top should be golden brown. The fruit juices should be bubbling up around the sides of the cake and appear syrupy.

Remove the cake, and cool on a rack for about an hour. The pan should be comfortable to hold but still slightly warm when you invert it.

Meanwhile, during the time the cake is baking or cooling, put all the reserved rhubarb juice in a saucepan, bring it to a boil, and cook, uncovered, until it has thickened into a ruby-colored thick syrup.

Inverting the *Invertita* and Serving

To unmold the cake, run the blade of a sharp knife around the sides of the pan. Cover the cake top with a round serving plate and, holding tight, flip the pan and plate upside down. The cake and rhubarb layers may drop neatly onto the plate. If they're reluctant, give the pan a quick shake to release the fruit, and pry one side of the cake from the pan to let air in and encourage it to drop.

Serve the cake still slightly warm or at room temperature. Slice it into wedges, and drizzle over a bit of the rhubarb syrup. If you want, top with unsweetened whipped cream, or flank with a scoop of vanilla ice cream, or just enjoy it plain, with a cup of good coffee.

RECOMMENDED EQUIPMENT

A 10-inch pie pan or cake pan, oven-proof glass preferred so you can see the fruit layer; I like the shape of a pie pan, and the tapering sides release the cake more easily

An electric hand or standing mixer, with beaters or paddle attachment

Torta al Vino with Grapes or Berries

Torta al vino is a traditional wine-country cake with white wine in the batter and seedless grapes (or any kind of berry) folded in. The acidity of the wine and the whole juicy fruits—baked grapes are luscious!—give this easy cake a delightful complexity of flavors and textures in each bite.

A 9-INCH CAKE, SERVING 8 OR MORE

1 ½ cups all-purpose flour, plus extra to flour the cake pan and to coat the grapes

1 ½ teaspoons baking powder

½ teaspoon baking soda

⅛ teaspoon salt

6 tablespoons soft butter, plus 1 tablespoon for the cake pan

¾ cup sugar

2 eggs

1 tablespoon extra-virgin olive oil

1 teaspoon vanilla extract

1 tablespoon lemon or orange zest, or a combination

¾ cup dry white wine

2 cups small red seedless grapes, stemmed, rinsed, and patted dry, or 2 cups fresh or frozen blueberries or raspberries

FOR TOPPING THE CAKE DURING BAKING

2 tablespoons butter, cut into small bits

1 tablespoon zucchero di canna or white sugar

Arrange a rack in the middle of the oven and preheat to 375°. Assemble the springform pan; butter and flour the insides.

Sift or stir together the flour, baking powder, baking soda, and salt.

With the mixer on low speed, cream the butter and sugar together in a big bowl; when blended, beat on high speed for a couple of minutes, until smooth and light. Scrape down the sides of the bowl, and beat in the eggs, one at a time, mixing well at moderate speed, then mix in the olive oil, the vanilla, and the citrus zest. Beat on high speed for 2 minutes or so, to lighten and smooth the batter.

Scrape down the sides and, at low speed, mix in the dry ingredients, alternating with the wine. Add a third of each at a time, and beat for a few seconds before the next addition. When everything's been incorporated, scrape the sides (and bottom) of the bowl, and beat on high speed for about 20 seconds to finish the batter.

Pour and scrape all the batter into the cake pan, and spread it in an even layer. Sprinkle a teaspoon of flour over the grapes, and toss so they're all lightly dusted. Scatter the grapes over the surface of the batter. Swirl a spatula or knife around them, folding and stirring them into the top of the batter—don't fold or swirl deeper than an inch. The fruits don't need to be completely covered, because they will sink as the cake rises.

Set the pan in the oven, and bake for 25 minutes, or until the top is set, though the batter underneath will still be loose and will shake. Carefully take the cake out of the oven—or just bring it to the front of the rack, where you can reach it—and scatter the butter bits and then the sugar on the top.

Return the cake to the oven, and bake another 15 minutes or so—a total of 40 minutes or more—until the cake is set and the top is golden brown and lightly glazed by the final sugar and butter. Test doneness by inserting a cake tester or toothpick into the middle to see if it comes out clean. Remove from the oven to a cooling rack.

Let the cake cool for about 10 minutes, then open the spring and remove the side ring. Let the cake cool thoroughly before serving. Remove the metal pan bottom, if you want, after an hour or so, when you can handle the cake: lay a piece of parchment or wax paper on the cake top (so the pretty surface doesn't get messed up), then a plate or a wire rack. Flip the cake over; pry and lift off the pan bottom. Invert the cake again, onto a rack if it needs to cool further, or onto a serving plate.

Serve at room temperature, sliced into wedges. I love the cake plain with just a dusting of powdered sugar, or garnish it with whipped cream.

FOR GARNISHING

Powdered sugar

Whipped cream (optional)

RECOMMENDED EQUIPMENT

A 9-inch springform cake pan

An electric hand or standing mixer, with beaters or paddle attachment

Two Fruity Desserts with Strudel Dough

In my family, strudel desserts—both making and eating them—are an Istrian tradition. Istria was part of the Austro-Hungarian Empire, which brought to it an element of Middle European cuisine. But this particular tradition of strudel stretches well beyond Istria, and is alive and well from Friuli–Venezia Giulia into the Trentino–Alto Adige regions of Italy. The beauty lies in the simplicity and versatility of this dough, which can envelop any form of a delicious fruit or savory filling.

The Autumn Strudel recipe that follows has the traditional form of a sweet filling rolled up and encased in many crisp and flaky layers of dough. The filling is an unusual one—sweetened winter squash and tart cranberries in their natural jelly. Any kind of hard squash with a golden flesh will be delicious here—butternut is always a good choice, or try some of the less common varieties, such as ambercup, buttercup, delicata, or other squashes in the farmers' market in the fall.

The prune-and-ricotta strudel is made in an entirely different form, with a single thin layer of dough enclosing a creamy filling. It's baked in a skillet to support the delicate dough as it bakes into a round *torta*. I've also borrowed a pastry technique used in Friuli (with savory *crostate*) to give the cheesecake a lovely top crust of rippling folds. This is fun to make—as you can see in the photos—and tastes wonderful too.

Homemade Strudel Dough

*T*his soft dough is a pleasure to knead on the table. You could mix it in a food processor, but since it only requires 3 or 4 minutes of kneading, and feels so good, I prefer to do it by hand.

Toss together the flour and salt in a mixing bowl. Drizzle the oil all over the flour and mix it in, then gradually add the water, in splashes, all the while tossing with the fork. When all 10 tablespoons of water are incorporated, mix vigorously to bring the dough together. Add more water if the dough seems dry or won't come together.

2½ cups all-purpose flour

½ teaspoon salt

3 tablespoons olive oil

10 tablespoons (½ cup plus 2 tablespoons) or more water

Scrape the dough onto the work surface, and knead with your hands until the clumps have disappeared and the dough is smooth and elastic, 3 minutes or more.

Press the dough into a disk, wrap well in plastic wrap, and refrigerate for at least 2 hours or overnight. Let very cold dough sit at room temperature briefly before rolling. Strudel dough can also be frozen for several months.

Rolling and Stretching the Strudel Dough

You may have heard that strudel dough should be so thin you can read the newspaper through it. That sounds difficult, but wait until you work with this dough: it is elastic and strong but quite cooperative, so it is surprisingly easy to extend it to any size and shape you want. Use the basic techniques of rolling and stretching, given below, to make either a large dough circle for the Strudel Purse (page 390) or a rectangle for the Autumn Strudel (recipe follows). In fact, your dough may stretch so readily that it will end up thinner than you need, so don't keep going until you can read the newspaper: use a ruler or yardstick and follow the measurements in the recipes.

• *Begin by rolling the dough:* Work on a large, preferably wooden surface, with at least a yard of clear space. Chilled dough should warm up briefly at room temperature. Lightly dust the work surface with flour. Press the dough flat with your hands and begin rolling it out from the center. For a circle, roll from the center out in several directions; to start forming a rectangle, roll in one direction and then at a right angle.

• *Turn the dough:* As soon as the dough has started to stretch, pick it up and turn it over. Roll to extend it several more inches (for either shape), then turn it over again. Dust the work surface again with flour, if necessary, each time you flip the dough over.

• *Stretch the dough on the board:* When it extends about 18 inches in any direction, the dough is thin enough to start stretching by hand. The easiest way to do this is on the table: lay one hand flat on the dough, near an edge, pressing only lightly, and with the other hand grasp the edge and tug it outward to stretch. To enlarge a circle, tug evenly all around. To maintain a rectangular shape, tug the sides and corners of your rectangle. As the dough sheet gets larger, and will stay in place, grasp the edge of the dough with both hands and

Rolling the dough out from the center

Picking up the dough and turning it over

Rolling the dough to extend it further

Stretching the dough on the board

tug it gently outward. Enlarge the circle evenly all around in this manner.

• *Stretch the dough while holding it up in the air:* This is a slightly more difficult stretch, but faster and more fun! Slide your hands under the dough, *palms down*, and lift the edge off the work surface. Cup your hands and turn your fingers toward each other, so the edge of the dough is supported by your wrists and extended fingers (as shown in photo). Raise the dough completely off the table, letting it hang from your hands so its own weight stretches it, as one does when making a pizza. Carefully move your hands apart to stretch the thicker dough along the edge; gradually shift the dough along your hands to enlarge it evenly.

To stretch a circle in the air, keep shifting the dough on your wrists and hands, stretching it on all sides (360 degrees). To stretch a rectangle, pick up the dough and stretch it along one side, lay it down, and pick it up with your hands under another of the four sides. Stretch the corners when the sheet is on the work board.

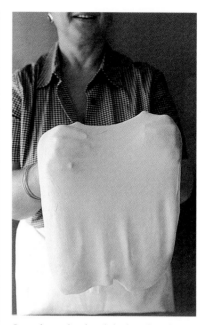

Stretching the dough by hand in the air

• *Stretch the dough with gravity:* A traditional trick. Pick up the dough sheet—or pull it gently toward you on the work surface—and position it so a third or a bit more of the dough is flat on the edge of the table and the other two-thirds is hanging toward the floor. The friction of the surface should hold the dough in place while gravity stretches the hanging portion down—don't let go until you are confident it won't all slide off. After a couple of minutes, lift and reverse the dough so the other edge stretches downward. (When I was little, my grandmother would leave the dough hanging down while she did other work in the kitchen.)

• *Mending the dough:* Strudel dough may get small tears in it during stretching, but they are easily repaired. When the sheet is the size you want, lay all of it flat on the worktable and pinch the edges of the holes together, then gently pat or roll them smooth.

Mending small tears in the dough

Autumn Strudel with Squash and Cranberries

2 tablespoons fine dry bread crumbs

2 tablespoons butter

FOR THE SQUASH

About 2 pounds winter squash, peeled, seeded, cut into 1½-inch chunks (6 cups)

1 cup *zucchero di canna* or white sugar

A pinch of salt

¼ cup freshly squeezed lemon juice

1 cup water

FOR THE CRANBERRIES AND FILLING

12 ounces (1 bag) whole cranberries, fresh or frozen

1 cup *zucchero di canna* or white sugar

½ cup freshly squeezed orange juice

¼ cup apricot jam, stirred to loosen, plus more if wanted

2 tablespoons soft butter

FOR ROLLING AND BAKING

8 ounces (½ batch) Homemade Strudel Dough (preceding recipe)

Flour, for rolling

6 tablespoons or more very soft butter, for the dough and baking pan

⅛ teaspoon cinnamon

1 tablespoon or more *zucchero di canna* or white sugar

Toast the bread crumbs in 2 tablespoons butter until golden brown. Let cool.

Making the Squash and Cranberry Filling

Put the squash, sugar, salt, lemon juice, and water in a large saucepan, cover, and set over medium-high heat. When boiling, lower the heat to keep at an active, bubbling simmer. Cook the squash, covered, for about 20 minutes, or until the chunks are *al dente*: soft enough to pierce with a fork but still holding a fairly firm shape. Lift them out of the liquid with a slotted spoon or spider, drain, and set in a bowl to cool. Boil the cooking liquid, uncovered, until it has reduced to ¼ cup or so of syrup; scrape it into a cup or bowl to stop the cooking.

Meanwhile, rinse the cranberries, put them in a small saucepan, and stir in the sugar and orange juice. (If using frozen berries, don't thaw: rinse and start cooking while they're still frozen.) Cover the pan, and bring the liquid to a boil over medium heat, stirring frequently to make sure the sugar dissolves. Uncover, and cook at a gentle simmer for about 25 minutes, until the sauce has thickened and the cranberries are thoroughly cooked (but still have their berry shape).

Let the berries and squash cool to room temperature, then fold them together gently, in a large mixing bowl, keeping the chunks intact. Fold in the apricot jam and the soft butter and finally the squash syrup—or as much syrup as needed, without making the filling too loose. It should be dense enough to stay in a mound when you heap it up, with no liquid seeping out.

Rolling Out the Dough and Arranging It on the Cloth

Before you form the strudel, arrange a rack in the center of the oven and preheat to 375°.

On a large, lightly floured work surface, roll and stretch the strudel dough into a rectangle that measures approximately 2 feet wide (left to right in front of you) and 18 inches long (from the nearest edge to the one farthest from you). Follow the strudel-stretching procedures detailed on pages 384 to 385: start by rolling the dough into a rectangular shape, then gradually stretch it with your hands until it reaches the size you want.

Now you want to cover the work surface with the cloth to help you roll the strudel. The best way is to have someone else lay out the cloth while you hold the dough up in the air (or lay out the cloth on another flat surface, then transfer it). Arrange the cloth so that its front edge is aligned with the near edge of your counter (it can drape over the edge a few inches too). The cloth should extend at least 4 feet left to right and 3 feet toward the far side of the counter. When the cloth is flat and smooth, flour it lightly, then lay down the sheet of dough with its longer side left to right in front of you, parallel to the cloth. There should be 6 inches to a foot of uncovered cloth all around the dough.

Rolling Up the Strudel

Brush the parchment liner of the baking sheet with about 2 tablespoons of the very soft butter; keep the baking sheet handy.

Brush the surface of the dough—gently—with soft butter all over, using about 2 tablespoons in all. Stir and toss together the toasted bread crumbs, the cinnamon, and about 2 teaspoons of the sugar. Sprinkle this evenly all over the buttered dough (it keeps the layers of dough separated when the strudel's rolled up).

Now you're going to create a long row of the squash-cranberry filling on the dough. The row will be about 18 inches long, running left to right in front of you, about 4 inches in from the edge of the dough nearest you. The row will start about 3 inches in from the left edge of the dough and end about 3 inches from the right edge of the dough. And it will be 3 to 4 inches high and 4 or 5 inches wide—leaving lots of dough to roll around it.

Got that? When you have a good idea of where the filling is going, scoop the filling out in cups all along the filling line onto the dough and use your hands to push it evenly into its proper place and shape, resembling a long, plump sausage of squash chunks in cranberry jelly. Wash and dry your hands. Now the rolling begins. Grasp the edge of the cloth nearest you, at the points close to the left and right corners

RECOMMENDED EQUIPMENT

A rolling pin or heavy wooden dowel

A linen tablecloth or sheet, or other smooth cloth

A heavy-duty rimmed baking sheet, 12 by 18 inches or similar size, lined with baking parchment

A small kitchen brush, to smear butter

of the dough. It is a good idea to have someone help you, at least the first time, so each of you can take a side. Lift the cloth, bringing the 4-inch margin of uncovered dough up and against the row of filling. Roll the cloth into your fists, so your hands are close to the dough and in better control; with your knuckles tight in a fist facing the filling, lift and push your hands, with cloth in them, forward, so the whole row of filling rolls over at the same time—and gets wrapped snugly in dough.

Keep gathering the cloth in your hands, holding it close to the strudel. Pull the cloth up gently as the strudel rolls over several more times, wrapping more dough around the filling, until you've created a long neat log. Get ready to roll the strudel right onto the baking sheet. First, make sure the seam of the dough is on top, so it will be on the bottom when you roll it onto the sheet: use the cloth to roll it seam up. Next, place the wide edge of the baking sheet against the strudel and lift the far side of the pan so it looks like you're going to roll the log up a steep ramp—get someone to help you hold the sheet.

Using the cloth, give the strudel a final forceful roll so it goes over the rim and onto the buttered parchment liner, seam down, on the near side of the baking sheet. The empty ends of the strudel dough are probably flopping off the sides of the pan. Twist these flaps (several dough layers thick) so they are snug against the ends of the filling and cut them off, leaving just an inch or two of twisted dough sticking out of the strudel. Tuck them under the strudel log.

Form the strudel into a horseshoe shape, carefully curving each end in on the baking sheet. Brush the strudel dough with the remaining soft butter all over. Cut ½-inch slits for steam vents all over the top of the pastry: plunge the tip of a sharp, thin-bladed knife straight down into the strudel, making sure it pierces through the layers of dough. Finally, sprinkle the remaining teaspoon of sugar all over the top of the strudel.

Bake the strudel for approximately 45 minutes, rotating the pan front to back once or twice, for even baking. The strudel should be deeply browned, with the juices of the filling bubbling out of the slits. If you want, brush any fruity juices in the baking pan on the strudel dough. You can also glaze the strudel with softened apricot jam, but wait until the pastry has cooled a bit. Glazing the hot strudel will cause the dough to lose all its crispness; glazing later on will soften it less. (I like crisp, flaky dough, so I don't glaze at all.)

Let the strudel cool on the pan briefly, then use a wide metal spatula to separate it from the sticky, caramelized juices on the parchment sheet. Use two spatulas—and a helping hand—to lift up the strudel in one piece and transfer it to a cutting board or platter. Or just slice the strudel right in the baking pan and serve on individual dessert plates.

Serve slices of the strudel warm or at room temperature—with cream, whipped cream, or ice cream, if you like.

Autumn Strudel, partially sliced

CANE SUGAR: ZUCCHERO DI CANNA

I play around when I'm making dolci—as I always do in the kitchen—using different and less refined sweetening agents. Recently, I've enjoyed baking with the pale-gold cane sugars (called zucchero di canna in Italy) that I've found in the supermarkets near home. These crystal sugars are less processed and refined than ordinary table sugar; some brands are also from organically grown sugarcane (in Florida and Hawaii, I am glad to learn). The tint of the sugar, like its hint of deep flavor, comes from a very slight amount of molasses naturally retained by the crystals—not added during processing, as is the case with conventional brown sugars. Use zucchero di canna exactly as you do white sugar (in the same amounts) in these strudel recipes.

Strudel Purse with Prune and Ricotta Filling

FOR THE FILLING

I cup (about 12) large pitted prunes

½ cup or so best-quality dark rum

3 eggs

¾ cup sugar

¼ cup heavy cream

⅛ teaspoon (2 good pinches) salt

½ teaspoon vanilla extract

Reserved prune-soaking liquid

2 pounds ricotta cheese, preferably
fresh, drained in a sieve for
3 to 4 hours

Zest of a medium lemon
(about I teaspoon)

Zest of a medium orange
(about I tablespoon)

I teaspoon or so all-purpose flour,
for dusting the prunes

2 tablespoons pine nuts, dry toasted
in a skillet

FOR THE CRUST, ASSEM-
BLY, AND GLAZING

2 tablespoons melted butter, or more if
needed

8 ounces (½ batch) Homemade
Strudel Dough (page 383)

Flour, for rolling

I teaspoon *zucchero di canna* or white
sugar, or I tablespoon apricot jam,
for glazing the crust

Making the Prune and Ricotta Filling

The night before making the dessert (or at least 3 hours ahead), cut the prunes into ½-inch pieces; pile them in a cup or bowl, and pour in enough rum to reach the top of the fruit. Cover, and let them soak at room temperature. Just before mixing the filling, pour off and save any liquid that the prunes haven't absorbed.

Crack the eggs into a mixing bowl (the one for your standing mixer, if using), add the sugar, and start mixing at low speed with the whisk attachment. As the sugar dissolves, add the heavy cream, salt, vanilla, and reserved prune-soaking liquid. Raise the speed to medium and whisk until the batter is smooth, about 2 minutes.

Scrape the ricotta into the bowl, and break up any big curds with a spoon or spatula (fresh ricotta can be lumpier than packaged varieties). Drop in the fresh citrus zests, and resume whisking with the machine. When the cheese is well incorporated, raise the speed to high and whisk for 4 to 5 minutes, until the filling is light and smooth.

Spread out the cut prunes on a piece of wax paper, sprinkle the spoonful of flour over, and toss to separate the pieces. Scatter the prunes and toasted pine nuts over the filling, and fold them in.

Rolling Out the Dough and Filling the Skillet

Arrange a rack in the center of the oven, and preheat to 375°. Brush a bit of the melted butter on the inside of the skillet.

On a large, lightly floured work surface, roll and stretch the strudel dough into a circle 2 feet in diameter or slightly larger. Follow the strudel-stretching procedures detailed on pages 384 to 385: start by rolling the dough into a round, then gradually stretch it with your hands until it reaches the size you want.

Lift the dough circle and hold it over the buttered skillet. If you have someone to help you, hold the circle out flat (like a trampoline) and lower it to rest, centered, in the bottom of the pan, covering the sides, and with a wide band of dough hanging outside the pan too. If you're alone, flop the dough down gently so it lines and covers the skillet completely and drapes over the rim. Make sure the dough is flat, not stretched in the pan with air bubbles underneath. If necessary, lift the overhanging edges and drape more dough into the pan, so it's comfortably settled.

Now pour and scrape the prune-ricotta filling into the dough-lined pan; smooth it flat with a spatula. Now comes the fun part.

Twisting, Cutting, and Finishing the Strudel Dough Shell

Have a sharp, thin-bladed knife or sharp scissors close by.

Lift one edge of the overhanging dough and hold it in one hand over the center of the pan, well above the filling. With your other hand, lift another section of overhanging dough and draw it up to the first hand. In this manner, gather all the excess dough together, so it forms a closed cone-shaped tent over the filling.

Now twist your hand—and all the dough it's holding—in one direction (as shown in photo on the next page). This will tighten the dough on the sides and top of the filling and form a pattern of spiral pleats. It should also form a big knot of twisted dough just above the

RECOMMENDED EQUIPMENT

An electric mixer, either a hand or standing mixer

A non-stick skillet or sauté pan, 12 inches in diameter. If you do not have a 12-inch skillet, you can use two 9- or 10-inch skillets, cutting the dough in half and dividing the filling between the two pans; the smaller pan will give you a thicker filling layer, the bigger pan a thinner cake but a larger shell of dough

Sharp, long-bladed kitchen scissors

Lifting the dough circle over the buttered skillet

Scraping the filling into the dough-lined pan

Drawing the overhanging dough into your hand

Twisting the gathered dough with your hand

filling. With a sharp knife, carefully cut beneath the knot of dough, parallel to the work surface, straight across, slicing through all the folds. Don't let go of your twist while cutting the dough: when the topknot is removed, the spiral pleats will fall onto the surface of the filling, covering it with ridges except for a hole in the center, where the filling is exposed. If your hole is too small or too large, or off center, trim or stretch the dough to get a satisfactory opening, but that's only a matter of aesthetics.

Before baking, brush the top of the dough with the remaining melted butter and sprinkle with *zucchero di canna* or white sugar. Set the skillet in the oven and bake for approximately 25 minutes, then rotate the pan for even baking (remember that the handle is very hot).

Bake for another 15 to 20 minutes, or until the strudel dough on top is deep golden brown and the filling is tinged with brown as well. Remove the skillet from the oven, and let it cool on a rack for about 15 minutes.

To remove the *torta* from the pan, cover the skillet with another rack or a large plate, and invert. Then cover the crusted bottom with a serving platter and invert again, so the *torta* is right side up. Now

Cutting off the dough beneath the knot

The baked Strudel Purse

brush the top with softened apricot jam, if it isn't already sprinkled with sugar. (You can also skip the inverting steps and serve the dessert right in the pan.)

Serve the *torta* warm or at room temperature, cut into wedges with a serrated knife to keep the strudel crust intact.

A Fruit Tart Trilogy

A tart—*crostata* in Italian—is a marvelously versatile form in which to present and enjoy fruit. And each of these *crostate* incorporates a different form of fruit as well.

The first is a free-form tart—a large round of dough folded into a rustic, crusty envelope around fresh fruit, with no pan needed. It's a great design: the fruit bakes inside the dough, releasing marvelous juices, but a cushion of sweetened bread crumbs absorbs them, and the central opening vents all the moisture, so the pastry stays crisp and flaky. The exposed fruit caramelizes too, adding to the beauty and the flavor of the tart. Small sweet Italian plums—*prugne*—are perfect in this crust, but you can fill it with any of the juicy fruits of summer—peaches, apricots, nectarines, or figs.

The second *crostata*, with poached apricots, is entirely different in form and filling. Inside a sweet pastry shell, formed in a pastry mold, is a soft, slightly chunky purée of cooked dried apricots and apricot jam, a combination that intensifies the flavors of the fresh fruit. Until you cut the tart, though, this treat is hidden under an elegant layer of almond macaroon studded with pine nuts, a traditional confection called *pignolata*. It's easier to make than you would think something this sophisticated could ever be. So I hope you will enjoy this often—both the tart and the pleasure you'll give your family—at holiday parties and special occasions in any season.

The last *crostata* in this group has fruit in company with something everyone loves, certainly in my house: chocolate. Truthfully, there's more chocolate than fruit, but that wasn't how I planned it. The original filling for the *crostata* used only a small amount of chocolate, along with orange zest, hazelnuts, and orange liqueur, in a base of butter and eggs (just as you'll still find in the recipe). But then the kids (and I mean my grown-up kids) wanted more chocolate, so I added the pure chocolate layer that covers the bottom of the tart. That seems to have satisfied them!

COMMENTS ON RIPE FRUIT

For this crostata, as for many desserts, I encourage you to use ripe fruit. But it concerns me that it is difficult these days—unless you have your own orchard—to get fruit that can truly ripen as nature intended. Much, perhaps most, of the fruit in our markets is engineered for commercial needs, for shipping and shelf life. It is bred to remain in a green, immature state for a prolonged period. This keeps the cellulose intact, so the fruit is firm when it's shipped, when it's on display, and when it's in your kitchen.

But fruit is not supposed to stay young. It has to ripen, to mature, and to die—and that's when it is at its best. Whether a pear, an apricot, a fig, or a berry, I want it precisely when its maturity has peaked and it begins to die—then the cells literally burst and release all their aroma and the flavor compounds of their mature development. The explosion in your mouth of a fruit at its moment of death, so to speak, is one of the great experiences we should have with food.

I guess I learned this when I was six or seven and we were sent to find the ripest figs. I remember looking at every fruit on all the branches, searching for ones that were split, on the verge of overripeness and fermentation. Out of the cracks, I had learned, would come a drop of the fig's essence, an elixir as sweet as honey. This made an impression on me I've never forgotten.

At my home today, right outside the kitchen window, is a fig tree. And whenever I'm at the sink, I find myself automatically looking for figs ready to explode. And then I can tell my grandchildren what I learned when I was their age—that is, if I can get them to stop racing up and down the driveway on their tricycles!

Free-Form Plum *Crostata*

Making the Filling and Rolling the Dough

Arrange a rack in the middle of the oven with a baking stone on it, if you have one. Preheat the oven to 375°. If the *crostata* dough is very cold, let it soften at room temperature for a few minutes while you make the filling.

Rinse the plums and pat dry. Cut them in flat halves, following the natural line around the fruit through the stem end, and remove the pits. Toss the halves with the lemon zest, apricot jam, and butter bits in a mixing bowl. (If you're making the *crostata* with large plums or fruit like peaches or nectarines, cut in quarters or wedges.)

Toss the bread crumbs, sugar, and cinnamon together.

On a lightly floured board, start stretching the dough into a circle, rolling from the center in all directions. Turn the dough over as it stretches, and flour the work surface as needed.

Cut a piece of parchment that will cover your baking sheet. Roll the circle of dough to a diameter of 15 inches, and lay it, centered, on the parchment. Now trim the outside edges of the dough, with a sharp knife or scissors, cutting away ragged or thin spots and making as perfect a round as you can, since this edge will be visible on the top of your *crostata*. Keep the circle at least 13 inches in diameter. Lift the parchment with the dough on it to the baking sheet.

Filling and Baking the *Crostata*

Sprinkle about ⅓ cup of the bread-crumb mix in a 7-to-9-inch-diameter circle in the center of the dough, as a base for the fruit. The bread crumbs will soak up the juices, so if you have very ripe and juicy fruit (like peaches) use more crumbs, to form a thicker layer; if using a drier fruit, like apricots, use less crumbs.

Arrange the coated plum halves, cut side up, on top of the crumb base. I place them in concentric rings, starting from the outside, and lean each inner ring on the plums just outside. In this manner, with a larger, 8- or 9-inch base of crumbs, you should be able to fit all the

1 batch (about 9 ounces) Free-Form *Crostata* Dough (recipe follows)

Flour for rolling

FOR THE FRUIT FILLING

1½ pounds small Italian prune plums or other ripe fruit

Freshly grated zest of a medium lemon

2 tablespoons apricot jam

2 tablespoons butter, cut in pieces

FOR THE SWEETENED BREAD CRUMBS

½ cup fine dry bread crumbs

2 tablespoons *zucchero di canna* or white sugar

¼ teaspoon cinnamon

FOR SERVING (OPTIONAL)

Whipped cream

Vanilla ice cream

RECOMMENDED EQUIPMENT

A baking stone or oven tiles

Baking parchment

A large baking sheet, 12 by 18 inches or similar size

plums in one layer, for a *crostata* with an even height. If the crumb base is smaller, you'll need to pile up the fruit. This will give the *crostata* more of a dome shape (as in the photo).

When you've assembled your fruit in the middle of the dough, fold the uncovered band of pastry on top of the fruit, as shown in the photo. The width of the band will vary with your arrangement of the plums, but you should have at least 2½ inches of dough to form the pleated top crust.

Finally, sprinkle 1 or more tablespoons of sugared bread crumbs over the visible fruit in the center. As before, use more crumbs on juicy fruit. If you have any left over, sprinkle them over the pleated dough.

Put the baking sheet with the *crostata* in the oven, on the stone if using one, and bake for 25 minutes; rotate the pan back to front for even cooking. Continue baking, and check the browning of the crust after 40 minutes: it should be light gold. If it is getting quite

Pulling the sides of the dough up onto the plums

The filled *crostata*, ready to bake

The baked *crostata*

dark, you may need to lay a piece of foil on top. Bake for another 15 minutes or more, until the fruit is bubbling and has caramelized on the edges. If you've filled the *crostata* with a mound of fruit, you'll probably want to bake it more than an hour—and cover the top—to make sure all the fruit is cooked.

Let the *crostata* cool on the baking sheet for about 15 minutes or more before lifting it, with the parchment, to a wire rack to continue cooling. When it has set, slide it off the parchment, supported by long spatulas, onto a platter.

Serve warm or at room temperature, cut into wedges, with whipped cream or vanilla ice cream, if you wish.

Free-Form *Crostata* Dough

ABOUT 9 OUNCES DOUGH, TO MAKE 1 FREE-FORM *CROSTATA*

1 cup all-purpose flour
2 tablespoons sugar
1/8 teaspoon salt
5 tablespoons very cold butter
3 to 4 tablespoons very cold (icy) water

Put the flour, sugar, and salt in the bowl of a food processor fitted with the metal blade, and process for a few seconds to mix the dry ingredients.

Cut the butter into 1/2-inch pieces, drop them onto the flour, and pulse the machine ten or twelve times, in short bursts, 20 seconds in all. The mixture should be crumbly, with only a few larger bits of butter visible.

Sprinkle 3 tablespoons of water on top of the dough; immediately pulse about six times, only a second or two each time. You want the crumbs to gather together in wet clusters, a bit like cottage-cheese curds—don't expect a mass of dough to form. If they haven't gathered, sprinkle on more water, a *teaspoon* at a time, and pulse two or three times after each.

When the clusters form, scrape them all out of the bowl, press them together, and knead just for a few seconds to form a smooth, tight dough. Flatten it into a disk, wrap well in plastic wrap, and refrigerate for 3 hours or up to a day before using. Freeze the dough for longer keeping.

(If the crumbs haven't clustered after you've added 4 tablespoons of water, open the top and press them with your fingers; if they're wet and stick together, just empty the bowl and press them into a disk of dough.)

Crostata with Poached Apricots and *Pignolata*

Pignoli (*pine nuts*) are an ingredient much loved and used in Italian cooking—from savory pasta dishes and pesto to meat dishes such as bracciole and rolla-tini, *and an infinite number of desserts. Here it is the topping of the tart, and hence its name, pignolata, lots of pignoli.*

For me, pignoli are delicious nuts that I recall harvesting from a cone of the big pine tree at the end of my grandmother's courtyard in Istria. It was a humungous pine tree—or maybe I was small. My brother Franco and the other boys would climb up the tree and shake or knock down the open cones. Burrowed in the open scales of the pine cone were the oval brown-shelled nuts, which the girls would crack open with stone on stone. First we would eat our fill, then we began collecting them for cooking. That fresh, sweet flavor of pine nuts is still vivid in my mind, and to me there is nothing worse than biting into a rancid old pine nut. So make sure that you get the freshest pine nuts, which should be sweet, nutty, and buttery at the same time. Buy them in small quantities, since they are expensive; use them quickly, and if you have some left over, seal them tightly in a plastic bag and freeze them for future use. To heighten their aroma, toast them just be-fore using—although not in this recipe, since you will be baking them.

A 9-INCH TART, SERVING 6 TO 8

FOR THE TART SHELL

1 batch (12 ounces) Sweet Tart Dough (page 402), chilled

FOR THE APRICOT FILLING

8 ounces dried apricots (about 1½ cups)

⅔ cup or more water

½ cup apricot jam, stirred to loosen

2 tablespoons sweetened condensed milk (optional—a nice touch but not mandatory!)

Making the Components of the Tart

Arrange a rack in the middle of the oven with a baking stone on it, if you have one. Preheat the oven to 350°. (If you make the shell or the apricot filling a day or hours ahead of time, turn on the oven be-fore you assemble the tart—be sure to leave extra time for the baking stone to heat up.)

Roll and press the dough into the mold to form the tart shell, as detailed in the box on page 403. If you're doing this ahead of time, refrigerate the tart shell so it is easier to handle and fill.

Put the dried apricots in a small, preferably narrow saucepan with the ⅔ cup water. Cover, and bring to a boil; reduce the heat to main-tain a steady simmer. Cook, covered, until the apricots are soft (but not mushy) and only 2 or 3 tablespoons of poaching liquid are left in the pan, about 20 minutes. If the water evaporates before the apricots have softened, add more water and continue cooking slowly. Let the apricots cool in the pan with the syrupy liquid.

To make the apricot filling, put the cooled poached apricots and syrup in a food processor and pulse in short bursts—about 4 seconds in all—to chop the apricots into a thick paste of very small bits. Don't purée: the paste should be chunky. Scrape the apricots into a bowl, stir in 6 tablespoons of the apricot jam, and blend well. (Refrigerate filling if prepared ahead.)

Make the macaroon base for the *pignolata* when you are ready to assemble the tart and bake. Crumble the almond paste into the food processor, and add the sugar. Process about 30 seconds, scraping down the workbowl if necessary, so the ingredients are completely blended, with the consistency of moist sand. Pour the egg whites into the machine, and process for another 30 seconds, scraping as needed, until the macaroon is a smooth white slush.

Assembling the Tart, Baking, and Serving
(If you haven't heated your oven and baking stone yet, do it now.)

Plop the remaining 2 tablespoons of apricot jam on the bare bottom of the tart shell, and spread it to cover the bottom dough thinly. Spoon the apricot filling into the tart, and spread it in an even layer—it should fill almost two-thirds of your dough shell.

If you like, drizzle the 2 tablespoons of sweetened condensed milk all over the apricot layer: don't bother to spread it, just streak the entire surface. (This adds a subtly different kind of sweetness that you should try sometime, but the tart is excellent without it.)

Scrape the macaroon slush in blobs all over the top of the tart. Spread it with a big spoon or spatula moistened with water (but not dripping). It will be sticky, but with a little patience you can push it into a smooth, flat layer that comes right to the sides of the dough shell and covers the apricot layer (but not the dough rim) completely.

To finish the *pignolata*, sprinkle the pine nuts, just a few at a time, on top of the macaroon. Take your time: you want to make a single layer of pine nuts, so dense that you can't see the macaroon at all. Drop the *pignoli* to cover small sections, and then fill in empty spots. Let them rest where you drop them—don't push them into the macaroon or across the top. Do not cover the rim of the dough.

FOR THE *PIGNOLATA* TOPPING

7 ounces (a standard package) almond paste

½ cup sugar

2 whites from large eggs

1 cup pine nuts

FOR SERVING (OPTIONAL)

Powdered sugar

Whipped cream

RECOMMENDED EQUIPMENT

A 9-inch tart mold, preferably a fluted metal ring with a removable bottom

A baking stone or oven tiles

A food processor

When the tart is assembled, set the mold onto the hot baking stone. If you're not using a stone, you can move and bake the tart on a baking sheet.

Bake for about an hour (or longer without a stone), until the *pignolata* and the outside tart crust are beautifully browned but not blackened. Rotate the tart on the stone (or the rack) for even baking. The pine nuts should brown gradually: if they're dark within the first 30 minutes of baking, cover them with foil and lower the oven temperature if necessary; if they're not taking on color at all in the first ½ hour, raise the oven temperature.

Let the baked tart cool completely on a wire rack—this can take several hours. If using a tart ring with a removable bottom, separate the ring from the tart. If you want, slide the tart from the round metal mold bottom onto a platter—use long metal spatulas to support the tart, if you have any.

Serve the tart at room temperature. You can top with unsweetened whipped cream, or just sprinkle with powdered sugar. It is such a deliciously rich tart that you don't want to give big portions (people can always have seconds).

Crostata with Chocolate, Hazelnuts, and Orange

Making the Filling

Arrange a rack in the middle of the oven with a baking stone on it, if you have one. Preheat the oven to 350°.

Roll and press the dough to form the tart shell, as detailed in the box on page 403. Put the shell in the refrigerator to chill.

Put the 5 ounces of chocolate chunks in a bowl, and set over a pot of very hot water (barely simmering). Stir as the chocolate begins to melt, enabling it to become molten at the lowest temperature. When completely smooth, pour the chocolate into the tart shell, and spread it to cover the dough bottom completely.

Put the hazelnuts in the food processor, and pulse to chop them into small bits—don't turn them into a powder or paste. Empty the nuts into a bowl, and wipe out the food processor (you don't have to wash it).

To prepare the orange zest for the filling, rinse and dry the orange, and remove only the outer, colored zest in strips, about 2 inches long, with a vegetable peeler. Stack up a few strips at a time and slice them lengthwise into very thin slivers with a sharp paring knife. Then cut the slivers crosswise into tiny bits, like glitter or small confetti; you should have about 2 tablespoons.

Now you'll blend the main filling in the processor, adding the ingredients separately; frequently scrape down the sides of the bowl to make sure everything is processed evenly. First blend the sugar and butter, processing about 30 seconds, until smooth. With the machine running, drop in the eggs and process for a minute or more, until smooth and slightly thickened (be sure to scrape the sides). Drop in the flour and blend until smooth; scrape the bowl.

With the machine off, drop in the chopped orange peel, chocolate, and hazelnuts, and pulse for only a second or two to incorporate. Finally, whiz in the orange liqueur for just a second. Take the processor bowl off the base, and scrape the filling from the sides and

FOR THE TART SHELL

1 batch (12 ounces) Sweet Tart Dough (recipe follows), chilled

FOR THE CHOCOLATE LAYER

5 ounces semisweet chocolate, chopped into chunks

FOR THE MAIN FILLING

1/3 cup hazelnuts, toasted in the oven, skins rubbed off

A medium-size orange, for zest (see recipe instructions)

2/3 cup sugar

6 tablespoons soft butter

2 eggs

1 tablespoon all-purpose flour

3 ounces semisweet chocolate, chopped in very small pieces (about 1/2 cup)

2 tablespoons orange liqueur, such as Cointreau or Grand Marnier

FOR SERVING (OPTIONAL)

Whipped cream

Crostata with Chocolate, Hazelnuts, and Orange (cont.)

blade. Stir one last time, and pour it into the tart shell. Smooth the surface with a spatula to form an even layer.

Filling and Baking the Tart

Set the tart mold on the hot baking stone, if you have one, or on the middle oven rack. Bake for 25 minutes or so, and rotate the mold for even baking. As the filling sets, it will start to crack around the edges (when it starts to crack in the center, it is done). Bake 35 to 40 minutes total, until the filling is puffed, and firm in the center, and a cake tester comes out clean. The tart crust should be nicely browned as well.

Set the baked tart on a wire rack to cool. If using a tart ring with a removable bottom, remove the ring; slide the tart off the round mold bottom onto a platter if you want.

Serve slightly warm or at room temperature, with whipped cream, if desired.

Sweet Tart Dough

This dough is one I use for both the apricot and chocolate tarts given above and other dessert tarts formed in a shallow tart mold. It has a delicate, cookie-crumb texture (with lightness from the baking powder) and great buttery taste. And it takes no time to make in the food processor.

This recipe gives you just the right amount of dough to form into a 9-inch tart shell—multiply the formula if you are making a larger tart.

12 OUNCES OF DOUGH, TO FILL A 9-INCH TART MOLD

1 ⅛ cups all-purpose flour
    (1 cup plus 2 tablespoons)

½ teaspoon baking powder

⅛ teaspoon salt (2 pinches)

2 tablespoons sugar

9 tablespoons cold butter
    (1 stick plus 1 tablespoon)

2 egg yolks

Into the bowl of a food processor fitted with the metal blade, drop the flour, baking powder, salt, and sugar. Process for a few seconds, to mix the dry ingredients.

Cut the butter into ½-inch pieces, drop them onto the flour, and pulse the machine ten or twelve times, in short bursts, 20 to 30 seconds in all. The mixture should be crumbly, with only a few larger bits of butter visible.

Drop the egg yolks into the processor and pulse in bursts, just until the dough starts to clump together in bigger crumbs—it won't form a single mass. Scrape out the wet crumbs, press them together, and knead just for a few seconds, to form a smooth, tight dough. Flatten it into a disk, wrap well in plastic wrap, and refrigerate for 3 hours or up to a day before using. Freeze the dough for longer keeping.

Let the chilled dough sit at room temperature for 10 minutes or so before rolling. Thaw frozen dough completely, preferably in the refrigerator, before using.

FORMING SWEET DOUGH INTO A TART SHELL

For either of the tart recipes here—or anytime you use this dough—follow these basic procedures to line a tart mold, turning the dough into a thin shell. I use a standard 9-inch metal tart mold with a fluted ring and removable round bottom, but this dough can line any 9-inch pan.

Let the chilled dough soften briefly, but don't let it get too warm. Put the disk of dough in between two pieces of wax paper or parchment (about 1-foot squares) and roll it out to an 11-inch circle: roll from the center, in all directions, trying to stretch the dough evenly. With 12-inch-wide paper, roll to a circle that comes right to the edge.

Chill the dough circle in the refrigerator after rolling, inside the paper—this always helps. Peel the top paper off the dough, and center it over the tart mold. Peel off the other paper sheet; if the paper doesn't come off easily, chill again, then remove. Press the dough gently down into the mold so it covers the bottom and comes up the sides.

If the dough is cooperative, it may line the shell perfectly, and all you will have to do is even out the sides. But if it breaks into pieces or is uneven, you can press it into shape with your fingers. Here are some tips that will help you:

Keep the dough cold: put it in the refrigerator whenever you have trouble.

Moisten your fingers lightly to press and push the dough without its sticking to you (but don't drip water in the shell). Move dough from thick spots to thin spots, until the bottom is evenly thick all over.

To shape the sides, press the dough against the fluted rim with your index finger to form an evenly thick wall all the way around. Remove any dough that's higher than the rim by flicking it against the sharp rim; put these bits back in the mold.

When the shell is finished, chill it in the refrigerator before filling.

Apple Crisp Parfait

A *parfait is a great party dessert—elegant-looking but essentially quite simple. This one is really fun to put together, and I have the kids help me: they love to crack and crumble up into hundreds of pieces the big brown sugar crisp I've baked, then layer them in the parfait glasses (and pop lots of crumbles into their mouths too, I've noticed).*

Like the crisp, the poached apple cubes are delicious all by themselves. You want to use flavorful, tart-tasting apples that will keep their shape when cooked but soften up nicely and remain moist too. Good varieties are Greening, Granny Smith, Northern Spy, and Golden Delicious. Some of the heirloom cooking apples that orchards are growing again would be fine too—we can never have too many varieties of apples to enjoy.

SERVES 10 OR MORE

FOR POACHING THE APPLES

4 pounds firm, tart apples for baking (see headnote)

Zest of 1 lemon, finely grated

Juice of 1 lemon (about 3 tablespoons), freshly squeezed and strained

1 ½ cups sugar

½ cup water

FOR THE PARFAIT

3 cups heavy cream, for whipping

2 to 3 cups Brown Sugar Crisp Crumbles (recipe follows)

RECOMMENDED EQUIPMENT

A large saucepan, 5- or 6-quart capacity, with a cover

Poaching the Apples

Cut the apples in thick wedges, peel, and cut away the cores and seeds. Slice the wedges into chunks and cubes, an inch thick or larger (don't cut them too small or they will overcook). As you work, put the apple chunks in a mixing bowl and toss with some of the lemon zest and juice, to prevent browning. When you're finished, you should have about 10 cups of apples mixed with all the zest and juice.

Pour the sugar over the apples, and toss gently to coat the pieces. Turn all the fruit into the saucepan, slosh the bowl with the ½ cup water to rinse out all the sugar, and pour that into the pan too.

Set the saucepan over medium-high heat and bring the water to a boil. Stir the apples gently (so they're all heating), cover the pan, and cook about 2 minutes. Remove the cover, and continue to boil, reducing the juices, stirring the apple chunks around a couple of times, but not mushing them up. After 5 or 6 minutes, when the apples have softened and turned translucent on the outside (they won't be cooked all the way through), remove the pan from the heat. If the chunks have started to fall apart, turn them out of the saucepan into a bowl to stop cooking; otherwise, let the apples and the remaining liquid cool to room temperature (the chunks will reabsorb some of their juices as they sit).

The apples can be cooked a day ahead and refrigerated; let them warm up a bit before serving.

Assembling the Parfaits

Have the apples, crumbled-up crisp, and serving glasses ready.

Whip the cream until soft peaks form, by hand or in an electric mixer. (No sugar or flavoring is needed, since the apples and crisp are quite sweet.)

Spoon about ½ cup of apple chunks into each glass, making a thick layer that fills the bottom. Scatter crisp crumbles on top—anywhere from 2 to 5 tablespoons on each parfait. Plop ½ cup or so of whipped cream on top of the crisp crumbles.

Now repeat the layers—apples, crumbles, cream—in each glass. These can be smaller amounts, or as ample as the bottom layers, for an impressive and generous dessert.

Parfait glasses (can be anything you have in the house, from parfait glasses and wine glasses, balloon-shaped or standard, to tumblers or even conic beer glasses; size should be appropriate for a portion, and you want the layering of fruit, crumble, and cream to be visible)

Brown Sugar Crisp Crumbles

¾ cup all-purpose flour

½ cup sugar

2 tablespoons dark-brown sugar

¼ teaspoon cinnamon

⅛ teaspoon salt

4 ounces (1 stick) cold butter, in
    ½-inch pieces

3 tablespoons cold water

RECOMMENDED EQUIPMENT

A food processor or a hand-held
    pastry cutter

A rimmed baking sheet

Parchment paper

Preheat the oven to 400°.

It is quickest to mix the crisp in the food processor, fitted with the metal blade. Put the flour, sugars, cinnamon, and salt in the work-bowl. Process briefly to blend the dry ingredients. Drop in the butter pieces and pulse a dozen or so times, until the butter has been uniformly cut into a sandy powder of small bits. Sprinkle on the water, and process for a couple of seconds only, just to moisten the dough; it should still be rather loose and granular.

To mix by hand, blend the dry ingredients in a large mixing bowl and cut the butter into the grainy powder with a pastry cutter. Toss the powder and water with a fork to moisten.

Line the baking sheet with the parchment paper. Sprinkle the loose grains of dough evenly—in one layer—in an oval shape about 8 by 12 inches, filling in any holes and keeping the layer thin; don't compress them.

Bake for about 10 minutes, then rotate back to front, for even heating. The crumbs will have melted together, spread out in a thin layer, and perhaps started to bubble. Bake for another 7 to 10 minutes or more, until the layer is deeply caramelized, golden brown all over (and probably very dark on the edges). It will resemble a giant brown sugar cookie.

Set the pan on a wire rack, and cool until the cookie is very crisp. Cut or break off any burnt edges. Crack the cookie into crispy flakes, an inch or smaller. This is a good size for munching; you can crumble them up a bit more when layering the parfait.

PAN-ROASTED CHESTNUTS

A Family Custom: Roasted Chestnuts to Finish the Feast

I love to prepare hot roasted chestnuts for the family after a big autumn meal, as a special treat of the season. While everyone's talking and drinking coffee at the table, the chestnuts "roast" in a big skillet right on the stovetop. When they're done—it takes about 20 minutes—I pile the chestnuts on a big platter and serve them with grappa we make at our Bastianich vineyard in Friuli.

Here's my pan-roasting method:

For a dozen or more guests—a typical Sunday gathering for us—I use my 14-inch skillet, to prepare 3 to 4 pounds of chestnuts. Use a smaller pan if you wish, but don't cook more chestnuts than will fit in the skillet in a single layer.

With a sharp paring knife, cut a short slit—an inch or less—in the shell of each nut. (You can cut anywhere, but the flat side of the shell is easiest, or the chestnuts explode.) Put them all in the skillet, pour in ½ cup or so of water, cover the pan tightly, and set it over high heat.

Let the water boil away, steaming the chestnuts until the shells have started to peel open at the slits, usually in 3 to 4 minutes. Check the pan before the water evaporates completely: if the shells are still closed tightly, add a bit more water and continue steaming until they begin to open.

Turn down the heat to low, and let the chestnuts roast, still covered, in the dry pan, for about 15 minutes. But don't go away and get lost in after-dinner conversation! You must shake the covered pan every minute or two: hold down the cover, and give the skillet handle a few strong jerks to roll all the chestnuts around. This is essential for even cooking and to prevent burning. Continue to roast until the shells are toasted and the nut meat is tender—peel one to taste and check. Serve hot.

Index

(Page numbers in italic refer to illustrations.)

Smooth Sweet Red Pepper Sauce, 364–5
Smooth Sweet Red Pepper Sauce with Eggplant, 365
soffritto:
    explanation of, 56
    for *sugo,* 148
Soup Base of Garlicky White Beans and Broth, 55
soups, 53–85
    All-Purpose Turkey Broth, 80–2
    Base of Garlicky White Beans and Broth, 55
    Cauliflower, with Poached Garlic Purée, 66
    Chicory and White Bean, 57
    Creamy Poached Garlic and Onion, 68
    culinary vocabulary for, 56
    Frantoiana—White Bean and Dried Bread Soup, 62
    Fresh Chestnut and Winter Squash, 70
    garnishes for, 60–1
    giving substance to, with rice and other body builders, 65
    Hearty *Minestra* Base with Cranberry Beans, Potatoes, and Pork, 73–4
    Hearty *Minestra* with Butternut Squash, 77
    Hearty *Minestra* with Corn, 77
    Hearty *Minestra* with Fennel, 78
    Hearty *Minestra* with Rice, 76
    with Lentils and Ditalini Pasta, 72
    Mushroom and Barley, 69
    Parsnip and Scallion, 72
    Passatelli for, 84–5, 84–5
    Savory Potato Broth, 63–4
    serving, 57
    Simple Vegetable, with Rice, 65
    with turkey broth, simple, 82–3
    vegetarian *minestra,* 75
    Zucchini and White Bean, 58
Soup with Lentils and Ditalini Pasta, 72
Spaghetti with Asparagus Frittata, 99–101
Spicy Tomato Sauce—*Salsa Arrabbiata,* 128–9

spinach:
    Cooked, Salad, 48
    Filling, Ricotta Manicotti with, 198–9
    Gnocchi, 212
    Gnudi, 213
    Noodles, Lasagna with Bolognese Sauce and—*Pasticciata Bolognese,* 200–5, *201–3*
    Pasta Dough, 178–9
    Sauce of Cannellini, Sun-Dried Tomatoes and, 113
Spinach Gnocchi, 212
Spinach Pasta Dough, 178–9
squash, winter:
    Autumn Strudel with Cranberries and, 382, 386–9, *389*
    and Fresh Chestnut Soup, 70
    Hearty *Minestra* with Butternut Squash, 77
    Roasted, 279
    Roasted Acorn Squash Salad, *xxiv,* 38–9
stoccafisso, explanation of, 5
strascinate, explanation of, 266
strudel dough, fruity desserts with, 382–92
    Autumn Strudel with Squash and Cranberries, 382, 386–9, *389*
    Homemade Strudel Dough for, 383–5, *384, 385*
    Strudel Purse with Prune and Ricotta Filling, 390–2, *391, 392,* 832
    Strudel Purse with Prune and Ricotta Filling, 390–2, *391, 392,* 832
stuzzichino, explanation of, 37
Suffocated Eggplant with Scrambled Eggs, 260
sugar, cane (*zucchero di canna*), 389
sugo (gravy):
    Cavatappi with Meatballs and, 196
    explanation of, 148
    Lasagna with Meatballs and, 206–8, *208*
    and Meatballs, Long-Cooked, 146–50, *148*
"Sunday sauces," custom of, 348

Sweet Corn Poached in Summer Tomato Sauce, 258, *258*
Sweet Gnocchi, 211
Sweet Onion *Gratinate,* 29–30, *31*
Sweet Tart Dough, 402–3

tagliatelle, 165, *166, 167,* 167–8
tagliolini, 165, *167,* 167–8
Tart Dough, Sweet, 402–3
tarts, fruit, 393–403
    Crostata with Chocolate, Hazelnuts, and Orange, 393, 401–3
    Crostata with Poached Apricots and *Pignolata,* 393, 398–400
    Free-Form *Crostata* Dough for, 397
    Free-Form Plum *Crostata,* 393, 395–7, *396*
tart shells, forming, 403
Thin-Cut Lamb Shoulder Chops in a Skillet with Sauce, 339–40
Toasted Bread Crumb and Butter Sauce, 122
Toasted Poppy Seed and Butter Sauce, 122
tomato(es):
    canned, San Marzano, 124
    Cherry, Baked Shells with, 195
    Fresh, Capellini with Sauce of Anchovies, Capers and, 91–3
    Fresh, Lemon *Salsa,* 308
    fresh, preparing for summer sauces (and winter suppers), 261–3, *262, 263*
    Garden, Elixir, 269–70
    loosening skins of, 262
    Mozzarella, and Basil Ravioli, 184
    peeling, seeding, and crushing, 262–3
    and Roasted Eggplant Salad, *xxiv, 41, 41*
    and Shrimp Ravioli, Fresh, 182–3
    Summer, Skillet *Gratinate* of Pork and, 287–8
tomatoes, sun-dried:
    Sauce of Cannellini, Spinach and, 113
    Sauce of Cannellini Beans and, 112
    Sauce of Marinated Artichoke Hearts and, 116

A Note About the Author

Lidia Matticchio Bastianich was born in Pula, Istria, a peninsula that belonged to Italy at the time and is now part of Croatia. She came to the United States in 1958 and opened her first restaurant, Buonavia, in Queens, in 1971. A tremendous success, it inspired her to launch Felidia in 1981 in Manhattan, followed by Becco and Esca (also in New York) and Lidia's in Kansas City and Pittsburgh.

Lidia Bastianich is the author of three previous books, *La Cucina di Lidia*, *Lidia's Italian Table*, and *Lidia's Italian-American Kitchen*, which won an IACP Cookbook Award. She has also been the host of several public television series, *Lidia's Italian Table*, *Lidia's Italian-American Kitchen*, and *Lidia's Family Table*, and she gives lectures on Italian cuisine across the country. Ms. Bastianich lives on Long Island.

A Note on the Type

The text of this book has been set in Goudy Old Style, one of the more than one hundred typefaces designed by Frederic William Goudy (1865–1947). Although Goudy began his career as a bookkeeper, he was so inspired by the appearance of several newly published books from the Kelmscott Press that he devoted the remainder of his life to typography in an attempt to bring a better understanding of the movement led by William Morris to the printers of the United States.

Produced in 1914, Goudy Old Style reflects the absorption of a generation of designers with things "ancient." Its smooth, even color combined with its generous curves and ample cut marks it as one of Goudy's finest achievements.

Composed by North Market Street Graphics,
Lancaster, Pennsylvania

Printed and bound by R. R. Donnelley & Sons,
Crawfordsville, Indiana

Designed by Cassandra J. Pappas